FROM CROCKETT TO CUSTER

MIKE MARTIN

© Copyright 2004 Mike Martin. All rights reserved.

No part of this publication may be reproduced, stored in a retrieval system, or transmitted, in any form or by any means, electronic, mechanical, photocopying, recording, or otherwise, without the written prior permission of the author.

Printed in Victoria, Canada

Note for Librarians: a cataloguing record for this book that includes Dewey Classification and US Library of Congress numbers is available from the National Library of Canada. The complete cataloguing record can be obtained from the National Library's online database at:
www.nlc-bnc.ca/amicus/index-e.html
ISBN 1-4120-1878-1

TRAFFORD

This book was published on-demand in cooperation with Trafford Publishing. On-demand publishing is a unique process and service of making a book available for retail sale to the public taking advantage of on-demand manufacturing and Internet marketing. On-demand publishing includes promotions, retail sales, manufacturing, order fulfilment, accounting and collecting royalties on behalf of the author.

Suite 6E, 2333 Government St., Victoria, B.C. V8T 4P4, CANADA
Phone 250-383-6864   Toll-free 1-888-232-4444 (Canada & US)
Fax 250-383-6804   E-mail sales@trafford.com   Web site www.trafford.com
TRAFFORD PUBLISHING IS A DIVISION OF TRAFFORD HOLDINGS LTD.
Trafford Catalogue #03-2256   www.trafford.com/robots/03-2256.html

10   9   8   7   6   5   4   3   2   1

ABOUT THE AUTHOR

Mike Martin is a keen and thorough self taught historian, whose particular area of interest includes the Old American West. Over a period of years, to research this book, he travelled extensively across the U.S.A., visiting the states of Colorado, Wyoming, South Dakota, Montana, Texas, Arizona, Nevada, Utah and California.

He originally studied film and television production at art college but ended up in the entertainment business as a concert and cabaret performer, with occasional forays into acting. In recent times he has worked freelance as a London tour guide, specialising in such subjects as the Jack the Ripper murders. Also, he is regularly commissioned as an article writer and reviewer for various publications.

Previously published book: *NODDIES THE FILM EXTRA'S GUIDE*
(Arlon House Publishing 1997) ISBN 0-946273-22-7

Mike Martin is an active member of the show business charity brotherhood The Grand Order of Water Rats.

....

ACKNOWLEDGEMENTS

With thanks to The Daughters of the Republic of Texas in San Antonio and their wonderful research library, the helpful and informative attendants at the Alamo itself and Jimmy at John Wayne's Alamo Village, Brackettville.

More gratitude is owed to the friendly staff at the Cowboy Artists of America Museum (Kerrville, Texas) for their patience, assistance and use of the highly useful library, likewise the Jim Gatchell Museum (Buffalo, Wyoming) and the troopers of the 2nd. Cavalry at Fort Laramie.

Further appreciation goes to the Chamber of Commerce in Deadwood, South Dakota, the Custer Battlefield Museum at Garryowen, Montana, Kitty Deernose (curator of the Little Bighorn Battlefield National Monument Museum), Josephine Littlelight (and other members of the tribe on the Crow reservation), Jim Court in Hardin, Bob Wilson and the Board of the Fort Phil Kearny/Bozeman Trail Association, the Rangers of Yellowstone National Park, the guides at the Buffalo Bill Heritage Centre (Cody, Wyoming) and Chief Henry Lane on the Navajo reservation, Nevada. Hats must also be tipped to the San Jacinto Monument Museum, the Presidio la Bahia and the people of the Texan towns of Seguin, Gonzales, Goliad, Galveston and Bandera. (Not forgetting the kind folk of Laramie and Cheyenne, Wyoming, and others towns, settlements and people on the roads all over the West who are too numerous to mention.)

And finally, thanks for the support from my fellow members of the Custer Battlefield Historical and Museum Association and the Custer Association of Great Britain, especially Peter Russell. (Also the patient technical advice I received from my good friends David Capri and Martyn Oram.)

Ultimately, this book owes everything to the souls of all nationalities who lost their lives in the 1836 Texas War of Independence and the 1876 Sioux Indian war.

****

Cover images: *David Crockett* by Mike Martin and *George Custer (1868)* courtesy of the Little Bighorn Battlefield National Monument, National Parks Service.

INTRODUCTION

Put simply, this is a book about The Alamo and Custer's Last Stand.

Although not hugely significant as events in the grand scale of history, most people in the Western world will at least have heard of them. The names ring a bell with many souls who do not give a hoot about the past. By this I mean that your average "man in the street" would probably be aware of Davy Crockett and General Custer and the stylised images they conjure up whilst not having a clue who Robespierre and Brunel were. (Even though both of the latter arguably had a far more practical effect on the progress of the human race.)

So why is this? Well, the likes of Crockett and Custer have emerged from history to join a select band of revered figures who have been placed on the pedestal of legendary symbolism. Proud Custer with his long, golden hair and tough frontiersman Crockett in his coonskin cap, both dying bravely as they face impossible odds. It is the stuff adventure films are made of, and, of course, there have been many, along with countless books and television portrayals. The image is a romantic one, both characters being flamboyant and larger than life as, by all accounts, they were in reality. Having lived adventurously, fate placed the pair of them in situations which would secure their unique notch in our imaginations. As symbols of the American Wild West they stand almost alone, but the West was far from devoid of such characters. Had they not died the way they did would they really be remembered in such a fashion? Almost certainly not. As it is, they make good movie material.

After all, that was how my interest was originally stirred. Growing up in the South of England in the 1950s I was very much influenced by cinema and the growing craze of television. Like anyone of my generation I was subject to Disney's version of the Crockett legend and wiled away my days singing "King of the Wild Frontier" in my synthetic long tailed hat, taking turns with school friends to sell my life dearly against the Mexican hordes in our simulated Alamo. (i.e. My parent's back garden shed and greenhouse!) And then along came John Wayne's epic version of *The Alamo* and the whole genre took a quantum leap. I cannot emphasise enough how much of an effect that excellent, though deeply flawed, film had on me. As a six year old it was like emerging into the light. Before that there had been other big screen versions of the Alamo story, good ones too like Sterling Hayden's *The Last Command*, but Wayne's effort was in a league of its own. Whatever one thinks of it now, with all its preaching, mawkishness and mistakes, the fact remains that in 1960 it was quite a milestone, certainly for me. Even now, having seen it countless times, I can still enjoy the experience of watching it all over again. Apart from anything else, I find it hugely nostalgic. Much of it is pretty accurate too, but, more than that, it certainly succeeds in portraying the spirit of the legend. More of that later.

And what of Custer? Well, he burrowed himself into my consciousness at such an early stage that I just cannot pin it down. Of course, there were the many films, notably Errol Flynn's vintage black and white version *They Died With Their Boots On*, a movie which did not exactly enhance historical fact but certainly played its part in romanticizing the boy general. Custer has been portrayed by Hollywood in many guises, (even by Ronald Reagan!) and since Flynn's heroic performance, the field commander of the 7th. Cavalry has usually been shown as a megalomaniac, Indian hating, incompetent idiot. This has largely been due to a backlash of opinion which has its roots in the hero worship which once surrounded Custer. After his dramatic death, his wife Libbie, who seems to have genuinely adored him, devoted the rest of her long life to promoting his image as the greatest American hero. She was a strong character, who naturally evoked much sympathy, and so for many years Custer's numerous critics, out of respect and fear, hid from the public eye whilst Libbie massaged the ego of her dead husband and thus created the legend. When she died, the darker side of Custer began to emerge resulting in a completely out of proportion view which so many mildly interested people have of him today. As usual, the probable truth can be found by observing the known facts objectively and without bias. That is when we get the impression of the complex character he undoubtedly was, with as many good points as bad. In other words, a typical human being! Actually one of the best filmed versions of the Last Stand did not even call Custer by name. This was John Ford's wonderful movie, part of his U.S. Cavalry trilogy, *Fort Apache*, in which Henry Fonda plays Colonel Thursday, a fiercely proud disciplinarian who leads his regiment to disaster. An obvious allegory of the Custer saga, even though Thursday's men are annihilated by Apaches instead of Sioux and Cheyenne, the film scores not only through Fonda's cold yet sensitive performance but by an emotive portrayal of life in a frontier cavalry regiment which really draws you in. Romanticized again, yes, but highly effective and moving, playing a great deal on camaraderie and pride. The most accurate effort to date has been the 1990 television mini-series *Son of the Morning Star* which obviously took great pains to get the look of the thing right. They succeeded. The costumes and general ambiance of the production are virtually faultless, but unfortunately this attention to detail makes the overall result unsatisfactory to all but the most ardent aficionado. Various incidents in Custer's life and the staging of the actual final battle are impressively accurate, but Gary Cole is miscast as Custer, coming across as a soldier lacking in bravado and confidence. If we know anything about the General, we can rest assured that he was certainly not in want of *these* qualities.

Anyway, for whatever reason, the Custer phenomenon was so deeply ingrained in my youthful consciousness it has left me with some of my earliest childhood memories. A blanket spread over cushions to simulate Last Stand Hill as my plastic toy 7th. Cavalrymen were wiped out by their whooping Indian counterparts. In my version, Custer was always the last to die! Later on I would use a toy garage building, the shape of which vaguely resembled the famed Alamo mission, to restage Crockett's last desperate battle. I had a few frontier types in buckskins amongst my toy soldiers and cowboys were close enough to make up the bulk of the defenders, but I had no Mexican army. My brother and I solved this by using figures from a Battle of Waterloo series. That was perfect. Santa Anna himself had modelled his troops on Napoleonic tactics. I wished I had possessed more of them though to overwhelm my Texians! The solution to this was found by adding ranks of British grenadier guardsmen and even Confederates. I console myself by thinking that the wryly humorous Crockett would have approved.

So this was my childhood. There were lots of kids like me I guess, but unlike most I didn't grow out of it. My games progressed to a curiosity about the truth and I began to read books on the subjects. The more I discovered, the more fascinated I became and I devoured material voraciously. I developed an avid interest in history in general, (as did my brother, which helped me) but in the American West in particular. I learned all about the gunfighters and cattle drives, Indian Wars and Civil War, frontier life and mountain men, but through it all two over-riding events emerged to outweigh all the rest put together, the two which had enthralled me since my earliest awareness. Fairly small military engagements, both of which could easily have been avoided, fought un-necessarily and which from a strategic point of view were pretty insignificant. And yet look at the legacy they have left. Back to symbolism again. Heroes fighting against impossible odds.

Some will ask why the need for yet another retelling of these well known tales. It is true that there appears to be no shortage of books on both subjects, especially in the United States where extremely obscure aspects are covered in great detail. What can I offer that is new and how am I qualified to do so? Well, here goes .....

First of all, although many writers have covered The Alamo and Custer's Last Stand I am unaware of any who have linked both engagements in one specific volume. So what is the link? My interest in the Old West is wide ranging so why focus on these particular events? Several reasons. Primarily it is because of my personal passion for them. As already hinted at, regardless of the films and so on, a spark of fascination was always there for me, something deep which stirs my soul. If that seems melodramatic then so be it, but I can honestly say that when I finally made it to Montana and Texas to walk across those battlefields the experience had a profound effect on me. I can only describe it as a feeling of belonging and it led to an overwhelming desire to write this book.

Quite apart from my personal inspiration, I think the names alone are familiar enough to the public in general to generate interest. And the two battles had much in common. There have been many "Last Stands" throughout history ..... the 300 Spartans who fell to the Persian horde at Thermopylae and the British Army disaster at Isandwhlana when the 24th. Regiment were wiped out by the Zulus for example. All incredible stories of courage, resilience and hopelessness, but those where Crockett and Custer fell do appear to have a relationship. Both fought on the North American continent in the 19th. Century, almost exactly forty years apart (one in 1836, the other in 1876), both fought on a Sunday (one in the early morning, the other late afternoon), about 200 victims died (on the losing side) in each engagement, each had a proud, stubborn commander who refused to be fazed by the superior strength of the enemy; other links will become apparent as we progress. Profound differences too, of course, the most obvious one being that in the case of The Alamo all the defenders were there by choice, volunteers fighting for a cause which ultimately they knew must lead to their deaths. Custer's men were just soldiers doing the job they had been ordered to do and probably the last thing on their minds was the possibility that they would be wiped out. Also, the 7th. Cavalry were attacking whereas the Texians at the Alamo were very much on the defence. They are also linked by something essentially human, a thought which chills the blood and moves the soul. What must it have been like for those men, cavalry troopers and Texian volunteers, in that sobering, spine tingling moment, shared across the decades, when they realised all hope was lost? Imagine it, if you can. The countless bayonets of the Mexican Army bearing down on you as you desperately attempt to delay the inevitable with your rifle butt or Bowie knife. With their backs against the wall there was to be no mercy for them. Likewise on that hot, dusty slope above the Little Bighorn River as those painted warriors surged in for the kill, the horrified soldiers burrowing behind their slain horses in a vain attempt to protect themselves. With the awful anticipation of hot lead or cold steel they died in confusion, terror and pain, in darkness, blinding light and amidst the cries of their comrades, choking on powder smoke, dust and their own blood. How sobering to think of that reality when you look now at the monuments, pretty gardens of remembrance, tourists and souvenirs.

I have not attempted to write a definitive book of the known facts. Many have done that already and their "facts" are often contradictory. Such is the nature of history for those who lived it are not around to give their interpretation. What we are left with is anecdotal evidence passed down through the ages and this must be considered carefully. We have the remains of old buildings too, of course, where we are told certain things took place. We can compare these with written descriptions and judge how the evidence mounts up. There are old accounts and letters from participants, official military and government reports, diaries, graves and archaeological finds. Paintings and etchings too, crumbling newspaper archives and the tales of living descendants who can show you their family heirlooms. We do not even have photographs from the Alamo period (too early for that) and the first known fuzzy image actually dates from the early 1850s after the United States Army had restored the building and altered its shape considerably from how it looked at the time of the battle. That said, a lot of people left vivid accounts and these often match well with the surviving physical evidence. Portraiture was the big thing then and so we have been left with some quite striking images of Crockett and one of Jim Bowie which I think we can take (artistic licence aside) to be largely accurate. Several decades later, when the new art of photography had become fashionable, prominent figures like George Armstrong Custer took advantage of it and there still survives numerous pictures of him taken throughout most stages of his colourful career. Not only studio shots but also several of him actually on campaign along with candid images of socialising at military posts and at home. Perfect for a man with an ego the size of Custer's and so at least we do not have a problem knowing what *he* looked like.

This book does not contain all of that evidence. You can find that elsewhere, especially serious historians who will know much of it already. I have been selective for my aim is to produce an entertaining but informative record of a slice of history. It was important to me to make this book accessible to those who have a very limited knowledge of the subject. There is a lot of information here but hopefully not so much that it will cloud the brain. I have tried to present it clearly, to set the scene and tell the tale without glamorising anything. There is no need for that for the apparent truth is stirring and dramatic enough as it stands. That is why these legends have endured so long. I have great respect and affection for my subject and feel I have treated it seriously but in a light enough fashion to keep the un-obsessed interested. Although I am not a professional, academic historian and have no formal qualifications in that field, my lifelong interest has furnished me with the necessary information and outlook. Be assured that I have completed the essential research and have done my utmost to present a balanced picture by looking at what is available for scrutiny and then subjecting it to a great deal of thought. My descriptions of all events and detailed incidents are based on careful analysis of the surviving evidence. If I have made assumptions based on probability I have made that clear in the text. All any of us can do is weigh it all up and come to our own conclusions.

In addition, I have actually visited the sites of The Alamo and Little Bighorn battles along with many of the related areas across the northern, western and southern States of America. These trips were lifelong ambitions and I carried them out with this work very much in mind. What I learned, in addition to all my studied research, was invaluable. There is no substitute for experiencing the actual places first hand. And so that is another essential element of this book; the history, the drama and how it compares with what remains today.

The stories of these conflicts, and the background leading up to them, are filled with as many acts of atrocity as they are feats of heroism. On *all* sides. When the zealous patriots speak of the Alamo defenders fighting for freedom, let us not forget that those Texians came from a society where slavery was big business. Jim Bowie had made a fortune from the slave trade and Travis's slave was beside him at the battle. Although prisoners were massacred in cold blood by Santa Anna's army, balance this against the terrible retribution meted out to helpless, defeated Mexicans when they tried to surrender at San Jacinto. Although Custer's troops were slaughtered and mutilated mercilessly, reflect on how the General had ruthlessly wiped out a Cheyenne village at the Washita and was intending to do the same had the tables not been turned on him. However, before making moral judgements, it is important to consider the context of the very different times, attitudes and situation in which these people lived. My intention, through these pages, is to make them live again.

So let us begin, as I take you along two trails which ended in the realms of legend.

PART ONE

"FROM CROCKETT ….."

PART ONE: **"FROM CROCKETT ….."**

CONTENTS

CHAPTER   PAGE

1	Remember the Alamo	11
2	Early Tejas	16
3	Sir Devil	20
4	The Raven and the War Dogs	23
5	From Law to Liberty	25
6	Duels, Deals and Destiny	28
7	War Fever	34
8	The Long March	44
9	Frontier King and Candidate	49
10	Armed and Ready	53
11	The Right to Command	58
12	Wolves at the Door	62
13	Thirteen Days	69
14	Siege Warfare	74
15	"Give me help, oh my Country!"	79
16	Hope versus Honour	84
17	Calm before the Storm	93
18	Attack	96
19	The Smoke Clears	107
20	Flight and Massacre	111
21	San Jacinto	115
22	Liberty	121
23	Texas Today	128
24	A Semi-Epilogue	134

REMEMBER THE ALAMO

Wednesday April 18th. 2001, early afternoon. The sun is shining brightly between wisps of thin cloud, the deep blue sky framing the roof tops of the city as they shimmer lazily in the heat haze. Texas, the Lone Star State, and it is hot, so hot .....

This is my first time in San Antonio, and with the annual Fiesta just two days away the streets are busy. I was lucky to find accommodation in the centre of town, in fact a short walk beneath the flyover approach road to the Interstate 37, just a couple of blocks down East Houston Street, and I was at my destination. A long journey, in miles and years, but I made it at last.

Lots of people around; fat men in garish shorts, women with loud voices and kids darting between the trees, "kapowing" away with toy weapons just purchased in the gift shop. I stopped to watch them, a wry smile on my face. That was me forty years ago, but I had re-fought my Alamo battles in rural England while these youngsters were acting out their fantasies on the very ground where the epic struggle took place 165 years ago. My attention was drawn to a chunky little boy wearing a coonskin cap (just like the one I had!), the butt of his plastic Kentucky long rifle scraping the ground as he dragged it along by the barrel. Pulling at his mother's sleeve he trilled, "Hey Mom, is this where Daddy killed the bad guys?"

She sighed and clasped his hand, reading the wording on one of the wall plaques as she answered him in her slow Texan drawl. "No, sweetheart ..... that was your daddy's, daddy's, daddy's grandaddy."

I perked up at this, looking long and hard at the boy whose interest was already directed elsewhere as he took aim at a bright green lizard darting along a low wall. Mesmerised by the thought that I might already be encountering a descendant of one of the Alamo's immortal defenders, I failed to speak up. The moment was lost as mother and child wandered away towards the restrooms and were swallowed by the crowd. Did the blood of a Tennessee Volunteer run in that kid's veins? A trooper from the New Orleans Greys? The Gonzales Ranging Company even? Now I would never know.

I wandered on in the shade of the trees and found an ornate fountain, on each side of which are carved the names of the four most prominent combatants; Crockett, Bowie, Travis and Bonham. This corner of the complex is like a haven from the milling crowds nearby and I stop to enjoy the gentle sound of the trickling water and the dappled sunlight reflecting on the surface. Birds sing in the branches and it all seems strangely still. I savour the moment, reflecting upon what happened here so long ago. Pretty gardens now, surrounded by a high wall with shrubs and beautiful flowers, but in the early hours of March 6th. 1836 this was open ground across which Colonel Morales led his column against the South Gate. More or less where the tree line ends, an area of paving marks the spot where Jim Bowie's room stood.

Emerging from the shade I see the front of the famous church, starkly white against the sky. A stunning sight, so familiar from pictures, films and legend and I actually feel myself let out a little gasp. I walk slowly backwards, taking in the scene. That ornamental entrance, with its double domed doorway, the four spiralled columns and twin insets which once held holy statues. The work is intricate, tasteful and shows much skill, well worth the 1,500 pesos they paid local craftsman Dionicio de Jesus Gonzales to create this back in 1767. Now it shows the strain of time, the stone worn away by centuries of relentless weather, but the real damage only becomes apparent when you look closely. Scarring in the patterns which could only have been caused by shot and shell, evidence of the fierce fighting which took place around this doorway in the last stages of the battle.

I make my way a couple of hundred yards distant and sit down upon some tiered seating which faces the building so that I can fully appreciate the whole picture. Thankfully, the skyline behind that famous humped shape of the mission is clear of buildings, even though the tall structures of modern San Antonio flank either side. Just to the right, the large brown sign of the Crockett Hotel stands in the distance but almost mockingly dominating the site of the long gone palisade, in front of the church, which was defended by Davy and his "boys". Tourists eating ice cream tramp endlessly across that hallowed ground now but that is not a criticism, just a rueful observation.

To the left of the mission, the State flag of Texas (the Lone Star on red, white and blue) flutters proudly in a gentle breeze above the remains of the Long Barracks where the museum has now been established. A well manicured rectangular lawn lies directly before the church entrance, the vivid green grass starkly contrasting the white stone walls. These walls are four feet thick and twenty two feet high, the chapel itself rising to thirty feet, just the place for a Last Stand. A large plaque has been set lying flat on the grass on which, cast for posterity, are the words of Colonel Travis' "Victory or Death" letter, the most famous of the many written appeals for help which he sent by courier during the thirteen days of the siege. Stirring reading even for the cynical. Immediately in front of the church doors a metal strip runs across the ground, apparently the line drawn in the earth by the tip of Travis' sabre the day before the Alamo fell. According to the legend, Travis, knowing that all was lost, assembled his garrison here, told them that he would go down fighting and asked all those willing to join him to cross the line. The story goes that all but one did so. Hmmm, maybe. We shall examine that later.

My eyes drift along the wall of the Long Barracks eventually resting upon the tall column of the gleaming white cenotaph, erected in 1936 slap bang in the middle of what would have been the Alamo Plaza.

In memory of the heroes who sacrificed their lives at the Alamo,
March 6th. 1836, in the defense of Texas.
"They chose never to surrender or retreat, these brave hearts with
flag still proudly waving, perished in the flames of immortality that
their high sacrifice might lead to the founding of this Texas"

Stirring stuff again, over the top for some, but Texans are deeply proud of their Alamo. Woe betide anyone who tries to voice criticism in your average bar from Laredo to Dallas! The "flames of immortality" are represented on the column, roaring from the saint like corpses of the slain defenders as a free spirit ascends to glory. On every side of the structure stand giant, carved likenesses of fine looking, armed men (Crockett and Bowie are there, naturally) along with the names of those known to have died within these walls. Texians anyway ..... no mention of the soldado dead here!

Further to the left is the area where the North Wall stood, where Santa Anna's men made their first breach in the defences and swarmed into the Plaza. Nowadays the Gibbs Building and Post Office stand on either side of the vanished cannon ramp where Travis breathed his last. Plaques are dotted here and there, marking significant spots in reverent terms. On the outside wall of the Long Barracks there are even two plates placed by The Grand Lodge of Texas Freemasonry. One of them, below the Masonic symbol, says;

Honoring these Masons
James Bonham
James Bowie
David Crockett
Almaron Dickenson
William Barrett Travis

*And those unidentified Masons
who gave their lives in the
Battle of the Alamo*

Well, Santa Anna was also a Mason but that did not save his Brothers in the Craft. The pretty gardens on the other side of the Barracks are interspersed with old cannon and more plaques, notably one specifically honouring the Immortal 32, the men from Gonzales who were allegedly the last to respond effectively to Travis' call for help. Throughout the day, knowledgeable guides stand here to repeatedly tell the Alamo saga through a P.A. system to a constant stream of enthralled visitors. A beautiful tree, with incredibly wide spreading branches shades the museum entrance. In here they have ongoing showings of a film and an excellently constructed display of artefacts and diagrams which outline the relevant history in clear but informative terms. The interconnecting rooms are gloomy and eerie. It is easy to shudder when you think of the soldados clearing out these rooms one by one, the Texians fighting desperately for every inch of their small arms armoury. The second story is no more but during the battle it was used as a hospital where the patients were slaughtered in their beds.

On to the church itself and a written request for gentlemen to remove hats because "brave men died here". The inner sanctum of the Alamo has a roof now, unlike the exposed version of 1836, and there is a feeling of hushed respect, regardless of the milling crowds. Rooms on either side of the chapel, (which *were* covered during the battle) are filled with paintings depicting incidents from the period and glass cases containing fascinating items. A colourful, embroidered waistcoat that Crockett wore along with one of his rifles, some of Bowie's personal effects and, especially emotive, Travis' ring which he tied to a cord and hung around the neck of Captain Dickinson's infant daughter just before the battle. Flags drape limply from the walls representing the different nationalities of those who traded their lives here for the Republic of Texas. England, Wales, Ireland, Scotland, Germany and Denmark, as well as men from numerous American States.

When the soldados broke through the doors into this chapel they were faced with a long timbered ramp running up to the back wall rampart where Dickinson had sited a triplet of cannon. The last organised resistance took place on this spot before the Alamo fell, and then the victors moved through the side rooms, cornering terrified non-combatants like Dickinson's wife and daughter and the Esparza family in the baptistry.

Appreciating all this takes on a dream like quality. So long ago yet somehow frozen in time. A brief, bloody episode which left an indelible mark on history and the human consciousness.

How could it have led to this? Why did it happen?

The Alamo, San Antonio, Texas, 2001. Note the Crockett Hotel.

An historical re-enactor, on guard at The Alamo in authentic Texian volunteer uniform. Surrounded by lady tourists, would he rather it were Santa Anna's *soldados*?

Idealized statues of the defenders on the monument at Alamo Plaza.

EARLY TEJAS

The "Kronks" were big Indians. With their faces painted yellow and blue, nipples and lips pierced with sharpened cane, naked bodies smeared with mud and animal fat, they made a hair-raising sight. They fought with clubs and huge bows which fired long, flesh ripping shafts. And they disliked strangers, displaying their hostility with demonstrations of cannibalism. Sometimes they even ate parts of their *living* prisoners!

Hardly a warm welcome for the first Spanish explorers when they began to make charts of the Gulf Coast in the 1500s. These savage Karankawas inhabited the region around present day Galveston and Padre Island, but the Spanish met further resistance from other tribes the deeper they penetrated into this new country, searching, as always, for gold. Gold they did not find but they did find land, plenty of it, vast open tracts of plains, forests, deserts, mountains and pastures seemingly there for the taking. The Spaniards were courageous and resilient, (although like all Empire builders cruel and grasping) as they fought Indians and the elements, starvation and disease but settlements were gradually established and a foothold found in this province of what was to become Mexico. Odd that by the end of the 17th. century they were calling this harsh place Texas, a derivation of the Caddo Indian word *tejas* (pronounced "TAY-has") meaning "friend"!

By this time the Spanish Empire in the New World was enormous, including Florida, most of the Caribbean Islands, present day Mexico and Central America as well as a sizeable chunk of South America stretching from Venezuela to Argentina. Having ruthlessly suppressed the native cultures (such as the Aztecs) the colonists sent a constant stream of rich spoils back to Spain. Ships laden with gold and silver were regular targets for pirates along the Spanish Main.

However, in the 1600s Spanish policy underwent a radical change. The Conquistadors, having bled the new lands dry of sparkling riches, began to embrace a more moral objective, the winning of new souls for the Catholic faith. With the many Native American tribes as their fodder, the Spaniards built a whole string of missions (more than thirty in Texas alone), their aim being to not only convert these "savages" into "good Christians" but to also make them Spanish subjects and therefore tax payers. In a volatile land these missions needed protection and so presidios (military forts) were built alongside them. The missionaries worked with dedication in their attempts to bring their Indian subjects into the fold, teaching them the Spanish language as well as how to build and farm, but by the mid 1700s these commendable efforts were being frustrated by the constant raiding of warlike Apaches and Comanches who were not so keen on being re-educated. The eventual effect of these attacks crippled the system, cutting off supply routes and making the mission outposts increasingly isolated. At around this time further complications were caused by French forces laying claim to parts of East Texas and over the years many of the missions were abandoned owing to mis-management, disease, massacre, endless skirmishes with Indians and French troops, lack of supply and a host of other disasters. By 1800 the mission system was well into decline and would soon vanish altogether.

Almost in the centre of this new province of Texas, one of these missions had a unique destiny. At the time it was just one of many, spread widely over the land, so who could know that one day it would become such a symbol for freedom and heroism?

In 1718, on the west bank of San Pedro Creek, a subsidiary of the San Antonio River, Father Antonio Olivares founded the Mission de Valero. The site was moved twice over the next few years, and after it was destroyed in a storm it eventually found its present place on the east side of the river in 1724. A Spanish military garrison had already been built here and the first permanent structure on the mission site was the Convent which became the Long Barracks. (Much of it still survives, as previously mentioned.) This original building had two stories, the ground floor comprising five equal sized rooms where the priests lived and ate. Construction of a church began here but yet another storm caused devastation and work on the new one, which we now know so well, commenced in 1758. They even inscribed the date above the doorway. Work on this church was never fully completed and so it is important to remember that the appearance of the front of the chapel was somewhat different to the famous humped shape immortalized in the John Wayne film. That hump and the two outer, upper windows did not exist in 1836 but the ornate, carved decoration around the doorway certainly did. Spanish troops established the usual presidio around the holy buildings and by the 1730s colonists had been imported from as far away as the Canary Islands, forming a local civil government and thus creating the settlement of Villa de Bexar. This was soon to become known as the town of San Antonio de Bexar (pronounced "BAY-har"), although the mission itself, east across the river, was eventually regarded as the separate self governing town of Pueblo de Valero.

For quite a while the mission thrived with members of such tribes as the Lipan Apaches, Cocos, Paraguas and Kiowas taking advantage of the facilities. At one point there were over 300 Indians living there, but following a sudden epidemic in 1739 which killed more than 100 of them, the population declined rapidly and by 1790 it was down to under fifty. Three years later the mission was officially closed on government orders but in 1801 a Spanish cavalry unit was sent to occupy the old mission building. They were the Second Flying Company of San Carlos de Parras and they had come from their base in Mexico, El *Alamo* de Parras! Alamo is the Spanish word for cottonwood tree, and although there were such trees growing in the mission's vicinity it is generally thought that the historic chapel gets its famous name courtesy of the troops from that Mexican village. It would forever afterwards be known as The Alamo.

*   *   *

As already stated, Texas is vast. (360,000 square miles.) Even today the land seems to stretch on endlessly and you can drive for hours without seeing civilization. In the early 1800s it was almost totally wild and untamed, the estimated population (not counting Indians) being only around 4,000, and most of these were centred around the presidios of San Antonio de Bexar and La Bahia (Goliad), some 95 miles south east of Bexar. So much empty land led to an inevitable, but gradual, invasion of American citizens who crossed the bordering Sabine and Red Rivers from Arkansas and Louisiana in their quest for a better life. As early as 1812 a serious attempt was made by Mexican rebels and American opportunists to gain independence for Texas but, having captured the two main towns, they were quickly crushed by the Spanish army.

From seeds great oaks grow, as they say, and this ill fated attempt led to the War of Mexican Independence which had, by 1821, succeeded in its aim. The new country of Mexico was thrown into further turmoil by disagreements between rival government factions but this was resolved, for a while, by General Agustin Iturbide who had himself proclaimed Emperor. He was swiftly ousted by another revolt which led to the creation of the Federalist Republic of Mexico.

During the war, a visionary American came onto the scene whose actions were to lead to the creation of the Republic of Texas and eventually follow on to its inclusion within the United States. His name was Moses Austin from Missouri. Austin had accumulated a fairly considerable fortune from lead mining, even gaining Spanish citizenship from his work in Louisiana before the Louisiana Purchase, but for various reasons this fortune was lost. Facing financial ruin and seeking a new direction in his life, Austin took a gamble. Still feeling that his Spanish citizenship could be viable, he presented a proposal to Spanish government representatives in Bexar. Would they consider allowing him to organise official American immigration of responsible colonists into the area? The authorities were already concerned about illegal immigration and saw this as a way to bring matters under control, so Austin was awarded his grant and thus became the first empresario or land agent. Unfortunately, returning excitedly to the U.S.A. with his historic offer, he fell ill and realised that he would never be able to fulfil his dream. On his death bed he managed to persuade his son, Stephen, to carry on where he had left off.

Stephen Austin now faced a destiny he had never considered. He had been educated in the Universities of the East, well versed in the classics, a true gentleman; more a philosopher than an adventurer, but not for a moment would he consider betraying his father's trust. He knew how much Texan settlement had meant to Moses and so he decided to dedicate himself to the old man's dream. By this time, 1821, the Republic of Mexico was in operation requiring Stephen to re-negotiate the now invalid Spanish grant. The Mexican authorities gladly agreed. Texas was a land in need of populating and perhaps Americanos were the ones to do it. The bulk of their own people, far to the South, were reluctant to re-settle in such a wilderness, isolated and in constant danger of evisceration by rampaging Comanches, but the adventure would certainly appeal to the American frontier spirit of the period. Concessions were made in a further attempt to attract these pioneers from the North and East when a Congress in Mexico City formulated the Constitution of 1824. This was a sweeping reform, modelled upon the democratic principles of the United States and, in theory, guaranteeing the rights of every individual in the land. The only conditions were that the settlers must agree to become Mexican citizens and also embrace the Roman Catholic faith.

Austin's initial colony of 300 hard working, dedicated families was set up around San Felipe on the Rio Brazos and, at first, all went well. They were responsible folk who took their pledge to Mexico seriously. Likewise Austin himself who believed sincerely that Texas should remain a part of Mexico, working diligently to that end as a member of various delegations. But in 1823 Texas officially threw open its border to American settlement, the result of which was an immediate flood of people from just about every American State. They were awarded permits which gave them huge areas of land, prairies of waving grass, magnolia and seas of bluebonnets, along with sparkling rivers from which arm length fish practically jumped into your hands. Grazing pastures which appeared to go on for eternity, enough wild game to feed the world, free ranging mustangs and buffalo.... it was nothing short of paradise. Or so it seemed. Word went back and before long the tidal wave of immigration was surging over the Red River.

From Arkansas and Louisiana they came, from New Jersey, Illinois, Alabama, Virginia, Tennessee and New York; men would shut up shop, load their families into ox drawn wagons and make the long trek South West. Throughout the Mississippi valley cabins had been locked up for good, the brazen message "GTT" ("Gone To Texas!") daubed across the door. The land opportunities were amazing; 4,000 acres could be snapped up for $100. Farms spilled profit with corn planted at San Felipe and sugar cane in the South, but the biggest cash crop, by far, was cotton. To enable this industry to thrive, owing to the large amount of manual work required to simply pick all this cotton, the settlers brought their slaves with them. With so much cheap land there was no free labour to be hired so slavery seemed the only solution. Cotton culture boomed and the oppressed blacks sang mournfully in the fields. To the average Southern American it seemed the way things should be.

It would be nice to report that this influx of Americanism blended harmoniously with its Mexican host but, sadly, this was not usually the case. Whilst taking advantage of the opportunities, most of the settlers kept very much to themselves, founding their own towns and avoiding their Mexican neighbours. East Texas, particularly, became dominated by American communities and the border with Louisiana grew into a haven for smuggling, gambling and all sorts of illegal activity.

For others life was hard but satisfying. Log cabins sprung up across the ranges and hill country and there were always Indians and outlaws to dodge. Around Gonzales, for instance, whooping Comanches often swept out of the hills to steal horses and cause general mayhem so the Mexican authorities presented the townsfolk with a small calibre cannon to help keep them at bay. (Little did anyone realise that one day this cannon would become the rallying point for the birth of the Texian Rebellion.) The fishing, hunting, riding and fighting made the men happy while the women kept the "home fires burning" amidst a dawn to dusk treadmill of endless toil. Some found it easier to enter the "oldest profession" to service the glut of sex starved gents who far outnumbered the ladies. No wonder the saying arose "Texas was heaven for men and dogs; hell for women and oxen"!

The old provincial capital of San Antonio de Bexar proved especially popular with these new arrivals. Since Mexico's independence the town had fallen into decline, with half the population it had enjoyed under Spanish rule, but it still retained a certain charm which drew Americanos into its spell. Days could be long and hot along the banks of the Rio San Antonio, the Mexican populace enjoying their siesta before the twanging of guitars and joyful singing drifted through the evening air. Farming, ranching and trading, a man could live a good life here. Nat Lewis from Massachusetts certainly had the right idea when he opened his store on the Main Plaza for he always did brisk business. The dominating feature of the town, which the Americans had now affectionately dubbed "Bear", was the old San Fernando church with its fat and thin domed towers. No one, it seemed, took much notice of The Alamo east of the river.

American settlers adopted a name for themselves; Texians. (As the years progressed this would adapt to Texicans, for a time, and finally Texans.) They saw themselves very much as their own people and, regardless of their vow of Mexican loyalty, attempted to solidify individual standards of liberty which they had brought from their original homes. Some began to openly criticise the Mexican system, especially judicial methods, a situation which brought considerable resentment from the Mexicans themselves. Who did these Americano ingrates think they were? Taking advantage of our country and then insulting our methods. They should know their place and be thankful they are here. The Texian response was one of pure contempt. After all, in twelve years nearly 28,000 Americans had taken up the original Mexican offer of Texas settlement. By 1835 they made up about 75% of the population. Did they not deserve a voice? Some even spoke of it being time to break away as a nation of their own. Treasonable talk but, for many, food for thought.

American expansionism had become a great cause for concern and was to all effects out of control. The two communities were being well and truly driven apart. Where would it end? Down in Mexico City the government, following years of worried talk, decided that the time had come to take action.

Before long the result of those actions would come to a head under the leadership of one man. His name was Santa Anna.

SIR DEVIL

Even as a youth, Antonio Lopez de Santa Anna cut a striking figure. At 5'10" he was tall for a Mexican and he carried his fine physique in an aloof and haughty manner. Strikingly handsome he strutted around with the bearing of a born leader.

However, at the Battle of Medina in 1813, he was a mere junior officer in the Spanish Army, watching wide eyed as his commandant, General Arredondo, inflicted a clever and crushing defeat upon the rebels who had dared defy the government. Santa Anna learned many lessons that day, not least of all that ruthlessness was the most effective way to deal with upstarts. He was also amused by, and contemptuous of, those loud, interfering Americans who had given aid to his enemies and were now fleeing in disorder from the field. They had proven themselves unworthy adversaries and were now paying for their mistake. The eighteen year old lieutenant even nodded grim approval as Arredondo gave the order for all prisoners, and their sympathisers, to be executed. Harsh but effective, such methods were to become deeply ingrained in Santa Anna's personality for the rest of his long, and volatile, career.

The conflict which was to lead to the War of Mexican Independence struggled on for years and Santa Anna served with distinction, honing his natural skill as a military commander. By 1821 he was a lieutenant colonel on the staff of General Iturbide himself and was instrumental in the chaos which eventually transformed into the Mexican Republic. From a Spanish army officer he had, by the age of 27, emerged as a brigadier general leading Mexican federalists. At first supporting Iturbide, who had proclaimed himself emperor, the ambitious young leader quickly realised that the future lay in the exploitation of liberal federalism. Ruthlessly changing his colours, he did not hesitate in helping to oust the emperor and, from that moment on, Santa Anna would remain dominant in Mexican politics for the next thirty years.

In 1824 he was partly responsible for creating the highly popular Federal Constitution. By this time the influx of American expansionism was gaining momentum and Santa Anna was one of the first to speak out against it, warning that the province of Tejas was in danger of being lost to "these perfidious foreigners". His power was growing rapidly but he was also going deeper down the road of megalomania. He soon proved himself to be so ruthless and corrupt that the people, out of earshot, were calling him "Don Demonio" (Sir Devil). Self preservation and personal advancement shaped his politics and he was known to lie, steal and gamble compulsively. He was also addicted to opium and used his suave good looks to fuel his insatiable appetite for women. One thing he could not be accused of was modesty!

And yet, his charismatic presence and undoubted abilities on the battlefield could not be successfully challenged. His influence surged to a higher level following the Battle of Tampico in 1829 when he effortlessly destroyed a gutless Spanish attempt to re-establish power. More revolutions and betrayals followed but Santa Anna always seemed to emerge one step ahead of his rivals, finally realising his goal in 1833 by being elected El Presidente. Not that this was enough for such a man. Already known as the "Napoleon of the West" the new president shamelessly declared "Were I made God, I should wish to be something more"!

*   *   *

Santa Anna inherited a hated law which had been instigated on April 6th. 1830, the first consolidated measure by the Mexican government to curb Anglo American influence in Texas. The conditions of this law were severe, including a complete ban on further American immigration and the abolishment of slavery, along with numerous other rules specifically designed to undermine the empresario system.

The Texians were horrified and outraged, for the immediate effect of this law would be to cut them off from their friends and relatives in the United States, many of whom had already been making plans to join them. Administratively adjoined with the neighbouring province of Coahuila; Texas, at a stroke, now appeared to have been relegated to second class status. That is certainly how the colonists saw it.

This resulted in increased open defiance. Meetings and rallies were called where men would grow red faced and breathless as they passionately put across their grievances. Resentment of all things Mexican began to reach boiling point and the diplomatic and sensible Stephen Austin had to use all his influence to try and establish an atmosphere of calm. Austin was sympathetic, of course, but stressed the need to remain loyal to the Mexican authorities, seeing co-existence as the way ahead. His "Peace Party" supported the 1824 Constitution but there was a growing tendency for the majority of disgruntled settlers to join the group that was becoming known as the "War Dogs". At first it was all mere talk but the flowery rhetoric of this "War Party's" spokesmen (characters like the fiery young lawyer William Barrett Travis) began to take practical effect. A strong movement was now unafraid to voice its desire to create a new republic, breaking away completely from Mexican statehood.

The Mexicans responded by establishing a much more obvious military presence in Texas in an attempt to stabilise their authority, but illegal immigration blatantly continued as if the law had never been installed. There were clashes and confrontations, threats and arrests (including the arrest of Travis for instigating trouble) but still Austin called for a more reasoned approach. He compromised by agreeing to present the Mexican government with a formal proposal for a self governing Texian community. This was officially drawn up in a meeting just north of San Felipe and, full of hope, Austin boarded a ship on the Gulf coast to take him on the quick route south to Mexico.

Initially, his meeting with the new president, General Santa Anna, looked hopeful. After all, the Americans, ironically, viewed this new blood in Mexico City as a liberal who would prove sympathetic to their cause. Unfortunately, whilst waiting for an answer to his proposals, Austin unwisely penned a letter to his compatriots in which he stated that whatever happened, Texian autonomy should be established. En route, this letter was intercepted and a furious Santa Anna had Austin arrested on suspicion of inciting rebellion. Bewildered and denied an opportunity to speak further, Austin was thrown into a cell and there he would remain, reflecting upon the doubtful wisdom of his reasonable nature, for nearly two years.

In the meantime, Santa Anna was taking the definition of "despot" to giddying heights. Having gained power with promises of democracy, he rapidly changed course once his hands were on the reins and had himself brazenly declared "Dictator". Arrogantly, he countered all protests, first with a dismissive declaration that only he knew what was best for the Mexican nation followed by ruthless displays of military suppression. Mounted on his gold plated saddle and with a $7,000 sword buckled to his waist, "Don Demonio" would gallop ahead of his army on his magnificent charger, surrounded by his escort of glittering dragoons and determined to let the peasants know who ran the show. Marching behind came his troops, always on hand to forcibly solidify the president's wishes. Cavalry, infantry and artillery, colourful and drilled in the style of the Napoleonic era, the soldiers were even equipped with vintage British army surplus weapons, the residue left over from Waterloo.

Time and again they swept aside a series of revolts which sprang up across the country until, at last, the Mexican people began to realise that their leader would always rule with an iron hand. Early in 1835, Santa Anna, perhaps bored with his mighty game, decided to let his brother-in-law, General Martin Perfecto de Cos, deal with another flickering rebellion, this time up north in Zacatecas, bordering Coahuila and right alongside Tejas. The troops moved in and the Texian settlers muttered, cursed and fidgeted.

Santa Anna himself, having suppressed his own people, began to turn an indignant and vengeful eye upon the upstart Americans who were daring to defy him. Here was a man who, despite his harsh methods, had brought some form of order to Mexico. He was as clever as he was vain, with an impeccable sense of timing and showmanship. Those good looks and that mesmerising way of speaking gained him many admirers who soon overlooked his brutality. He knew how to use his charm and as a figurehead he was way ahead of the shambolic array of uncertain and shabby characters who had ruled over the last few years. This was a man to look up to, especially as he was focussing the people's frustrations and anger towards a simmering issue that had been around for a long time. Santa Anna exploited this for all it was worth. Already he had abolished the popular 1824 Constitution, replacing it with oppressive centralist rules which seemed designed to antagonise the free spirits of the Texians. It would not be long before he decided to deal with the problem personally.

Antonio Lopez de Santa Anna......

"Were I made God, I should wish to be something more"

THE RAVEN AND THE WAR DOGS

The big man stretched in the saddle, tipped back the crown of his broad brimmed hat and peered thoughtfully west across the rippling currents of the Red River. Quite possibly, once again, a question that he had so often voiced out loud entered his mind.

"What the devil am I going to do in Texas?"

It was December 1832. Comanches were raiding along the frontier and American president Andrew Jackson knew just the man to deal with it, his great friend Sam Houston. Houston understood Indians, he had lived with them and had an affinity with tribal ways. If anyone could negotiate a settlement with these wild savages, he was the one.

Houston himself was glad to take the assignment. He had been looking for a new direction in his life and needed to get away, the further the better, and the untamed stretches of the American/Texan border seemed to fit the bill. Ever since the collapse of his marriage to his beloved Eliza, Houston had been a changed man. What had gone wrong? True, she was so young, not yet twenty, and he was a seasoned veteran pushing forty, but he had thought she was happy being married to the Governor of Tennessee. Within months she had returned home to her parents leaving the normally unflappable Houston shattered. The great soldier and statesman, brought to his knees by a girl in her teens. Heartbroken and confused it affected him so much that he resigned from his post as Governor and headed west.

It was not the first time he had run away from a situation. Born in 1793 in Virginia of Celtic stock, Houston's father died when Sam and his eight brothers and sisters were still very young and the whole remaining family packed up a wagon and headed for Tennessee where they quickly established their own plantation. Sam was a dreamer with visions of grandeur, a voracious reader who devoured the classic books from his late father's extensive library. Inspired by the tales of battle, heroism and honour which he picked up from such works as Homer's *Iliad*, Houston became obsessed by the notion of an adventurous life. He developed a rebellious attitude, especially to the family business. When his brothers tried to force him to work in their general store he decided to vanish, travelling south for more than ninety miles before meeting up with a band of Cherokee Indians. Aged only sixteen, he decided to settle down with them and he was to spend the next three years adopting their way of life, the Chief actually accepting him as a son and naming him The Raven. He learned to track and hunt and developed a great love for the forests, rivers and wide open spaces. Eventually, one of his brothers found him and tried to coax him back into the family fold but Sam's answer was he "preferred measuring deer tracks to calico".

Requiring money, Houston, aged nineteen, returned to civilization for a while to work as a schoolteacher but in 1812 war broke out with Great Britain and he immediately enlisted in the American 7th. Infantry. Keen to impress, he was always at the forefront of the fighting and was wounded several times during the war, notably at the Battle of Horseshoe Bend where he was shot twice and came to the attention of General Andrew Jackson. Jackson took a liking to the courageous and spirited young man and Sam was invited to become a personal staff officer. This was the beginning of a lifelong and very deep friendship, but Houston was a man of principle and in 1818 he resigned his army commission because of a certain point in government policy regarding the removal of Indians from their territory. Sam always had a soft spot for his native American brothers.

Studying law, he also worked as an Indian agent and began to dabble in politics. With Jackson's help he was elected to Congress and in 1827 became Governor of Tennessee. It was during this time that he made another close friend, fellow congressman David Crockett. Houston was a natural politician who understood the importance of image and media manipulation in a way that seemed to place him years ahead of his time. He knew how to work an audience, portraying himself in many romantic guises. That is why we have today so many surviving portraits of him dressed as a Roman senator or in traditional Indian costume. He was flamboyant alright, aggressive even, but the people loved him.

He seemed set for a conventional political career. Influential men were talking about him in terms of a potential president, but then came his disastrous marriage, a personal tragedy which put paid to such ambitions. He sought refuge in Arkansas with his Cherokee brethren and began to drink heavily, so much so that the Indians gave him a new name; "Big Drunk"! And then came Jackson's offer to help solve the Comanche problem. At a loose end, Houston's attitude was probably "Why not?"

However, once in Texas, his attitude began to change. Like so many other American arrivals he became entranced by the beauty of the country and the boundless opportunities it appeared to offer. He spent little time on the frontier and was soon heading deep into the interior, applying to Stephen Austin for one of those desirable land grants. Once established, he set up his own community at Nacogdoches just west of the Sabine and, in true Houston style, became delegate for the area.

Before long he had become an advocate for the cause of Texian independence and, with Austin off the scene, imprisoned in Mexico, the settlers began to look to him for guidance. Houston took to the role with ease and made no secret of the fact that his sympathies lay very much with the aggressive talk of the War Party. However, he was no rash fool and, whilst stimulating the energies of the settlers, he proceeded with caution and sought to encourage the much needed aid of the United States. By now the radical's hero, Houston tactfully began to suggest to his old friend President Andrew Jackson that the possible acquisition of Texas might be worth considering. Jackson sympathised but, realising the enormity of such a bold question, remained non-committal.

In 1835, around the time that General Cos' troops were moving into Texas, Stephen Austin was released from Mexican confinement. If Santa Anna thought that he had broken this honourable man's spirit he could not have been more mistaken. Austin arrived back in Texas with a very different attitude to the peacemaker he had been two years before. Now he darkly declared, "Santa Anna is a base, unprincipled, bloody monster. War is our only recourse ... war in full... there is no other remedy but to defend our rights, our country and ourselves by force of arms!"

This was just what the War Dogs had been waiting for. Full support from their leadership. War fever spread like wild fire and men all across Texas began to reach for their weapons, calling out for the expulsion of their Mexican oppressors.

Not a moment too soon, thought War Dog Travis, ruefully. As far as he was concerned, he had already been at war with Mexico for years.

FROM LAW TO LIBERTY

As early as May 1832, several months before Sam Houston first appeared in Texas, William Barrett Travis had already gained a reputation as a severe agitator. As a leading light of the growing War Party he did all he could to add fuel to Texian discontent, calling for action against Mexican oppression while Austin did his diplomatic best.

Travis was young for one so influential. Still only in his early twenties, he had already achieved a great deal and was highly respected as a professional and authoritative figure. He was excitable yet moody by nature, flamboyant like Houston, and he possessed a flair for dramatic rhetoric. Also he had a strong sense of destiny, a quality which is most evident from the writings he left us, penned from behind the walls of the besieged Alamo.

Originally he hailed from South Carolina but his family moved to Alabama. He grew up tall and with looks which appealed to the ladies, an asset which he took advantage of with gusto. His diaries contain many clues to his numerous sexual liaisons with prostitutes, washerwomen and farmer's daughters; "Screwed Miss C. ... paid her a dollar", "Paid Melinda two dollars" and about one lady " ... reception cold but conclusion very warm"! Even so, he was religious and well educated in the ways of the world. Studying law he was admitted to the Alabama bar before he had reached the age of twenty. He also worked for a while as a schoolteacher, joined the militia and even published his own newspaper. As a prominent member of society in Claiborne town it was perhaps inevitable that he should become a freemason, an interest which he apparently pursued enthusiastically. By the time he was 23 he had completed his autobiography, but that certainly did not ease his raging sense of ambition. There was something simmering within him, the bursting aura of a man who seemed to know he was destined for immortality.

His story was to mirror Houston's in several ways, notably in the fact that it was a failed marriage which also sent him en-route to Texas. Travis had married into a prosperous farming family and soon had a child. His wife Rosanna was pregnant for the second time, in 1831, when he apparently accused her of infidelity. Other problems arose and the marriage grew stormy, giving rise to a family legend that Travis actually killed his wife's lover. True or not, something dramatic enough happened to make him leave home and head west, although it could have been something as mundane as escaping from the debts of his failed business interests.

And so W.B. Travis ended up in Texas where he was to find the outlet for his ambitious energy. From the port of Anahuac he settled in Austin's town of San Felipe where he set up another law practice. The business was successful and he became quite a man about town, standing out amongst the buckskin and hickory clad populace in his fancy shirts, bright red trousers and large white hat. He loved to gamble and party, drifting from girl to girl, the period when he began to keep the notorious diary of his conquests. At one point he wrote "Hell among the women"!

However, there was a deeply serious side to Travis and he embraced the cause of Texian rebellion with fervour. Involving himself in numerous public issues, he became one of the earliest, and most vocal, of the pro-independence lobby, much to the annoyance and embarrassment of Austin's Peace Party. Always a man to back his words with actions, Travis caused a furore in May 1832 by upsetting the Mexican commander at Anahuac.

The Texians had continually flouted the laws against smuggling (as they had regarding slavery and other matters) and there was a strong feeling that the authorities were turning a blind eye to the constant illegal coastal traffic. So, when, at Anahuac, forceful tactics were suddenly used to curb the landing of contraband goods, Travis seized the opportunity to make a name for himself by making open threats to the officer in charge. Infuriated, the port commander had Travis arrested but by this time the fledgling revolutionary had enormous support amongst the colonists and a huge mob surrounded the building where he was held to demand his release.

In a desperate attempt to disperse this mob, the Mexicans threatened to kill their prisoner but Travis, in a moment he must have relished, encouraged his supporters to open fire saying he would rather die than permit such injustice. It was a mad, courageous gamble but it worked. The Mexicans backed down but it left an atmosphere of dangerous unease.

Within a couple of years Santa Anna had come to power, proving his anti-American stance by his hostile, despotic policies. For a while, men like Travis had become frustrated by the colonists lack of will power to do anything positive about their grievances, but now the time was growing ripe for steadfast resistance. With Austin in prison and Mexican troops tightening their hold on the colony, Santa Anna ordered a series of restrictive moves. The Monclova legislature was closed down, effectively leaving the Texians with no government of their own, the campaign against smuggling was stepped up and a Texian schooner was seized off Galveston Bay. There was also a heavy handed attempt to collect long overdue custom's duties and for that purpose the hated Custom's House at Anahuac was re-opened under a new commander, Captain Tenorio.

It was June 1835 and Travis launched what was to be the first real step of the Texian revolution by taking a chance again. He raised an unofficial company of 25 men and, with armed threats, forced Tenorio to surrender his headquarters, but it was a short-lived success. Many Texians were shocked by Travis' rash action. Protests and harsh words were one thing but open rebellion? Most were still not quite ready for it.

Seething at the lack of support, Travis retreated and lay low for a while but Santa Anna's response was to send an even greater number of troops into Texas. What is more, he demanded the arrest of all troublemakers, Travis himself being at the top of the list. Now the colonists were facing martial law, complete lack of representation and the constant threat of incarceration if they dared speak out of turn.

Events were now moving swiftly. With Austin back home from his Mexican prison and, for the first time, speaking of armed resistance, the Texians succumbed to war fever. The Mexican General Cos landed over 400 soldiers at Copano and headed straight for San Antonio de Bexar where the authorities were busy trying to eradicate growing signs of revolt. Cos immediately occupied the old mission east of the river, the place the locals called The Alamo, noting its potential as a possible fortress should the need arise.

Right now though, the real trouble was brewing about seventy miles east at the town of Gonzales where it was reported that the Texian colonists had responded very aggressively to word they had received regarding the surrender of their old cannon. The cannon itself was a mere symbol, only an ancient six pounder which did not even work properly. It had been given to the town years ago by the Mexicans, in friendlier days, to help the townspeople frighten off marauding Indians and was largely forgotten until the new Mexican demands (and fears) insisted on its return.

The Gonzales settlers became most indignant about this demand and suddenly found a great new desire to keep their cannon. Dusting it off, they brought it into the open and remounted it on a carriage with sawn down tree trunks serving as the wheels. It looked absurdly small, but the Texians were determined to keep hold of it.

Anxious to not see his authority usurped, Cos ordered a squad of 100 men to march on Gonzales and take the cannon by force, if necessary. They were met by a small group of determined armed Texians who shouted defiant threats, enough to make the Mexicans hesitate. These men were all local townspeople, led by such individuals as the blacksmith Almeron Dickinson and store owner Albert Martin, but the word was out and volunteers rushed to the scene. Pretty soon the Texian force outnumbered the Mexicans.

Swallowing his doubts the Mexican officer, Lt. Castaneda, once more demanded the surrender of the cannon as the two sides faced each other about 300 yards apart. He was met with hoots of derision and the cannon itself was wheeled into view to taunt him. Above it the Texians had raised a crude homemade flag, made from a white silk wedding dress, which sported a black star of independence, a roughly etched picture of a cannon barrel and the bold, defiant message "COME AND TAKE IT".

Suddenly the muskets of both sides sputtered into life and the old cannon roared as it spewed out a shower of metal debris. A Mexican soldier fell, the Texians cheered and Castaneda ordered his men to withdraw.

It was October 2nd. 1835. The War of Texan Independence had begun and Travis had not even been present to witness it. He was in bed in San Felipe, not, this time, with a lady, but with a bad cold.

DUELS, DEALS AND DESTINY

Wednesday September 19th. 1827; on a sand bar in the Mississippi River between Vidalia and Natchez, Louisiana.

Twelve noon, the appointed hour. Colonel Robert Crain and Major George McWhorter, as seconds in this affair of honour, glanced at their pocket watches and nodded in grim agreement. Although late in the year the climate was oppressively hot and sticky, a wispy steam rising from the shallows of the river as the two parties faced each other across the grubby sand. Two Negro servants stepped forward to offer the chosen weapons to the opponents. Mortimer pistols, .36 calibre, London made, fine pieces.

Dr. Thomas Maddox and Samuel Levi Wells removed their frock coats, stiffened aggressively, but with dignity, then grasped the butts of a pistol each. Eying each other coldly they had waited a long time for this moment. Enemies for years over numerous matters, events had recently culminated in mutual slights on each other's honour. Dr. Maddox's recent indecent accusation regarding Wells' sister's chastity was the final straw. Their differences could now only be satisfied in the age old manner of the duelling field. The seconds, Crain for Maddox and McWhorter for Wells, checking that the weapons were primed and cocked, stood back alongside Doctors Denny and Cuny who were present to administer any necessary medical aid. Nearby, in the shelter of the trees stood other groups of men observing the proceedings with interest. Most of them had their own scores to settle and saw this meeting as an ideal opportunity to do so. One of them, present to support his friend Sam Wells, was a big strapping figure who had already become quite a legend throughout the land. His name was Jim Bowie.

Wells and Maddox were directed to stand back to back, pistol barrels held close to their bodies and pointing skywards. As a properly conducted dispute between gentlemen, each duellist was asked if he wished to make an apology and thus avoid bloodshed, but an unflinching shaking of heads allowed things to proceed. The count began, a precise ten steps in opposite directions before the men turned and fired simultaneously. As the smoke cleared with both men still on their feet, it was obvious that each had missed his target. Methodically and patiently the process was repeated. With pistols reloaded Maddox and Wells, perspiring in the heat and pressure of the moment, spun again on the count of ten pulling their triggers a split second apart. They had missed again!

For a long moment the parties stood motionless, staring at each other, unsure what to do. Then, abruptly, all the tension appeared to evaporate and one or two present even smiled and exhaled with relief. "Is honour now satisfied?" asked one and it seemed that all on the sandbar agreed. Calling for a bottle of wine Wells relaxed and said, "Come, let us all share a glass", then he turned to beckon those in the shade of the oaks and willows to join them.

Emerging from the trees, a group of men began to make their way cautiously towards the prior antagonists. Almost at the same moment a second bunch of men, seven or eight strong, appeared from the cover of a cluster of sweet gum trees and strode purposefully over to the sand bar. They were armed and one at least was brandishing a double barrelled shotgun.

Glasses were offered as the distance between the groups narrowed but Colonel Crain is said to have declared to Wells "Be damned! I'll not drink with you or your blasted friends ... especially those rascals Cuny and Bowie!"

Tension mounted once again at these harsh words but Bowie appeared unaffected. Calm as ever he sauntered casually onto the sand and cast his cold grey eyes over the approaching group, swiftly registering the familiar faces of those present. The Blanchard brothers, Alfred and Edward, and Bill Barnard who carried the shotgun. Bowie had dealt with trouble from these characters before. His main concern however was the presence of Major Norris Wright, the sheriff of Rapides Parish, a dangerous and vindictive man of action who had sworn on several occasions to rid the world of his arch enemy Bowie.

Wright glared back at Bowie, his lip curling into a sneer. Their enmity went back a long way, starting with conflicting business interests and culminating in open insults from Wright about Bowie's status as a gentleman and entrepreneur. Wright dabbled in such diverse interests as banking, land swindles, gambling, slave trading and counterfeit money. He was ruthless and vicious and, as an expert shot and swordsman, was not averse to dealing out his own brand of rough justice. Men who he owed money to would simply be challenged to a duel and killed, it was said. Only the previous year, when Bowie had confronted him on the streets of Alexandria for an explanation regarding a blocked loan, Wright had responded by branding his rival " a carouser, womaniser, drunkard and brawler" who he did not wish to do business with. As Bowie reacted to this, Wright drew a pistol and shot him point blank. Some said that Bowie was saved by the ball being deflected by his freemason's amulet, but, whatever, he recovered swiftly enough to seize the treacherous Wright and undoubtedly would have destroyed him had he not been dragged away by a group of bystanders. Since then their problems had grown and festered.

General Sam Cuny (brother of Dr. Cuny who stood nearby) was outraged by Crain's slight. "And damn you, Crain," he responded, reaching for a pistol in the pocket of his coat, "this is a good time to settle our problems!"

Unfortunately for the general, the hammer of his pistol snarled in the material giving Crain time to draw his own weapon. As Crain aimed, Bowie stepped between them, raising his hand as if to ease the situation but Crain let fly and Bowie fell, a ball in his hip. Freeing his pistol, General Cuny fired, wounding Crain slightly but the Colonel was a tough and cool customer. Pulling a second pistol, he aimed again and put a slug directly into Cuny's body. The General was pitched back into the sand dying.

This started a free for all with everyone drawing their weapons. A rattle of discharged guns filled the air and pandemonium ensued as some stood their ground and others ran for cover. Bowie was already picking himself up from the ground, his eyes fixed on the man who had shot him. It was always said that Bowie's icy stare froze the blood in his enemy's veins and now he was launching himself towards Crain, dragging his injured leg but moving frighteningly fast. Crain's eyes almost burst from their sockets when he saw Bowie draw his big knife, the sunlight glinting off that keen edge which would reputably send so many future rivals to their Maker.

Panic swept over Crain and in desperation he hurled his empty pistol as hard as he could at Bowie's face. The pistol connected against Bowie's forehead and the big man fell again to his knees, dazed and momentarily out of action. As shots flew all around, Dr. Maddox attempted to wrestle Bowie to the ground but the wounded man soon rallied and shrugged Maddox off as if he were a child.

To see the feared fighter Jim Bowie on his knees was a rare sight and several sought to take advantage of it. Norris Wright, the renowned duellist was the first to act, damning Bowie to hell and shooting him yet again. No amulet saved him this time and he fell onto his back with Wright rushing in to administer the *coup de grace*. The sheriff had unsheathed a concealed sword from his cane and, with a twisted grin, raised it high then drove it down with all his strength into Bowie's chest.

Thinking he had killed his rival, Wright placed a foot on the stricken man's chest and attempted to pull his sword free, but even using both hands he could not do so. It was stuck fast in Bowie's sternum. Exerting more effort, the sheriff merely succeeded in pulling the handle from his weapon, staggering back and cursing. At the same moment, Bowie burst back into life, reaching up and grabbing Wright's arm, dragging him down in the same motion. As he did so, Bowie's broad bladed knife flashed upwards, plunging into the sheriff's stomach.

Wright screamed but Bowie methodically followed through, his knife ripping far up through flesh, muscle and sinew, all the way to the breastbone whereupon he gave the hilt a sharp twist. Wright's blood spilled out onto the sand before he sank down, his legs twitching convulsively. Part of his dying body had fallen across Bowie who pushed the corpse away and struggled to his feet, the sword still protruding from his chest. Other shots hit him as he remained standing but this time Alfred Blanchard sought to try his luck. He also had a sword which he used to lunge at Bowie, but Big Jim parried the blows with his knife and then neatly slashed down into Blanchard's forearm, almost severing it at the elbow. Blanchard cried out and fled, holding his ruined arm and leaving a wide trail of blood in his wake.

When it was all over, two men were dead and several wounded. Bowie himself, according to Dr.Cuny's medical report, had been shot four times (once through the lung) and grazed by three more pistol balls. He was concussed by the thrown pistol which raised a large swelling on his head and had suffered a deep gash to his hand. Cuny was unable to remove the sword from Bowie's chest and had to have him taken to a nearby tavern. Obtaining a pair of blacksmith's tongs, the doctor finally managed to extract the blade but it was a long struggle, two men holding Bowie steady as he did so.

Cuny said his patient was a "testimony to the human spirit".

*   *   *

The Vidalia Sand Bar Fight has the distinction of being the best documented of James Bowie's many battles (Alamo excluded) and that is because so many people were involved. Therefore, we have been left with what can be considered a pretty accurate picture of what happened. (As per the previous dramatization.) Numerous accounts exist of other adventures he was involved in, but very often the details are hazy. However, enough has survived to assure us that he was an exceptional character even by the wild and heroic standards of his day. You do not need to exaggerate the details of Bowie's life because the proven material is impressive enough as it stands.

His father was a soldier of Scottish descent who had fought in the thick of the American War of Independence. It seems Bowie Senior, though a man of strong mettle, had a cultured side and brought his family up to respect commendable principles. He raised his sons, Rezin, John, Stephen and James to fend for themselves, both physically and with business acumen. They were taught to be fiercely proud of their Scot's Highland heritage, learning much, it is said, from the adventures of Rob Roy and other classic tales.

The Bowie family moved from Kentucky to Missouri to Louisiana, finally settling in the rich sugar cane country where they built their wealth with sheer hard, back breaking work and shrewd deals. They hauled logs out of the swamps, planted crops, sold livestock and dealt in land, more than once warding off brigands and other ne'r-do-wells with their fighting ability. In their spare time Jim and his brothers loved to hunt, fish and explore the expanses of wild territory, indulging in such dangerous sports as riding wild bulls. Occasionally they would venture into the swamps to take this leisure activity to new levels by riding alligators! No wonder they became known as the Wild Bowie Boys. And yet they all apparently possessed a passion for literature and music, along with a highly developed appreciation of the world around them. Jim learned three languages and could converse with people on all manner of topics, be it politics, machinery, history or beaver skinning!

As an adult, Jim was a large man, over six feet tall and weighing about 220 pounds, which was mostly hard muscle. "Amazingly well knit with a hearty constitution" said Dr.Cuny, although after the injuries he received in the sandbar fight his health was never quite the same. He had thick, sandy coloured hair, not quite red, steely grey eyes which communicated authority, and a most calm and collected way of going about his business. His conversation was well informed and eloquent and he possessed considerable charm. He was courteous and helpful by nature and would often put himself out to support the underdogs of life. Often he would be quiet but when he spoke people listened to a cultured voice that was rarely raised in anger. It seems he put his sense of honour above everything else and could mix with all types from the cream of New Orleans society to the roughest of frontiersmen. Jim Bowie possessed the knack and presence for simply fitting in. Unless a man was foolish enough to question his honour, it was difficult to rile him but once riled he was a formidable foe. He was far more than a backwoods brawler. His fighting skills were based on quick wittedness, agility, ruthlessness and sheer strength. He never held back and fought to win, thereby leaving a host of crippled adversaries behind him.

His flair for adventure drove him and he travelled far and wide from the family home in his attempts to make his own fortune. And he succeeded, but some would say this is where a darker side of Bowie emerged, for most of his money was made in fraudulent land deals and slave trading. Much of the latter came from his dealings with the famous pirate Jean Lafitte around Galveston.

And, of course, the legendary tales grew around him. Duels with buccaneers, saving damsels in distress, surviving impossible scrapes, but there is probably a good dose of truth within the hogwash. Some spoke of his run-ins with the cannibal Kronks and of how Sam Houston allowed him to steal his horse. No one else would have got away with that!

And then there was the Sans Saba Fight in 1831 which went down in history as one of the most renowned battles with Indians. It occurred on the Sans Saba River at Calf Creek, Texas, when Bowie, his brother Rezin, and about ten companions were on an expedition searching for some lost silver mines. One day they found themselves trapped in a thicket by 200 or so Caddo braves. For a long period Bowie and his party held them off, repulsing relentless head on attacks and indulging in clandestine fighting in the bushes until the Caddo chief was sent to the happy hunting grounds and his followers dispersed.

It was around this time that the famous Bowie knife came into existence. Although Jim himself is credited with its invention there is considerable evidence that his brother Rezin was more likely responsible, although Jim became notorious for its murderous use. Many individuals claimed to be the maker of the original knife but it was perhaps a cutler named Black who forged the first one to the Bowie design. Bowies were fighting knives, designed specifically for that purpose. There were different styles but a typical one would be twelve to fourteen inches in length with a wedge shaped blade for slashing, more like a short sword than a knife. Often they would have a brass back strap for catching rival blades in combat along with an S shaped cross guard, also the full tang was weighted to give it balance when thrown. The classic curve to the point of the blade gave it the renowned Bowie shape. How many of Bowie's enemies died on the receiving end of this vicious weapon is lost to history but, regardless of hard surviving evidence, it was reputed to be more than a few. Sometimes it was known as the "Arkansas Toothpick".

Land opportunities took Bowie to Texas and by 1830 he had settled in San Antonio de Bexar. Unlike most American settlers, Bowie made a supreme effort to ingratiate himself with the Mexican populace and he became a revered figure in Tejano society. He gladly converted to Catholicism and became a Mexican citizen. It was soon being said that he owned a million acres of prime Texas land and he became great friends with Juan Seguin, a rich and influential Tejano rancher who served several terms as *alcalde* (mayor) of Bexar. Seguin also was active in the Coahuilan/Texan state legislature and Mexican Congress and had enormous sympathy for the Texian cause. This made him a most important figure in the coming conflict.

Jim Bowie began to court Ursula Veramendi, the teenaged daughter of the vice governor of the territory. When they married, this actually made Bowie a relative, technically, of Santa Anna, a fact which Don Demonio constantly tried to disassociate himself from, but in 1833 Ursula, and her parents, were killed by a cholera epidemic. Bowie received the news whilst on a business trip in Mississippi. He took it badly and plunged into a terrible black depression from which he never really recovered. For months he brooded alone in Louisiana, finally wending his way back to Bexar where he attempted, half heartedly, to pick up the pieces of his life. Regardless of attempts by his many friends, like Seguin, to comfort him, Bowie gradually became a shadow of his former self. He grew short tempered and difficult until people, out of fear, began to keep their distance from him. Truly alone now, he sulked in the cavernous, empty house of Veramendi, yearning for his beloved Ursula. Always a drinker of moderation, it was now noticed that Bowie was drunk for much of the time.

It would take something dramatic to renew Bowie's interest in life. By now he was nearly forty years old, usually inebriated and ready to quarrel. He needed a cause in which to channel his suppressed resentment.

Along came the first seeds of the Texian rebellion and, at last, a spark resembling the old Bowie was re-kindled.

A Bowie Knife. These vicious fighting weapons were typically used with the cutting edge facing upwards, the idea being to disembowel an opponent with a vertical slash.

 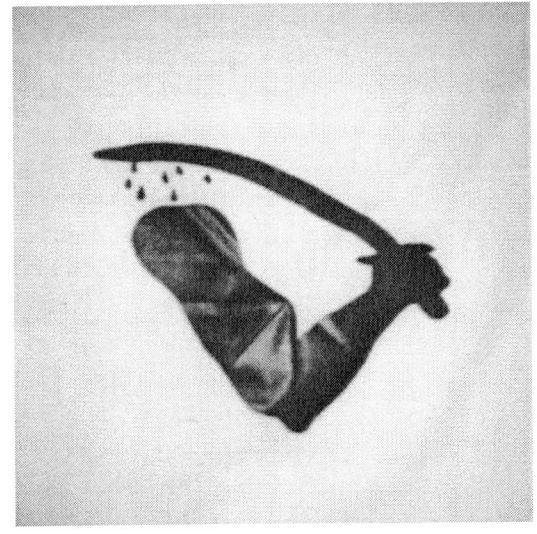

Texian volunteer flags. Gonzales and Goliad.

WAR FEVER

Although the Texian success at Gonzales could hardly be called a great victory, it had a tremendous effect on morale. Within days hundreds of volunteers had flocked to the town baying for blood. The mood was joyous, though perhaps, for many, naive. Also, not every man in this newly declared "Volunteer Army of the People" shared the same aim. Many were calling for total independence from Mexico while others were still only insisting on re-instatement of the 1824 Convention.

Stephen Austin was immediately declared commander of this army but he was soon out of his depth, unable to keep control of what initially amounted to little more than a rag-tag mob of brave hearts, patriots and adventurers waving guns. Also, Austin had never pretended to be a military man. His strengths lay in diplomacy and organisation and he was anxious to travel to the United States to make an appeal for assistance. For the meantime, though, he had little choice but to go along with the wishes of the majority, and that meant a march upon General Cos and his men at Bexar. Waiting in the wings, Sam Houston quickly sold 4,000 acres of his Red River land so that he could purchase a uniform, sword and sash for the command he knew he would soon hold. He also sent out an appeal for more volunteers to rally to the cause, offering vast land grants in return for armed service and declaring "Let each man come with a good rifle and one hundred rounds of ammunition ... and come soon!"

Confidence was further bolstered just a week after the Gonzales clash when another Mexican force surrendered to Texians a few miles south at Goliad. Flushed with success, a force of about 300 Texians set out for Bexar, with Austin somewhat doubtfully leading them. They must have seemed a happy band, marching proudly along as they sang old Irish songs of rebellion like "Rising of the Moon", played soldier's favourites like "The Girl I Left Behind Me" and roared defiant and raunchy new lyrics to "Yankee Doodle" and "Auld Lang Syne". Anyone would have thought that they had won the war already.

Over in Bexar, General Cos grimly listened to Lt. Castenada's report then swiftly set about preparing for an Americano attack. Barricades were thrown up across the streets of the town and sharpshooters took up positions in the houses, trenches were dug and a cannon was placed in the tower of the San Fernando church. However, Cos knew that his main line of defence would be best positioned in that old mission building he had noted on his arrival; The Alamo. It had strong stone walls but had not been strictly built as a military garrison and would need work to fortify it.

He did not have much time but a lot was achieved very quickly. The walls lacked terraces, bastions and gun ports and Cos' men did much to rectify this. Earth was piled up against the walls to form ramps and platforms for cannon to fire over and a timber stockade was erected running south west across the vulnerable open area in front of the main church building. The roof of the church itself had been demolished and the rubble was piled against the back wall (facing east) and covered with hard packed earth to form another cannon platform.

Cos had more than a thousand men under his command and although they were poor quality troops (because mainly the worst calibre of soldado was sent to Texas at this stage) the General felt that his position was sufficiently strong to meet any threat these rebels could throw against him.

Austin's Texians arrived in the town's suburbs to be met by the likes of a newly inspired Jim Bowie and a totally committed Juan Seguin who offered his services to the Volunteer Army. Both these men, with their immense local knowledge and influence, were to prove invaluable to the Texian war effort. Even so, Austin never took to Bowie and considered him a "wild adventurer".

Regardless of his superior numbers, Cos decided to mount a defensive action, closing ranks within Bexar and The Alamo while the rag-tag Texian army threw a loose ring around the whole area. Action came quite swiftly at first when Bowie, supported by Captain James Fannin, routed a Mexican force at the Mission Concepcion on October 28th., losing only one man against Cos' losses of almost seventy. This, naturally, served as another great boost to Texian confidence and there was more celebrating, but then things started to slow down. The Mexicans dug in and the Texians settled around their camp fires. It seemed as if no one was sure what they should do next.

Day by day reinforcements were arriving to bolster the Texian strength. Word had spread far and wide and it was now well known that enormous support was on its way to further the cause of liberty. That word "Liberty" had certainly caught the American public's imagination in a way that it is difficult for us to appreciate in more cynical modern times. As far away as Boston and Philadelphia men were dropping everything to flock to Texas "with their good rifles and ammunition" to assist their countrymen. Idealistic but most effective.

They came as individuals or small groups of friends. Some travelled in officially formed companies, often with elaborate names and garrishly tailored outfits. The Texians at Bexar were impressed by the arrival of the New Orleans Greys who actually looked like proper soldiers in their grey jackets, knapsacks and U.S. Army surplus forage caps. The Greys even had an impressive looking flag, a pretty blue fringed with gold, which bore a noble eagle and the statement "God and Liberty". There was also room for the proud boast "First Company of Texan Volunteers from New Orleans". These men were a mixed bunch who hailed from lands as far distant as Germany, Ireland and England. Amongst them was Captain John Baugh and 55 year old Robert Moore, both from Virginia. With Captain Carey's artillery company came Sergeant John McGregor, a jolly Scotsman who brought his bagpipes with him. Soon he was serenading the ranks with favourite tunes from his homeland, like "Flowers of Edinburgh".

Activity continued throughout November. Bowie was elevated to the position of unofficial colonel of militia and Seguin was given authority, and the rank of captain, to form his own cavalry company. His men were all local Tejano vaqueros, expert horsemen who knew the surrounding land like the backs of their hands. Immediately Seguin set them to work, fanning out south, east and west to scout for enemy activity, particularly any sign of reinforcements for Cos' beleaugured garrison.

Another asset for the Texian cause came in the form of a hard bitten, leather skinned frontier veteran named Erastus Smith. Known as "Deaf" because of a lifelong hearing problem, this disability did not detract from Smith's legendary reputation as the most highly skilled scout in the land. Deaf Smith had been settled into the Mexican community for a long time and was thus reluctant to become involved in any dispute against them. However, when General Cos made the bad mistake of refusing to allow Deaf to visit his wife and children in Bexar, the scout responded by throwing in his lot with the rebels. With a man like Smith opposing them, Cos' decision was to ultimately prove costly to Santa Anna.

Travis was on the scene by now, impatient as ever and urging action as Austin uttered his usual words of caution. Desperate for something to happen, Travis occupied himself by scouting the area and capturing horses but pretty soon he was so frustrated he threatened to resign. Typical hot headed behaviour but there was much in the young lawyer's bravado and patriotism to be admired. Austin spoke reassuringly that his time would come. Indeed it would.

In the meantime Austin turned his command over to General Edward Burleson and declared that he was travelling to the United States to make a concerted appeal for official American assistance, backed up by military might. The men cheered him on his way but soon became despondent when Burleson proved himself to have no enthusiasm for a fight. Days dragged into weeks of virtual inactivity and it did not help matters when the weather grew damp, grey and miserable. Inevitably this led to frayed tempers which culminated in the Texians turning on each other. In one dispute a man was killed. His killer was swiftly strung up from the nearest tree but the Texian leadership were now worried by the prospect of their men murdering one another.

Fortunately, by the end of November another episode occurred to distract them from their brooding. Deaf Smith rode into camp with a report about a Mexican column outside of town and from somewhere a rumour arose that this enemy party was carrying a fortune in silver to pay Cos' trapped men. Burleson ordered Bowie to ride out with 100 men to observe the column, but he was not to attack it unless necessary. With such an open brief, Bowie must have smiled wryly as he led his keen riders out to obvious battle. They were like starving dogs on a leash. "Attack" would be necessary alright.

It was the 26th. when Bowie's men reined in to look down upon the slow moving column of Mexican troops, half heartedly guarding a tantalising looking string of pack mules and wagons. Without hesitation, Big Jim led a charge and the startled Mexican guards formed up to meet them. A short but lively skirmish resulted in the Mexicans fleeing in disorder, leaving their wagons and mules in Texian hands. The Americans wasted no time tearing into the packs, expecting glittering silver but finding only cut grass! The Mexican mission had merely been to collect fodder for the hungry cavalry horses back in the besieged garrison.

A disappointment, yes, but one tinged with positivity. The Grass Fight, as it became known served to boost Texian morale at a time when it was becoming sorely needed. It was another victory, after all. The Mexican army was beginning to seem like a bit of a joke.

Things were happening elsewhere too. In San Felipe Texian political leaders were meeting to thrash out the creation of a provisional government of their own. Austin was now officially declared Commissioner to the U.S.A. and Sam Houston took his place as Commander of the Volunteer Army. In Bexar the time had come to make an effort to oust General Cos from his cosy fortress.

In early December word came, via a pair of escaped Bexar residents, that the Mexican troops were sick, cold, demoralised and low on food and ammunition. Surely a Texian assault must now be imminent, but Burleson still dithered.

Enter Ben Milam, a man destined to become the original heroic martyr for Texian liberty. Milam's whole life had been one big adventure. A Kentuckian, he had fought in the War of 1812, had served as a sea captain, an Indian trader, an "empresario" and even as a Mexican soldado! Recently he had escaped from a Mexican prison (where he had been shut up for his pro-rebel sympathies) but by the time of the Bexar siege he was in his mid-forties and serving as a volunteer scout for the Texians. Returning from a mission on December 4th., Milam was distressed to discover his countrymen sitting around and failing to press home their advantage. He was like a breath of fresh air, calling the men around him, berating them for their lethargy and challenging them by demanding, " Who will follow old Ben Milam into Bear?"

Their shouts of agreement were deafening. Dithering Burleson was forgotten as the Texians primed their weapons and prepared to attack the town. With Milam leading them the Texian army advanced on Bexar at dawn on the 5th., taking the tired Mexican defenders completely by surprise. However, the fighting was fierce and intense and it was quickly obvious that Cos' men were not going to be dislodged easily. The conflict raged from house to house as the Mexicans gradually gave up their various strongholds and were pushed back towards The Alamo, but it was slow, bloody work. For four days the Battle of Bexar raged relentlessly and on the third day Ben Milam himself became immortal in Texas history when he was shot dead by a sniper. Spurred on by their hero's sacrifice, the Texians redoubled their efforts to take the town and by the 9th. Cos had entered into negotiations to surrender.

It was a huge and significant victory for the rebels and it had an air of finality about it. After all, just 300 or so Texians had managed to defeat something like 1,400 Mexican soldiers entrenched in fortified positions. Terms of surrender were agreed and Cos suffered the humiliation of having to promise that he would never again take up arms against Texian independence. With his army's weapons seized, greatly bolstering the rebel armoury, Cos and his men withdrew south towards the Rio Grande, back towards Mexico with their tails between their legs.

Now it was time for celebration and many Texians prematurely assumed the war must be over. With Bexar and The Alamo now firmly in Texian hands Burleson went home, turning his command over to Col. Frank Johnson. Many other volunteers left too, anxious to spend Christmas with their families and get back to their farms and other businesses. Even Deaf Smith left, cautiously transporting his family to the safety of Gonzales. Juan Seguin and his Tejanos were not so confident, however. True there had been some easy victories, but most of the Mexican army that had been sent to quell the Texian rebellion were of poor quality, all that was thought necessary. Santa Anna would undoubtedly learn a lesson from these setbacks and now he would be seeking revenge, using the full force of his huge, combat experienced army to re-establish his authority. The Tejanos knew, from bitter example, what Don Demonio was capable of.

Jim Bowie, too, was sufficiently long in the tooth to know that it was far too early to sit back on his laurels. He and Seguin immediately sent out a whole wave of scouting parties far to the south to watch for any sign of Santa Anna's approach which they knew must come, probably sooner than later. Having set up their scouting network, Bowie and Travis then left the area, making their way east towards the Rio Brazos to seek further guidance from Houston.

In Bexar, the celebrations soon turned into a shambles. Those who had not deserted the newly won garrison now entered into a lively debate regarding their next move. Some wished to stay put but a proposal was made to actually invade Mexico! The country south of the Rio Grande was full of liberal Mexicans who, it was thought, could easily be persuaded, with a little armed help, to turn against the tyrant Santa Anna. That was the theory anyway. Many Texians, flushed with their own recent success, became enamoured by the idea and a plan was hastily formulated to march upon the Mexican port of Matamoros. There would be a lot of booty to be had and from such a base, they could launch a strike into Santa Anna's heartland. If the Mexicans continued to put up as poor a fight as they had done to date, then it would be childsplay to take the whole country.

Col. Johnson was fully behind this scheme and so, when the ill fated Matamoros expedition set out, the command of Bexar changed hands yet again, this time under the leadership of Col. James Neill. (If all these names are getting confusing, then I apologise. I am doing my best to keep it as simple as possible!) With Johnson went about 200 men, leaving Neill with an impossibly small force of about 100. Johnson's men also cleaned out the garrison taking almost all the supplies and much of the armament with them, forcing Col. Neill to write to San Felipe informing Houston of the stronghold's "alarming weakness".

By mid January 1836 the situation in San Antonio de Bexar was critical. Owing to further desertions, there were now only about eighty die-hard effective volunteers under Neill's command, all of them lacking adequate clothing and food. They had received no pay since at least October and their spirits were declining rapidly. Miserably, Neill ordered them to pull back from the town itself and base themselves in the dilapidated Alamo. There were not even enough of them to man the walls and so they sunk down beside their camp fires, hungry, shivering and longing for the good times to return.

And yet these were the men with true backbone, those who had chosen to stay and defend that which had been won at such cost. Perhaps some of them had nowhere else to go, but for the most part they were volunteers who simply believed in what they were doing. After the euphoria of the Mexican defeat, when the celebrations had ended, these eighty or so men must have looked around and thought long and hard about their situation.

The Alamo was a sprawling place covering some three acres which they could not realistically hope to defend alone, but there were barracks and strong stone walls. Much of it was in ruins and the Mexican's attempts at building fortifications had not been very successful. However, when they surrendered they had left behind quite a few fine cannon in good working order so maybe the old mission did have some potential after all.

Assembling his shabby band of determined volunteers, Col. Neill cannot have felt too optimistic as he looked them over. Neill was a capable officer but not a man to inspire high hopes. He lacked fire but the men paid morose attention as he grimly spelled out their situation. No food, no apparent line of supply, no pay and seemingly no hope. And all this with a huge Mexican army on its way to annihilate them. Was there any point in staying here and prolonging the agony?

Surprisingly, the men unanimously seemed to think so. Miserable as they were, they resolved to remain, come what may, becoming the first of many who were to fall under the mission's strange spell.

*   *   *

Further east matters had escalated into a hive of activity with General Sam Houston and the newly appointed Texian Governor Henry Smith desperately attempting to establish some form of order. The ragged, ever growing army of volunteers were impressive in their enthusiasm but were becoming increasingly difficult to control. Houston was particularly horrified at the prospect of Col. Johnson's ill advised Matamoros expedition and had to use all his powers of persuasion and authority to convince the naive hotheads not to go. In the end, to Houston's relief, only about seventy followed Johnson.

Arguments regarding policy raged between the Council and Governor Smith which ended in them dismissing one another! However, the volunteer army, as individuals, were strongly behind Smith because they approved of his stance on independence. The council, by contrast, seemed too vague in their aims and there remained a strong feeling that a compromise might be offered to Santa Anna. The men were in no mood for that.

All this turmoil made it difficult to arrange such things as a supply line to Neill and his men at The Alamo, but the situation was more in hand at Goliad. Another old mission, but this one was surrounded by a much stronger fort, the Presidio la Bahia, which the men were eventually to proudly name Fort Defiance. Promoted to Colonel, the commander here was James Fannin, a veteran of the battles of Concepcion and Bexar and, as a West Point trainee, one of the only proper soldiers in the Texian army. Unlike the miserable Alamo defenders, Fannin's 400 or so men were well equipped and supplied which naturally made them brimming with confidence. (Amongst them were the distinctively dressed and newly formed company of the Alabama Red Rovers in their bright red, fringed smocks.)

Houston took stock and decided that the best way to confront Santa Anna's army would be with patience. Instead of an immediate pitched battle, General Sam's strategy would involve drawing the Mexicans deep into the interior, extending their supply line and wearing them down with hit and run raids before picking the right moment to strike. This made sense, but could his hell raising, blood lusting volunteers be counted on to wait? Probably not. Whilst putting on a brave front, Houston was racked with doubt.

One thing he decided made an unecessary complication was The Alamo itself. This isolated outpost was proving more trouble than it was worth and so, in mid-January 1836, Houston entrusted Jim Bowie with the task of destroying the defences of the place and drawing the garrison (including their captured Mexican cannon) back to Gonzales where they could be put to better use.

Riding at the head of about thirty men, Bowie reached The Alamo on January 19th. but his analysis of what he found left him with mixed feelings. True the garrison was a sprawling mess in need of repair and Neill's men were certainly a ragged bunch, dejected and hungry, but they *had* remained at their posts whilst others had deserted or gone off on that crazy Matamoros jaunt. Beneath their grumbling, Big Jim saw fighters with true mettle. What was more, they had a fine collection of cannon, about twenty in fact, with no means of transporting them out of the area. Could the Texian army really afford to abandon such a force of much needed artillery? There was even a big eighteen pounder, the largest gun in Texas.

Within a day or two, Bowie had decided to adapt Houston's express orders, cunningly exploiting the part which told him to act at his own discretion. He simply could not bring himself to blow the place up and he began to see it as playing a key role in the defence of Texas. After all, did it not stand directly in the path of any invading Mexican army? Could he really abandon a place which had been won at such high cost? (Ben Milam had been martyred here, after all.) And would not a stand here buy precious time for Houston to organise his army? Another factor was undoubtedly the character of Bowie himself. He had never run from anything and the sheer drama and potential glory of the plight here appealed to his frontier spirit.

Bowie had brought good men with him too; tough, determined volunteers who fired Neill's motley crew with a new sense of purpose. They included fifty year old Louis Rose, a Frenchman who had actually fought in Napoleon's army, and a good looking aristocratic fellow with piercing eyes and thick black wavy hair. This was James Butler Bonham, a 29 year old lawyer from Carolina who had been brought up as part of one of the highest bred families in the south. He had breeding and the qualities of a true gentleman but he was also a born hero whose undoubted courage and deeply held convictions would serve Texas well. Three years older than Travis, Bonham was raised in the same area, but W.B. was of more lowly stock and therefore the two boys probably had little to do with one another, although it seems they undoubtedly met as youngsters. Bonham was a dashing soul who ran his law practice as if it were part of a plot from a romantic novel. Once he even thrashed a judge who dared to insult his female client! He was working in Alabama by the time he heard the Texian call to arms, a distress signal he immediately responded to. Within days he was helping to organise the Mobile Greys, soon leading them to assist in the Battle of Bexar. They arrived just three days too late for that, but Bonham straightaway immersed his talents in the continuing struggle, roaming the countryside and making himself useful. Commissioned as a lieutenant in the cavalry, the young aristocrat was more than happy to follow the renowned Jim Bowie back to The Alamo. When word came that they would be staying he was delighted.

Major Green B. Jameson, 29 like Bonham and also a lawyer by trade, was another volunteer whose worthy streak was fired by the irresistible aura which seemed to emit from The Alamo. He was appointed chief engineer of the garrison, a role he took to with considerable enthusiasm and inventiveness. After an initial tour of the defences, Jameson swiftly drew up plans and set the men to work strengthening the place. Platforms of earth and timber were raised against the walls, weak points were bolstered, guns were mounted and before long the old mission finally began to resemble a formidable fortress, even though there were still nowhere near enough men to realistically defend the place.

After considerable thought, Jameson and Bowie agreed to mount their finest gun on the summit of the wall at the south west angle, its long iron barrel pointing towards the main plaza of Bexar, about 800 yards away. They knew that this big eighteen pounder could lob an iron ball more than half a mile, beyond the western boundary of the town, if necessary.

Bowie knew everyone and everything in the area and he was soon using his contacts to resupply The Alamo. The local Tejanos were more than happy to co-operate, delighted to see their beloved Don Jaime back in the land of the living after his long period of mourning. Bowie also re-established his network of scouts with Juan Seguin and this time the hard riding vaqueros were sent further south than before, for now it was more urgent than ever to know of Santa Anna's movements.

The men were so inspired by the famous knife fighter that many were looking upon him as their new leader, with Col. Neill beginning to take a more supportive role. Bowie must have gleaned satisfaction from this, but it would need more than the men's heightened spirits to defend the place effectively. Hard cash was required. At least $500 immediately to cover expenses. Requests for assistance through official channels could not be depended upon and Bowie's own considerable fortune had dwindled dramatically over the last year or two, owing to his troubles and inactivity. He was forced to take a loan locally, and this probably came from the ever supportive wealthy rancher Seguin.

Day by day the garrison took more shape and by the end of the month a rally was held within the walls wherein the men unanimously voiced their determination to remain at their posts. It was then that Bowie took the step of writing a strongly worded letter to Governor Smith in which he declared "Colonel Neill and myself have come to the solemn resolution that we will rather die in these ditches than give it up to the enemy." On a more practical note he also emphasised that he believed the security of Bexar would prove essential for the defence of Texas and that reinforcements must be sent forthwith.

General Sam Houston had already received word of Bowie's failure to carry out his orders. Houston liked Bowie, admired him greatly, but this was the final straw. Frustrated by his wayward subordinates and their maddening tendency to do as they pleased, Houston took leave for a while and disappeared into the wilderness to deal with further Indian affairs. His attitude must have been "Let them get on with it!"

At The Alamo, Maj. Jameson was demonstrating his inventiveness with remarkable degrees of efficiency and energy. Constantly coming up with grand new ideas to strengthen the defences, he kept the men busy digging and building. Bowie was glad to see all this activity, for not only did it serve a very useful purpose but it kept the men's minds off of what they might be facing in the near future. Previous lethargy had proved to be a bad enemy. Stoical Virginian Captain John Baugh was working industriously in his new role as garrison adjutant and Gonzales blacksmith Almeron Dickinson, recently installed as a captain of artillery, was positioning and maintaining the guns as if he had been born to it. All these men had adapted to their military assignments with ease.

Even so, a dark cloud of uncertainty hung over the high spirits of The Alamo volunteers, and this was due to Jim Bowie himself. The men were beginning to cast concerned looks at the great man, he who had always seemed so indestructible, for Big Jim was beginning to resemble a shadow of his former self. His health had been slowly declining for some time, almost certainly due to the heavy drinking and depression which had followed the loss of his wife. Although he was now freshly enlivened by the spirit of Texian Independence, the hard times had visibly taken their toll. His ruddy complexion had grown pale, his eyes sunken with dark shadows below them, his cheeks hollow. The broad, upright physique now showed signs of a slight stoop and his movements seemed slower. And then there was that terrible hacking cough that seemed to be torn from the very base of his spine, no doubt complicated by the severe lung wound he had taken at Vidalia years before. Although he tried to make light of it, the pain and trauma were obvious. Still no one dared to take issue with him and he carried on bravely, managing the day to day affairs and encouraging the men as he had always done. In effect, a fearfully ill Jim Bowie was still a towering figure amongst normal men.

And there was plenty to occupy him, not least of all an opportunity to exercise his legendary gallantry to the ladies. He may have lost his beloved Ursula, but her adopted sisters remained very much alive and in need of protection. These were the nieces of the late Governor Veramendi, strictly speaking cousins to Bowie's late wife, and Jim made it his business to ensure that they were safe. Juana had recently married a Texian volunteer named Alsbury and had an infant son. With her husband away from Bexar on military business, Juana was now living with her son and sister, Gertrudis Navarro, at the old Veramendi house. Bowie took them under his wing and could not do enough for them. In his darkest moods, this surrogate family brought out the best in him

Then came grim news from one of Seguin's riders who had galloped full pelt some 300 miles from the Mexican border. Within a few days more detailed news arrived and The Alamo's leadership were forced to face facts. An advance guard of Mexican infantry and cavalry were already across the Rio Grande, carrying out drill on the banks as they awaited the arrival of Santa Anna's main force. It was estimated that the enemy numbered in excess of 5,000 men.

*   *   *

Santa Anna was not the only one making his way to The Alamo. William Barrett Travis was returning at the head of forty newly mustered cavalrymen.

Travis, true to form, had shown himself anxious to get back into the thick of the action and had been pestering Governor Smith and Sam Houston. Eventually he was granted the rank of Lieutenant Colonel in the cavalry. This satisfied him partially, but as he rode towards Bexar he inwardly seethed that he had only been given a supporting role. Travis made no secret of the fact that he felt he was born to command.

Of course, he knew The Alamo needed reinforcements, but could that not be left to a more junior officer? And what was the point of the place anyway? Surely Houston's plan to destroy the old mission, pull back the men and reform properly was the sensible course to take. Why would no one listen to him? Why were his letters ignored? For now, at least, he must do as he was told.

Travis had spent the weeks since the Bexar battle making preparations and putting his affairs in order. Up in San Felipe he carried out a little work in his law office, then left it in the capable hands of his business partner. He also spent some time with his young son, Charles, who was now living with him following some wrangling with his ex-wife. Leaving the boy in the care of relatives and friends, Travis then began to make ready for his route to glory. He had already ordered a fancy uniform from the renowned tailors McKinney & Williams but it was far from ready by the time he had to leave, so he was forced to ride out dressed in his plain Texas jeans tail coat. However, he made sure he was well armed with a sword, pistols and his lethal double barrelled shotgun. As usual, official money was in short supply so Travis had to dig deep into his own pockets to furnish his men with rations, blankets, horse fodder and other essential trappings. With a final touch of patriotism and personal honour, W.B. even spent $5 having a flag made so that his group could have their very own banner to rally to.

The ride to Bexar was not a happy one and the men grew as gloomy and miserable as the weather. Hunched in their saddles, heads bent against the wind and drizzle, their thick blanket coats drawn up around their ears, some of the volunteers began to have second thoughts about this adventure. Within a few days, a quarter of Travis' little band had deserted taking essential supplies with them.

Travis reacted furiously to such treachery and sent a courier with a message to Governor Smith. Whilst praising the loyalty of those who had remained with him, W.B. complained that volunteers were unreliable and that he could see no point in turning up at The Alamo with such a paltry force. He stressed that he was keen to play an active role in the rebellion but he thought his talents were being wasted, the truth being that he actually felt embarrassed to be associated with what he saw as an insignificant command. He begged to be released from his mission to Bexar, hoping for a more important assignment elsewhere.

Camping on the banks of the Colorado River, Travis and his men halted for a day or so to await a response. None came. Governor Smith probably knew that, given time, Travis would overcome his petulance and this seemed to be the case, for W.B.'s patience was quickly exhausted and he resentfully carried on to Bexar, arriving on February 3rd..

Few as they were, Travis' party received a warm welcome from Bowie and Neill which obviously elevated the newcomer's spirits. And Travis himself was pleasantly surprised by what he saw. The industriousness and optimism of the men in The Alamo, the impressive work that Jameson was doing on the defences, the strong case that Bowie put forward for holding the place. Like so many others, Travis was soon under the spell and his mood changed. Yes, The Alamo must be held at all costs. This would be the place where he would find his destiny, after all.

43

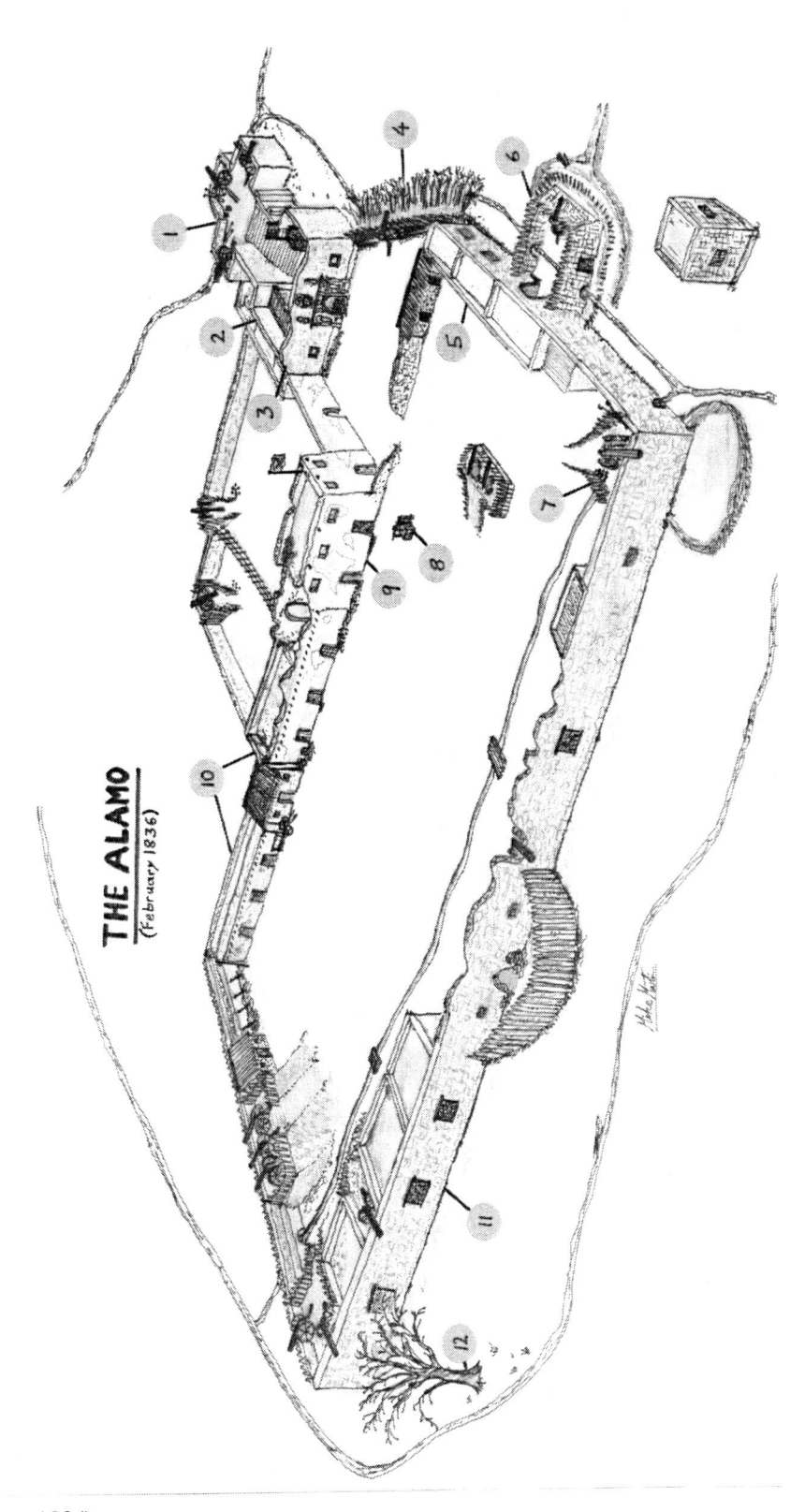

The Alamo (February 1836)
1. Dickinson's battery
2. Sacristy where the non-combatants sheltered
3. Powder magazine
4. Abatis at the south east palisade
5. Jim Bowie's sick room
6. Outer fortifications at the main gate
7. The 18 pounder
8. Well
9. Dr. Pollard's hospital (2nd. floor)
10. The Long Barracks
11. Travis' headquarters
12. Pecan tree

THE LONG MARCH

The Alamo garrison, still numbering less than 140 men, may have been full of fire and optimism but very few of those defenders knew the true implications of what was being sent against them. How many of those gallant souls would have remained behind the walls had they been able to see the thousands of troops assembling at San Luis Potosi, outside of Mexico City, preparing for their long march north?

For Santa Anna this had become a personal matter, not just a strategic and political one. He saw the taking of Bexar and the humiliation of his brother-in-law, General Cos, as a personal slight on his honour and he was determined to wreak vengeance upon this rabble of rebels. His original plan had been to mount his campaign against the Texians in the spring, when the weather grew fine, but when Bexar fell he decided to act without delay.

Raising the money for such a huge enterprise was never easy, even for His Excellency El Presidente, but by forcing contributions and loans Santa Anna soon amassed the required amount and the army was on its way. Their next stop was at Saltillo where for two weeks the masses of troops, many of whom were recently conscripted, were endlessly drilled and generally whipped into shape. Strangely enough, however, their actual combat training was almost non-existent despite the theory that the cavalry, infantry and artillery should work tactically together, in the style of the European armies of Santa Anna's hero, Napoleon. The reality of the Mexican army was that most of the men only understood the concept of a frontal attack. They would advance firing from the hip and then it would all be down to the cold steel of the bayonet. The average soldado did not like to level his weapon from the shoulder as he disliked the heavy recoil. Consequently, generally speaking, their marksmanship was pretty atrocious.

By the end of January 1836, following a grand review, the army was on its way again, heading for the border where the First Division, or Vanguard Brigade, under General Sesma, was already awaiting them, numbering about 1,500 men and eight cannon. Santa Anna himself led the Second Division which was made up of two infantry brigades under Generals Gaona and Tolsa, a cavalry brigade, led by General Andrade, and twelve more cannon. There was also a small force of Zapadores (or "Sappers") numbering 185 men under Lt. Col. Amat. The Zapadores were Santa Anna's crack troops, for although they were essentially an engineer corps whose main function was to build bridges and forts, dig trenches and raise batteries, they were often used as assault infantry, a function in which these highly trained, experienced soldiers excelled. In all, the Second Division amounted to around 4,000 men. (A further brigade, under General Urrea, separated from the main column and marched east where they would follow the line of the Gulf Coast to cover Santa Anna's right flank. Also they would be expected to deal with Texian activity in that area, such as Johnson's Matamoros expedition.)

The backbone of the Mexican army was made up of fusilier infantrymen. Some of them, "permanentes", were professional troops, regulars who were experienced in action at frontier posts fighting Indians, but the majority were "activos" who were usually just called up for campaigns such as this. The activos, therefore, were generally the most poorly equipped soldados and often wore open sandals instead of shoes. Their tunics were single breasted, blue with red piping and they wore tall, black leather shakos, topped with a multi-coloured plume or pom-pom. For marching or camp work, these troops usually wore white cotton or linen fatigue clothing. They were armed with British "Brown Bess" muskets (1809 India pattern), a heavy weapon which produced quite a kick. Loaded with a single charge it fired a .75 calibre lead ball, but the real fear for a soldado's opponent was the seventeen inch length and vicious point of the needle like socket bayonet.

Each battalion included two companies of elite troops who were better equipped, one of "granadaros" or grenadiers (heavy infantry) and one of "cazadores" (light infantry). The cazadores (which means "hunters") were well trained (by Mexican standards) to fight in skirmish order and tended to be armed with another British made weapon, the light Baker rifle. Shorter barrelled than the Brown Bess it fired a .625 calibre ball. The blade of its brass hilted sword bayonet was double edged, and it actually had a longer reach in close combat than the Brown Bess.

The cavalrymen made an impressive sight. They were excellent riders and wore scarlet tunics. Their helmet was moulded from tanned cowhide, fronted with a gleaming brass shield and topped with a brass comb of black goat fur. Heavily laden with weapons, their arms consisted of a brace of pistols, short paget carbines and a light sabre. Their favoured accoutrement was without doubt the nine foot long lance, tipped with a broad, sharp blade and red pennant. In the hands of a skilled horseman, these lances were the scourge of an enemy foot soldier. Presidial cavalrymen were equally capable and colourful.

Officers often wore large, black bicorn hats, heavily adorned with plumage. Moustaches were common amongst the troops and sometimes they sported long, hanging sideburns, curled in a jaunty fashion. It was a tradition in the Zapadores for the men to wear full beards. Physically, the average soldado was usually under nourished and his average height measured between 5' and 5'6". Not exactly an army of giants.

It was never thought by the Mexican leadership that the march into Texas was going to be easy, but none of the Generals, especially Santa Anna himself, could have foreseen the nightmare which lay ahead. Something like 400 miles of harsh country lay between Saltillo and Bexar and the long column of troops and camp followers set off with woefully inadequate preparation.

They appeared impressive enough, particularly Santa Anna's personal entourage. As always on campaign, Don Demonio cantered far ahead of his troops, aloof in the saddle of his charger, resplendent in his ostentatious uniform and anxious to get to grips with those "perfidious foreigners". Immediately behind him rode his escort of magnificent looking dragoons, the polished metal of their weapons and equipment glinting in the winter sunshine, the pennants of their lances fluttering in the chilly breeze.

Far to the rear, but easily reached when needed, the president's luxury, ornamental carriage lumbered along the dusty trail. Then came his personal baggage train, bursting with the essentials of war, such as his big multi-striped marquee, fancy hand painted china, monogrammed slippers, tea sets, cut glass decanters, a silver chamber pot and, naturally, his ample supply of opium.

The long lines of infantry began their march briskly, but the well ordered formations soon broke up and the soldados slouched along wearily, hands and bandanas held against their mouths to shield the billowing clouds of choking dust. It was not much easier on the cavalrymen who were often forced to dismount and lead their plodding horses along rocky, treacherous trails. The artillerymen struggled to keep up, hindered as they were by their twelve cannon, munitions wagons and gun carriages.

Then came the supply train which reached back like a drunken snake for miles. Almost 2,000 heavily laden mules, thirty odd gigantic wagons (the wheels were seven feet in diameter), hundreds of ox drawn carts and a countless array of barrows and various other modes of transport. Most of these were not even military but were owned by a seperate army of "hangers on", sutlers who brought along their wares to sell en-route. There was a whole host of women too, soldaderas as they were known, wives, mothers, sisters, mistresses and, of course, the much in demand prostitutes. Many of these females accompanied their men folk out of sheer concern for their welfare, but they also carried out practical tasks such as cooking, laundering, foraging, mending clothing and basic nursing. Lots of them brought their children with them. Although this offered considerable comfort and assistance to the oppressed soldados, the presence of the soldaderas was also a huge distraction, not to mention the fact that they consumed vast amounts of food.

This particularly concerned General Filisola, Santa Anna's second-in-command, waiting for the column to reach him at Monclova where he had been attempting to organise more supplies. He was horrified at the sight of such a rabble and he formally protested that the army's efficiency would suffer accordingly. Santa Anna took him to one side and smoothly made the point that the presence of the soldaderas was the lesser of two evils. True, they were a nuisance, but dismiss them and probably half the army would desert in their wake.

Also waiting at Monclova was the disgraced General Cos. Having lost Bexar to the Texians, thereby forcing his illustrious brother-in-law into the fray, Cos no doubt attempted to make excuses for the poor show put on by his troops. Santa Anna dismissed these explanations contemptuously. All that mattered now was the retaking of the town and garrison to reassert Mexican pride. When Cos mentioned that he had given his word not to take up arms again against the Texians, Don Demonio's face reddened with fury. Staring hard at the nervous, shamefaced General, Santa Anna declared that no one, least of all his own officers, was to make any kind of pact with traitors. Knowing that the pressure was now upon him to make amends, Cos uttered no further protests, quietly joined the column and found himself back in the war.

And so the huge, chaotic expedition rolled on into the bleak hills of northern Mexico. There seemed to be little sign of any order, just a general agreement that they were heading for the Texan border. The clatter of hooves, the lowing of oxen, the incessant grumbling of disgruntled troops, the shouting of their officers, the chatter of women, the piercing creaks of unlubricated wagon wheels, the cries and laughter of children, it must have added up to an infernal din.

In theory, soldados below the rank of first sergeant were allotted food which should have consisted of a daily allowance of one pound of meat, along with some hardtack, beans or corn. Anything extra they had to buy for themselves out of their measly wage of just twenty pesos per day. Needless to say, the sutlers overpriced all their wares, taking advantage of the troops helpless position. Officers had to pay for their own food and supplies which caused resentment and created a climate of corruption. Quite a few of them actually bribed the quartermasters so that they could plunder the private trooper's woefully inadequate rations. On top of this, Santa Anna had made virtually no provision whatsoever for the medical care of his army on this campaign. No medicine, no ambulances, no surgical equipment and certainly no doctors. Any ailments along the way and the men had to rely on self help or the limited nursing skills of the soldaderas. Any that died could not even depend upon the comfort of a proper Christian burial, for in this vast array of devoutly Catholic troopers no one had thought to officially contract any priests.

The hardships of the long march gradually turned into real suffering and progress slowed to a virtual crawl. Merry banter and children's playful cries soon became depressingly silent, broken only by the shuffle of long weary columns on the move, punctuated here and there by wailing and pitiful pleading. And it was growing colder too. The soldado's white linen marching clothing proved totally unsuitable for the harshness of a Texan winter and they huddled together as they marched in a desperate attempt to keep warm. By night they did not even have any tents to shelter them. It all grew much worse when, in early February, the columns were suddenly, and savagely, hit by a blizzard which howled out of the hills, stopping the army in its tracks. Horses panicked and many oxen were lost in the swirling snow storm, men were temporarily blinded and dozens collapsed, some permanently.

Even when the storm was over and the army had staggered on into drier country, its suffering was far from over. Now it faced a critical water shortage and an almost complete lack of grazing land for the livestock. Animals and humans alike grew so thirsty their tongues swelled to such a degree that their mouths bulged open. A few stagnant pools were found but those who drank from these became victims of a fever which often proved fatal. As stocks dwindled, Santa Anna ordered the troops rations halved, a terrible blow as they had been inadequately supplied in the first place. Now they were existing on eight ounces of toasted corn cake per day. Starving, soldados and their followers broke away from the columns, scouring the surrounding bleak land for anything they might be able to eat. They resorted to chewing the long bitter beans of mesquite trees and the berries of any plant they happened to find, but this resulted in mass sickness, dysentery and itchy skin complaints.

The ranks were decimated as men dropped from illness or sheer fatigue. Sometimes the soldados were so shattered, no amount of screaming and beating from their sergeants could get them on their feet again and so they were just left behind to fall victim to the circling buzzards. Many tried to desert but usually ended up lost in the wilderness. And then there were the raids from hostile Indians who would often attack isolated pockets of the column, swooping down when the men were at their lowest ebb, running off horses, stealing what they could and, in some cases, taking captives. Women and children would be kept as slaves or held for future bargaining but captured men knew their fate lay as the tormented playthings of Apache or Comanche braves. These unfortunate's tortured screams would split the night, chilling the blood of their surviving compadres who huddled around sputtering camp fires counting their blessings.

The army left behind a veritable "trail of tears". Crippled wheels, wagons with broken axles, discarded military equipment, dead animals and human corpses too; even the army's giant howitzer which had proved too much of a burden for the journey. As for Santa Anna, he was the least affected by all this misery. Naturally he would procure the most and best of whatever there was to be had and was always far ahead of his suffering army. Therefore he and his dragoon escort were amongst the first to reach the border.

It was February 12th. when the president trotted his horse along the antiquated streets of Presidio de Rio Grande, another old Spanish town which had seen better days. This was where General Sesma had established his headquarters over the last few weeks, making himself and his men comfortable on the banks of the river while they awaited the arrival of their leader. Now Santa Anna had come with his army lagging shortly behind.

Sesma had spent his time antagonising the local populace, requisitioning livestock and grain and generally disrupting their normally uneventful lives. To stem boredom and lethargy, Sesma had been drilling his troops relentlessly, the result being that El Presidente was greeted by a rather snappy force of enthusiastic soldados who were itching to meet the enemy. Unlike his own men who were slowly dragging themselves into town, appearing more like an army returning from a defeat rather than fresh troops on their way to war. The march had been so harsh that many of them had already worn out their shoes and sandals. In many cases their shirts had rotted on their backs.

But now the worst of it was over. Allowing them a short period to recuperate, Santa Anna was swift to issue his officers with fresh orders. There was no time to waste. The rebels would be growing stronger by the day and Bexar must be retaken before any significant Texian reinforcements could reach it. Sesma's men should prove an inspiration and the newly arrived soldados must shake off their self pity and make themselves ready for the fight which lay ahead.

The Alamo was now only 160 miles away.

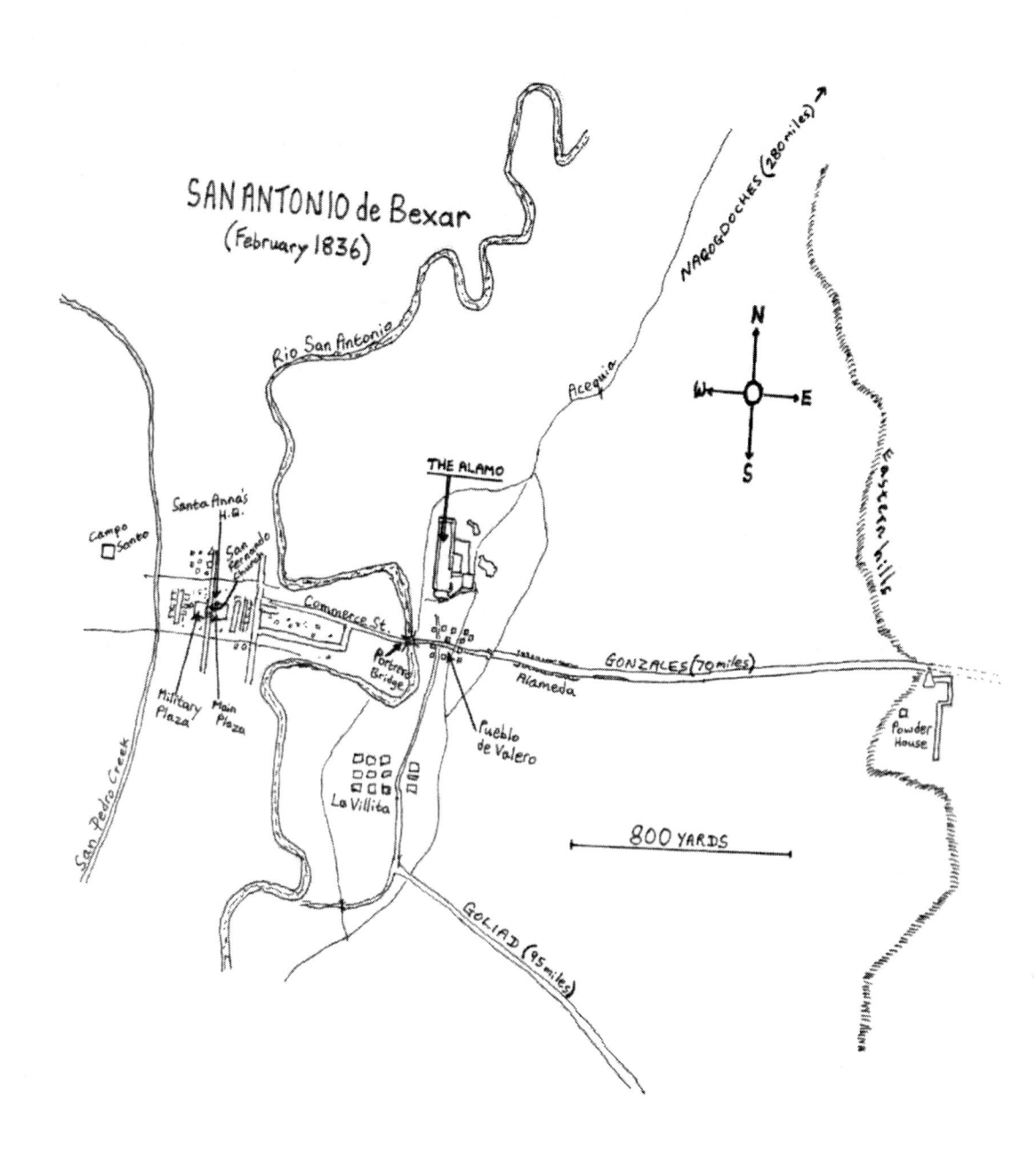

FRONTIER KING AND CANDIDATE

So we come at last to one of the men who shares the dual title role of this book; David Crockett.

Born in 1786 in the wilds of rural Tennessee, (although perhaps not quite on a mountain top as the well known Disney song tells us!) Crockett was never too fond of people calling him Davy, despite the fact that plenty did. It seems he possessed a sparkling personality, was universally liked and without doubt knew how to spin a yarn. He was a natural showman and loved to "hold court", achieving a legendary reputation during his lifetime by doing little more than entertaining people with his tall tales. That said, his golden tongue did get him quite far in life but he was not very much like the caricature which John Wayne would have us believe. In actual fact that other giant of the frontier, Kit Carson, turned out in reality to be much more like the Crockett legend than "Ol' Davy" was in real life.

If you study Crockett's portraits you will see the face of a gentle looking fellow, almost feminine in his mild demeanour. The long nose, thin features, easy smile and kind eyes convey intelligence and sensitivity, hardly the classic image of a fierce frontier fighting man. That is not to say that he was a weakling, far from it, but there was definitely a deepness and unexpected bearing in him that most people would not be aware of. He had a favourite motto which has a ring of homely wisdom about it; "I have this rule for others when I am dead ... be always sure you are right then go ahead".

Probably the main thing to emerge from the Crockett legend, which has not been subject to exaggeration, is his renowned skill as a marksman. There is much evidence, from his earliest years, which underlines the fact that he was a crack shot who certainly knew how to use his Tennessee long rifle. Brought up in the woods, Crockett developed an affinity with the flora and fauna which taught him to be a natural hunter. He had a magnificently attuned sixth sense when at large in the wilderness and would often disappear for weeks on end. Even at the peak of his fame, he never lost his love of adventure and exploration and always sought pastures anew. He claimed to have shot 108 bears in a single eight month period and he regularly enjoyed telling the tale of how he had once aimed at a raccoon only to have the creature scurry up to him and surrender! Not exactly politically correct by today's standards but it certainly impressed people back in Crockett's lifetime.

He may not have been well educated (he ran away from school at the age of twelve) but he could read and write and was naturally articulate. At first he tried farming but this was not a successful venture for him as his heart was not in it. He found a much more satisfactory outlet for his talents serving under General Andrew Jackson in the war against the Creek Indians between 1813-14. His first wife died in 1815 leaving him with three children to raise, but he soon took aboard another spouse; a young widow who needed a father for her own two offspring.

With this large family to support, Crockett tried his hand at various businesses, never satisfactorily, until he discovered his flair for politics. Using his oratorial skills and natural communion with people, he had himself elected as a local magistrate. Before long he had acquired a widespread reputation as a man of words and homespun philosophy which led to a position in the Tennessee state legislature between 1821-25.

There was no one else quite like him. Wearing Indian moccasins, a long, beaded and fringed buckskin shirt and his famous raccoon skin cap, complete with the striped tail hanging down his back, Crockett made a real impression. (Although this was to become his perennial image, he eventually much preferred to be perceived as a gentleman in city clothes.) Even his trusty rifle, "Old Betsy", became famous and, by all accounts, he played a mean fiddle too. A character indeed, who in spite of the entertaining though outlandish stories, proved himself a man of integrity who was trusted and liked by one and all. Well, by most anyway.

Never willing to compromise, "Ol' Davy" went from strength to strength and by 1827 he had served the first of three terms in Congress. The capital, Washington, welcomed him as a breath of fresh air amidst other stuffy politicians and he became the darling of society. He was a particular champion of frontier folk and fought hard for their land squatting rights. It was on this issue that he made an enemy of his old military commander, Andrew Jackson, who was now president, for Jackson and his Democrat government opposed the concept of free land. This was very much a platform upon which Crockett could pillory his simple distaste for authority and he spoke up eloquently, but in a language ordinary folk could understand, for the underdogs of this new nation. It was during this period that he made a close friend of Sam Houston.

Crockett was lauded by the Whigs who cunningly used his popularity to retrieve some of the respect they had lost as a party. With such a people's champion on their side, they could no longer be accused of elitism. In very public displays they presented him with gifts; a beautiful, inscribed gold watch and a new rifle which was so ornate that he dubbed it "Pretty Betsy". The Whigs put their full power and influence behind their new figurehead, sponsoring rallies for him, publicising his book (the hugely successful *A Narrative of the Life of David Crockett, of West Tennessee*) and writing his speeches. These speeches were particularly vehement against President Jackson.

Having thrown in his lot totally with the Whigs, Crockett was backing a lone horse and had burned his political bridges behind him. Campaigning for his fourth Congressional term in 1835, this would be all or nothing and so he milked the sympathy of his constituents for all it was worth. But Jackson was not known as "Old Hickory" for nothing and he fought back with a most contemptuous attack upon the "Backwoods Colonel". Regardless of his popularity, Crockett lost the election by a surprisingly large majority. This was a stunning blow to him, underlined by the rapidity with which he was deserted by the Whigs. Now seemingly unwanted by anyone, Crockett quickly pulled himself together and with great resilience and dignity declared "You can all go to hell while I go to Texas"!

This was more like it. With his political career behind him, but many laurels to sit back on, David Crockett, ex-congressman and bear hunter extraordinaire, could return to his true love, the wide open spaces without a care in the world. He was understandably bitter about Washington and needed a complete change of scene.

He could have chosen any area of the vast untamed frontier; north, west or south, there was so much of it back then, all waiting to be explored and settled. He chose Texas purely because he liked the idea of escaping from civilization for a while. Although he set out just as the War of Texian Independence was getting into its stride, it seems that, initially, getting involved in the cause was far from his mind. For now he was all for the simple life. Taking a handful of close friends with him he was seeking nothing more than riding, hunting, laughter and rest.

The emphasis of the Crockett expedition was to eventually change, but in early November 1835, as he began his journey down the Mississippi River, he must have felt a huge sense of relief. Word of his coming stretched far ahead and wherever he arrived he found a welcoming committee of adoring sycophants. Parties were thrown, banquets arranged, from Memphis to Little Rock and beyond. At one stop Crockett even distinguished himself, yet again, in a shooting match. He was truly in his element and wiled away the time re-telling his favourite tales to endless crowds who had gathered to see their great hero in the flesh. It is safe to say that he never disappointed them.

Transferring from steamboat to horseback, the Crockett party took a leisurely path south west, never in any hurry but gradually picking up companions along the way, for there were always adventurous types willing to seize such an opportunity to ride out with a legend. Throwing off the past, Crockett gladly traded in the gold watch given to him by the Whigs and it did not go un-noticed that he was carrying his original rifle "Betsy", not the fancy one which had also been a cynical political present.

Crossing the Sabine, Crockett and his followers rode into Houston's town of Nacogdoches, Texas, on January 5th. 1836. The reception here was exceptionally warm, the townspeople cheering him as he rode cheerily down the main street, doffing his famous coonskin cap and exchanging greetings and jokes. The town's cannon was even fired in salute as if royalty itself had arrived. That night at the welcoming dinner, Crockett's speech was even more emotive than usual. Obviously moved and doubtless prompted by reminders of the precarious situation regarding the Texian rebellion, the famous Tennessean drew gasps of approval and a standing ovation. He thanked the people of Texas for the wonderful welcome and expressed great concern for their present difficulties. Furthermore, he was horrified by what he had heard of Santa Anna's despotic policies. If anything was worth fighting for it had to be the Liberty of Texas. More cheers. He spoke of a desire to form a "constitution for this province" and of his willingness to enrol in the Volunteer Army. The crowd went wild.

Asked to sign the oath of allegiance, Crockett pointed out that it required loyalty to "any future government". He refused to sign such a document and the onlookers gaped at him non-plussed. Milking the moment for maximum dramatic effect, Crockett insisted that the wording be altered to "any future *republican* government". Of course, this was instantly done, the great man signed and rose another notch in Texian estimation. He could do no wrong.

A group of Nacogdoches volunteers had already been preparing themselves for service under Capt. William Harrison but now they were all overcome by the desire to ride with Davy Crockett. Crockett was flattered but graciously insisted that the command should remain in Capt. Harrison's hands. He made a statement, repeated several times in the coming weeks, in which he said that his interests lay in defending the "liberties of our common country" and that he wished to serve only as a "high private". His existing colonelcy was actually only an honorary rank bestowed upon him by local militia back home.

All kinds of men joined him and, although he would not take official command, it was decided to name the group in his honour, the "Tennessee Company of Mounted Volunteers", even though not many of them were actually from Tennessee. A Pennsylvanian doctor named Reynolds was one, also a young lawyer from Kentucky called Daniel Cloud. (There was certainly no shortage of lawyers in The Alamo!) Another was 42 year old Micajah Autry. He had left his family in Tennessee some time ago, coming to Texas on the promise that he would make a better life for them. Since then he had attempted to settle in many careers. Farmer, shopkeeper, schoolteacher and, (surprise, surprise) lawyer, but it appears his real love lay in aesthetic matters for he sketched beautiful pictures, wrote sensitive poetry and played the violin. He obviously adored his wife as is evident from the romantic letters he regularly sent to her. One of them conveys his pride and delight at having joined up with Col. Crockett. Micajah is a typical example of how these volunteers became caught up in the euphoria of the moment and how the notion of liberty inflamed their sensibilities. As you can see, the men who rode with Crockett were not quite the bunch of roughnecks who accompanied John Wayne. And bear in mind Crockett himself was 49 years old, a little flabby and spoiled by rich eastern living, not exactly in his prime. However, he was apparently happy and contented for he wrote an optimistic letter to his children telling them to feel no concern for he was "among friends".

They were only a small group, probably less than twenty in all, but they were awarded the grandest of send offs. The problem of where to go was never an issue. By now word had already filtered through of that isolated outpost to the west where brave volunteers were gathering to stand up to the might of Santa Anna.

The Alamo would need all the help it could get.

ARMED AND READY

Down on the banks of the Rio Grande, as the Mexican army re-organised itself from a shambles to a fighting force, Santa Anna would have had precious little information about what level of resistance faced him. No doubt he had received colourful explanations from General Cos, obvious excuses to explain the loss of Bexar, but Don Demonio was a seasoned enough soldier to be able to read between the lines. He knew that the rebels were enthusiastic and well armed but they could hardly be called a proper army. Could they really pose a dangerous threat to his drilled host of patriotic soldados?

Well, the first thing that would have encouraged Santa Anna, had he known, was the lack of manpower in the Alamo garrison. The Texian force at Bexar, at this time, certainly numbered well under 200 men, although volunteers were still constantly coming and going. This is one of the many confusing aspects of The Alamo story for there are many contradictory accounts giving "exact" figures for the amount of defenders. Traditionally it has been largely accepted that there were 183 men defending the walls on the day of the final assault, but more recent evidence points to the likelihood of there having been perhaps as many as 250. Even so, this would still put the odds in the Mexican favour by about eight to one.

So let us take a look at the situation. As previously explained, San Antonio de Bexar was a small, rural town which had originally been built alongside the mission. Expanding over the years, the town itself was now centred around the San Fernando church which had the old military plaza on its west side and the main plaza on its east. Well ordered streets of adobe, flat roofed buildings and thatched huts spread away on every side, surrounded by sprawling farm land and scattered trees. Still further east of the main plaza, the deep, fast flowing San Antonio River took a sharply winding course around the town. Cutting a long straight line through the buildings was the main thoroughfare, Commerce (or Portrero) Street, which ran for several hundred yards from the plaza down to a bend in the river which was crossed by a small wooden bridge. Some distance to the right of the bridge lay the huts of the outlying hamlet of La Villita while immediately to the left stood the tiny village and plaza of Pueblo de Valero. About 200 yards north east of the bridge was The Alamo itself.

The four main corners of the garrison covered about three acres with the dominant spectacle of the famous Alamo church standing at the south east apex. From the air, you would be able to observe that the nave, transept and chancel were built in the shape of a crucifix but the roof had never been completed. A series of arches had been constructed across the inner chapel but these had been demolished by Cos' men during their occupation as material for fortification. The stone from this and rubble and earth from elsewhere had been used to raise a high mound in the chancel. Wooden planking covered a quite steep slope from the church doorway, leading up to a timbered rampart about twelve feet high. Almeron Dickinson had positioned three cannon on this rampart, their barrels pointing in differing directions over the summit of the walls, but his gunners must have been severely restricted for space. It seems that the doorway of the church itself had no doors and was probably filled with a barricade of sandbags or maybe a breastwork of earth and wooden stakes. To the left of this, high up on an observation post of timber, flew a flag which was most likely a tri-colour (red, white and green) bearing two stars to represent Texas and its neighbour Coahuila, which had recently had its uprising crushed by Santa Anna's men. This was probably the nearest piece of symbolism possessed at the time by the Texians to show their opposition to Santa Anna, although there were other flags raised at The Alamo which we shall get to later. (It has been said that the main Alamo flag bore the date "1824" to represent the discredited Mexican constitution, but by mid February 1836 it is doubtful that any of the combatants would have seen that particular issue as anything more than a lost cause.)

To the right of the doorway, alongside the rampart, stood the sacristy which was used as a storeroom and shelter for non-combatants, and this was connected to large and small rooms which were similarly occupied. The powder magazine was located here in what had been the confessional. In front of the church was the inner courtyard (which had at one time been the site of a cemetery for the mission's Indian converts) to the right of which was the old convent building, the ground floor serving as an armoury and the upper floor as a hospital. Attached to this were the "long barracks", but the second story was mostly in ruins; the result of the pounding it had taken from Texian guns when the garrison had been captured from Cos the previous year. Horse and cattle corrals stood outside of this, but the barracks extended as the whole length of the east wall until it met the junction of the north wall.

New research has shown that the entire north wall needed a complete overhaul. Before Maj. Green Jameson got to work on it, the adobe brickwork was so cracked and brittle it was virtually falling over but the industrious engineer officer had it reinforced by piling earth on its outer sides which was then supported by horizontal piled logs and further bolstered by the addition of strategically placed vertical timbers. The gaps were filled with tightly packed dirt and rubble. This made a somewhat formidable obstacle for any assault as the wall was now about five feet thick and eight to nine feet high, but, unfortunately, the outer surface had been roughly finished. As we shall see later, this was to prove advantageous to the attacking soldados. In the centre of the north wall stood a stockaded battery, the ramp of which led up to three eight pounder cannon. Further along, at the apex with the west wall, was a similar two gun battery.

The west wall was a hotch potch of various buildings which included the officer's quarters, the garrison's command post and Travis' room. There was also a warehouse and workshop along with a mess of breastworks and embrasures which had needed a great deal of work to make secure. Along here, dotted in the crumbling walls, there had been portholes but Jameson had deemed it necessary to block up most of these and replace them with raised gun platforms. At the south west angle, as mentioned previously, stood The Alamo's pride and joy; the big eighteen pounder with its nine foot iron barrel pointing towards the distant San Fernando church. Weighing about two tons, the eighteen pounder had its very own rampart and platform and was much larger than anything the Mexican artillery had to offer. It had come from New Orleans, reaching Bexar in December just after Cos' defeat and was obviously a great addition to the Texian arsenal. However, cannonballs were in short supply and this proved eventually to be quite a problem. Also, some thirty feet south of the eighteen pounder's position stood an awkward, flat roofed stone building which partially blocked the field of fire. Something else which would prove beneficial to the Mexican army when the time came.

And so to the south wall where the main gate was situated. Contrary to previous assumptions, it now seems that this gate was protected by a rather formidable outer structure, probably made of stone and with a secondary defensive palisade of stakes, loopholed and with firing platforms. Inside the gate, positioned in the plaza, was an inner redoubt; a raised platform which had two naval style cannon pointing at the opening for the express purpose of mowing down any enemy troops who might manage to breach the gate. There were several small rooms along this wall, one of which would eventually be occupied by a gravely ill Jim Bowie.

The south wall ended here leaving a gap of about thirty feet at an angle leading up to the front of the church. This was The Alamo's renowned "weak point" and in the John Wayne film it certainly does look pretty feeble. However, in reality, the Southern Palisade, as it was known, actually proved to be such an obstacle the attacking soldados avoided it altogether. It was, in fact, protected by a single wall of upright timbers about eight feet high, behind which was a two foot high firing step of hard packed earth and stones. Loopholes had been cut well down in the timber giving the defenders excellent cover. There was also a single cannon here mounted half way along the palisade, in front of which was a fairly deep ditch and a whole line of felled trees. This was an ancient form of defence known as an "abatis", with the branches of the fallen trees sharpened into pointed stakes and pointing out towards any potential attackers.

To complete the picture, the whole of the fortress was surrounded by an "acequia" (water course) which brought irrigation to the surrounding farmland, and there were also two fairly large ponds just outside the east wall. Running parallel to the west wall, inside the garrison, was a long dry ditch, a branch of the acequia which had its water supply cut off by the fortifications. At the junction of the north and west walls stood a large but lonely looking pecan tree. There were many places around the walls where the ramparts were low or virtually non-existent, meaning that the defenders would often find themselves totally exposed to enemy fire.

So this was how The Alamo looked just before the famous battle, but what of the men who defended it?

*   *   *

The Alamo defenders were a mixed bunch, to say the least. Remember, they had come from all walks of life, responding to the call of Liberty for their Texian brethren. This naturally meant that there was no typical appearance to an average Texian volunteer. Very few of them had actually served as professional soldiers although a handful were regulars from the United States Army who had deserted to rally to the cause. These men, therefore, would be dressed in their old uniforms of sky-blue kersey tunic and a leather, foldable forage cap as well as some individualistic additions of their own now that they were away from Uncle Sam's discipline. They brought their weapons and equipment with them, of course, so this would include the U.S. musket 1816 pattern. I have already mentioned the New Orleans Greys who wore a lot of U.S. Army surplus gear, and therefore resembled proper soldiers. Originally, two companies of Greys had been formed but while one remained in The Alamo the other marched off with Col. Johnson's abortive Matamoros expedition although they eventually joined up with Col. Fannin at Goliad. They were to meet a tragic end there.

Generally, though, the men with Crockett, Bowie and Travis were ordinary citizens who had given up their normal lives to seek ideological satisfaction (or perhaps just adventure). There were several doctors and numerous lawyers, farmers, storekeepers, students, boatmen, blacksmiths, plasterers, surveyors, hunters and goodness knows how many other occupations. Henry Warnell was a jockey, Jesse McCoy a sheriff, Marcus Sewell a shoemaker and James Northcross a Methodist minister, for instance. There were at least two Negroes present in The Alamo; Travis' slave Joe and another black man identified only as John. John was possibly a slave as well but he served as a rifleman with the others. So many nationalities too; from France, Germany, Ireland, Scotland, Wales and England. Lt. Charles Zanco was from Denmark and 54 year old Englishman (and gunner) Anthony Wolfe had his two young sons with him. However, Wolfe was not the oldest of the defenders. Several of them were well past the first flush of youth, like Gordon Jennings and Robert Moore who were both in their late fifties. (Incidentally, on the subject of diverse nationalities, it is worth relating a little story. I know of a man who was present at the London premiere of The Alamo film and actually got talking to John Wayne. When told that a large proportion of the defenders were not red blooded American boys, The Duke apparently grew very agitated and said he didn't want to hear any "Limey pinko crap!")

At least fifteen of the defenders were only in their teens, one of them being a mere fifteen years old. The vast majority of the others were in their twenties and early thirties. Then there were the three Taylor brothers, farm hands from Liberty, Texas. Edward, George and James were inseparable as they served together as riflemen. And, of course, we must not forget that several Mexicans fought alongside the Alamo Texians. These were Juan Seguin's Tejanos (meaning Texan residents of Hispanic origin). Acting largely as scouts, the Tejanos were of great benefit to the rebel cause although not all the native residents of Bexar were totally committed. Many of the townspeople kept their heads down, carrying on with their business as they waited to see which way the tide would turn. More than a few would serve as informants to Santa Anna.

In appearance then, the Alamo defenders would be dressed in a mixed array of store clothes, frock coats, business suits, hunting shirts, buckskins, Indian leggings, coats of crumpled calico and blanket coats (typically in grey, green or white). On their feet they wore brogan shoes, moccasins, riding boots or perhaps crudely stitched, undressed coverings if their original footwear had worn out. Heads would be adorned with high crowned straw hats, toppers, fur caps, rounded hats and narrow brimmed felt hats. Many, but not all, would be bearded with long hair reaching at least to their collars; not the Tejanos though for the average Bexareno resident considered facial hair unfashionable. These Tejanos favoured colourful serapes and bandanas, waist sashes, wide slit trousers with silver buttons and broad brimmed sombreros. This gave them a striking and romantic appearance but there were real individuals and characters amongst the Americans too. Elaborately fringed and beaded attire was looked upon as very stylish.

As for weapons, the first volunteers arrived armed with their hunting rifles and double barrelled shotguns but after Cos' surrender the Texian Army acquired hundreds of Brown Bess muskets and other Mexican equipment, including 66 highly useful Presidial Lancer's hats and some band instruments! Backwoodsmen and frontier types came with their long barrelled Kentucky rifles, a weapon originally of German design but by now regarded as real Americana. Its effective range was four times the distance of the Brown Bess, making it chillingly accurate at 300 yards. As a rule, the Americans, regardless of profession, were mostly good shots owing to a deeply ingrained tradition for hunting. As a concession to some form of military appearance, the men usually wore cross straps to hold their shot pouches and powder horns. Water was held in canteens or Spanish gourds.

There were also pistols and hilted swords, as well as the ever popular Bowie knife, seen around in its various styles. Many men carried plain butcher knives, not as impressive as the Bowie but deadly just the same. Belt axes were popular too along with Indian style tomahawks, very effective in close quarter fighting. Tejanos often had double bladed dirks tucked in their sashes.

Artillery-wise, The Alamo was not short of guns, not only its prized eighteen pounder but also about a score of three, four, six, eight and twelve pounders mounted on wagon wheels or garrison carriages. These fired cannon balls of iron or brass (which were in fairly short supply) but there were also a few powder filled shells to be used sparingly. What would prove really effective, however, was the use of "langrage"; pieces of chopped up horseshoe, nails and any other small scraps of metal refuse tightly packed into a canvas or sacking bag, or rammed loose into the gun barrel to be discharged as grapeshot or canister. When fired into ranks of attacking infantry the result was truly devastating, as well as horrific.

The Alamo was a small, under-manned but significant garrison. It could be said that its importance was over rated by Bowie and Travis, for did it really stand in the way of Santa Anna's march into the heart of Texas? Not really. The fortress could easily have been contained by a single regiment while the rest of the Mexican army marched around it, but

Santa Anna was determined to settle a score before he dealt with the bulk of the rebel army under Houston. He knew it could be taken, although at great cost, a sacrifice he considered worth making to re-establish his honour.

As for Houston, it may surprise many to know that he only realised the significance of The Alamo *after* it fell. As we shall see, regardless of numerous pleas for assistance, it seems that General Sam failed to take the defender's plight seriously until it was too late.

TEXIAN WEAPONS

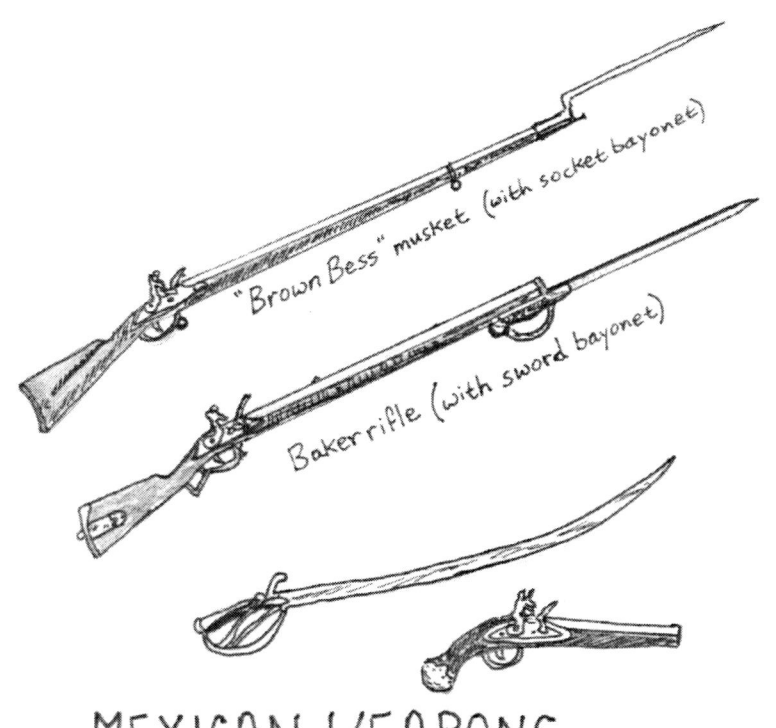

MEXICAN WEAPONS

THE RIGHT TO COMMAND

David Crockett's arrival at The Alamo on February 8th. seemed to come at exactly the right time.

Travis himself had only been there for five days but had already made his mark, full of ideas and bolstering the men's morale with his own fiery brand of patriotic optimism. Quite a contrast to commander Col. Neill's cautious and bland leadership. Further complicating matters was the presence of Jim Bowie who despite any formal qualifications of command was very much looked upon by many of the men as their true leader.

From the start there were personality clashes between Travis and Bowie, but they were both strong characters in different ways, also realists who knew that the overall crisis facing The Alamo rose above any personal difficulties. In any case, Bowie was heavily distracted by many issues, not least of all his concern for Gertrudis, Juana and her son, his constant liaisons with the locals and his deteriorating health. This last factor was becoming increasingly difficult to ignore. Likewise, Travis was well involved in the garrison's affairs, even ensuring that The Alamo would have its own two official representatives at the coming Convention. These elected men, Jesse Badgett and Sam Maverick, were duly despatched to Washington-on-the-Brazos to be part of the setting up of a permanent and independent Texan government.

Like the rising sun, Crockett and his small party of amiable companions rode in from the east, a breath of fresh air with their happy demeanour and news from the home country. As always, "Ol' Davy" rose to the occasion, shaking hands and displaying his warm smile to one and all. The local populace flooded into Bexar's Main Plaza to welcome him, for it must be remembered that Crockett was a legend in his own lifetime and his presence would have meant a great deal to them. Here was one of the most famed figures in America, in its entire history in fact, who had chosen, voluntarily, to come all this way to their aid.

His back slapped raw, Crockett happily stepped up onto a packing case and addressed the hushed crowd with the skill that had earned him his name. The speech was laced with his characteristic humour, but he knew how to milk a moment, bringing in the elements of emotive drama just when they were needed. He stressed how he had journeyed to Bexar devoid of "selfish motive" and said "I have come to aid you all that I can in your noble cause". Women wept and hard men brushed away tears as they cheered and whooped approval. Capt. William Harrison was probably glad to stand aside and let the glory of his Tennessee Mounted Volunteers be taken from him, while Dr. Reynolds, Daniel Cloud, Micajah Autry and the others beamed proudly in their association with the great man.

Crockett acted as a mediating influence between the volatile relationships of the various Alamo commanders and pretty soon his genial personality had calmed the waters. For now, at least. Most of the garrison's men were living within the comfort of the town itself, rather than inside the walls of the fort and it was seen as fitting that a fandango should be thrown in the Plaza to celebrate Crockett's arrival. This was done on the night of the 10th. and, by all accounts, it was a wild affair with the men blowing off steam and forgetting the past weeks of hardship in an orgy of laughter, song, drinking and dancing. The local senoritas were more than happy to share their favours with the Americanos, in fact many had already formed relationships with them. After all, The Alamo defenders had become pretty familiar in recent times. At the height of the party most of those present probably would have forgotten the predicament they were in. They would not have cared anyway. The average feeling, at this time, would have been that they were invincible.

In the early hours of the morning, with the carousing at full swing, a Tejano rider came galloping into the Plaza, virtually un-noticed in the chaos until he pushed his way through the crowd and found Jim Bowie. This courier had ridden hard from the border and the letter he clutched bore grim news. It seemed that Santa Anna was much closer than had been thought possible and was already hastening his huge army north to Bexar. Bowie read the letter and immediately sought out Travis. He found the insatiable young colonel in the arms of a raven haired Mexican girl and apparently Travis' response was, "I cannot stay to read letters for I am dancing with the most beautiful lady in San Antonio"! A surprising reaction perhaps, even bearing in mind the balance between Travis' military professionalism and his fervent passion for the opposite sex. It enhances the confidence that must have been felt deep down by the likes of Travis. When he was finally persuaded that night to devote a little time to more pressing matters, he, along with Bowie and Crockett, decided that the news was not worth worrying about at this stage. The soldados were coming, of course, but not before the better weather of Spring, surely. Satisfied, the immortal three went back to the party.

It is significant that, apparently, Col. Neill was not even consulted on this matter and so, perhaps, it is not coincidental that the very next day he decided to hand the garrison over to the command of Col. Travis. Neill's official reasons for leaving were rather vague but he said he was taking an extended leave and everyone knew that he had no intention of returning to a command where he had been largely over-ruled. The choice of Travis as The Alamo's commander-in-chief was the obvious official one as W.B. was the senior regular army officer. Crockett was a new arrival and regardless of his huge popularity still saw himself as a "high private". Bowie was a different matter but, like Crockett, his rank of colonel was not really recognisable and had only been earned by his long membership of the freewheeling Texas militia.

This new situation created something of a rift. Travis did his best to assert his authority and he was doubtless a most capable leader, but he was up against strong resentment from the rank and file. Many of the men had known Bowie for years, had fought alongside him in all kinds of scrapes, so they simply could not accept the superior command of one they saw as an upstart 26 year old youth. Bowie himself could not accept it either and would find it difficult to take orders within a command that he knew like the back of his hand. The general feeling was that, regardless of the logistics, Big Jim was the obvious colonel of the garrison. He was the only one who could command ultimate respect.

The two men argued until, at last, Travis took an ill advised gamble by allowing the volunteers to vote on who they wanted to command them. The result was highly predictable and Bowie won by a landslide. Travis fumed and brooded over this ridiculous split in loyalty, especially at such a critical time. He retained official command of the regular troops and volunteer cavalrymen but it was an impossible situation to have the other volunteers under seperate leadership.

Travis and Bowie's relationship reached rock bottom and all of Crockett's mediating skills could not appease them. By the 12th. tensions were reaching boiling point and Bowie, swigging whisky in an attempt to ease his vicious, hacking cough, grew violently drunk. In a dangerous mood and seemingly out of his mind, Big Jim appeared riotously in the centre of town at the head of his men. Demanding the attention of the townspeople, he loudly declared that he was taking command of the entire garrison. Furthermore, he had the town's jail cells thrown open and all the prisoners released. When word reached him that one of these prisoners, Antonio Fuentes (a Seguin man), had been put back in his cell, Bowie flew into a fury. An enraged Bowie was definitely a figure to avoid and Travis, regardless of his humiliation, wisely decided to keep a low profile for the time being. However, while Bowie's contingent "hurrahed" the town,

Travis did take the precaution of writing a letter to Governor Smith in which he berated such drunken behaviour and refused to accept responsibility for it. In the same letter he underlined the importance of The Alamo as a garrison and actually called it the "Key to Texas".

Everyone knew that it was best to let Bowie, horribly sick and inebriated, get his frustrations out of his system and on the 14th. a big change came over him. Shattered but reasonable at last, Bowie made an effort to offer a conciliatory gesture to Travis, apologising and stating the importance of the pair of them finding a compromise. This was agreed, the result being that from that moment on they would share joint command of The Alamo with all decisions being taken together. Happy with this arrangement, the first thing they did was write a joint letter to Governor Smith, informing him of their plan and urging him to send reinforcements "as speedily as possible to our aid".

With matters now settled, the garrison soon fell back into the day to day business of killing time. There was always work to be done, of course. Maj. Jameson's efforts to improve the fortifications were never ending and he was still coming up with new ideas. Men were still drifting away, sometimes not to return, but generally the garrison had become a tight-knit little group of diehard adventurers, fiercely proud of their fortress and anxious to get to grips with the enemy.

That said, Travis and Bowie knew they had no chance of successfully defending the place until they received a considerable relief force. At this stage they believed they had ample time and they had no reason to believe that help would not come. Volunteers were still streaming into Texas and surely everyone knew that The Alamo was the first obstacle in Santa Anna's path. New found respect for Travis was growing by the day as the men realised that no one's heart was more strongly at the core of The Alamo than that of their young commander.

Seguin's scouts were ranging far and wide and each day reports came in, from a variety of sources, telling of Santa Anna's approach. Some of this information was absurdly exaggerated and it was difficult to extract the wheat from the chaff, but finally, on the 20th., a scout arrived with the shocking news that he personally had seen the Mexican army streaming across the Rio Grande which meant that by now they would be deep into Texas. Santa Anna could arrive in Bexar any day.

This new information was taken seriously enough for Travis and Bowie to call a council of war with their officers. They debated for long into the night, with voices raised between the pessimists and the optimists. Or should we say the realists and the wishful thinkers? It must be remembered that planning for warfare in those days was conducted very much on a hearsay basis. Communications moved slowly and were notoriously unreliable, so in the end decisions were usually taken on past experience, gut feeling and probability.

So was this Tejano to be believed? Why should he lie? Or was he just mistaken? After all, it simply did not make sense that Santa Anna would have begun his campaign so soon. In the end The Alamo's high command made a decision. The Mexican army could not realistically be expected for at least two more weeks and by that time the garrison would have received ample reinforcements for sure.

Would they have slept so easily that night had they known that as they spoke Santa Anna was less than 50 miles away?

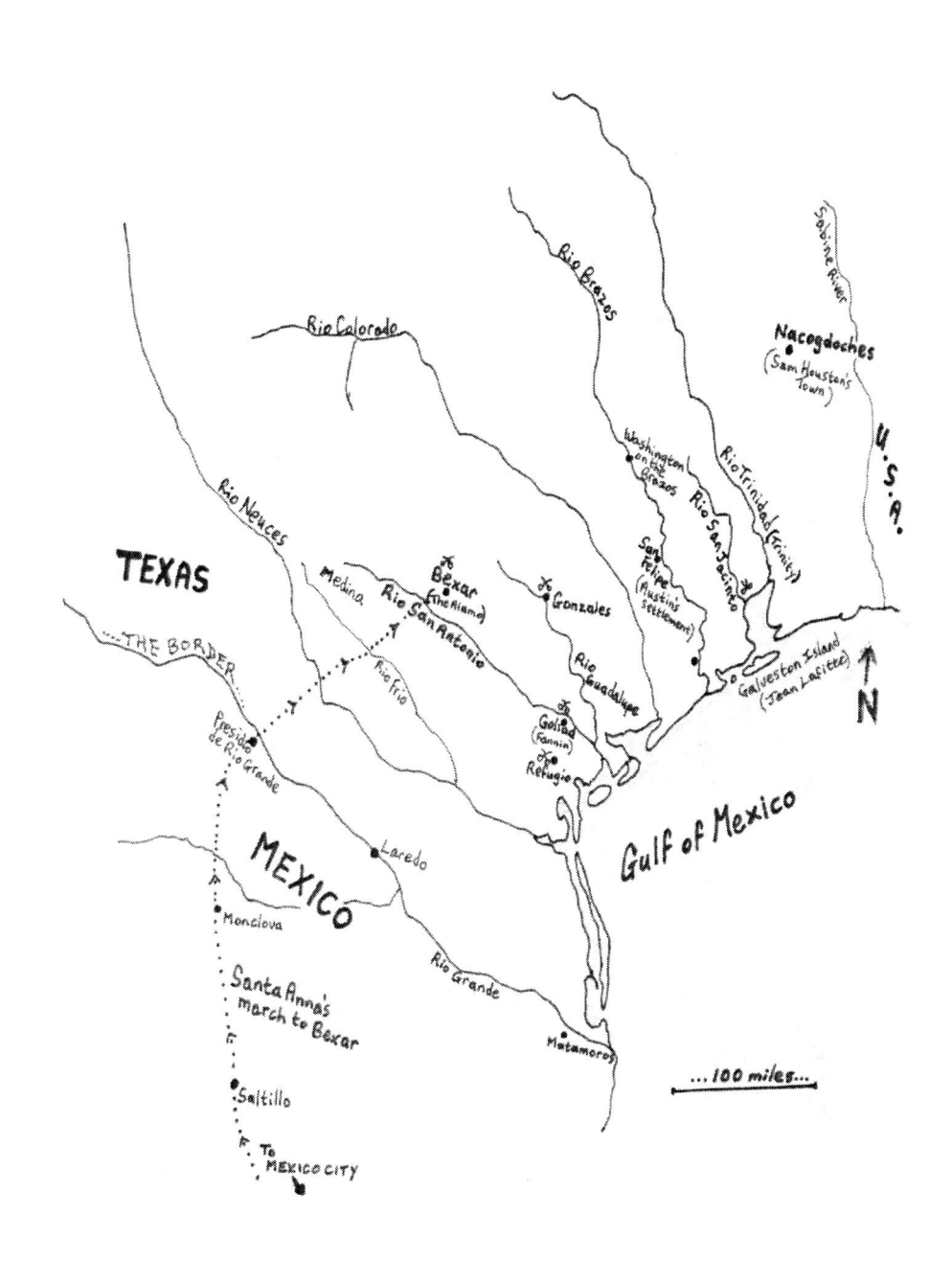

WOLVES AT THE DOOR

Dr. Amos Pollard was seriously concerned about Jim Bowie's rapidly deteriorating condition. 32 year old Pollard was The Alamo's chief surgeon and he had been working hard establishing a neat, reasonably equipped little hospital on the second floor of the Long Barracks. As Bowie grew weaker, the doctor tried several times to persuade him to take to his bed but Big Jim just shrugged it off, insisting on soldiering on. There was simply too much work to do, and in any case Bowie was not the type to give in to anything. Unfortunately, it was reaching the point where he would have no choice.

Pollard called in Dr. John Sutherland for a second opinion. Sutherland, a 43 year old Alabaman, was serving as a rifleman with the rank of private but Pollard was so baffled by Bowie's symptoms he needed another diagnosis. The big man was coughing up great gouts of blood, his eyes had developed an ugly yellow cast and he had lost a frightening amount of weight. It was a miracle he was still on his feet. Between them, the doctors concluded that it must be some kind of advanced consumption, complicated perhaps by pneumonia and some unidentifiable fever. Sometimes Bowie's coughing fits were so violent he struggled to breathe. Sutherland was convinced that it must be a fatal condition.

Regardless, Bowie continued to put on a brave face and actively shared his responsibilities with Travis to command the garrison. Strangely, despite their soldierly qualities, it seems that a certain neglect descended over the defence arrangements in the days leading up to Santa Anna's arrival. Since the message brought on February 11th., very little active reconnaissance had been carried out and the Texians generally disregarded whatever intelligence they received. Although Jameson still laboured away at the defences (a labour of love, apparently), most of the men were still billeted in Bexar town, enjoying the comforts and seemingly without any sense of urgency. Not much effort had been made to actually stock the garrison with food supplies, the cannon had not been ranged and the huts of La Villita and Pueblo de Valero extended almost all the way up to The Alamo's south wall. Clearing these buildings away should have been a priority as they would obviously give cover to attacking troops. And then, on the 22nd., two days after that sobering message from Seguin's scout which told of Santa Anna's proximity, it was decided to throw another party, this time to celebrate George Washington's birthday!

It says a lot for the confident, and perhaps irresponsible, nature of The Alamo's defenders that they were happy to drink and dance the night away with advance units of the enemy literally just a few miles distant. Over the last few days, Santa Anna's army had been advancing rapidly, crossing the network of little rivers which laced the prairie south of Bexar. Receiving news from his spies about the Texian's complacence, Santa Anna decided on a bold plan. He ordered General Sesma to take a detachment of the Dolores cavalry and ride ahead through the night. With the element of surprise this flying column should be able to catch the defenders outside their fortress and probably still in their beds. Bexar could be taken with barely a shot being fired.

It could have worked but, unfortunately for the Mexicans, the night of the 21st. into the 22nd. suffered from a severe deluge of rain. Sesma's dragoons were forced to halt on the banks of the Medina River, unable to ford what had turned into a raging torrent. Santa Anna caught up with them within hours, frustrated and infuriated that his plan had been foiled. Summoning up reserves of patience, Don Demonio would now give his army one more day to dry out, reform and allow the current of the swollen Medina to recede so that they could cross it. Then a forced march of under 25 miles would take them to The Alamo.

*   *   *

As usual, the men from The Alamo had enjoyed themselves. Celebrating Washington's birthday had been another good excuse for a wild fandango and the Texians had drunk, danced and caroused far into the night. By the time the sun rose on the morning of Tuesday February 23rd., most of them were sleeping soundly, blissfully unaware of the activity which was taking place all around them.

The town of San Antonio de Bexar was already buzzing with life, but it was in the form of a kind of hushed, determined atmosphere with the Bexarenos dashing silently to and fro, speaking in whispers as they loaded their belongings onto carts or the backs of mules. Before long an intermittent stream of men, women and children were hurriedly making their way north, south and east out of town.

True to form, Lt. Col. Travis was one of the few Texians up and about early enough to take note of this strange behaviour. What was going on? Anxiously he began stopping passers-by but they were evasive, many of them unable to meet his eye as they mumbled lame excuses about heading out to the country for farm work. Ridiculous! Travis huffed and cursed and by 9.00am. had roused enough of his men to enforce an embargo on the town, issuing strict orders that no one else was to leave unless he was satisfied with their explanation. People panicked and protested, several were arrested and interrogated, but it was mid-morning before Travis finally learned the truth. One of his closer Mexican informants nervously gave the news that reliable information had arrived the previous night, for the ears of the townspeople only. The courier was from Santa Anna himself stating how the vanguard of the army was bivouacked on the Leon Creek just eight miles away. El Presidente was sending a warning to the Bexarenos to make themselves scarce if they knew what was good for them. Few needed reminding of what had happened back in 1813 when the Spanish Army had executed ordinary civilians alongside revolutionaries, an event during which a young Santa Anna had been present to serve a bloody apprenticeship.

Travis absorbed the news soberly. There would be precious few moments to spare. Without delay he rushed to the San Fernando church which dominated the town, racing up the winding steps of the taller tower to the belfry. It had turned into a bright, sunny morning, but the glare far out across the prairie made visibility limited as the colonel squinted and peered hard out to the west. Joined by Dr. John Sutherland, the two of them spent a long time scouring the horizon for signs of activity but they detected nothing untoward. Travis then stationed a sentinel in the belfry giving him strict instructions to ring the bell the moment he saw anything suspicious. W.B. then made his way back to his quarters, issuing further orders as he went and putting the garrison on full alert. Bowie and Crockett appeared as a hum of expectancy descended over the town.

Shortly after noon the rapid clanging of the bell sent Travis hurtling back up to the belfry, the sentinel crying out "The enemy are in view!", but, once again, nothing could be seen. However, the indignant lookout was insistent that he had not been mistaken, swearing an oath that he had definitely spotted distant horsemen riding between the thickets of mesquite. They must be hidden by the slopes and brushwood. As Travis pondered what best to do, Dr. Sutherland offered to ride out and scout the area, as long as he could be accompanied by someone who knew the country well. Travis agreed and a local man was found to go with the doctor. This was Missouri John Smith (not to be confused with Deaf Smith who had by now long retreated to the east with his family), known to the locals as El Colorado because of his bright red hair. Smith was the town's middle aged carpenter, also a boarding-house keeper and respected engineer who had made his mark during the fighting in December. Sutherland and Smith told Travis that if he saw them returning at the gallop, that would be the sign that they had discovered something worth worrying about.

The two men cantered cautiously out of town towards the western horizon, only covering about a mile and a half before they reached the summit of a slope and were able to see down the other side, a view which would be invisible even from the belfry. Abruptly reining in their horses, they must have gasped at the sight of hundreds of Mexican cavalrymen, formed up in lines between the scrub oak as their sword wielding commander rode along the ranks issuing orders. With the sun glinting on their polished helmets and lance tips, Sesma's dragoons had arrived at last.

The doctor and the carpenter spent just seconds absorbing the shocking sight before turning their mounts, digging in their heels and racing pell mell back towards town. They had been within 200 yards of the enemy and Santa Anna always said afterwards that if General Sesma had exercised enough gumption to pursue them, the Texian garrison could have been defeated in the streets of Bexar before they had a chance to take cover inside The Alamo. The ground was muddy owing to the recent heavy rain and, in their haste to return to town with their pressing news, the two Texians threw caution to the wind. Consequently, Sutherland's galloping horse lost its footing, pitching the doctor over its head and rolling heavily across his legs. Smith glanced back, wheeled his mount and cantered back to help the stricken man up into the saddle again, but Sutherland was wincing with pain, his leg badly wrenched. Regardless, they carried on to the sound of the sentinel frantically ringing the church bell at their approach.

Now, as they say in Texas, all hell broke loose. Travis immediately rushed into the Main Plaza, calling out to his officers to rally the entire command. They must withdraw back into The Alamo without delay. Shaking off their hangovers, the men jumped into action, grabbing their weapons and equipment and rushing bleary eyed down Commerce Street, out towards the fortress. Pretty soon the small bridge to the south of the main gate was choked with bodies as the defenders hastened across it.

Capt. Almeron Dickinson straightaway thought of his wife Susannah and their infant daughter Angelina who were staying in an adobe house to the south of town. Riding his horse right up to the front door he instructed his wife to hand him the baby before telling her to climb up behind him. She did so without question and they galloped off towards the bridge along with a host of others.

Over in the Military Plaza, a few of the men were riding or running around excitedly, discharging shots from their rifles and pistols into the air, whooping like demons as if another party was about to take place. It was at this point that someone apparently decided to raise a flag in the middle of the Plaza which was clearly seen by the Mexicans approaching from the west. Col. Juan Almonte described it as bearing two stars, so it was quite likely the Texas/Coahuila standard, but it had been taken down again by the time the Mexicans arrived in town.

Jim Bowie's first concern was for his newly adopted family, Juana, Gertrudis and the baby. Coughing and unsteady on his feet, Big Jim made his way as fast as his fading strength would take him to the Veramendi House where he courteously urged the women to gather their things. This done, he escorted them into The Alamo before painfully dragging himself back into town to assist with the preparations for defence. One of his first tasks was to raise a squad of volunteers to collect as many sacks of grain as they could from the surrounding huts. The siege might be a long one. Likewise, other men were rounding up cattle which lowed and kicked as they were herded hurriedly across the bridge and into the pens along the east wall.

By 3.00pm. the last of the Texian combatants had left the western part of town. The Mexican army was streaming down from the Alazan hills and, with Santa Anna himself at their head, were soon marching into the Military Plaza in the shadow of the San

Fernando church. El Presidente had ordered his soldados to change out of their grubby, white marching fatigues and they stepped smartly in formation dressed in their blue and red tunics, impressing the Bexareno children and terrifying their nervous parents. As the long lines of grenadiers and cazadores, flanked by sergeants and led by officers and standard bearers, continued on past the church, pouring into both sides of the Main Plaza, the regimental bands played melodious marching tunes, national airs and, very likely, stirring pieces such as "The Blood of the Patriots" to recall the 1821 revolution. Santa Anna took the presence of his bandsmen very seriously as he felt they were essential to morale. In fact, his army included over 300 musicians; drummers, fifers, buglers, numerous other players of brass instruments and distinct pieces such as the "jingling johnny" (a brass pole topped with multi-tiered bells).

As the soldados established themselves in the middle of town, fanning out to scour the surrounding streets, Santa Anna ordered half of his division, under General Mora, to sweep to the south towards the Mission Concepcion, for at this point he was unsure exactly where the main Texian defences were placed. Mora would later lead his cavalry far round to the hills north and east of The Alamo, setting up pickets around the old Spanish military powder house and earthworks.

By the time Capt. Dickinson had reached the vicinity of Commerce Street bridge, it was clear that the route was unsafe. Advance units of cazadores were already appearing beyond the buildings, cautiously making feints within range of the fort's defences. Dickinson reined in his horse, his baby daughter in his arms and his wife, Sue, clinging tightly to his back. A quick decision would have to be made before he found himself cut off from the garrison. Jerking the reins to the right, he cantered down to the river's edge, seeking out a ford he knew. Splashing into the water, his horse surged through the strong current, struggling up the slippery east bank before galloping the last few hundred yards to The Alamo's south gate. With the jubilant men cheering him on, the Gonzales blacksmith turned artillery officer thus brought his family to safety. Sue Dickinson's soaked skirt and stockings must have seemed like minimum sacrifice for such sanctuary.

Travis did not waste a moment. From his quarters in the west wall, he had already dashed off the first of many notes calling for assistance. He and Bowie were painfully aware that they would be unable to hold out for long unless their small command received reinforcements. The best hope of that, initially, would have to come from Col. Fannin's strong force at Fort Defiance, located some 95 miles to the south east at Goliad. As the defenders and a sprinkling of their dependants took up residence behind The Alamo's walls, Travis' courier set out at the gallop, keeping just ahead of the Mexican cavalrymen who were fanning out behind him. Travis then turned again to the faithful Dr. Sutherland who had arrived in the colonel's office limping from the injury he had received when his horse fell on him. He was supported by the ever reliable Davy Crockett who stood by awaiting instructions. The doctor was in great pain but he confirmed that he was still fit enough to ride. Nodding, Travis returned to his desk, this time addressing an appeal to the inhabitants of Gonzales which lay seventy miles to the east.

As Sutherland hobbled out to mount up, Crockett caught Travis' eye. Quietly but firmly he reportedly said, "Colonel, here am I. Assign me to a position and me and my boys will try to defend it". It was at this point, it seems, that Travis gave Crockett and the Tennessee Mounted Volunteers responsibility for the defence of the south east palisade.

It was now late afternoon and the Mexican army was well and truly in control of the town, while keeping a sensible distance from The Alamo itself. Santa Anna had already found a suitable headquarters for himself in the Yturri house on the north west corner of the Main Plaza. Anxious to know where he stood, the town's mayor, Francisco Ruiz, managed to secure a swift audience with El Presidente and was relieved to be told that he could retain his position as long as he co-operated. Ruiz's sympathies lay with the Texians (he was even Bowie's uncle by marriage) but he knew what he must do for the sake of self preservation. As for Santa Anna, he was determined to make an immediate display of his intentions. Cazadores were ordered to the summit of the San Fernando bell tower (the very same belfry where Travis had stood just a short time before) to attach a banner to the large metal crucifix on the upper dome. Unfurled and snapping in the crisp breeze, this ominous looking blood red flag was known by all to mean "No Quarter". Don Demonio was emphasising his oft stated contempt for the Texian rebels whom he regarded as no better than pirates. As such they would receive no mercy.

800 yards away along The Alamo's west wall, the defenders paused in their work to glare darkly at this chilling symbol and, perhaps for the first time, many of them would have begun to ponder their fate. Travis was infuriated by such a display of dismissal for his command. As far as he was concerned, he and his men were soldiers fighting a conventional war. His response to the red banner was characteristically defiant for he ordered a shot fired from the eighteen pounder. The roar of the big cannon stopped everyone in their tracks as an iron ball sped its way crashing through the streets of Bexar. First blood to the Texians but the Mexicans did not let it go unanswered. Within moments they had unlimbered their two howitzers, replying with four shells which exploded harmlessly inside The Alamo's compound.

At this point it appears that the ailing Bowie took stock of the fast deteriorating situation and decided to act of his own accord. Without consulting his hot headed co-commander, he addressed a note (written on a torn page of a child's copy book) to the "Commander of the Mexican Army", in which he apologised for the rash opening shot. He explained that this had been fired before it was realised that the Mexicans "might" be requesting a parley. Signing it "God and Mexico" he then obviously thought he was being too conciliatory, for, as an afterthought, he crossed it out and wrote instead "God and *Texas*", just to reiterate where his loyalty lay.

Bowie chose the reliable engineer officer Green Jameson to take the message, so before any more shots could be fired, the major was riding out of the south gate displaying a white flag of truce. He was received by a high ranking representative of Santa Anna's but the president was not open to any concession. The written reply stated "The Mexican Army cannot come to terms under any conditions with rebellious foreigners" going on to state that if the rebels wished to save their lives, their only hope was to surrender immediately. As Jameson made his way back to the fort with this mournful news, another courier passed him. This was Capt. Albert Martin, sent by Travis, for W.B. was angered by Bowie's decision to break their agreement of joint command. How dare that wild, knife fighting adventurer over ride his authority by making overtures to the enemy! To underline his own importance, Travis wanted it known that he too wanted his voice heard. Martin's message from Travis was a verbal one in which he expressed the colonel's willingness to discuss the situation in a civilized manner, but Santa Anna's view, through his representative, Col. Almonte, had not changed. Unconditional surrender or the garrison would be slaughtered.

When Travis received these replies his resolve deepened. Climbing back up onto the parapet at the south west corner, his slave Joe at his side, Travis gave a curt order to Capt. Carey's gunners. Once again the long barrel of the eighteen pounder spurted smoke and flame in the direction of the town. Santa Anna had his answer.

The distant roar of the gun was heard by Dr. Sutherland who was by now well on his way to Gonzales. Taking the old Goliad road and doing his best to keep out of sight, Sutherland had caught up with John Smith (his cavalry spotting companion) going in the same direction. Smith had spent his time securing his house in town before deciding to take his own message to Gonzales. Recruiting reinforcements was foremost in his mind too, he said. Other fugitives were on the road as well, not always for such noble reasons. Sutherland had already passed the desperate figure of storekeeper Nat Lewis, hurrying away on foot and loaded down with as much of his fortune as he could carry. The pain in Sutherland's leg was troubling him badly but he knew he must push on. He and Smith could only assume that the sound of cannon fire was a sure sign that battle had commenced.

Smith need not have bothered securing his home. Like all other abodes in Bexar, the Mexican occupiers were methodically working their way through all the buildings, battering down any doors they could not easily open. Anything that could be used for the comfort of the army was seized. Santa Anna was not really surprised by Travis' defiant cannon shots and was already consulting his staff officers about the practicalities of a siege. He was in no great hurry for although he had arrived with many men, the bulk of his army was still strung out for miles across the distant prairie and would not reach Bexar for days. This included the heavier cannon which he would need before sensibly attempting an assault on The Alamo.

As the sun set over the town and fort, both bustling with the excitement of preparation, one of many smaller dramas was unfolding in North Flores Street, at the home of Gregorio Esparza. Esparza was a lifelong Bexareno, one of Seguin's recruits whose loyalty lay well and truly with his Texian friends. He had learned from them the skills of a gunner and knew he would be needed to help man the cannons in the coming battle. It must have been most poignant as he looked around at his family, his wife Ana and his young children, three boys and a girl aged between three and ten. They stared back at him expectantly, their innocent dark eyes shining in the lamplight as he told them they must abandon their house and go to The Alamo, if they could make it without being caught by the Mexican patrols. He had already tried to convince Ana to take the children to a safer haven but she had insisted that their place was to remain with him. Matters were further complicated for Gregorio when he gave thought to his brother who was a soldado in Santa Anna's army.

Gathering together as many of their possessions as they could carry, the Esparza family slipped quietly out and made their way towards the river, the steady militaristic beat of soldado drums rattling in their ears. All around they could hear the sound of marching feet, shouted orders and the odd crash and cry of protest in the surrounding streets, but they ignored it all. With bundles and cases they made it across the river, hurrying unseen between the trees and jacales (huts) to the south gate of The Alamo.

The sentries peered over the wall at them in the gathering dusk. Ana lost her temper at the delay and started pounding on the gate, but the officer of the guard soon recognised their ally Gregorio and motioned for them to make their way down to the church itself. Swiftly the small group did as they were told, passing the south east palisade where Crockett and his men perhaps called hushed words of encouragement to them. They could not enter the fort here because of the high breastwork and virtually impregnable wall of felled and sharpened trees. Instead they carried on down to the old church walls, alongside the famed chapel. Here there was a small side window near the rear of the building in the sacristy, the ledge about seven feet above the ground. One by one, the Esparza children were lifted up by their father and pulled through by the men inside, then came Ana and finally Gregorio himself, the wooden shutter of the window battened down behind him.

The Alamo was as secure as it would ever be.

ALMERON DICKENSON
JAMES BOWIE
JAMES BUTLER BONHAM
Mike Martin

THIRTEEN DAYS

"There were thirteen days of fighting at the siege of The Alamo ...."

So trills the familiar theme song from Duke Wayne's movie, but those thirteen days were not quite like what Big John would have us believe. For a start, the Mexican army was sensibly cautious in its approach to the fort, keeping well out of small arms range. At first, The Alamo's defenders had to be satisfied with hurling verbal abuse at the distant figures who could be seen fanning out between the streets of east Bexar. Although the Texians and Tejanos must have felt quite secure behind the walls, now that they were all together with the enemy at bay, this would have been the first time that the full extent of their vulnerability became clear. It was now overwhelmingly obvious that the defenders were spread very thinly along the walls. Some of them were even positioned outside in chest deep ditches which had been dug in strategic places mainly along the north and west walls, the object being to counter any approaches which might be made by Mexican scouts or skirmishers. With great foresight, Jameson and Bowie had also ordered the creation of inner defences in the likely event that the walls would be breached. Consequently inside the Long Barracks, which stretched most of the length of the east wall, trenches had been dug between the scattered rooms along with semi-circular parapets across the doorways. (These took the form of stretched ox-hides filled with earth and to this day you can see a recreated example of one inside The Alamo's Long Barracks museum.) The idea behind this was that it would be very difficult to dislodge even a small group of defenders from such a labyrinth; anything to buy more time. However, it did not need to be spelled out that it would require the addition of at least another 400 men to realistically have any hope of repelling a serious Mexican assault.

And then there were the non-combatants to worry about. Quite a number of women and children had been brought into The Alamo, most of them being the families and dependants of the Tejano defenders. Of course, this included the Esparzas, but there was also Sue Dickinson and her eighteen month old daughter, Angelina, who were the only Anglo-American females inside the garrison. However, as previously mentioned, the English gunner Anthony Wolfe had his young sons Benjamin and Michael with him. Both under twelve years of age, they were placed under the protection of the women. Bowie's dependants, Juana, Gertrudis and the baby, had their own quarters which they shared with Big Jim himself, but the others were all located inside the sacristy of the church. This was a strongly built room thirty five feet long by fifteen feet wide, flanked by eighteen foot high walls and topped by two Moorish domes in the ceiling. Without windows and lit by flickering candles, this crowded refuge must have been stuffy and oppressive, but at least it was secure. Bedding took the form of a few cots or piles of hay and no doubt artillerymen Almeron Dickinson and Gregorio Esparza spent the nights with their wives here. After all, it was very close to their posts manning the guns on the church's roof rampart. There was even a resident cat skulking in the shadows which, from want of things to pass the time, probably received considerable fuss and attention from the children.

Whilst well aware of the seriousness of their plight, Travis and Bowie were not, at this stage, unduly alarmed. Although the Mexicans had arrived in force much earlier than expected, the Texians remained optimistic. After all, they had managed to withdraw into the safety of the garrison unscathed and morale was still high. Santa Anna's army may have been deploying around Bexar and making feints, but Travis was confident that a major assault would still be several days away. By then, surely, his various appeals for help would have instigated the arrival of reinforcements, his best hope still being Col. Fannin's large force at Goliad.

As for Santa Anna, he knew he could take his time. He had the rebels pinned down where he wanted them, to be dealt with at his leisure. However, soon after he had settled into his new quarters, he consulted his staff officers and gave orders for major reconnaissance of the surrounding area. By the end of this first day, it was obvious that the Texians had no intention of surrendering so taking The Alamo by storm was inevitable. It was just a question of when. The defences would need to be softened up first and the eight pounder cannon and howitzers currently available would not be capable of doing enough necessary damage to the walls. Santa Anna needed his twelve pounders and they were still far away to the south, along with several battalions of infantry. Don Demonio immediately sent couriers back along the trail to tell General Gaona to stop dragging his heels. In the meantime, batteries for the smaller guns were established at advantageous sites during the first night of the siege.

By the following warm but cloudy morning, the pandemonium of the previous afternoon had calmed down and the Mexican army was settling into the business of acclimatising to its new surroundings. By 9.00am. Santa Anna had personally taken it upon himself to supervise the distribution of decent new footwear to his preferred military companies, the grenadiers and cazadores. The long march from Mexico had taken its toll on the soldado's shoes but the president was determined that his men should be adequately shod for the coming battle. Rather than being issue items, which were in short supply, these new shoes probably came from confiscated local inventories, not just Bexar cobblers but from anyone who could give a soldado foot coverage. As usual, the poor relation of the army, the fusilier activos, probably had to make do with open sandals, if they were lucky.

Also during the morning, the Mexican artillerymen began constructing a new gun battery on the banks of the river, some 350 yards from The Alamo. With guns of such small calibre, it was important that they were placed as close as possible to the walls so as to effect any kind of significant damage. That said, the soldados soon learned to exercise great caution when straying within range of the eagle-eyed Texian sharpshooters. Well before noon Santa Anna, at the head of a cavalry detachment, was carrying out his own survey of the area, at one point even passing within musket shot of The Alamo. He ordered the entire town stripped of everything that could be of use to his army and, in some cases, this resulted in quite rough treatment of the locals. Also, by early afternoon, he had instructed his gun and howitzer batteries to commence a steady fire upon the rebel garrison.

The Mexican cannon threw solid shot directly against the perimeter walls, the notion being to weaken them by constant battering. The howitzers were angled so that the trajectory would send grenades (or shells) arching through the air so that they would land inside The Alamo's compound. These "grenades" were hollow iron balls packed with black powder and lit by fuses. The defenders quickly became accustomed to these hissing bombs landing at regular intervals all around them. As the fuses sputtered, the Texians would duck down and take cover inside buildings, against the walls or simply by throwing themselves flat on the ground or in the dubious shelter of the dried up acequia. Such exploding shells, though noisy and messy, caused nominal damage and, apparently, no casualties, but they cannot have been of any benefit to the defender's nerves.

Although the bombardment continued relentlessly, the Texian guns only replied at sporadic intervals. Travis ordered the gunners to return fire just enough to demonstrate determined resistance, for the garrison's stock of cannon shot was fairly limited and might have to last throughout a lengthy siege. On the plus side, it was soon realised that the Mexican guns dispensed shot which was of the same calibre as several of The Alamo's guns, so these balls, once cooled down, could be picked up, loaded and fired back at their original owners.

And then the Mexicans scored a bulls eye, cheering and waving their shakos as a lucky shot shrieked into the fort's south west corner and, with a loud crash and splintering of wood, sent the prized eighteen pounder spinning off its carriage. Grim faced at this setback, Carey's gunners ignored the distant jeering of their enemies and wasted no time in repairing the shattered wheel and mounting of their big gun, resetting it into position as quickly as they could.

During the night Jim Bowie's condition had worsened dramatically. By the morning of the 24th. he was scarcely able to rise to his feet, let alone take any further active part in the defence of the garrison. His efforts to soldier on had reached the end of their tether. He was rambling and weaker than a new born kitten. Dr. Pollard, summoned from the hospital, shook his head sombrely. Concerned, Travis found time to rush to his co-commander's side. Although they had endured their differences, Bowie and Travis still had a mutual respect for each other, and now the problem was a more practical one. Bowie was still coherent enough to understand what was at stake here. Beckoning Travis to lean closer he said that, under the circumstances, he was willing to let the young lawyer take over full command of The Alamo. Travis, despite the tragic reasons for such promotion, must have been delighted at this turn of events for he could now run things his way unhindered. Bowie, suffering terribly, was probably past caring, but he did express concern to the doctor that he did not wish to expose Juana and Gertrudis to any risk of infection. He decided to isolate himself and when the women protested managed to gasp, "Sisters, do not be afraid. I leave you with Col. Travis and Col. Crockett ... they are gentlemen and will treat you kindly." He was then placed upon a litter and carried by two of his men across the compound to a small room in the low barracks, just east of the south gate. The sight of the great Jim Bowie, stricken by illness, must have been a terrible blow to the defenders. Many of them had followed him personally for a long time and were there only because of his presence. There was no way they would desert him. Juan Seguin would later say how heartbroken he was to see his close friend, Don Jaime, coughing so fiercely that it seemed his lungs would burst from his body.

With the position of new command made clear to all within the walls, Travis retired to his quarters in the west wall to pen a letter which has become one of the great symbolic items in American history. Travis certainly relished the use of flamboyant and dramatic language, and he wrote many letters using similar stirring terminology, but this is the one that really made its mark. To this day the wording is set in a plaque which has pride of place on the pretty lawn in front of The Alamo chapel. Written in the Colonel's strong, sloping hand, punctuated by sweeping dashes and bold under linings it reads ...

Commandancy of The Alamo
Bexar February 24th. 1836
To the People of Texas & all Americans in the world.

Fellow citizens and compatriots - I am besieged by a
thousand or more of the Mexicans under Santa Anna -
I have sustained a continual Bombardment & cannonade for 24 hours
& have not lost a man - the enemy has demanded a surrender at discretion,
otherwise the garrison are to be put to the sword, if the fort is taken -
I have answered the demand with a cannon shot, & our flag still
waves proudly from the walls - I shall never surrender or retreat.
Then, I call on you in the name of Liberty, patriotism &
everything dear to the American character, to come to our aid,
with all dispatch - The enemy is receiving reinforcements daily &
will no doubt increase to three or four thousand in four or five days.
If this call is neglected, I am determined to sustain myself as long as possible & die like a soldier who

*never forgets what is due to
his own honor & that of his country - Victory or Death*

    *William Barret Travis
    Lt. Col. Commandant*

    *P.S. The Lord is on our side - When the enemy appeared
    we had not three bushels of corn - We have since found in
    deserted houses 80 or 90 bushels and got into the walls 20
    or 30 head of Beeves - Travis*

Darkness was descending over the garrison when Travis called for a courier to relay his message. Once again he chose Capt. Albert Martin, a veteran of this campaign since the very first engagement when the residents of Gonzales had defied the Mexicans over the return of that small, useless cannon. Martin hailed from Gonzales and that is where he would be bound to spread word of Travis' plight. Further north than Goliad and some twenty miles closer it made sense to keep the Texians there informed. It would also be a stepping stone to send word to possible larger relief forces.

The day's relentless bombardment had actually ceased for a while as both sides assessed their losses, so the moment was chosen for Martin to make a run for it. Slipping out of the south gate, the young officer stepped nimbly into the saddle and was soon cantering away towards the powder house on the eastern hills. He was barely noticed as he zigzagged in and out of the shadows. Still deploying and short of men, the Mexican army were not too bothered at this stage by lone couriers.

Travis watched him go, content with the way things were shaping up so far, but he was determined to make his defence arrangements anything but passive. Showing incredible reserves of energy, he paced out yet another of his endless patrols around the walls, checking up on everybody and everything. Although missing their hero Bowie, the men recognised that this young colonel was certainly proving himself to be an able and brave commander. Anxious to instigate events, Travis ordered a series of patrols to make recces outside the walls. The boldest adventurers amongst the defenders (Gregorio Esparza being but one) responded to this, creeping on their haunches towards the Mexican lines and soon returning with at least one soldado prisoner. During the remainder of the siege this terrified fellow was used to interpret enemy movements, including explanations of the various Mexican bugle calls.

Another boost for Texian morale came late in the evening, just as it was assumed that all would be quiet until the sun rose. A small group of soldados, led by a high ranking officer, was spotted making their way across the Commerce Street bridge, no doubt confident that in the darkness, and at such range, they would be safe on their scouting foray. How wrong they were. A volley of rifle fire rang out from The Alamo's south wall and one soldado fell dead. As the others scurried back to the safety of their lines the Texians whooped and hollered.

Santa Anna decided that it was time to show that things would not always favour the rebels, shut up so smugly in their cosy fortress. For the first time he implemented a tactic that he would use constantly throughout the remainder of the siege. He ordered his bands to start playing loud, martial music for long periods throughout the entire night, punctuated by orchestrated cheering from his men and occasional blasts of fire. At first these unorthodox concerts were merely a novelty to the defenders but they would soon lose their appeal, wearing away at the men's good spirits, shredding their nerves and depriving them of sleep.

Inside The Alamo, during the siege, Crockett entertains some of the defenders with one of his " tall tales". On his left stands a trooper from the New Orleans Greys, his tattered uniform reflecting the months he has spent living rough in the garrison. Travis, in a rare relaxed moment, leans upon his sword while one of Seguin's Tejano volunteers, clad in his colourful serape, looks on. A rank and file volunteer sits at their feet toying with his Bowie knife. The remaining figure, in hunting garb, is a Kentucky rifleman.

SIEGE WARFARE

The third morning of the siege proved to be a most eventful one. Under grey skies and chilly, drizzling rain, the Mexicans attempted to advance against The Alamo's south wall but the Texians were alert and ready for them.

About 400 soldados from the Matamoros and Jimenez battalions, supported by detached units of cazadores, crossed the river and began moving up through the scattered huts of Pueblo de Valero. To cover this advance, the Mexican batteries commenced a fire which was immediately returned by the Texian guns. Under this explosive exchange, Alamo defenders rushed out of the south gate and took up positions in the network of ditches which graced the outer fortifications. By all accounts Davy Crockett was notably active in this action, rushing from place to place, encouraging the men with cheers and good humour and directing their small arms fire. Some of the Mexicans got as close as fifty yards from the defences, but brisk volleys from the Texians and a deadly "firing at will" soon stopped them in their tracks. Firing as they withdrew and taking their wounded with them, the soldados took shelter in the nearby jacales. From here the musket and rifle fire was almost continuous throughout the morning as the two sides blasted away at each other. It became almost a stalemate until the Texians at last decided that something had to be done about those huts which had proved so convenient to the enemy. If the Mexicans were allowed to establish themselves there, right in the shadow of the fortress walls, things could prove prematurely disastrous.

It was then that a small group of daring defenders, clutching burning torches, rushed the buildings of Pueblo de Valero, setting fire to the thatch and causing general mayhem. Miraculously, although operating right in the heart of the enemy positions, these few brave men managed to avoid harm or capture and made it back to the Texian positions, mission accomplished. The huts and outbuildings burned healthily, depriving the soldados of their precious cover. Under a renewed onslaught of Texian fire, the Mexicans were forced to withdraw towards the outlying hamlet of La Villita further south.

The Texians, suffering only three men slightly wounded, must have felt very pleased with themselves. For many of them it was their first taste of combat and even Crockett had not been involved in a fully fledged battle for over twenty years. Once again, it was an event which did much for the defender's morale but it had not gone entirely their way. The Mexicans had now managed to establish themselves on The Alamo side of the river and were soon digging entrenchments and placing new gun batteries. By nightfall cavalry detachments had been posted along the eastern hills.

This minor setback had not been too worrying for Santa Anna, in fact in its way it had been valuable. His casualties were also light and the action had proved a good testing ground to sound out the rebel's fire power and fighting ability. Admittedly the Americanos had disported themselves well, but the president had only committed a fraction of his troops to the attack. The situation would be very different when the bulk of his army, plus the heavy guns, arrived. Santa Anna had also learned the powerful lesson not to attempt an open assault on the defences in daylight. He would not repeat that mistake. What he did do, however, was turn his attention to one of his keenest past times; the pursuit of pretty women. The small matter of putting down a rebellion did not stop him from quickly finding a mistress in Bexar who kept him entertained throughout the duration of the siege!

During the afternoon the weather grew calmer, becoming quite hot again as the opposing sides glowered at each other with new found respect. The Mexicans worked on industriously, a steady stream of reinforcements arriving for them from the south west, while the Texians congratulated themselves on the morning's success and gave more thought to improving the defences.

Of course, what they really needed was more men. Travis sat at his desk and composed another of his eloquent appeals, this time addressing it directly to General Sam Houston and giving a detailed description of the siege so far. His tone was optimistic but he did emphasise his desperation for assistance in holding off the enemy, saying, " ... it will be impossible for us to keep them out much longer. If they overpower us, we fall a sacrifice at the shrine of our country ... Give me help, oh my country!"

Now that the garrison was almost totally surrounded, the business of sending out messengers was becoming a more risky one. That evening, Travis called a war council for his officers during which the question arose as to who should attempt to take this latest news to Houston. General opinion strayed strongly in favour of it being Capt. Juan Seguin who spoke the language and knew the country well, but Travis opposed this saying that those were the very reasons why he wanted the Tejano leader to stay in The Alamo. His local knowledge would be invaluable. It was put to the vote and Travis lost. Seguin would take the message.

Before he left, Seguin went to see his old friend Bowie who lay soaked in feverish sweat, tossing and turning on his bed. They exchanged a few words and Bowie managed to tell the faithful rancher that he could use his horse for the mission. Deeply saddened, Seguin said goodbye to "Don Jaime", saddled up and made his way out of the south gate under cover of darkness, promising to return as soon as he could. Reaching the Gonzales road, and after a scrape or two with Mexican dragoons, he made it through.

Several Alamo defenders slipped over the wall that night and gave themselves up to the enemy. Evidence tends to suggest that they were Tejanos although at least one report gives credence to the notion that some of them may have been American. Arrogantly, Santa Anna refused to see them until the morning when it seems they supplied the Mexicans with some valuable information, including the location of fifty Texian rifles which had been hidden in town. What happened to these men is not known but if they survived the war they cannot have been too popular with their erstwhile friends.

Also during the night, as the weather worsened again, the Mexicans tried their luck with another small foray, this time, probably, against the east wall. Travis noted, in a later message, that the attackers were repulsed by a "discharge of grapeshot and musketry" and "took to their scrappers immediately", whatever *that* means!

Friday, February 26th. began miserably with a famous Texas "Norther" blowing in. The temperature plummeted and men braced themselves against the savage wind, huddling behind the walls or close to their cooking fires, but the business of the siege had to go on. Water was becoming a problem for the defenders as the Mexicans had already discovered they could affect the garrison's supply by blocking the irrigation ditch in the north. Green Jameson sought to remedy this by putting a squad to work on a half completed well, just to the front of the hospital in the plaza. They did find a new source of water this way, eventually, but unfortunately their digging efforts succeeded in also weakening an earth and timber parapet by the low barracks, causing it to collapse. It was quickly re-bolstered but left severely weakened.

At dawn Mexican cavalrymen were seen cantering in a circular direction, making their way towards The Alamo's eastern ramparts, but a Texian detachment soon drove them off with determined rifle fire. Taking advantage of this, another group ventured out from the garrison, this time to try and collect fire wood and water from the pond at the junction of the north east corner. They came under fire from Mexican riflemen who were positioned in the nearby cover of an orchard and the surrounding brush on the slopes above the acequia. Naturally, the Texians responded to this sharp shooting with volleys of their own before the bold water gatherers made it back into the fort. It was a fairly brief but intense exchange and it seems hard to believe that by now, regardless of Texian claims that the defenders received no fatalities until the final fateful day, no Americans had yet fallen to Mexican guns. Could the soldados really have been such atrocious marksmen? Despite the limitations of the Mexican issue "Brown Bess", it must be said that the cazadore's Baker rifle was a fine weapon.

The bitter Norther raged for two more days making conditions for both sides difficult and miserable. Determined to keep up morale, Travis kept his men busy. At least two more sorties ventured out to burn more huts but the Mexicans were well entrenched by now in hastily built fortifications all around the garrison. They did most of this work under cover of darkness, "advancing the sap" as it was called, for any soldado who showed himself within range to the Texians during the day was likely to be shot down. In this way, the Texians became accustomed to a constant re-arrangement of the surrounding landscape when they would awake to find earthworks and entrenchments a little closer each morning. On the subject of danger from sniper fire, a Mexican captain later wrote about a tall, long haired man dressed in buckskins who would take a regular position on The Alamo's south west wall to fire upon any soldado who was foolish enough to stray from cover. The tall Texian was very cool, apparently, and a deadly shot who claimed several victims, taunting his enemies in a resonant tone as he reloaded. Legend grew that this heroic figure must be Ol' Davy Crockett himself, but, of course, there is no real evidence to support such a romantic notion. However, it is interesting to note that the Mexican captain said that he later learned that the rifleman's name was "Kwockey".

Santa Anna, too, was not idle and spent much of his time surveying the results of his men's efforts. At La Villita he regaled the officers of the Matamoros battalion for shoddy workmanship and ordered them to rebuild their entrenchments, then he set off to ride along the lines again, inspecting his troops. In his colourful, glittering uniform, flanked by his smart dragoons, as usual, Don Demonio brightened up the greyness of the day. Cantering arrogantly along, his horse's hooves splattering mud upon the crouched bodies of his troops, the president must have presented an inviting target to the Alamo defenders, but they blasted away to no avail for he was just out of range. Later that day, Santa Anna sent a written message to his government officials in Mexico City informing them that he had captured Bexar. He also sent additional couriers back along the trail to General Gaona and his second-in-command, General Filisola, urging them to hurry on with their much needed troops and heavy artillery. At present there were eight Mexican guns in position around The Alamo, but nothing heavier than an eight pounder.

As the wind howled around the walls on the night of the 27th., Travis was busy at his desk again making yet another written appeal to Col. Fannin at Goliad. W.B. was growing impatient. Fannin should have received his previous message and surely would have mobilised by now. Why had nothing been heard from him? Lt. James Butler Bonham, the young, feisty lawyer from South Carolina was summoned and given the responsibility to get the message through. Bonham was a valued officer who had proved his worth by making it back into The Alamo after the siege took hold. He left via the northern postern vowing to return to his post as soon as he could, with or without help.

Each night Santa Anna continued with his policy of psychological warfare using his bands, sudden bugle calls, musket volleys, stage managed warlike cheering, in fact anything that could be thought of to un-nerve his enemies behind those defiant walls. The Mexicans had now succeeded in cutting off the Texian's water supply direct from the river so Jameson's well was much appreciated. As for the Mexicans, they too had general supply problems and foraging parties were sent out into the surrounding countryside to scavenge whatever was available. This included ransacking the nearby ranch of Juan Seguin.

The combination of several days of skirmishing, lack of water, noise, uncertainty and bad weather was beginning to take its toll of the Alamo defenders. They were tired and growing increasingly worried, wet, hungry and often bored. Those distant figures and earthworks were creeping nearer each day. Where was the help and reinforcements they so desperately needed? Had their friends forsaken them in their hour of need? Sue Dickinson later recalled that even the normally unflappable Crockett was heard to say, "I don't like to be penned up like this. I would rather march out into the open to die ..."

Generally, however, Crockett was a tower of strength who the men always seemed to look to for a cheerful word of encouragement. His tall tales were never ending and the defenders never lost their perception that this famous man had given up a luxurious life back east to come and assist them in this forlorn corner of Texas. On Sunday 28th., with the Norther dying down but persistent rain taking its place, Crockett decided to do something positive to improve the garrison's dark mood. Taking out his fiddle he began to play a string of jigs and reels, stomping his foot as the merry music drifted to the ears of the men huddled at their grim posts. The defenders gathered around him, smiles creasing their faces, hands clapping, feet tapping. Soon it seemed that everyone was enjoying this impromptu, free for all concert. With the bow flying across the strings, Crockett spotted artillery sergeant John McGregor in the crowd, calling upon him to bring out his bagpipes. McGregor needed no persuading and to ribald cheers, the Tennessean and the Scotsman formed a duet. Within moments their playing had turned into a kind of musical duel with each man trying to outplay the other, as to who could be louder and faster. Amongst the many tunes played, such classics as *Soldier's Joy* and *Temperance Reel* were heard, pieces which are still standards in Bluegrass/Country circles to this day. I think we can safely assume that this jolly interlude must have helped to take the defender's minds off their troubles for a while. Even Jim Bowie, immobile and barely conscious on his cot, managed to insist on playing his part by having two volunteers carry him around the ramparts to speak to his men as best he could. These courageous and inventive gestures were doubtless much appreciated by Travis.

At around this time it seems that an unofficial amnesty was agreed upon by the opposing forces. Word came that Santa Anna would be willing to allow any Tejano volunteers inside The Alamo to give themselves up, provided they made no further resistance. He gave them three days to decide. Most of these Tejanos had their homes in Bexar, of course, so the offer was tempting to them. The strain of the siege and rising tensions must have diluted many an initial dose of heroic fervour. Confused and feeling guilty probably, several of them went to Bowie's bedside for advice. They always trusted the word of Don Jaime. Weakly, Bowie was able to say, "All of you who desire to leave here may go in safety". Travis could only agree. That was good enough for the Tejanos and several of them disappeared that very night, taking their families with them. A few chose to remain at their posts, one being Gregorio Esparza who gave his wife the option to leave and save herself and the children while she could. Gregorio's young son, Enrique, recalled his mother Ana saying, "No, if you're going to stay, so am I. If they kill one they can kill us all". (Actually, by all accounts, Ana became the unofficial matriarch of the non-combatants gathered in the sacristy. She kept her head while most of the other women wailed and wallowed in self pity, completely helpless. Enrique said that even Sue Dickinson, long regarded as a pillar of strength, seemed "not to know what to do". As the enemy bombardments rocked the building, Ana soothed the others with her calm words and fine cooking.)

By the 29th. intelligence reports had informed Santa Anna that help was indeed imminent for the rebels inside The Alamo. Col. Fannin, with heavy guns and hundreds of men, was apparently marching from Goliad and would arrive very soon. Don Demonio knew this would need an immediate response but he really required Gaona's men. Where were they? To still contain the siege and send a force to repel Fannin would spread his troops very thinly, but he had no choice. Making rapid plans, Santa Anna ordered detachments from the Dolores cavalry and the Jimenez battalion, under the direct command of General Sesma, to advance down the Goliad road to meet the threat. This left a gap in the siege works which was plugged by men under General Castrillon, spread out in a thin line between the powder house on the eastern hills to a new earthwork some 800 yards north east of The Alamo.

Before General Sesma led his men out on their mission to stop Fannin, Santa Anna spoke strong words to him. A final reminder.

"In this war, you know," said El Presidente, sternly, his eyes full of intense black determination, "there ought to be no prisoners."

"GIVE ME HELP, OH MY COUNTRY!"

Col. James Fannin was suffering from a dilemma; a crisis of conscience. He was well aware of the desperate situation endured by his countrymen at The Alamo, but he had to be realistic. Fannin was one of the very few men in the volunteer army who had actually undergone proper military training and, as such, his tactical mind came into play.

The situation lay thus ... Fannin was indeed in a strong position, his 420 well armed men and cannon entrenched behind the walls of sturdy Fort Defiance, adequately supplied and probably capable of holding off the enemy. 95 miles to the northwest stood The Alamo, woefully undermanned and completely surrounded by the might of the Mexican army. Obviously they needed help. In fact it was essential for them and Fannin knew that his force was their best hope, even though other Texian forces would be gathering in the east. The message signed by Travis and Bowie on the 23rd. had reached Goliad on the following day but the fort's commander had perused it ruefully.

" ...we hope you will send us all the men you can spare promptly ..." it said, " ...we deem it unnecessary to repeat to a brave officer, who knows his duty, that we call on him for assistance."

Well, Fannin did not feel that he needed to exercise further evidence of his courage. Already he had seen action in most of the war's fights to date, including Gonzales, Concepcion and the taking of Bexar, his efforts resulting in his promotion from captain to colonel. It was how he had found himself responsible for the command of such an important post and, as such, could he afford to lay it open to risk? Santa Anna may have chosen to enter Texas by the back door at Bexar but Goliad was the front door. Would it be sensible to leave the front door bare and vulnerable whilst rushing to the back?

So these were the doubts, but the notion of ignoring The Alamo's plea and abandoning those heroic souls to certain death was unthinkable to the majority of Fannin's men. Somewhat reluctantly, Fannin began issuing orders for the formation of a hasty relief force and by the 26th. they were moving out, leaving a skeleton guard of 100 men to defend their garrison.

It seems this relief force was dogged by bad luck from the start, as if some divine intervention was at work to prevent their righteous actions. Struggling against a hostile, searing wind, Fannin and his men filed out of the fort, trudging towards the river. Before they reached the banks of the Rio San Antonio the problems began when several of their wagons began to come apart. Still well within sight of the fort, they halted to make repairs. Anxious to cross the river before dusk, the necessary work was rushed through, but the oxen dragging the wagons and quartet of cannon proved exceptionally stubborn. There was more frustrating delay while they were double teamed to give the animals enough strength to drag the heavy loads across the river, but by nightfall a large proportion of the column was still on the fort's side of the banks. And so this desperately needed relief force was forced to camp for the night, having barely made any progress at all.

Fannin's night of increasing doubt was made worse by the morning. The oxen had all wandered away! More hours were wasted as search parties were sent out to bring them back and by this time a grim mood had descended upon everyone. Fannin's officers formed a delegation, daring to question the wisdom of this unfortunate enterprise. Probably Fannin secretly welcomed this and he underlined the overall scenario. This courageous mission of theirs was actually going to expose the entire Texian left flank. More than a few of the diehards were outraged by this line of thinking. Moral outbursts and accusations flew freely but in the end sound good sense won over suicidal heroics. It was decided that for the good of the "complete cause", the relief force should retire back into Fort Defiance to think again.

With terrible feelings of guilt and still hoping they would yet be able to assist The Alamo somehow, the Goliad Texians tried to take their minds off their troubles by setting to work on improving the defences of their already rock solid fort. Then, during the evening of the 28th., news came via an excited, weather worn horseman, which would put paid to any further plans to march to The Alamo's aid. A day's ride to the south at San Patricio, General Urrea's soldados had inflicted a crushing defeat on Col. Frank Johnson and his optimistic Matamoros expedition. Those who had sought to invade Mexico had died in battle, or, worse still, had surrendered and been immediately executed. Johnson and a handful of others had somehow managed to escape the massacre but the message was painfully clear. The Mexicans were truly following Don Demonio's "no quarter" policy to the full.

Chilling news which sent a shudder through the garrison and had a sobering effect. This was the first real setback suffered by the Texians in the war and it was a severe one. They could expect no mercy from *this* foe.

*   *   *

Travis' other original messengers, Dr. Sutherland and John Smith, made it to Gonzales on the afternoon of February 24th.. They had pushed themselves hard to cover the seventy miles from Bexar so quickly and their arrival was met by an excitable and attentive crowd in the street. The news spread like wildfire. The Alamo needed help and the men of Gonzales were determined to answer the call.

Not a moment was wasted. Bravehearts, patriots, anyone with "fire in his belly" rushed home to make swift preparations. The little town had recently organized its own militia unit, "The Gonzales Ranging Company of Mounted Volunteers", and they were being called into action sooner than any of them expected. Not that they had any objections. Enthusiastically the members came forward while newcomers jostled to join them. They already had a leader, newly elected Lt. George Kimball, a hatter by trade who had originated from New York and now ran his own successful small business creating headwear for the good folk of Texas. He was happy and content in his new life with his pregnant wife and baby son, and it was a lifestyle he was determined to preserve. That would mean playing his part at The Alamo.

Others were equally committed, and a wide ranging bunch they were too. Farmers Dolphin Floyd and Jacob Darst, Sheriff Jesse McCoy and English shoemaker Marcus Sewell, for instance. Louisianan Charles Despallier stepped forward too. He had already been in The Alamo, leaving after Santa Anna's arrival as one of Travis' couriers. Now he could not wait to return. Some were in their teens, like young firebrand Johnnie Kellogg (19), his brother-in-law John Gaston (17) and even 16 year old Galba Fuqua, a boy who was close to the Dickinson family. Even he was not the youngest. That dubious honour went to 15 year old Will King who somehow managed to insist on taking the place of his father whom he said would be needed at home. By contrast Isaac Millsaps was in his forties and would be leaving behind a blind wife and seven children.

Late on the 25th., while preparations for the mission were in full swing, another courier arrived from The Alamo. This time it was Capt. Albert Martin carrying Travis' famous "Victory or Death" letter, a message which stirred the Gonzales spirit to even greater heights. Martin paused just long enough to scribble his own note on the back of the dispatch, "Hurry on all the men you can", before handing it to another horseman who would immediately hurry it on its way to the next town, San Felipe. Some might say that Martin had already played his part but he too insisted on joining the relief party, stressing how every extra man would count.

The group was finally mounted up and ready to leave by mid afternoon on the 27th., sent on their way by loving wives and sweethearts. There must have been many a tear proudly shed. With Lt. Kimball at their head, they trotted out of town silhouetted against the western sky, picking up others along the way until they totalled a healthy little squad of 32. Not quite Fannin's 300 plus but it would all help.

Their guide was John Smith, who also could not wait to return to his home and comrades. Dr. Sutherland, whose injured leg was still giving him trouble, said he would follow on later, perhaps with the next party of volunteers. Across the Cibolo Creek they rode, halting a few miles east of Bexar on the 29th. to wile away the daylight hours before risking their dash into The Alamo under cover of darkness. Smith took the precaution of sending a scout ahead to inform the garrison that they were coming. No one wished to be fired upon by mistake.

Under the blanket of nightfall they set off cautiously, riding in silence in single file, descending from the eastern hills just north of General Sesma's cavalry positions around the powder house. At some point here they were suddenly confronted by a stranger on horseback who addressed them in perfect English. They could not see him well in the gloom as he appeared to keep his distance, but he acted like an ally, asking the group if they wished to be escorted to the fort. Gingerly, the Gonzales men agreed to follow him, but as they rode on doubts grew. "El Colorado" Smith became particularly suspicious. Just a gut feeling but he trusted it. Instinctively the experienced scout suddenly said to those around him, "Boys, its time to be after shooting that fellow!"

The stranger heard, dug his heels into his horse's flanks and was away into the bushes before anyone could raise their gun. Who the stranger was and what his motive could be was a mystery that was never solved. Jittery now, the relief column hurried on, sensitive to any movement or sound around them. Across the open plain they trotted, shielded by the blackness until, at last, to their great relief, they saw the eastern adobe walls of The Alamo. As they drew nearer, the details lost their haziness. There was the corral and the semi-circular palisade and ditch just below one of the main eastern gun emplacements. Picket guards would be on watch here in the ditch and had probably already spotted the approaching riders.

Smith was not worried. His outrider would have made these guards alert to the impending arrival of friends. Unfortunately, it appears a breakdown in communication had taken place. Maybe the guards did not expect them to arrive at this particular spot. Whatever, a shot rang out from the garrison and a Gonzales man yelped in pain, hit in the foot. Curses and cries of rage. Not a wonderful welcome! Behind the walls the defenders abruptly acknowledged their error, waved a lantern and beckoned their snubbed allies to carry on through the open postern.

Although the edge had been taken off their arrival by this embarrassing retort, the Gonzales men entered The Alamo to a very warm welcome. To hell with the fact that they were only 32 strong. These were the first to respond to Travis' call and as such they were Saints! It was 3.00am. on Tuesday March 1st..

Although the day dawned clear but cold, the Texians spent the morning celebrating the arrival of the Immortal 32 (as they became known to history). Travis was particularly euphoric, convinced that other larger parties would be close on their heels. To signal his confidence and contempt for the enemy, Travis ordered Carey's gunners to fire a couple of rounds from the twelve pounders at the town. With cannon shot in short supply this was a rare luxury, but such was their joy. Using the blood red flag on the San Fernando church tower as their general target, the artillerymen let fly. Their first ball crashed noisily into Bexar's Main Plaza but the second shot could not have been better placed if they had carried it there by hand, for it smashed through the roof and walls of the Yturri house, Santa Anna's headquarters! There were casualties but not Don Demonio himself who, fortunately for him, was out inspecting his troop's positions at the old mill to the north west of The Alamo. Even so, it gave great cause for celebration and the Texians must have danced and sung themselves giddy to the strains of Crockett's fiddle and McGregor's bagpipes. Young Enrique Esparza remembered that others joined in on drums and one tooted on a fife.

As for the Mexicans, their day was otherwise uneventful, apart from the usual trench digging and keeping their heads down from Texian sniping. General Sesma returned from the south, his Dolores cavalrymen redeploying on the eastern hills and the Jimenez battalion trudging tiredly back to their posts around the town. Although they had advanced far down the Goliad road, no sign had been found of Col. Fannin and his so called relief force.

*   *   *

March 2nd. also proved to be a quiet day in Bexar, this time for both sides as Texians and Mexicans took advantage of the lull in hostilities. The Mexicans carried on digging and raising earthworks along with a little more foraging. Seguin's ranch was raided again for additional corn supplies and a hitherto undiscovered roadway was found by Mexican scouts just to the north east of The Alamo. This was quite a revelation, for this hidden path, concealed by dense foliage which apparently stretched almost to the garrison walls, came within fifty yards of the Texian fortifications. Santa Anna immediately exploited this by posting elements of the Jimenez battalion there. The president was also pleased to hear news that an aide had arrived from General Gaona's division with promises that substantial advance units of his brigade would arrive in Bexar within 24 hours.

As for the Texians, they were in a more relaxed mood than they had been for some time. The arrival of the "Immortal 32" had given the weary defenders new cause for hope. They would have felt even better had they known about events which were taking place that very day far to the north east, beyond San Felipe, at Washington-on-the-Brazos. Here in the Texas capital, the delegates had assembled to make history. Sam Houston, of course, was prominent among them. Amidst wild celebration and patriotic zeal this convention officially declared Texas to be an independent state, separating it forever from Mexico. This was exactly what the men of The Alamo were fighting for but, sadly, they would never get to know about it.

That day the Mexican losses were far from severe, although it doubtless concerned the family of cazadore Trinidad Delgado from the San Luis Potosi battalion who drowned whilst bathing in the river. No matter to Santa Anna. Within a day this unfortunate soldado would be replaced many times over.

Santa Anna's soldados gather before the final assault, making their way to their various units. On the left stands a bearded Zapadore, still dressed in his work fatigues, while beside him an Activo trooper shoulders his Brown Bess musket. In the foreground an unhorsed cavalryman from the Dolores company walks arrogantly by, watched by a high ranking officer and a Cazadore.

HOPE VERSUS HONOUR

From a position approximately half a mile to the north of the Powder House, high up on the eastern hills, Lt. James Butler Bonham reined in his lathered horse and observed the scene around him. He was wary of being spotted, for away to his left new Mexican positions had been established which had not been present when he had last been in the vicinity just five days before. Crouching low in the saddle, the young lawyer looked down towards The Alamo less than a mile ahead, the pale walls looking so isolated and vulnerable now. Although not unexpected, Bonham must have been affected by the sight of the many fresh Mexican entrenchments, fortified positions and bodies of troops which now hemmed in the garrison on every side. From such a vantage point he was truly able to appreciate the extent of the defender's predicament. Dozens of soldado camp fires, dotting the terrain like stars in a night sky, those hundreds of distant figures, marching in column, digging trenches, going about the daily business of siege work, and those formidable looking gun and howitzer batteries. What hope did The Alamo have if help did not come?

It was 11.00am. on Thursday March 3rd.. The morning was clear, still chilly, but without a breeze. Bonham had ridden through the night, anxious to bring greatly anticipated news to his comrades in arms. How he must have wished he was returning at the head of 500 volunteers instead of riding in alone again. In fact, would he be able to make it? It was no short dash across that open plain, in broad daylight with the enemy on every side.

Bonham sat upright in the saddle, took a deep breath and summoned up his deepest reserves of courage. Reaching into his coat he took out a clean, white bandana which he wound around the crown of his broad brimmed hat. That, at least, would identify him to the trigger happy sentries. Choosing a spot as centrally between the two closest Mexican positions as he could estimate, Bonham spurred his horse into the open, reaching full gallop within moments. Heart pounding, he dashed for The Alamo's eastern postern, the same one used by the Gonzales men just two days before. So near and yet so far. Any moment he expected a fusillade of shots to topple him from the saddle but the surrounding Mexicans let him pass with barely a raised gun. His sudden dramatic appearance startled them but it was of no great consequence. Let him go, they thought, for he would be dying with his foolish friends soon enough.

The Alamo sentries spotted the galloping figure and, in the brightness of the day, recognized him almost immediately. Cheering him on, the gates swung open and Bonham hurtled into the fort, his horse rearing to a halt as the excited defenders gathered around. Dismounting and acknowledging the warm greetings and back slapping, the young officer extracted the packet of letters he was carrying and made straight for Travis' quarters.

The Alamo's commander was waiting for him, urgently taking the dispatches and leafing through them as Bonham told his story. He had reached Goliad's Fort Defiance on February 29th. catching Col. Fannin at his lowest ebb. Just ensconced back in the fort after his luckless attempt to march out with a relief force, Fannin was in no mood to respond to Bonham's appeal. He was now concentrating on the reality of conducting his own defence but all his reasonable talk, excuses and apologies cut no ice with the bold Carolinian. Bonham had never liked the cautious Fannin anyway and now he felt pure contempt for him. Turning down Fannin's invitation to remain safely in the fort, he indignantly replied that he had promised the stalwarts of The Alamo that he would get help. If Fannin chose to let them down then he would have to try elsewhere. Many of those in the Goliad garrison stressed that if they had their way, they would definitely follow Bonham, but their hands were tied by their reluctant commander.

Darkly but determinedly, Bonham turned to the north, riding hard and arriving in Gonzales the next day where he found quiet streets populated only with women, children and other non-combatants. All those willing to fight had already left. George Kimball's Ranging Company had set out a couple of days ago but Bonham was satisfied to think that they should have reached The Alamo by now. Also, Dr. Sutherland, along with Horace Alsbury (the husband of Jim Bowie's sister-in-law, Juana), had recovered sufficiently to fulfil his promise of riding out with a second group. Alsbury, naturally, had an extra motive to return to The Alamo as his wife and baby son were still there. Bonham was also told that Juan Seguin, having delivered his despatch, had raised a further group of Tejano volunteers and had ridden on to join Sutherland. Both groups were hoping to catch up with Kimball but, as it turned out, were unable to do that.

Assured that more help was coming from San Felipe and beyond, Bonham mounted up again. Many tried to tell him that he had done his duty, but he would not be persuaded that his rightful place lay anywhere but inside The Alamo. He solemnly declared that he must report the result of his mission to Travis or die trying.

En route back to Bexar, Bonham did not find either Sutherland or Seguin, as he thought he might. Having missed Kimball, these two groups (numbering less than forty in all) decided to settle down on the Cibolo Creek to await the arrival of Fannin's expected army. It would be a fruitless wait which would cost The Alamo those desperately needed men.

Travis read through the letters and his spirits soared. The news was good. Especially a message from his close friend and fellow Texian officer "Willie" Williamson which promised hundreds of men from Bastrop, Brazoria, San Felipe and other towns. It finished with the plea "For God's sake, hold out until we can assist you ..." Williamson also wrote of Fannin and the 300 men on their way from Goliad but, having heard Bonham's report, Travis dismissed this ruefully. It was obvious now that he should give up any hope of help from Fannin, but he was confident that other sources would not let him down. If he could just hold out for a few more days .....

Late that afternoon the tide turned again. Waves of cheering and cries of "Viva Santa Anna!" could be heard from the direction of Bexar's Main Plaza while the bells of the San Fernando church tower rang out gleefully. Something was happening. The men of The Alamo crowded together along the south and west walls, shielding their eyes against the glare of the setting sun. Gloomily they watched as long lines of fresh Mexican troops marched into town. Santa Anna's bands were in full swing once more. His impatient demands had born fruit at last for these were the men of General Gaona's brigade, nearly 900 of them with two additional cannon. Not the twelve pounders that Don Demonio had requested, but it would all help. The main thing was the manpower. Led by Col. Francisco Duque, Gaona's acting commander, these soldados were made up of advance units of the Toluca and Aldama battalions, the latter being experienced permanentes. However, even these Toluca troops, who were normally raw activo recruits, had seen action in the recent Zacatecas campaign and were therefore battle tested veterans. More important, perhaps, to Santa Anna, was the fact that marching with them came 185 of his crack troops, the bearded, highly professional Zapadores. In all, this brought the strength of the Mexican army surrounding The Alamo to about 2,400 men and 10 cannon. And that would not be an end to it. Gaona and the remainder of his brigade were still on their way.

With an impeccable sense of timing, word then arrived of General Urrea's success defeating Col. Johnson at San Patricio, along with news of another victory he had won annihilating a smaller Texian force at Agua Dulce Creek. The Mexicans cheered themselves hoarse. They were long overdue in hearing such splendid news. Now they could really get down to the business of removing this stubborn outpost of cocky rebels.

Up at the Powder House a second blood red banner was raised to complement the one which still flapped in the breeze on the San Fernando church belfry. Once again the Texians, as they watched in sullen silence, were reminded that their foes would, when the time came, give "no quarter".

The Zapadores, with their engineering skills, were straightaway put to work improving the Mexican's advancing sap. Already the soldados had taken advantage of The Alamo's acequia, which had been dammed to deprive the garrison of its water supply, for now that it was dry it served as a convenient sheltered road along which troops could get close to the garrison itself. The Zapadores, working in drilled teams, now enlarged upon this by beginning new ditches leading off the acequia. In this way, several new frontal assault positions were established along with the re-siting of the north eastern gun battery, which had soon been placed within 200 yards of The Alamo. It was now the Mexicans turn to feel ultra confident.

Travis was unbowed. It would take more than a few thousand Mexicans to make him throw in the towel. Defiantly, he took to his desk again to write a long, eloquent letter to the President of the Convention up at Washington-on-the-Brazos. If only he had known he was now addressing the officially declared nation of Texas! How much prouder this proud man would have been. In the letter, Travis gave an updated and detailed description of events, not smoothing over the seriousness of his plight yet retaining his optimistic tone. Stressing the need for immediate provisions, cannon ammunition and, of course, troops, he also found space to attack the loyalty of certain Tejanos, saying, "we have but three Mexicans now in the fort; those who have not joined us in this extremity should be declared public enemies, and their property should aid in paying the expenses of the war". Yet again he signed off with his famous phrase "Victory or Death!" Obviously feeling that time was running out, W.B. also penned some other messages, personal ones to various friends throughout Texas in which he explained his deeply held beliefs in liberty and loyalty. Most moving of all is a note he included to the Ayers family who were looking after his little son Charles at their home up on the Rio Brazos. The sensitivity of this courageous, if outwardly flamboyant, Texian hero was never more apparent than in these words; "Take care of my little boy. If the country should be saved, I may make him a splendid fortune; but if the country should be lost and I should perish, he will have nothing but the proud recollection that he is the son of a man who died for his country."

The courier selected to take these messages was already waiting out in the moonlight of The Alamo's plaza. John "El Colorado" Smith again. Even though he had only just returned, no one else was better qualified to make it through the Mexican lines. Other Texians were gathered around him, whispering messages for him to relay to their loved ones or handing him hastily scribbled notes. Smith received them all patiently then turned to take the official despatch from Travis.

W.B. shook the hand of this seasoned scout, wishing him luck and explaining that from now on he would order a round fired from the eighteen pounder three times a day; first thing in the morning, at high noon and last thing at night. In this way any approaching relief force would know that as long as they heard this signal The Alamo would still be resisting the enemy. Smith nodded and tried to assure his commander that help would surely come.

From the northern postern, Travis apparently arranged for a party of men to venture out to cause a diversion. In the ensuing crackle of fire and confusion, Smith was able to disappear into the darkness of the east and by first light was well on his way back towards Gonzales.

The fragile, uncertain amnesty was well and truly over. The Mexican guns opened fire again with a vengeance, seven cannon pounding the north and west walls and three howitzers lobbing their fizzing shells into the garrison's plaza. Santa Anna's artillerymen had now concentrated four of their cannon together at the new northern battery which was painfully close to The Alamo's north wall. The whole length of this previously re-bolstered fortification took terrible punishment as the nine pound iron balls smashed at point blank, short range directly into the crumbling adobe and earthwork structure. Green Jameson rose to the challenge gamely, but he knew it was a losing battle. As soon as his teams of sweating overworked men rushed to plug a weakness or gap in the wall, another blast would send them scurrying for cover, showered with dirt, stone splinters and shattered timber. No amount of piled dirt and extra bracing could withstand such an onslaught indefinitely. The west wall suffered a similar bombardment but the Mexican gunners seemed to be particularly concentrating on the north. As they huddled into corners and ditches for shelter, or peered warily over the ramparts, an air of expectant gloom hung over the defenders.

Travis' remarks in his last despatch regarding the loyalty of certain Tejano volunteers and their families was not totally unfounded. As previously stated, quite a few of these Mexicans had already decided to hedge their bets and slip over the wall to throw in their lot with Santa Anna. To be fair, they cannot be admonished for this without considering the whole picture, which was far from being painted in plain black or white. We must remember that this battle was taking place on the very doorsteps of their homes. A great deal was at stake for them and also the emphasis had largely shifted as to what this conflict was really about. Initially, many Mexicans had allied themselves with the Texian cause because they felt they were standing together with the Americanos for a fair *Mexican* based constitution, the idea being merely to defy an arrogant dictator and return to the terms of the 1824 agreement. Now it had become a fight between Americans and Mexicans. Many of those with Mexican blood began to wonder where they would stand should they end up under the control of an American government. Santa Anna was ruthless and undoubtedly had the upper hand in this conflict. What real motive did most Tejanos have to remain loyal to Travis? Of course, many had become personal, long term friends and that could not be dismissed lightly. Men like Juan Seguin and Gregorio Esparza could always be trusted, but how far could most of these Bexar residents be expected to extend loyalty when their families and homes were at risk? The odds were stacked against them as long as they remained in The Alamo. Don Demonio had offered them an escape route and time was running out. Back in Bexar, at least they could lay low and see how things panned out.

On the evening of March 4th., therefore, one or two Mexican women left the shelter of the sacristy, crept out of The Alamo unseen, and presented themselves at the Yturri house to see Santa Anna. He welcomed them and was most intrigued by what they had to say as they betrayed details of conditions within the garrison. They spoke of weakened defences that barely held up, demoralised, tired men at the walls, lack of cannon ammunition, talk of surrender; the place was obviously ripe for the taking. Santa Anna felt strongly that the time had come to mount an immediate assault. Wait any longer and the rebels might just receive their long awaited reinforcements from the east.

That same night he called a council of war at his headquarters and, uncharacteristically, asked for the opinions of all his assembled officers. Although there was general agreement that an all out assault should be imminent, the subject of exactly when it should take place was open to much debate. Several officers proposed that it would make sense to wait for General Gaona to arrive with the rest of his brigade and the all important pair of twelve pounder cannon. These bigger guns would make final mincemeat of the Texian defences, clearing the way for a simpler, obstacle free attack. This would mean a delay of just another day or two, at most, but Santa Anna insisted that even that could be too late. Fannin and his men could be on their doorstep. The

Tejano women had confirmed that The Alamo's defences were weak enough already and the Mexican forces present now were more than adequate to take the place, outnumbering the defenders by about twelve to one.

Some of the officers hinted at their doubts over any kind of frontal assault. True, The Alamo could be taken but the cost in soldado lives would be immense. Was it worth such sacrifice when the fort could just be contained by siege while the rest of the army marched on into Texas? Don Demonio brushed their whispered arguments aside. It was a matter of pride that he felt the need to take the garrison by shot, shell and bayonet. He also claimed that the blood soaked defeat of this symbolic rebel garrison would infuse his soldados with ""the enthusiasm of the first triumph that would make them superior in the future to those of the enemy".

The subject also arose of taking prisoners. Santa Anna was still 100% insistent that there should be no quarter. Any of these "perfidious foreigners" who surrendered should be immediately executed as the "pirates" that they were. He cited the example he had witnessed as a young Spanish Royalist lieutenant in 1813, during the Federalist rebellion, when hundreds of rebels and their sympathisers had been hanged. This was the only way, declared El Presidente forcefully. However, several officers were shocked by this, particularly General Manuel Castrillon who pleaded for clemency on the grounds of honourable principle and the rights of men. Castrillon was one of Don Demonio's most valued confidantes, a fine, experienced officer and gentleman of advanced years who believed in knightly codes of conduct within warfare. Santa Anna let him speak but would not be dissuaded. There were to be no prisoners and that was his final word on the matter.

This conference went on for so long that eventually Santa Anna grew tired of it, dismissed all of these generals and colonels and made the decision himself. There would be no further waiting. Preparations for the assault would begin without delay. By early afternoon the next day, Saturday March 5th., he had thrashed out his meticulous plan of operations and the top brass were re-assembled to hear his instructions.

The attack on The Alamo would commence at 4.00am. the following morning, the garrison being hit at four points simultaneously by massed columns of infantry. The first column was to be led by General Cos, giving him a chance to assuage the shame of losing the fort in the first place. At the head of 300 men from the San Luis and Aldama battalions he was to strike the north west corner while more soldados from the San Luis contingent and others of the Toluca battalion (about 400 in all) were to concentrate on the north east corner under the leadership of Colonel Duque and General Castrillon. This would be the main thrust of the assault, but there would be another strike at the east wall, in the area of the horse and cattle corrals, carried out by Colonel Romero and 400 men of the Matamoros and Jimenez battalions. The final column would find a point to scale along the south wall. In the hope that all the Texian attention would be focussed on the main attacks to the north and east, it was deemed necessary to only designate 100 men, all cazadores, under Colonel Morales for this southern assault. Another 400 soldados would be kept in reserve under the direct command of Santa Anna himself at the north east gun battery. Don Demonio made sure he had the best troops surrounding him, for these men would all be tough grenadiers, the pick of the army, along with the entire contingent of his favoured Zapadores. He would only commit them to danger if unavoidable. The first and second columns were equipped with a score of scaling ladders between them, along with crowbars and axes to demolish the defences. The third column was to carry six ladders and the fourth column just two. Sesma's 300 cavalrymen were not to be used in the assault itself but had to position themselves in the area of the Alameda to the south east. Their function was to watch out for any foolhardy defender who tried to escape over the south or east walls for they could easily be cut down by horsemen in such open country. Another 400 men were to remain in camp but these were all conscripts, reservists and those who were generally considered to be unreliable. Santa Anna wanted only hardened men to fight this battle for him.

*   *   *

Regardless of these preparations, the Mexican bombardment did not lessen throughout that long Saturday. If anything it intensified until, abruptly, at around 5.00pm., it ceased altogether. The Texians within The Alamo had become so mesmerised by the incessant pounding of shells and cannon balls that the sudden onset of silence fazed them. Slowly, they began to emerge from shelter to try and see what new developments could be occurring beyond the Mexican lines. There certainly seemed to be intense activity but it was difficult to assess exactly what might be going on. Columns of troops were moving back and forth, many of them, it seemed, marching determinedly away from the town. What could this mean? At the very least it meant a chance for the defenders to re-organize themselves. Some even built fires out on the plaza and began preparing supper. Young Enrique Esparza remembered at least one Texian courier getting into the fort but the news was grim. Communications were cut off and it seemed the likelihood of reinforcements arriving in time to save the garrison was slim.

Whether or not Travis truly believed this will never be known. It is probable that he never gave up hope that hordes of flag waving saviours would come swarming over the eastern hills to his rescue at any moment. Whatever, by early evening on The Alamo's final full day a heavy mood of melancholy had descended over the garrison. It was best described as a terrible feeling of the world closing in on every side and leaving them horribly alone. Travis knew that he must address it.

Just before dark he passed the word around that he required the entire garrison to assemble in the plaza so that he could speak to them. Nobody protested. They all wanted to hear what he had to say about their situation. How depressing that the mood had sunk so low in just two days. As one, the men of The Alamo postponed whatever they were doing and ambled purposefully down into the plaza, assembling in one large group facing the chapel. Hungry men left their cooking, Dr. Pollard removed himself from his duties in the hospital, Dickinson came down from his gun post on the church roof, Crockett's volunteers turned away from their stockade and even Green Jameson put aside his never ending repair work. And then there was Big Jim Bowie, barely recognisable now that he looked so emaciated. He had insisted on being carried out on a stretcher so that he could hear Travis' words along with everyone else. Men tutted and shook their heads. By the look of him it was a miracle he was still alive. Sue Dickinson was there too, watching from the shadows of the church doorway.

Travis faced them sombrely, leaning on his sword as he cast his eyes across the faces of this noble band whom he had grown to know so well. To one side stood his loyal slave, Joe, head bowed in sadness. There are several accounts of his words; even those who were present and lived to tell the tale contradicted their own stories as they retold them over the ensuing years. However, the general gist of what he had to say remains fairly certain. Speaking in a bold, clear tone, he told his command that there now seemed to be very little chance of help arriving before the Mexicans staged a serious assault. Their hope of resisting such an attack with the resources and men they had at present was pretty futile, therefore, sadly, The Alamo was likely to fall. As the men mumbled amongst themselves, Travis carried on to say that he did not expect any man to choose certain death but that he personally was resolved to remain at his post whatever the outcome. If the Mexicans were to taste victory here he was determined to make it very costly for them, more costly, in fact, than defeat. Urging his men to join him he also stressed that he was giving every man under his command a choice. They could attempt to escape with his approval but all who wished to do so should step out of the ranks and make themselves known.

It was at this point that, apparently, only one individual stepped forward, the fifty year old former soldier from Napoleon's army, Louis Moses Rose, who had ridden into The Alamo with Jim Bowie himself. Rose was forever afterwards considered to be the only coward in The Alamo but, in actual fact, stepping forward like that in front of his comrades must have required a certain brand of courage in itself. Also, he had fought courageously enough alongside everyone else all these hard days past. He was an old soldier who did not need to prove his worth to anyone and did not feel ready to die. Fair enough. "I have done worse things than go over that wall," he is said to have muttered, mysteriously, then he gathered his things together and with barely a backward glance vanished into the dusk.

Here we must consider the romantic idea of Travis drawing a line in the dirt with his sword and inviting all those who wished to stay and fight it out to cross it. Legend says that virtually the entire command did so. In actual fact, although there exists several accounts which claim that this *did* happen, unfortunately they are all subject to serious doubt, mainly because the story did not surface until years after the battle and was not mentioned in any of the early recollections by survivors. Once the notion had captured the public's imagination, figures like Sue Dickinson and Enrique Esparza, suddenly, in their old age, began to recall it! No doubt they were often encouraged and inspired by news hungry reporters. So, this perhaps is a victory for the cynics, but before they crow too loudly, let us remember that there is no evidence which definitely refutes the possibility that Travis drew the line. It certainly would have been an act typical of the man's character. In any case, the main point is that, with the exception of Rose, all others in the garrison *did* choose to stay and fight. That in itself is worthy of the creation of a legend.

As the evening advanced the sky grew cloudy, enveloping Bexar and the surrounding countryside in an even deeper darkness. It was peaceful, a welcome change to the endless days and nights of cannon shots, gunfire and the Mexican's noisy tactics of disorientation and false alarms. But there were still sounds from the Mexican lines, barked orders and the rustle and crunch of marching feet. They were definitely up to something.

Travis could not afford the luxury of spending too long on supposition. The lull had to be exploited for all it was worth. Not having to duck from shells and shrapnel, the men of The Alamo were able to throw themselves back into work, albeit in the blackness of night. There was still a lot to be done shoring up the walls, plugging gaps, stacking sandbags. Jameson was everywhere, checking every detail while Travis took stock and made his rounds. The men were all comfortable with him now. He had proved his worth and they looked up to him as an able commander. Whatever his failings, no one could deny that William Barret Travis was a man not lacking in principle, honour and great courage. Scouring his mind for the notion of anything he might have missed, W.B. decided there was nothing to be lost by making a final plea for help to Fannin. He must have known it was pointless. If the Goliad contingent were coming they would have arrived by now but Travis felt he could not let it lie. At the very least underline their guilt by stressing how much they were needed.

In contrast to the seasoned scouts who had acted as couriers previously, Travis now chose a sixteen year old youth to act as his final messenger, probably because he felt he would need the most experienced men for the coming battle. In any case, young James Allen was a superb horseman and was even going to ride his mare bareback for extra speed. Hidden by the pitch blackness and un-noticed in the hubbub of Santa Anna's assault preparations, he got away safely.

Travis carried on with his rounds, speaking words of encouragement to each man he encountered, stirring their spirits with his insistence on making the Mexicans pay dearly for their time at The Alamo. Some defenders had a strong feeling that something was about to happen while others complained that the siege was dragging on intolerably and would probably do so for some time to come. Whatever, most felt they were safe enough for now. Many of those who had not yet written a will settled down, when they found a quiet moment, to write one. More than a few expressed concern that should the worst happen, they desired that their bodies be decently buried.

Although cannon shot was in short supply, the defenders did not want for small arms and ammunition. Apart from their own weapons, much had been seized from Cos' men in December and now virtually all the Texians could take to the ditches and ramparts with three, four or even five loaded muskets or rifles lined up beside them. They may be few in number but their fire power would be phenomenal. This, at least, must have made Travis nod contentedly.

At the south east palisade he exchanged a few words with Crockett whose gentle charm and wisecracks remained as solid as ever. Those Tennessee long rifles, tall, spiked stockade and sharpened tree stumps should prove a worthy obstacle. No worries there. Travis walked on to that small room just east of the main gate in the south wall where Jim Bowie lay alone. It must have been a sad sight. One can only guess what went through W.B.'s mind as he gazed upon the prone figure of his ex co-commander. Bowie was stretched out on his cot, too weak now to even toss and turn, the sweat on his pained, fleshless face glistening in the candle light. Someone had placed a loaded rifle next to the bed, the tip of the muzzle leaning against the wall. Also within reach were a pair of primed pistols and, of course, the huge, savage looking knife that this living legend had made so famous. Quite an armoury but what could a man in this condition hope to do to defend himself?

On to the hospital, two rooms, one large, one small, on the second floor of the long barracks, containing perhaps a dozen bunks and mattresses. A wooden stairway led from here down to an arcaded gallery at the edge of the horse corral along the fort's east wall. How many sick and wounded were housed here is unknown, but there could well have been a handful more bedded down in the low barracks near to Bowie. Apparently a few had been laid up since the Battle of Bexar three months ago. Although testy about his lack of medical supplies, Dr. Pollard seemed to have it all in order.

In the church, Travis inspected Almeron Dickinson's high placed gun positions, satisfied as ever by this conscientious artilleryman's efforts. Blacksmith to ace gunner. A transition indeed. Tending the guns, Gregorio Esparza, skinny little Jacob Walker and others looked up and acknowledged their commander. James Bonham was there too, cheerful and bold. With men like this perhaps they could hold out yet. Irish New Yorker Robert Evans, chief of ordnance, approached and pointed towards the supplies of gunpowder and ammunition stocked securely in the safety of the baptistry. Travis dourly reminded him of an order he had issued earlier. If The Alamo fell to the enemy, the last capable defender was to destroy this magazine. Evans understood his duty and nodded knowingly.

Finally, Travis visited the non-combatants in the sacristy, peering at each of the innocent, worried looking faces as they stared back at him in the gloomy lamplight. Ana Esparza and her children, Anthony Wolfe's two boys, other women and youngsters and that ever present, spoiled cat. Sue Dickinson too, nursing her little daughter, Angelina. Mrs. Dickinson often looked like she had the weight of the world on her shoulders but she had good cause for concern. Still, at least her husband was nearby and spent his nights with her.

Travis' military bearing softened as he looked at them. Perhaps he thought of his own little boy so many miles away. Stepping forward he dropped to one knee and whispered gentle, coaxing words to the baby. Smiling, he took a heavy gold ring from his finger and threaded a piece of string through it. Tying a knot in the string, he placed it carefully around the girl's neck, an historic souvenir which would eventually find its way, many years later, into The Alamo museum. It was a poignant moment which Sue Dickinson would never forget.

It had been a long day and night for Travis and he still found much to do before finally making his way back to his quarters in the west wall. It was 4.00am. and he must have been very tired, regardless of the many things racing around his mind. Wearily, and still fully dressed, he wrapped himself in a blanket, his weapons close to hand, and lay down upon his cot. Joe, his slave, was already sleeping in the far corner of the room.

As he drifted into welcome oblivion, could The Alamo's commander have had any notion that this was to be his last night on earth?

CALM BEFORE THE STORM

As Travis indulged in his duties, military and personal, much activity was taking place in the Mexican camp. All through that Saturday afternoon Santa Anna busied himself supervising the carrying out of his most specific orders, right down to the finest detail. He was determined that this should be a model military operation and was leaving nothing to chance.

As the Mexican guns stopped firing around 5.00pm., the heavy set troopers of the grenadiers amalgamated with Lt. Col. Amat's Zapadores, marching through the streets of Bexar to their assembly point. Throughout the evening, at staggered intervals, similar scenes were staged throughout the Mexican lines as company officers relayed Don Demonio's instructions to their subordinates. Particular attention, said the president, was to be paid to each man's bayonet. They must be well secured and deadly sharp for the close combat that lay ahead. And every soldado must turn in for sleep as quickly as he could for it would be a long hard day tomorrow.

Consequently, in the hours approaching midnight, all became still and quiet in the Mexican lines. Up on the hills around the powder house the soldados of the Jimenez and Matamoros battalions were trying to rest as best they could and the Aldama and Toluca troops, in town, had stacked their weapons and were doing the same. The last to be stood down from duty for the evening were the fusiliers of the San Luis Potosi battalion who were allowed a little cold supper of tooth cracking hardtack before they dozed.

No sooner had they settled when it seemed they were being raised again. On the stroke of midnight, officers and sergeants were moving methodically along the rows of huddled soldados, prodding them awake and barking softly in their ears. They were stern and insistent but silence was the order of the day this time as the big sleeping giant of the Mexican army was roused from its dreams. Quickly, but with an eerie noiselessness, the soldados were mustered into line so that their officers could check that all was in order. Every man had to be shod with either shoes or sandals, all blankets and packs were to be left behind (nothing was to slow the advance), the scaling ladders must be sturdy and ready for use. Shako chin straps must be tight above the neck, two spare musket flints to be carried by all those in the lead companies, plus extra cartridge packs. There was to be no smoking or unnecessary talking. And how were those sword and socket bayonets? Keen enough to impale a rebel like a hot knife through butter? Very good, compadres!

As all this was going on, Santa Anna was having a midnight meal with General Castrillon and Col. Almonte in the Yturri house. Regardless of the Mexican government's anti-slavery policy, Don Demonio, just like Travis, had his own Negro servant. This over worked black man of American origin, Ben by name, was certainly feeling the brunt of Santa Anna's nervous impatience this dark night. Drinking endless cups of strong coffee, the Mexican commander swore oaths and threats whenever his cup grew empty. The strain of what was to come was weighing on him heavily. More than once the officers left the house, and Ben was able to relax, but they were soon back again, as waspish as before.

During this period Castrillon and Almonte tried further reasoning with their president over the risks of this enterprise but he brushed them both aside. Castrillon pushed for a delay again, to wait for the heavy guns and more men so that the casualty figures might be reduced. Nibbling at a leg of chicken, Santa Anna thrust it towards the general's face, contemptuously saying, "What are the lives of soldiers more than so many chickens?" Later, Almonte dared to comment that the fight would be a costly one only to have the president snap, "It doesn't matter what the cost is; it *must* be done! The Alamo *must* fall!"

At 3.00am., finally leaving poor Ben to get his breath and nerves back, Santa Anna made his way towards the north east battery where he would station himself with his reserve grenadiers and Zapadores. For the last couple of hours the troops had been silently moving to their positions, the four columns spreading out in the darkness. Morales' cazadores moved up from the south through La Villita, cautiously approaching the south west corner of The Alamo where the eighteen pounder was posted. Sheltering behind the surviving stone and mud jacales, they were able to advance to a close position undetected. Romero's men tramped over the plain from the eastern hills, skirting the ponds and crossing the acequia before settling down on the cold, damp ground within 300 yards of the east wall. Likewise, Duque's and Cos' columns huddled together, sitting shivering on the wet grass, some of them only 200 yards from the north west wall. Clutching their weapons, these men endured a long, uncomfortable night in near freezing temperatures. Ordered to remain motionless and silent, they pressed close together in a desperate attempt to keep warm. At 3.00am. Sesma's cavalry walked their mounts on a circular route to the vicinity of the alameda. Despite the fact that Travis had posted sentries, notably in the ditches outside the garrison walls, the Mexican manoeuvres were carried out with such silent precision not a thing was seen or heard to arouse untoward suspicion. Quite a feat.

By 4.00am., just as Travis was turning in, the Mexican assault force had achieved the first stage of its objective right on schedule. All the soldados were in their allotted positions, straining their ears for that long awaited signal to attack.

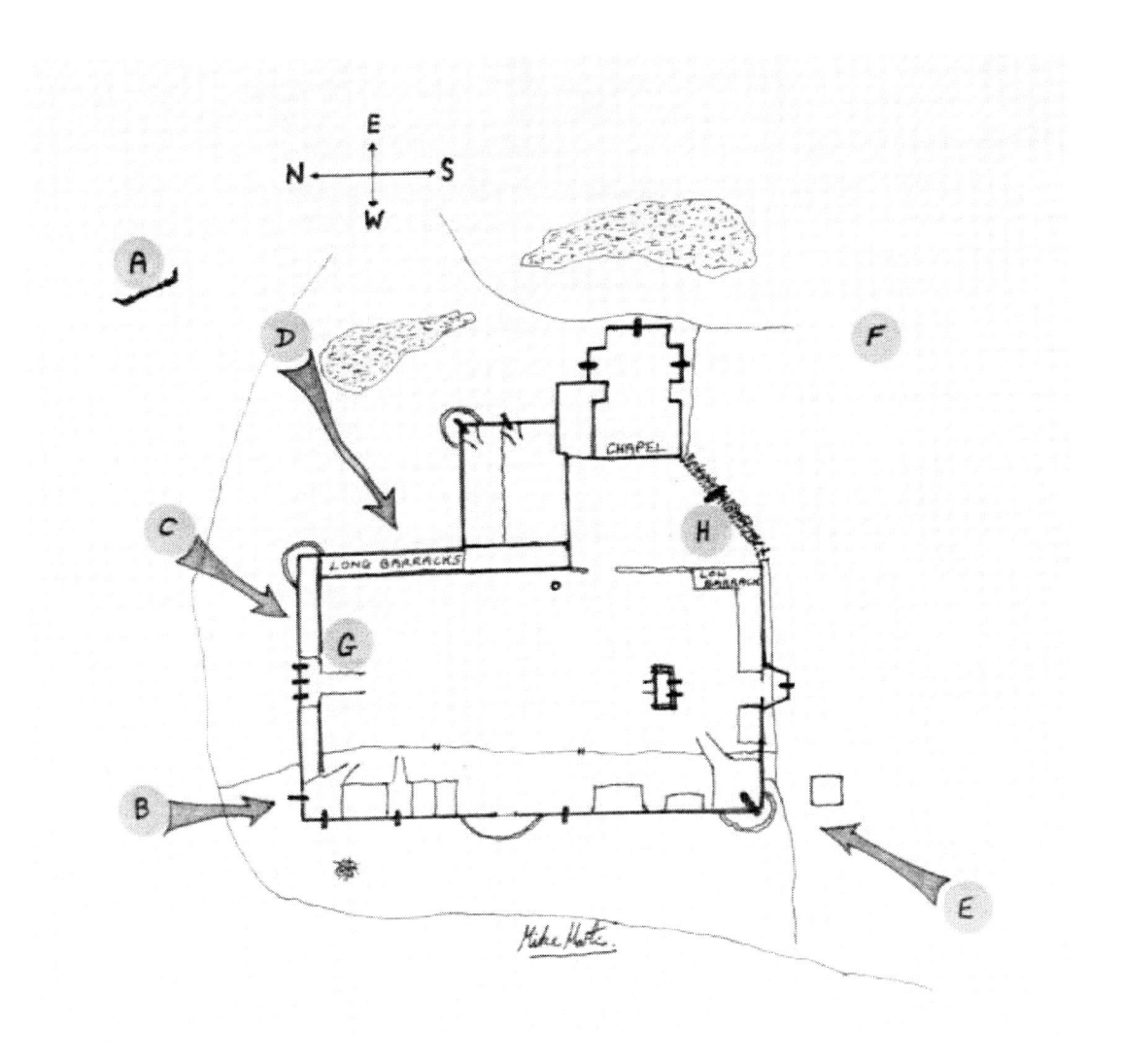

ASSAULT ON THE ALAMO (5.00am. Sunday March 6th. 1836)

A. Santa Anna with reserves, plus staff officers and bandsmen
B. General Cos
C. Colonel Duque and General Castrillon
D. Colonel Romero
E. Colonel Morales
F. General Sesma and the cavalry, positioned to cut off escapees
G. North wall position where Travis fell
H. David Crockett's position

ATTACK

5.00am.. The Alamo lay in peaceful silence. With the chill of pre-dawn darkness still very much in the air, stern faced Capt. John Baugh pulled his thick grey cloak around his shoulders, raised his flickering lantern and climbed the rough parapet of the north wall. As officer of the day Baugh was one of the very few Texians alert and on his feet after the strenuous efforts of the previous day. Rifle crooked in his free arm and a sabre hanging from his waist, Travis' Virginian adjutant trudged along the stockaded rampart, doubtless noting the first feint streaks of grey in the inky eastern sky above the distant powder house.

Although the moon occasionally peeked through the scudding clouds, visibility on every other side of the garrison remained almost non-existent. Just a few feet of coarse grass and then blackness. Baugh stared idly into the gloom, but it was just another night, quieter than most had been during this seemingly endless siege. Perhaps he chose such a tranquil moment to reflect on how much had happened in the four months since he had arrived here in Bexar. A keen, fresh faced new volunteer he had been then, first lieutenant of the second company of New Orleans Greys, proud in his uniform. Only the cloak of that uniform remained now, civilian attire replacing the military garb which had long since worn through after all these weeks of harsh weather and fighting. He had come a long way .....

Something made him hesitate and he froze. What was that sound out there in the blackness to the north? Leaning on the wall he raised the lantern and strained his eyes in the direction of the noise. There it was again. Rustling to the left, a crack and clink to the right. That low murmuring ..... could it be voices?

Behind the earthworks of the north eastern Mexican gun battery, Santa Anna himself, within musket range, scoured the dim outline of The Alamo's walls through a telescope. Surrounded by his staff officers, artillerymen, massed ranks of bandsmen, grenadiers and Zapadores, Don Demonio stood at a gun embrasure, the cannon itself moved aside to allow him access to a safe observation post. The tension was almost unbearable, for the original set time for the attack order had long since passed. What could he be waiting for? Anxiously, the officers glanced towards the eastern hills where the early tinges of dawn were beginning to lighten the horizon with a pale golden hue. Leave it much longer and the dense lines of infantrymen, waiting patiently for orders on every side of the fort, would soon be visible to the defenders.

Santa Anna was aware that his men were growing restless. The long hours of silence and immobility were beginning to tell on them. Mumbling and fidgeting could be heard from the ranks. Now was the time for Travis, Bowie and their rebellious pirates to pay the price for their insolence! Turning to the nearest bugler, El Presidente gave the signal.

The harsh, brass notes blasted through the darkness, startling soldado and Texian alike, but the call was taken up from company to company, through the hushed battalions, as other buglers echoed the signal like some bizarre relay race. "Viva Santa Anna!" came the cry from some activo fusilier as he grabbed his Brown Bess and struggled to his sandalled feet. "Viva the Republic!" yelled another as he and hundreds of his comrades surged upwards into action like a gigantic whale rising from the waves. Lifting their swords, the Mexican generals and colonels, at the head of their men, thrust their weapons symbolically towards those hated adobe walls with cries of *"Arriba!"* (attack) and *"Adenlante!"* (forward). Within moments, the disciplined lines of troops had sprung from their lumbering uncertainty, adrenalin coursing through their veins as they ran headlong into their assault formations. Bayonets pointing rigidly before them, ladders held aloft, pickaxes and crowbars aimed at those crumbling walls, Don Demonio's soldados split the night with their roaring determination.

The din must have been blood curdling and deeply shocking to Baugh as he gaped blindly into the darkness. Within seconds he could make out the first surging ranks of the enemy as they ran full pelt towards him, indistinct but obviously deadly. This was it! No more sniping at distant shapes. This was real war, and it would be close up and bloody!

Already Texians were beginning to stir, roused by the deafening cries of the soldados and the reverberation of hundreds of pairs of running feet, pounding the earth all around them. Bleary eyed, defenders began to appear at the doorways of the Long Barracks, slapping themselves awake as they rushed to the walls, most of them struggling under the weight of several rifles, muskets, pistols and other small arms. They were taking up position and commencing a withering fire when Baugh jumped down from the wall and ran as fast as he could towards the officer's quarters, hollering out warnings all the way. Reaching Travis' room, he virtually kicked open the door, bellowing into the shadows, "Colonel, the Mexicans are coming!"

Travis was out of his bed in an instant, barely having slept an hour. Grabbing his jacket, he buckled on his sword and reached for his shotgun, looking over at Joe who was rubbing his eyes as he sat up in bed. Illuminated in the dim glow of Baugh's lantern, Travis was composed but determined. "Follow me, Joe," he said sternly, "and bring your gun."

It was sheer pandemonium out on the plaza as men rushed to and fro, mostly heading for the north wall where most of the action seemed to be taking place. The picket guards positioned in the ditches outside were the first casualties, overwhelmed before they knew what was happening, but their Texian comrades at the walls soon avenged them with a vicious barrage of firepower, raining a thick and constant wall of lead into the packed soldado ranks. The first volleys stopped the momentum of the initial Mexican charge, bowling men over by the dozen and causing hesitation in those who saw them fall or stumbled across their twitching, moaning bodies. General Cos was everywhere, waving his sword and urging them on, determined to make amends for the previous shame he had suffered at the hands of these rebels. So far his men were well on line to their objective at the north west wall while Duque and Castrillon were proving to be equally effective, bravely leading their battalions in a reckless charge against the north east. All according to plan, Romero had also begun his assault on the east walls where his 400 odd men were proving to be the clearest targets yet as they advanced with the early tinges of the rising sun at their backs. They suffered accordingly as the two Texian cannon positioned at the edge of the corrals began to rake them with grapeshot. To the south, Morales and his 100 cazadores were alert but biding their time, waiting for the right moment to strike.

Travis had reached the north wall gun battery where the gunners were already levelling the barrels of their pieces at Duque's yelling soldados as they charged out of the shadows. As he raced to this position, W.B. had been highly vocal in his demonstrations to the men. "Come on, boys!" he cried, relishing the moment for all its peril, "The Mexicans are upon us and we'll give them hell!" As he climbed the battery slope he was heard to cry, "Hurrah, my boys!" and other such stirring phrases. This was the kind of drama William Barrett Travis had been born for and, in its odd way, he probably loved it. The heat of battle, the shot and shell, leading from the front.....

Leaning on the parapet between two of the cannon, the young commander of The Alamo stared down into a sea of advancing Mexican faces. Cocking both barrels of his shotgun he raised it to his shoulder and let fly at the soldados with a double blast. At such short range, he almost certainly hit his mark and probably felt the satisfaction of seeing his victims fall before a returning Mexican salvo rang out. With half his body exposed at the low rampart, he made a perfect target and a musket ball struck him in the head. Dropping his gun, Travis span away from the wall, the impact of the heavy slug like a blow from a club. Staggering back, he fell and rolled a little way down the slope where he sat up and held his hands to his head, dazed and trying to staunch the flow of blood.

Standing just behind his master when he was hit, Joe's eyes widened in disbelief. The colonel felled so early in the fight? It was more than the young black man could comprehend. Glancing once more at the attacking horde and again at his dying master, Joe, still clutching his gun, took to his heels and ran back towards the officer's quarters. Such irony that Travis was denied the right to see his battle through to the bitter end.

With W.B. out of action, responsibility of command fell upon Capt. Baugh but the Virginian adjutant would have had little time to dwell upon the significance of this sudden promotion. He too was at the north wall and, along with so many others, was engaged in pouring a heavy fire upon the enemy who had almost reached the base of the ramparts. The north and east walls were now continually lit by the rapid flashes of cannon and small arms fire and soon a thick, acrid pall of powder smoke hung over the scene, blinding and choking the combatants of both sides. Up on the roof of the chapel, Dickinson's triplet of cannon were hard at work blasting away at Romero's hard pressed men, checking their advance and slowly beginning to turn them away from their objective of storming the corral walls. The men under Cos, Duque and Castrillon were also suffering terrible casualties along the whole length of the north wall and they began to waver. However, there would be no retreat for them, for the front ranks were pushed forward by the massed bulk of those coming up from the rear. Fearsome corporals and sergeants added incentive too, screaming threats at reluctant soldados, beating them with their staffs and switches until they found fresh reserves of courage and threw themselves into the fray.

The chasseurs of Duque's Toluca battalion suffered a particularly heavy blow when they got carried away in the heat of the moment, giving an especially loud communal cheer of *"Muerto alos Tejanos!"* ("Death to the rebels!") Coming out of the pitch blackness, this exposed their position and gave the Texian gunners an ideal point to aim their cannon at. The big gun roared, spewing a lethal hail of grape and canister which ripped through the cheering troops. Their patriotic cries turned abruptly to screams of agony, bodies mangled by searing chunks of metal, flesh torn from bones and limbs blown off. An horrific price to pay for high spirits which did away with a good forty of them in one salvo. Other blasts and volleys did similar damage; even Col. Duque was hit in the thigh by a chunk of shrapnel. Falling amongst the torn corpses and writhing wounded, Duque bravely continued to shout encouragement to his men as they pushed on, heads bowed against the hail of Texian lead. General Castrillon now took over full command of the second column assaulting the north east wall, leading them with all the courage of the seasoned soldier that he was.

At this point the Mexican attack reached its lowest ebb. For about fifteen minutes the three columns assaulting the north and east walls had been subjected to a merciless and continual fire, halting, wavering and pressing onward, time and time again. To the east the barrage was so intense that Romero's men were forced to turn to their right, encroaching upon the massed ranks of the second column under the new command of Castrillon. With Cos' column pushing in from the north west, this resulted in a huge, disorganized mass of humanity crowding in against the north wall, the front ranks actually crushed against the timber and earth ramparts by those moving up from behind. Many attempts were made to scale the wall but several of the ladders had somehow been lost in the attack, perhaps concealed by the heaps of bloody corpses of those who had carried them. Such ladders that reached the wall were quickly employed to do their task, but the first soldados to climb them were instantly thrown back by the hard fighting Texians. As the Mexicans reached the top of this eight to nine foot high rampart, defenders would rush forward to skewer them with bayonets, blast them with pistols or chop them down with hatchets. Their bodies were then hurled back down onto their comrades.

One advantage to the Mexicans at the base of the wall was the fact that they were now safe from the dreaded cannon blasts, for the Texians were unable to deploy their big gun barrels at a steep enough angle to reach them. The defenders now had to lean right over the parapets to fire down upon their foe, but although this still caused fierce damage to the attackers, the Texians exposed themselves much more to soldado muskets. Gradually, more and more Americans began to topple from the walls or fall back from them, clutching at their wounds.

The first column under Cos had, so far, more or less managed to maintain its intended formation, but they now found themselves facing a new threat, from their *own* men. Doubtless due to panic, soldados from the second column were firing blindly ahead, paying little attention to what they were actually aiming at, the effect being that Cos' men were being struck in the rear and left flank by *friendly fire*. Quickly recognising this danger, Cos gave orders to turn the direction of his advance, moving obliquely to the right to concentrate on an unplanned assault against the west wall. This proved to be a wise move for there were still more than enough troops to occupy the thin line of Texians spread along the north wall. Most of The Alamo defenders had flocked to this position, where the heaviest pressure was forming, leaving the other areas of the garrison weaker than ever. Cos exploited this, throwing his San Luis and Aldama fusiliers in force against the west wall, employing those of his ladders which still remained. Other soldados began attacking the blocked up windows and portholes which perforated this wall, using their pickaxes, crowbars and heavy timber beams to break through the hastily assembled blockages of stone, adobe bricks and sandbags. Apart from the use of ladders, the wall here was low enough for the activo troops to scale it by simply standing on one another's shoulders. Such Texians as could be spared to counter this threat were soon dealing with far more than they could handle.

Watching through his telescope at the north east battery, Santa Anna did not like what he could see. It actually looked worse than it was, because although the Mexican advance had been temporarily checked it appeared to Don Demonio that his forces might actually have been repulsed. Observing only flashes of fire and jumbled heaps of men, Santa Anna pondered the notion of defeat, a concept he could not tolerate. Worried and desperate he called on his reserves, all the grenadiers and the 185 men of Lt. Col. Amat's crack Zapadores. *They* should turn the tide. Ordering them to advance, the president even turned to his staff officers and all those around him, even his personal secretary, demanding that they too should enter the fray for the glory of Mexico! This order sent a further 400 men into action, pushing the already present columns from the rear and adding a huge surge of momentum to the attack (though more than a little additional confusion).

The Zapadores were especially pleased to be included in the fight, at last. Cheering and leading the charge, these tough, bearded veterans rushed the north wall, firing as they ran. Unfortunately, the grenadiers and others, following behind, also opened fire, ostensibly upon the Texians at the palisade, but many of their shots fell low, striking the heads and shoulders of their comrades who were attempting to scale the wall. The chaos and slaughter was dreadful to behold, all accompanied by a terrible jumbled din of gunfire, cannon blasts, hacking, clashing, the agonized cries of the dying and wounded, along with the screaming, shouting, oaths and curses of hundreds of desperate men fighting for their lives. And yet there was another sound which almost seemed to dominate the hellish scene, adding a bizarre element of high drama, for Santa Anna had ordered the bandsmen of all the battalions to play his troops into battle. The tune they played, Don Demonio's express choice, was the chilling "Deguello", an old Moorish hymn of merciless hate which translates as "cut throat".

Stirred on by this martial music, the Mexican attackers re-doubled their efforts. The Texians resisted them with an almost superhuman ferocity, but no matter how many soldados they killed, there always seemed to be many more to fill the gap. Over at the south wall, where things were initially pretty quiet, Col. Morales led his cazadores slowly through the darkness, creeping up to shelter unseen around the handy stone hut which lay, to their advantage, only about thirty feet from The Alamo's south west corner. Here on the garrison's ramped platform, the crew of the eighteen pounder had wheeled their big gun around to point into the garrison towards the inner side of the north wall. With all the activity going on up there, these gunners, under Capt. William Carey, were distracted from their own post. It seemed that the Mexican attack was entirely concentrated on the north and so Carey's men were intending to help out if they could, perhaps with a blast or two if and when the soldados began to swarm over the ramparts. Consequently, they almost certainly did not notice the first rush made by Morales' 100 light troopers, advancing in open order as soon as their colonel decided the time was right. This was indeed a daring move, cleverly executed, which completely avoided the heavily fortified main gate and Crockett's formidable palisade.

By the time the gunners realised what was happening, the cazadores already had their two ladders up against the wall and were nimbly rushing over the parapet. Totally taken by surprise, Carey's men turned and attempted to defend themselves. Probably all they had to hand at that precise moment were the accoutrements of their gun handling, so it would have been a quick struggle hitting back with hand spikes, sponge rammers, linstocks and priming wires before they fell beneath those deftly wielded Baker rifles and sword bayonets. The Alamo's prized eighteen pounder was now in enemy hands. Pushing home his advantage, Morales wasted no time resting on his laurels but immediately ordered his men to rush on, down inside the garrison compound to take the main south gate and other positions along the low barracks.

At the same time, at the north wall, the huge impetus and extra weight supplied by the reserve column resulted in the front Mexican ranks (who had been more or less trapped beneath the ramparts) almost being swept up and over the parapet. As more and more Texians fell to their incessant firing, the soldados here realised that, with a little effort, they were actually able to climb the roughly finished timbers of Jameson's re-bolstered stockade. Lots of footholds and helping hands from their compadres below. In this way, with the defence slowly thinning out, the first Mexicans were able to roll over the barricades. Still many were struck down, but enough made it in one piece to gain a solid base for others to follow suit. Finally, a breach was made and the soldados began to swarm through in a cheering torrent.

Almost simultaneously, a similar scenario was being enacted at the west wall where Cos' troops had either gained a foothold on the top or had simply succeeded in breaking through the barricaded gaps. For the Texians these Mexican triumphs were a triple handed disaster. Resistance at the north and west walls had collapsed almost entirely and matters were getting desperate to the south. Surrounded by swarms of the enemy, the defenders barely knew which way to turn for the best and those who were not trapped or had not already fallen retreated from the parapets down into the plaza, firing as they went.

Maj. Green Jameson must have stoically observed this with a sinking heart. All his hard work, the planning, rebuilding and coverage of all eventualities, he thought, swept away in minutes, soaked with the blood of his friends. Maybe he died with them here at his precious north wall. Adjutant John Baugh, still unable to comprehend the swiftness with which this was all happening, pulled himself together long enough to order a withdrawal and as the men jumped from the walls or raced frantically down the battery slopes, he oversaw it all with dignity. Travis and Bowie had always planned for a secondary redoubt and Baugh was now attempting to organize it as best he could. Shouting at the men to pull back into the shelter of the Long Barracks, Baugh was most likely one of several defenders who stood their ground in the centre of the plaza, coolly taking aim at the Mexicans who were pouring over or through the walls. The soldados also came under fire from a deadly fusillade directed from the Long Barracks roof where quite a few defenders had taken up sharpshooting positions. With all live Texians gone from the parapets, Dickinson's guns on the chapel roof could now be turned inwards to rake the Mexicans and these barrages took a terrible toll.

This covering fire did the job of supplying precious moments to the defenders who were intending to fight on from inside the Long Barracks. It was about now that some, including Joe, spoke of seeing Travis breathing his last. Apparently, as the Texians drew back, hotly pursued by their jubilant foe, W.B. was spotted by the slope of the northern battery, close to where he had been hit. He was sitting up, still holding his bleeding head, with his back against the stockade. A Mexican officer rushing past saw him and raised his sword, apparently intending to decapitate the stricken man but Travis was not done yet. Lifting his own sword, he ran the Mexican through the body. Whether or not this recollection is accurate, Travis did meet his end here, of that we can be reasonably sure.

Driven back, selling their lives dearly, the defenders of The Alamo knew they had nothing to lose. Surrender would be pointless. Better to fight on to the last and take as many of the enemy with them as they could, just like Travis had vowed. Did George Kimball, the hatter who commanded the Gonzales Volunteers, have time to dwell on his unborn child? Probably not. What thoughts crossed the minds of the rest of his Immortal 32 who had entered this doomed garrison so fearlessly? Did Albert Martin regret his decision to return when he could so easily have stayed safely away? Shoemaker Marcus Sewell was certainly a long way from his English homeland and Isacc Millsaps would be leaving behind a large family with only a blind wife to fend for them. Surely, at fifteen years old, young Will King must have longed for a longer crack at life. And farmer Dolphin Floyd ..... what a way to celebrate, for today, March 6th., was his 21st. birthday. As for sixteen year old Galba Fuqua, he had more than enough to occupy him, for a musket ball had smashed him in the face, leaving his shattered jawbone hanging limp like some horrific mask. Whatever, none of them would be granted much more time on earth but, right now, they were doing their utmost to wring out their last moments to the full.

Like a tidal wave of glinting steel, the wall of Mexican bayonets advanced resolutely towards them but from inside the Long Barracks, the remaining defenders were able to draw a second breath. Throwing up ready made barricades across the doorways, firing from here and through loopholes cut in the walls, their renewed volleys cut further swathes in the soldado ranks. The Texians did not intend to be dislodged from this secondary fortress with ease but Cos and Castrillon had the answer to that. In their haste to retreat, the defenders had not had time to spike their abandoned guns, an oversight which they would now regret, for the north and west wall eight pounders were wheeled around and brought up close to the Long Barracks where rounds were fired point blank at the barricaded doors. Once this was done, the soldados would rush the smoking gap, fire a volley into the choking interior and then leap inside, fanning out to engage the surviving rebels hand to hand once more. Some of the fiercest fighting took place in these restrictive spaces and it was a gruesome business. The Texians even had trenches dug inside these rooms along with further barricades of ox hide stuffed with earth. Struggling in the darkness and smoke combat became intensely personal with pairs of men engaged in groping, throttling, stabbing, clubbing, eye gouging duels. Regardless of the vow, a few defenders did, it seems, attempt to plead for their lives. In one or two of the rooms white cloths or pale socks were displayed on the end of bayonets poked through windows, but few Mexicans paid them heed. In one long room of the convento some heavy resistance was wiped out instantly by a cannon being pushed right up to the door, double loaded with grape and canister and discharged. No more sound came from within after that.

Baugh was gone, the three devoted Taylor brothers too, fighting side by side. Likewise Tejano Antonio Fuentes who less than a month before had been languishing in the Bexar jail. How trivial it now seemed that he had been the subject of a dispute between Travis and Bowie. The remnants of Baugh's New Orleans Greys, who had thus far been displaying the only truly disciplined and formal military style resistance amongst the Texians, were now reduced to a handful of desperate individuals. It had become every man for himself and those who did not make it into the dubious sanctuary of the Long Barracks looked towards the chapel as their only chance of salvation.

On the church roof's elevated platform, Dickinson had been joined by Bonham and together they supervised the continuing cannon fire from their three overheated guns. As Robert Evans kept the powder supply coming from the baptistry below, the gunners were doing a commendable job, loading and firing mechanically, the sweat pouring down their faces and bodies. In the sacristy the women and children huddled together, trembling as they listened to the terrible din of battle beyond the walls. At one point Dickinson himself appeared in the doorway to spend a few precious, snatched seconds with his wife and baby. Grabbing her by the shoulders, his face etched with emotion, he gasped, "Great God, Sue, the Mexicans are inside our walls! All is lost! If they spare you, save my child ....."

With a last hug and stroke of his daughter's cheek, Dickinson composed himself, drew his sword and dashed back towards the roof, leaving his wife in tears. Ana Esparza gathered her children into a group, the little ones clinging to her skirt in fright. Her son Enrique recalled the dignity and fearlessness she showed and he thought of his father, Gregorio, bravely manning the guns above. As for the cat, the poor terrified creature backed into a corner, hissing and arching its back.

*   *   *

Romero's men spread out across the horse and cattle corrals, over-running the north eastern gun batteries as they had originally been assigned to do. Texian survivors from these positions were pushed back towards the church where it seemed a last stand would have to be made. Inside the Long Barracks the final desperate struggles were taking place. Francisco Beccera, a sergeant from the San Luis Potosi battalion, burst into one small room to find an American lying prone on a bed, evidently sick and unable to defend himself. Disregarding the "no quarter" order, Beccera took pity on the man, lowered his musket and turned to leave but another Mexican sergeant entered, along with a Toluca fusilier. These newcomers had no intention of being so merciful. The sergeant raised his gun to shoot the seemingly helpless fellow but the Texian suddenly found a new lease of life, produced a brace of pistols from beneath his blanket and shot them both down. Beccera, shocked by the turn of events, killed the "invalid" with a single bullet.

The soldados had now reached the hospital on the second floor of the convento. Not withstanding Dr. Pollard's probable pleas for clemency, he was slaughtered along with the sick and wounded, the blood crazed Mexicans moving between the beds, bayoneting and shooting them where they lay. There is no record of any resistance here, however on the roof of this building the blue silk banner of the New Orleans Greys still flickered proudly in the dawn breeze. Several soldados had already attempted to tear this rebellious symbol down and had been shot for their trouble, but Zapadore Lt. Torres was determined to succeed. Helped by another officer, dodging Texian bullets all the way, Torres reached the roof, ripped the hated flag from its pole and hastily hoisted another in its place. No sooner had they completed this task when the two of them fell beneath a hail of newly determined and angry fire, leaving the multi-coloured flag of the Mexican Republic flying above their corpses. To see the enemy banner raised on the garrison must have been an enormous blow to the morale of those Texians still fighting.

Events were moving too quickly now for anyone to ponder their fate. In their quarters in the west wall, Gertrudis, her sister Juana Alsbury (and her baby son) cowered in the corner, listening to the carnage and last stages of defence going on unseen above and around them. It was obvious that the defenders here had been annihilated but one of them, a Texian named Mitchell, managed to stagger in to join the women. He was wounded so Gertrudis rushed to the door, calling out to the troops that the room sheltered only women. She was answered by coarse and offensive language from the soldados, then one barged in and roughly tore her shawl from her shoulders. Terrified, Gertrudis ran back into the corner to join her sister just as other soldados entered the room. Mitchell made an effort to place himself between them and the women but he was quickly struck down. Then another defender appeared, as if from nowhere, a Tejano this time who grabbed Gertrudis by the shoulders and held her in front of him as a shield. Struggling and panic stricken, this man was pulled away from her and within a second half a dozen bayonets had plunged through his body. Before he hit the ground, the soldados made sure he was dead by shooting him several times as he fell. The Mexican troops then began to ransack the room, breaking open trunks and taking money, clothes and other items before an officer arrived and managed to restore order. He, fortunately, was a gentleman who put the women under his protection, saving them from any further ordeal.

In the meantime, Morales' cazadores had been doing a fine job mopping up resistance along the south wall, even though they too had come under fire from their compadres who were taking the north. The cazadores made short work of the gunners manning the pair of naval style cannon on the platform which covered the inside of the main gate. Working their way from room to room along the low barracks, these nimble soldados eventually came upon Jim Bowie in his sick room just to the left of the gate. Entering cautiously, their sword bayonets at the ready, it is doubtful that the dying adventurer even knew they were there. Legend has it that he sold his life dearly, blasting them with his pistols before dying beneath the bayonets, blood soaked knife in his hand. Had he been well enough, that is doubtless the way he would have gone, but the disappointing truth is that he was almost certainly delirious or even in a coma. Ironically, the soldados, unaware of his condition, saw him in bed, away from the fight, and within weeks the Mexican newspapers were speaking of "...that perverse and haughty James Bowie" who "died like a woman, in bed, almost hidden by the covers". Unjust indeed that one of the greatest fighters and characters American history has ever known should be remembered thus. Whatever, the bayonets and bullets ensured that his name would be forever enshrined in the legend of Texas Liberty.

It is not entirely clear what happened at the south palisade, but it was probably not assaulted from the front at all. As explained, Morales' cazadores took the south west corner of the wall, along with the eighteen pounder, by stealth, then worked their way along the southern defences advancing towards the chapel. Crockett's men at the palisade, distracted by the chaos at the north wall and no doubt itching to get into the fight, very likely put pressure on their commander to go to their comrade's aid. Capt. Harrison, as leader of these Tennessee Mounted Volunteers, and Crockett, would have seen the folly of leaving the palisade totally undefended but, even so, quite a few of these lion hearted souls most likely insisted. However, they would not have got very far before new action broke out at the south west corner, probably forcing them to change course again, going back to their posts. Here in the plaza, immediately in front of the church's ornate doorway, ferocious fighting raged as the cazadores, now joined by advance elements of the first three columns, advanced in overwhelmingly superior force. Crockett and his men, along with any other fugitives who may have joined them, fired frantically upon this horde until, with their backs to the church wall and no more time to reload, they turned their guns in their hands to use as clubs. With a great shout, hundreds of soldados fell upon them, bayonets slashing and stabbing as the Texians fought back to their last breath. This is the image that remains in public perception more than any other of The Alamo. Clubbed rifles, Bowie knives and fists; the last desperate struggle of heroes.

Micajah Autry probably fell here, along with Daniel Cloud, Dr. Reynolds and Capt. Harrison, but mystery still surrounds the actual end of Crockett himself, although a Mexican sergeant told of a dark skinned man in a long buckskin coat who fought like a tiger before being struck down by an officer's sword and pinned to the ground by a score of bayonets. That description could easily have fit many of the defenders, but at some point, near the end of the battle, Crockett was identified inside the chapel, kneeling and whispering a swift prayer.

Not all the defenders made the decision to fight to the last. Quite a number, perhaps sixty or more, decided to make a daring attempt to break out to fight another day. In three separate groups, as organized resistance collapsed and the situation grew hopeless, these fugitives vaulted the walls of the horse corral close to the church while others clambered over the southern palisade, tearing their way through the abatis before running pell mell towards the rising sun. Racing through the long shadows into the underbrush, leaving the conflagration of death behind them, these men must have initially felt a great sense of relief. The path looked open and safe; soon they would be out of harm's way and en-route to a friendlier refuge. Unfortunately, the lancers of General Sesma's Dolores cavalry had been poised, hiding behind the avenue of trees at the alameda, waiting for this anticipated moment. Like a swarm of enraged bees, 300 colourful horsemen galloped from cover, bearing down upon the startled Texians who were now totally exposed. Sesma had waited until they were too far from The Alamo walls to attempt a return before he gave the order to charge, so now the fugitives had no choice but to try and run for it or fight it out.

This is a little known, but extremely significant, episode in the battle which went on for some time as the expert horsemen rode the running men down, skewering them with their nine foot lances or hacking at them with sabres. It was hopeless for those on foot, but several turned and stood their ground, choosing to resist rather than be cut down from behind. These men fought back desperately with their guns and knives. Inevitably, they were soon wiped out, but not before inflicting considerable casualties on their hunters. Others tried to hide in the thick vegetation but were soon flushed out and killed.

The massed columns of soldados were now pressing heavily upon the church, the only area that was still offering any real resistance. About a dozen men, including Dickinson and Bonham, still fought from the high platform, their guns as busy as ever. Now they were loading up with langrage, ripping the closely packed Mexicans with wicked showers of nails, pieces of horseshoe and scrap metal. The soldados were scythed down in droves, screaming and spraying their compadres with blood and flesh, but no amount of return musket fire could bring down those accursed rebels, safe behind their strong stone walls. That is until Col. Morales ordered the captured eighteen pounder to be used. The infantry momentarily drew back as the big gun began to pound the church, first concentrating upon the platform to silence Dickinson's deadly twelve pounders, then a single blast to blow away the barricade which blocked the portal entrance. As soon as this was done, the soldados swarmed forward again, leaping through the doorway over the smoking rubble and any mangled defender who had been caught in the blast. More Mexicans fell here as small arms fire came from the pitch blackness in the eastern recesses of the building, but as more soldados filled the gap, returning fire blindly, resistance began to slacken. Now the men of Santa Anna, enraged by the lust of battle and tasting victory, fanned out through the church and its various rooms. Once through the doorway, the first thing they faced was the long ramp which ran up to the gun platform. Although enveloped in smoke and dust from the pounding it had just received, movement could still be seen there so the soldados fired a series of musket volleys directly into the area. Moments later they ascended the ramp at the run, finishing off any signs of life with their bayonets. This is where Dickinson, Bonham and Gregorio Esparza died.

Fearing for her husband, Sue Dickinson had already suffered the terrible sight of their young family friend, Galba Fuqua, all but falling through the sacristy doorway. She gasped at his hideous injury but the boy was determined to tell her something. Wincing with the pain he actually tried to hold the shattered parts of his face together to speak but could only manage a strangled, gurgling sound. Finally, shaking his head hopelessly, he staggered back outside towards the sound of the guns. She never saw him again.

At the top of the church wall a Texian was seen silhouetted against the rising sun with a child in his arms before plunging headlong to the ground. It is suggested that this could have been the English gunner Anthony Wolfe with one of his sons. A terrible game of "cat and mouse" then ensued as the remaining, scattered defenders were chased through the shadows and rooms of the church by the homicidal soldados. One, at least, put up a particularly impressive defence and it was said that this man was the mysterious "Kwockey". His end, described in detail by two Mexican officers, involved him being cornered in a small room. Standing just inside the door he bellowed defiant challenges to his enemies but as it was such a narrow opening, they could only attempt to approach him one at a time. As each man entered, "Kwockey" would grab and kill him with a long knife and in this way he held out for some time. Unable to bring their guns to bear properly upon him, because of the lack of space, the soldados finally managed a lucky shot which broke the Texian's right arm. Dropping his knife, "Kwockey" then moved to the centre of the room, clutching the barrel of his rifle with his good arm, butt held forward. The Mexicans then attempted to rush him but he brained several more of them before a corporal ordered the men out of the way so that he could organize a volley to be fired at point blank range. That finished off "Kwockey".

A Mexican defender called Brigido Guerrero was brought to his knees in another room, begging for his life. He swore that he was a soldado, captured by the defenders and forced to help them. Incredibly, his countrymen believed him and he was spared. Most of the others were not so fortunate. The Mexicans were firing continuous volleys into the darkest corners, nervous of venturing into such areas. Dead defenders were being bayoneted and clubbed repeatedly. Remembering Travis' ominous orders, ordnance officer Robert Evans, streaming blood from his wounds, grabbed a burning torch and staggered towards the powder magazine but he was shot down before he could make it.

Finally, the soldados found their way into the sacristy, in hot pursuit of gunner Jacob Walker and two others. The latter pair were quickly shot but Walker was wild eyed with desperation. He knew there was nowhere left to run. His eyes met those of Sue Dickinson and she gazed back at him pitifully. Many times throughout the siege this little man had spoken to her fondly of his wife and children. He turned and backed into a corner but the soldados went for him without mercy. Plunging their bayonets into his twisting, shrieking body, at least four of them lifted him into the air as if he were a bale of hay. The soldados grinned wickedly as he continued to writhe and scream, lifting and lowering him several times before he died. Sue Dickinson turned away, sickened.

More Mexicans entered the room, eyes straining in the gloom to see what awaited them, searching for someone or something else to kill. Some of the women screamed and the children whimpered with fright. Wolfe's other son, less than twelve years old, was murdered here along with another young boy who faced his killers with a blanket wrapped around him. He was standing next to Enrique Esparza who felt certain he would be next. For some reason they spared him, turning instead on the cat which they shot for "looking American".

THE SMOKE CLEARS

It was all over. After such an extended build up, the preparations, the hopes and aspirations, the emotion; Travis and his noble crew were gone. In little more than an hour they had been transformed into a ragged bunch of mangled carcasses strewn across the smoking ruins of The Alamo.

6.30am., Sunday March 6th. 1836. The sun was well above the powder house now casting its golden rays over a grim scene of misery and devastation. Weather wise it looked like a bright, pleasant day was coming. Sporadic firing could still be heard in odd areas of the defeated garrison but none of it came from Texian guns. Many soldados were still caught up in the euphoria of the moment, blasting away at the dead bodies, plunging their bayonets repeatedly into them. It was anger, revenge, frustration, blood lust and, simply, human nature amid the spoils of war. The ultimate power of the victor and the ugly face of triumph which can bring out the worst in the best of men.

Immaculate in his military frock coat, Santa Anna strolled haughtily through this scene of horror, observing it all with his customary expression of arrogance. Behind him came his staff officers while others, who had taken a more active role in the attack, approached with their varied reports. Don Demonio listened smugly, commenting on this and that and snapping an occasional order. In all, he was deeply satisfied. Gesturing towards the heaps of dead, dying and wounded he callously remarked, "These are the chickens. Much blood has been shed but the battle is over. It was but a small affair."

Maybe it was, to him, but not so for those who had lost their lives as the price to pay for retrieving his pride. At present there was confusion but before long the casualty figures would be available. About 200 Mexicans killed outright in the assault with at least a further 400 wounded, totalling about a third of the attacking force. A further 80 or so of the injured would die from their wounds. There is no record of how many were put out of action permanently with lost limbs and such. Indeed, it had proved costly but Santa Anna shrugged it aside. General Gaona was approaching with reinforcements so the army was still strong enough to carry on with the task in hand. The destruction of the garrison here would send a chilling message to any other Texians who dared to continue with this foolish rebellion.

The bodies were already being stripped and looted. An activo sergeant claimed Travis' coat, for example. Whoever got Bowie's fabulous knife obviously won himself a true prize and McGregor's bagpipes must have intrigued the Mexican bandsmen. Santa Anna ordered that the faces of the dead, if still recognisable, should be wiped clean of filth and gore so that there would no confusion as to which nationality they were. As this was going on, General Castrillon approached his president, leading a small group of men under heavy guard. Castrillon, the noble old officer, was streaked with the grime of battle having been in the very thick of it. He believed in a code of gentlemanly warfare. About half a dozen Texians had been found alive, some of them trying to hide under a pile of mattresses in the barracks. The soldados were going to kill them immediately but Castrillon had managed to avert the slaughter, insisting on bringing them to Santa Anna in the hope that he might take pity on them. Surely their bravery in putting up such a spirited defence would earn them clemency as worthy adversaries, at least.

Santa Anna would not hear of it. In fact he exploded with rage at the general, demanding to know why his very clear orders regarding "no prisoners" had not been carried out. Castrillon kept calm and tried to reason with him but Don Demonio turned his back and stalked away, barking orders at the nearest men to carry out his bidding. At this point it seems that several of the staff officers decided to grab the chance to show that they could draw blood for the Republic too. Unsheathing their swords, they advanced upon the helpless prisoners and commenced hacking and stabbing them.

Enthused by the terrible sight, other soldados joined in with their bayonets.

Many of the Mexican officers were sickened by this dreadful and un-necessary deed. Castrillon never forgave Santa Anna for such heartless cruelty and felt that this kind of act would harm their cause. Just to complicate matters, quite convincing evidence exists which claims that Davy Crockett himself was one of these last victims. This came in the form of several Mexican eye witness accounts which do appear to hold weight. Naturally, this sordid demise of one of America's greatest heroes does not sit well with the patriots and romantics who love to think of "Ol' Davy" going down *a'la* John Wayne, swinging Betsy before falling on heaps of Mexican dead, but in a serious appraisal we must consider it. Anyway, if Crockett did surrender, is that really a bad reflection on his reputation? His courage is certainly not in question as there is plenty of evidence to show the active and beneficial part he played during the siege. As for the battle itself, when it became obvious that all was lost, could any of the defenders be blamed for at least attempting to save their lives by surrendering? Their deliberate choice of death would serve no real purpose (apart from historic glory for future generations) so let us be realistic here. Of course, the Texians were aware of Santa Anna's "no quarter" policy and that is why so many of them fought ferociously to the end, but maybe Crockett thought his fame might save him from the president's wrath. Who knows? Whatever, it was stated that those Texian prisoners died with dignity.

Trembling with fright, Travis' slave, Joe, had been found skulking in the officer's quarters where he had ensconced himself ever since running away from his master's death. He narrowly escaped joining Travis at the hands of over keen soldados, but before long he was brought before Santa Anna himself, certain that he would be executed. Surprisingly, Don Demonio's attitude to Joe was one of benign kindness. The president greeted him pleasantly and told him he was now free from the evils of slavery; the Mexican government did not make war on enslaved Negroes. Breathing a huge sigh of relief, Joe agreed to the president's request of being shown the dead bodies of his arch enemies, Travis and Bowie. Joe knew where to look; the north wall and the low barracks.

Having gloated over the corpses, Santa Anna had his battalions assembled in a hollow square in The Alamo's plaza so that he could address them. His speech was full of predictable platitudes, praising their courage and loyalty for a job well done, inferring that the war was all but won. Later that day he would send his official report to his government officials in Mexico City, a document filled with boasts and exaggerations, such as his claim to have slain 600 Texians. He also sent the battle ravaged flag of the New Orleans Greys which had been torn down from the Long Barracks roof. This would serve as a perfect symbol of his triumph.

Mayor Ruiz, of Bexar, was given the grim task of disposing of the Mexican dead. He was told to inter them in the town's burial ground at Campo Santo, just to the north west of the Military Plaza but there were simply too many of them. Exasperated, Ruiz finally had the excess corpses dumped in the river where they crowded up to such a degree that they embarrassingly blocked the flow. As for the Mexican wounded, the old problem of no army medical facilities or doctors was proving to be a nightmare. The women of Bexar were asked to help out as best they could to tend the battle injuries but, naturally, their powers were limited. All along the banks of the river and at the roadsides, lines of moaning men sat and lay in misery, squirming with pain. It is a miracle that so many did manage to eventually recover.

The Texian dead were treated appallingly. Ropes were tied to their ankles and they were dragged by the Mexican cavalrymen to three separate areas, two on either side of the avenue of trees at the alameda and one at Pueblo de Valero. Vast amounts of kindling were collected to make funeral pyres and the corpses were arranged in layers with wood between them. Combustible camphene was poured over these piles and they were lit in the late afternoon, burning throughout the night, enveloping the town in a terrible stench. Ruiz gave an official figure of 182 defenders disposed of in this way in the largest pyre and that is where the traditional number comes from, but it does not include at least sixty to seventy more who were consumed in the two smaller pyres. These were the men who tried to break out only to be slaughtered by Sesma's dragoons. This may have been a convenient and swifter way for the Mexicans to rid themselves of offensive bodies but it was another mistake which they would eventually pay for. In 1836 cremation was an insult to the Christian dead and Santa Anna would have been well aware of it.

*   *   *

In the last moments of the battle, Sue Dickinson smothered little Angelina in the folds of her apron, praying hard that her death would be an easy one, but not all the Mexicans were obsessed with slaughter. As the firing slackened and the last cries of the defenders faded away, the Dickinson's, the Esparzas and other non-combatant survivors were taken under escort out of the sacristy into the plaza. Here, for the first time, they saw the full horror of the battle, recognizing the dead faces of those they had been speaking to just a short while before. Mrs. Dickinson swore she spotted the body of Crockett lying near the church, his coonskin cap beside him. Also, before being taken out of the chapel, she had witnessed the terrible sight of her husband's bullet riddled corpse suffering the indignity of mutilation by the bayonets of laughing soldados. It made her faint. Enrique found his father's body draped across a wrecked cannon and his mother wept as she led him away. (Actually, Gregorio Esparza was the only Alamo defender to be granted a decent burial because his brother, Francisco, was a loyal soldado in Santa Anna's army.)

Relieved to be removed from this terrible place, the women and children from the sacristy were put with Juana Alsbury and her sister and together they were taken into town. The latter women, with Juana's child, returned to the Veramendi house, but the others were incarcerated in a big building on Bexar's Main Plaza. That afternoon they were summoned to the Yturri House where Santa Anna wished to meet them.

One at a time the family groups were led in to be interviewed by His Excellency. Enrique Esparza remembered the president having a "cruel, hard look" and how his mother, Ana, angered him with her defiant attitude. Juana Alsbury was particularly concerned that Don Demonio should not find out that she was married to a Texian rebel, even though he had not been present at The Alamo. However, Santa Anna turned on his charm for these ladies and treated them gallantly, although he did lecture them on the folly of their men folk which had led to such self inflicted tragedy. He was especially impressed by little Angelina Dickinson and, amazingly, made a most generous offer to ship the girl to Mexico City where he would ensure that she was raised properly with the best education and finest opportunities Mexican society could offer. The thought must have appalled Sue Dickinson, having just lost her husband to this tyrant, and she made it clear that she could not possibly agree to such a proposition. Rebuffed, Santa Anna said that if she wanted to deny her daughter such an opportunity, she could take her instead back into Texian obscurity with word of what had happened at The Alamo. The women were given two silver dollars and a blanket each in recompense for all they had endured.

Within a few days, Sue Dickinson and her daughter were sent on their way. Santa Anna even let his Negro servant, Ben, act as their escort, riding to the east heading for Gonzales. When they were well away from The Alamo they were joined by Joe, Travis' ex-slave who had fled from Santa Anna's hospitality saying that he did not trust the man. Two days after this, the little group were met on the road by the scout Deaf Smith who had been sent out from Gonzales by Sam Houston to see how things fared at The

Alamo. He did not need to go further for he was told the complete harrowing story by those who had seen it fall. Turning in his tracks, Smith led them the last twenty miles into town. Sue Dickinson had come home.

Back at Bexar, General Gaona arrived as planned, more than doubling the strength of Santa Anna's force. Don Demonio wasted no time in planning the next phase of his operation but more than one of his officers felt deeply depressed by the losses they had suffered. Observing the graves, the swollen corpses in the river, the suffering of the wounded and the wailing of the bereaved, Col. Juan Almonte, the president's own aide, was heard to ruefully say, "Another such victory will ruin us".

FLIGHT AND MASSACRE

General Sam Houston, commander of the Texian Revolutionary Army, felt ashamed. Hearing the terrible news first hand from Sue Dickinson he could scarcely believe it. Taking her hand in his, he hung his head and wept.

For weeks, regardless of the numerous pleas for assistance, Houston had not really felt that The Alamo was under as great a threat as was claimed. He could not comprehend that Santa Anna's forces had managed to gain a foothold in Texas so swiftly and, although he would later deny it, it seems he may have believed that reports from Travis and Fannin were exaggerations. There had been much to occupy him, but after the Declaration of Independence had been confirmed, Houston had finally made an effort to assemble a force with the apparent intention of relieving The Alamo. The Declaration having been made on March 2nd., the General took to the road on the 6th., the day the garrison fell, riding leisurely towards Gonzales. The journey from Washington-on-the-Brazos took him five days, and could have been completed in half the time.

At Gonzales, Houston found a small army of volunteers awaiting him, almost 400 of them and all anxious to get involved in the war. For days rumours had been circulating about The Alamo. Were they still holding out? Travellers from the vicinity spoke of the ominous silence from Travis' promised signal gun. People began to fear the worst and Sue Dickinson's arrival in town merely confirmed their nightmares. A huge wave of despair, anger and grief swept over Gonzales, for it was now known that many loved ones and friends were lost.

Facing the awful truth, Houston could only assuage his feelings of guilt by acting with previously unseen haste. It was too late to save The Alamo, of course, but something could be done, maybe, to salvage the rest of Texas. Realising it would be suicidal to plunge his few men into an open conflict with hopelessly superior odds, Big Sam came up with a new plan. His original idea had been to amalgamate with Fannin to march on Bexar but that would be pointless now and would just subject both forces to unnecessary risk. Advance units of the Mexican army were already bearing down upon Gonzales but although many of the Texians were itching to get to grips with them, Houston ordered a withdrawal. He also sent word to Fannin at Goliad to do the same, a decision which was far from popular in many quarters, although it was a sensible one. "By falling back," he said, "Texas can rally".

By the evening of the 13th., the same day Sue Dickinson had arrived, the townspeople and volunteers had begun their rapid evacuation. Houston ordered the town burned to the ground so that nothing would be left that may assist the enemy. The plan now was to head east, drawing the Mexicans far from their homeland. On the far side of the Colorado River, vital supplies and reinforcements could be gathered until such a time as Houston could pick his ground to stand up to Santa Anna. Word spread quickly with couriers riding around the clock to bring the news to the outside world. Washington-on-the-Brazos was also abandoned. Newly elected Texian president David Burnet and his officials were soon on the run too, heading east to the hastily established temporary capital of Harrisburg, which lay a few miles to the west of San Jacinto Bay.

Soon it seemed that all of Texas was on the move. The colonists became gripped by a kind of panic, although in years to come, as things turned out, they would look back upon this period with discomfort and embarrassment. All over the country people packed up their belongings and headed east with Houston and his men trailing them, forever keeping an eye on any pursuit which may come from the west or south. This flight became known in history as the "Runaway Scrape".

By contrast, Santa Anna was feeling supremely confident. Having celebrated their victory over The Alamo, the Mexicans spruced themselves up for their next move. They were all tired and anxious to get this business over with but the feeling was very much that the war was as good as won and would now merely be a mopping up operation. Leaving a small force to garrison Bexar, Don Demonio now divided his army, sending his various generals on missions to take a mixture of objectives. Sesma, as usual, acted as the spearhead, plunging towards Gonzales while another force was to target Houston's own town of Nacogdoches. Col. Morales was sent south east to amalgamate with General Urrea for an assault on Goliad. Santa Anna himself, proud as a peacock and more arrogant than ever, followed Sesma. There were now something like 6,000 Mexican troops on active service in Texas. No wonder the colonists were on the run.

*   *   *

At Goliad, Col. James Fannin was still acting with characteristic caution. Here he was, safe behind the strong walls of Fort Defiance with hundreds of well armed men, including cavalry and artillery. He had little reason to feel nervous but he was unsure what to do. Receiving orders from Houston to abandon this sturdy position and head east to join the rest of the fleeing volunteer army, Fannin was reluctant to do so. So much work had gone into the establishment of this fort. It was a real stronghold where he could hold out indefinitely, but to what end? Pondering and worrying, Fannin eventually came to his senses and realised, above everything else, that he could not ignore a direct order. The problem was he left it too late.

As he prepared to evacuate, Fannin sent a company of men to the south to warn colonists in that area to make themselves scarce. When they failed to return, he then sent his Georgia battalion to look for them, but they too vanished. Both of these unfortunate groups had run into General Urrea and his soldados, advancing northwards from their victories at San Patricio and Agua Dulce Creek. Urrea, a skilled soldier, had vanquished them with ease.

At last, under pressure, Fannin got moving, abandoning his cosy fort and heading into open country, his force still numbering well over 300 men. It was March 19th. and he did not get very far. Heavily weighed down by baggage and suffering from the misfortune which seemed to plague them, the Goliad Texians ground to a halt just two miles short of Coleto Creek. Here they would have had water and cover in the timber but instead they became sitting ducks for Urrea who was hot on their tail. The Mexicans surrounded them but Fannin formed his men into a square, putting up a brisk resistance until nightfall. By morning the industrious Texians had dug in and felt safe behind their breastworks of piled earth and baggage, but Urrea had received reinforcements and there was no way out. Water was in short supply and all the cannon shot had been used up. The Texians had lost about ten men dead with a further seventy or so wounded, including Fannin who had been shot in the thigh. The brightly clad Alabama Red Rovers led those who wished to fight on, but the decision was finally made that their position was hopeless. Even if they could fight their way out, they would be unable to take the wounded with them and nobody wanted to leave their injured friends in the hands of such a ruthless foe. With much reluctance, the whole force surrendered on the understanding that they would be treated honourably.

Dejected, Fannin and his men were taken back to Goliad and put under heavy guard. They were joined by prisoners from other actions, including the survivors from the Georgia battalion and a group of fresh volunteers who had been captured at Copano. Fannin's men were distressed to hear that the survivors from the original company sent south from Fort Defiance had been tied to trees and shot. Many of the prisoners were interrogated and several dozen were singled out and ordered to wear a white cloth wrapped around their sleeves. Nobody thought much about this at the time but it would soon become significant.

For almost a week, now numbering over 400, the Texian prisoners pondered their fate, frustrated that so many of them had been removed from the war. Then, on March 27th., Palm Sunday, they were instructed to collect their things and assemble outside. Fannin and the rest of the wounded were kept behind, but the others were told that they were to be sent back to the United States. Humming "Home Sweet Home", the elated Texians were marched away in four separate groups, then, about fifteen minutes away from the presidio, they were told to halt. Bewildered, the unarmed volunteers turned to find themselves facing the barrels of hundreds of muskets. As the terrible realisation of their fate swept through the ranks, the Mexican officers gave the command to fire. Texians were cut down in heaps, those who had not fallen in the first deadly volley jumping this way and that as they desperately sought an escape route. More volleys followed and scores more fell dead. Some Texians tried to rush their killers but were swept away before they even got close. Others broke free, hidden by the thick veil of powder smoke, only to be run to ground by the ever vigilant cavalrymen wielding swords and lances. The wounded were systematically despatched by soldado bayonets, knives and gun butts.

Back at the fort, Fannin limped out of his room, demanding to know what all the distant firing could mean. Callously, he was told that his men had been executed under the rules of the Tornel Decree of 1835 which stated that all foreigners entering into armed attack against the Mexican government would be treated as pirates and would receive no privileges. This would not include existing colonists or those captured not bearing arms. In this way, some, along with medical personnel who would be needed to treat the Mexican wounded, had been spared. These were the men who had been told to wear white arm bands. Once again, this had been a personal directive from Santa Anna.

Fannin, by all accounts, resigned himself to his fate bravely. Having witnessed the massacre of the other wounded who were led or carried into the courtyard to be shot, the colonel slipped ten pesos into the hand of the supervising Mexican officer asking only that his body should receive a decent Christian burial and that his pocket watch be returned to his family. He also requested that there be no wounds above his neck.

As if mocking his final wishes, the officer allowed Fannin to tie on his own blindfold and permitted him to sit in a chair before promptly shooting him through the head. The officer then took Fannin's watch for himself and ordered his body to be burned along with the other executed men.

The massacre at Goliad was an appalling atrocity which claimed the lives of about 340 helpless Texians, far more than had been slaughtered, under arms, at The Alamo. And yet few people know of it, over shadowed as it is by its far more famous predecessor. As previously stated, it must be stressed that many Mexican officers were horrified and totally opposed to Santa Anna's ruthless policy, but others defended their actions by claiming that they were only following orders. Familiar sentiments which would one day be heard from Nazi Germany.

The chapel at the Presidio la Bahia (Fort Defiance), Goliad

SAN JACINTO

These were dark days for Texas. It seemed that everything the Texians were doing was ending in disaster. Now they were fleeing with the widely spread tentacles of Santa Anna's army pushing at their backs.

The situation appeared hopeless. Houston's small army was getting smaller by the day as previously keen volunteers deserted in droves, returning to their families to organise personal escape plans. From a peak of 1,400 men under arms in March, Big Sam's brave hearts had, by mid April, been reduced to about 900. And all the time they were withdrawing, backing off to the east under dismal skies and torrential rain. These tactics of constant retreat led to much criticism, in fact almost to mutiny. Some elements of the volunteer army were still spoiling for a fight and were desperate to stand their ground, but Houston was resolute and pushed on, threatening to order the execution of any man who opposed his orders. Even President Burnet came out openly against Houston, lambasting him for not standing up to the enemy but Big Sam let it all flow over him. He knew what he was doing and would only say, "If I err, the blame is mine".

Contrary to appearances, Houston did indeed have a positive plan, realising that if he could extend the Mexican's line of communications and separate their various forces he might have a chance to hit back. East of the Rio Brazos, Houston began to bring his demoralized force into some semblance of order. Two regiments were formed, the first under Edward Burleson (who had originally commanded The Alamo), the second under Col. Sidney Sherman, a flamboyant Kentucky businessman who was said to wear the grandest uniform in Texas. The army had also received a gift from the citizens of the American city of Cincinnati; a pair of six pounder cannon which were quickly dubbed the "Twin Sisters". A mounted troop of scouts was also established, dominated by the celebrated Deaf Smith, and these men were soon put to work, ranging all over the countryside gathering information.

They did their job well. Houston was kept up to date with the movements of the enemy as they spread themselves far and wide across Texas. General Gaona pushed north, Urrea south to Matagorda while Santa Anna personally drove ahead of Sesma, intent on capturing the president and delegates of the Texian government before they fled too far to the east. In his enthusiasm to achieve this, Don Demonio became over confident and careless, putting too much distance between his relatively small force and the bulk of his army. It was the moment Houston had been waiting for.

President Burnet and his entourage took flight again, leaving Harrisburg and heading for the Galveston coastline. Frustrated by his failure to catch them, Santa Anna halted his force to consider his next move. His own scouts told him that an even better target could be for the taking; Houston's rabble of an army, still on the retreat and heading for Lynch's Ferry, the crossing point where the San Jacinto river flowed down into Galveston Bay. Excited by this news, Don Demonio ordered a rapid advance for it was important that he should reach the ferry before Houston and thus trap him.

However, Houston was no longer retreating. After weeks of uncertainty, the Texians now had something to cling to. Deaf Smith was able to report that Santa Anna himself was in command of this Mexican force which was within striking distance, news that created a wave of blood lust and renewed enthusiasm in the Texian ranks. The notion that they might have a chance of getting their hands on the "butcher" himself restored their interest in the war no end. To underline the drama of the moment, Smith brought in a Mexican prisoner who actually possessed Travis' captured saddlebags, stamped with his name.

Unknown to Santa Anna, Houston now began edging his army in a cautious flanking action, trailing the route of the supposedly pursuing Mexicans. Don Demonio raced on, leading his soldados across the rickety little Vince's Bridge, on past the swampy sludge of Buffalo Bayou on their left with the marshes of Galveston Bay and Peggy Lake on their right, towards the estuary of San Jacinto and Lynch's Ferry. There was water on every side of them now, an insane position to put themselves in, but Santa Anna thought only of the certainty of success, although he did send back word for reinforcements.

Houston reached the Buffalo Bayou on April 18th., the day that Smith was able to confirm that Santa Anna was within their grasp. The next day Houston assembled his men and regaled them with a stirring speech. Victory was certain, he said, Santa Anna was cut off from his main army and soon they would all be able to avenge the deaths of their friends at The Alamo and Goliad. Telling them to trust in God, the General ordered his men to move out, following the path of their enemies over Vince's Bridge by moonlight. Early the following morning their campfires were spotted by Mexican scouts who instantly raised the alarm. Battle was imminent. Deaf Smith's scouts rushed ahead to seize Lynch's Ferry, which they accomplished against little resistance.

Alerted to the Texian's proximity, the Mexicans were advancing now, marching determinedly through the knee high grass but they were met by a double blast from the Twin Sisters and a barrage of rifle fire. Faltering, the Mexicans responded with a less than forceful charge which was quickly driven back. Later that afternoon, Col. Sherman led his Texian cavalry in a cantering feint towards the enemy lines but a skirmish ensued which did not go too well for them. However, during the clash, an incident occurred which could have been plucked from the pages of a romantic novel. A young trooper named Walter Lane was knocked from his saddle and tried to make his way back to Texian lines on foot, but he was attacked by some Mexican lancers. He would have been impaled for sure had it not been for the impressively named Mirabeau Bonaparte Lamar, a Georgian volunteer, who rode between Lane and his attackers, coolly took aim and shot one of the lancers dead. As the Mexican tumbled from his mount, the other lancers drew to a halt, stunned by such casual bravery. A Texian scout galloped up and dragged Lane up behind his saddle before riding to safety, an action which, apparently, drew a round of appreciative applause from the enemy! Before trotting away, Lamar faced his foe and presented them with a gallant bow! Houston was so impressed by Lamar that he immediately promoted him to the position of commander of the Texian cavalry, replacing Sherman.

This engagement was an anti-climax after so much expectation. Houston's men withdrew to the shelter of the woods alongside the bayou while the Mexicans went back to their camp next to the bay to await the next development. Santa Anna fully expected Houston to follow up with an attack of his own, but nothing happened. The evening wore on in silence, apart from the odd patch of sniping from the trees and ridges, and by the next morning, Thursday April 21st. 1836, the Mexicans had comfortably entrenched themselves in what they considered to be an impregnable position. They were strung out on the summit of a gentle slope with heavy woods on their right and open ground to their left, the waters of the bay stretching out behind them. It was a beautiful, sunny, warm start to the day and by 9.00am. the soldados confidence had been bolstered by the arrival of General Cos and 400 reinforcements, bringing the total Mexican strength at San Jacinto to about 1,300 men. A barricade was raised, constructed from earth and strengthened by packs, provision crates, saddles and other surplus equipment. Their single six pounder cannon was mounted in position, but as the morning wore on with nothing happening, the soldados began to relax. Santa Anna felt sure that the expected Texian attack would not take place so late in the day and so he ordered his troops to stand down. Weapons were stacked and the soldados took to their tents. It was such a lovely afternoon, Santa Anna even forsook the shelter of his big, fancy marquee, laying instead in the shade of an oak tree where he dozed contentedly. It was siesta time and all was well.

Over in the Texian lines things were far from relaxed. At midday Houston held a war council where much time was spent on debating the wisdom of an all out assault on the Mexican positions. The Texian strength still stood at only about 800 men, cavalry and infantry, so the Mexicans outnumbered them considerably, but Houston's men had inspiration and fervour on their side. They were aching to get at the enemy, furious at the tales of Mexican atrocities, desperate for revenge and eager to ease the gnawing shame of having failed to go to The Alamo's aid. Knowing that he could afford to wait no longer, Houston finally made the decision to attack, first of all ordering Deaf Smith to destroy Vince's Bridge so that there would be no chance of further reinforcements reaching Santa Anna.

Mounting his horse, a big white stallion named Saracen, Houston rode along the lines of his assembled and eager troops, calling out last minute instructions. Leading a detachment of nineteen Tejanos, Capt. Juan Seguin had presented himself to the General offering their services. At first Houston had excused them from duty, nervous that these loyal Mexicans might be confused with soldados in the thick of the fight, but Seguin was insistent that they be allowed to play a part. They too had lost many friends and Seguin, perhaps more than most, had good reason to feel anxious to make amends for his failure to return to The Alamo in time. At last, Houston relented, allowing the Tejanos to join the Texian ranks provided that they wore identifiable pieces of card in their hat bands.

Drawing his sword and raising it high, Houston finally gave the order to advance. The Texian infantry swept forward in a long line with Mirabeau Lamar's cavalry trotting along on their right flank. At first their discipline was commendable, surging silently towards the long awaited conflict, spurred by hatred and a desire for vengeance, and this good order helped enormously for them to achieve the essential element of surprise. Inexplicably, the Mexicans had not even placed sentries and this enabled the Texians to advance within just 200 yards of Santa Anna's breastworks before any sleepy soldados began to spot them bearing down determinedly through the long grass. In many ways this mirrored the last throes of The Alamo when the soldados had surprised the defenders in their sleep. Now, in a supreme moment of wry justice, the tide had turned.

At 4.30pm. the silence of that balmy afternoon was broken abruptly. Not possessing a full military band, Houston sought something to serenade his men into battle. A couple of men came forward who played the fife, also a free black man named Dick who was willing to beat a drum. Their repertoire being somewhat limited, they were unable to play the requested "Yankee Doodle", settling instead for a driving and angry rendition of an old love song. And so it was that Houston's army of fearsome volunteers descended upon their enemy to the strains of "Will you come to the Bower?"

As the fifes began to toot and the drum rattled its stirring rhythm, the Texians broke into a run, a huge roar bellowing from nearly 800 mouths. On the far left of their line, at the edge of the trees, Col. Sherman, leading the Second Regiment, emitted a battle cry which would immediately be taken up by one and all; "Remember The Alamo! Remember Goliad!" One man, at least, had his own personal slogan, crying, "Remember Wash Cottle!" in deference to his nephew who had died with Travis.

Wheeled right up to the line, the Twin Sisters crashed out in unison, ripping gaping holes through the barricades and peppering the bewildered soldados with grapeshot. The Mexicans barely realised what was happening before the Texians were upon them, opening up with ragged but deadly volleys. Sherman's men were the first to strike the enemy hand to hand, but Burleson's first regiment quickly followed suit, vaulting the centre breastworks as Lamar's horsemen galloped over the dismounted Mexican dragoons.

The Mexicans had no time to rally or formulate any cohesive defence. Already

Sherman's vigorous assault was driving their right flank down into the heart of the camp causing confusion and panic. Santa Anna himself had a rude awakening but his efforts to try and restore order were hopeless. His men were flailing around like headless chickens. It must have been terrifying for them as they did not know which way to turn. Also, it soon became obvious that these Texians were in no mood to be merciful.

Waving his sword, Houston did his best to try and control his men, calling on them to behave like gentlemen, but it was to no avail. Reaching the barricade, Houston's horse was suddenly hit by five musket balls, the result of a rare Mexican volley. As Saracen buckled and collapsed beneath him, men rushed forward to help their commander and he was soon up in the saddle of a second mount, pitching himself back into the fray. Before long this horse was also hit and Houston had his right ankle shattered by a Mexican bullet. Still game, Big Sam called for a third horse which he mounted with his injured leg draped over the saddle pommel.

It was a savage and bloody affair. In the close quarter fighting, the Texians used their gun butts, tomahawks and knives to deal death to the soldados, ignoring all those who tried to surrender. Many of the Mexicans fell to their knees, weeping and crying out, "Me no Alamo!" or "Me no Goliad!" but the vengeful Americans carried on killing. It was their kind of battle, fought on an individual basis and the Mexicans, effective only when organized, were completely out of their depth. There were many incidents of atrocity. A Mexican drummer boy, both legs broken, was spotted hanging onto the coat tails of a Texian volunteer as he pleaded pitifully for mercy, but the Texian shot the lad in cold blood. One Tejano, Antonio Menchaca, was recognized by a Mexican officer as an acquaintance from Bexar. "Save me, brother!" he begged but Menchaca cursed the man, saying "I am no Mexican, I am an American!" before having him slain. Deaf Smith struggled with another officer, wrenching the man's sabre from his hand before killing him with it. Smith then used this captured weapon to strike another Mexican so hard the blade snapped. The scout, his blood lust up, was then heard to yell, "Heeyah, take prisoners like the Meskins do!" Another Texian captain instructed his men, "Boys, you know how to take prisoners ..... knock their brains out!"

That grand old officer, General Castrillon, bravely tried to rally a crew to man the Mexican's six pounder, but the artillerymen fled leaving him to face the Texians alone. As his men begged him to retreat with them, Castrillon stood proudly erect, saying, "I have been in forty battles and have never showed my back. I am too old to do it now." He then turned and folded his arms, glaring with sad defiance at his enemies before being struck down by a salvo of bullets.

Most of the Mexicans had by now thrown aside their weapons and, realising that they would not be taken prisoner, were seeking to escape the field. Their flight to the south being blocked by Lamar's cavalry, who was doing an effective job immobilising Santa Anna's dragoons, the soldados sought refuge across the marshes into Peggy's Lake, alongside the bay. Hundreds of them were driven into the water where they were caught like rats. There was nowhere left for them to run. Helpless in the chest deep water, they cried out in terror as the Texians lined up along the bank, firing their rifles and pistols point blank into the surging mass of desperate humanity. Many Mexicans were trampled in the chaos while others ducked beneath the surface of the lake to try and win themselves a few extra moments of life. It proved to be a brief salvation, for as soon as their heads appeared again they would be blasted by the constant stream of lead from the shore. As they thrashed and struggled, the white foam of water turned a deep shade of crimson. Despite the efforts of some Texian officers who tried to halt the slaughter, there appeared to be no end to it. One snarling volunteer turned on his colonel to bellow, "Sir, if Jesus Christ himself were to order me from Heaven to stop shooting these yellow bellies, I wouldn't do it!"

Turning away in despair, the Texian high command realised that they would have to let the men have their way. Houston ordered Dick the drummer to beat the retreat in an attempt to restore order but when this was ignored, Big Sam yelled, "Gentlemen, I applaud your bravery, but damn your manners!" He then rode away from this field of death leaving the slaughter to continue.

The Battle of San Jacinto lasted a mere eighteen minutes but the cold blooded killing of helpless soldados continued for hours. Only nine Texians lost their lives in the fighting with a further thirty or so wounded, but the Mexican casualties were staggering. Well over 600 killed outright, far more than the Texians had lost at The Alamo and Goliad combined. When the Texians at last tired of the killing, hundreds more soldados were finally allowed to surrender, herded together in a shivering, terrified group and under threat of annihilation at any moment. After Goliad, how could they expect mercy?

If many of the blood crazed Texians had got their way, no Mexican would have left that place alive. Santa Anna's policy of "no quarter" had backfired on him and his men had paid a terrible price. The Alamo and Goliad had been avenged, the stain of slaughter washed clean with Mexican blood.

But what of Don Demonio himself?

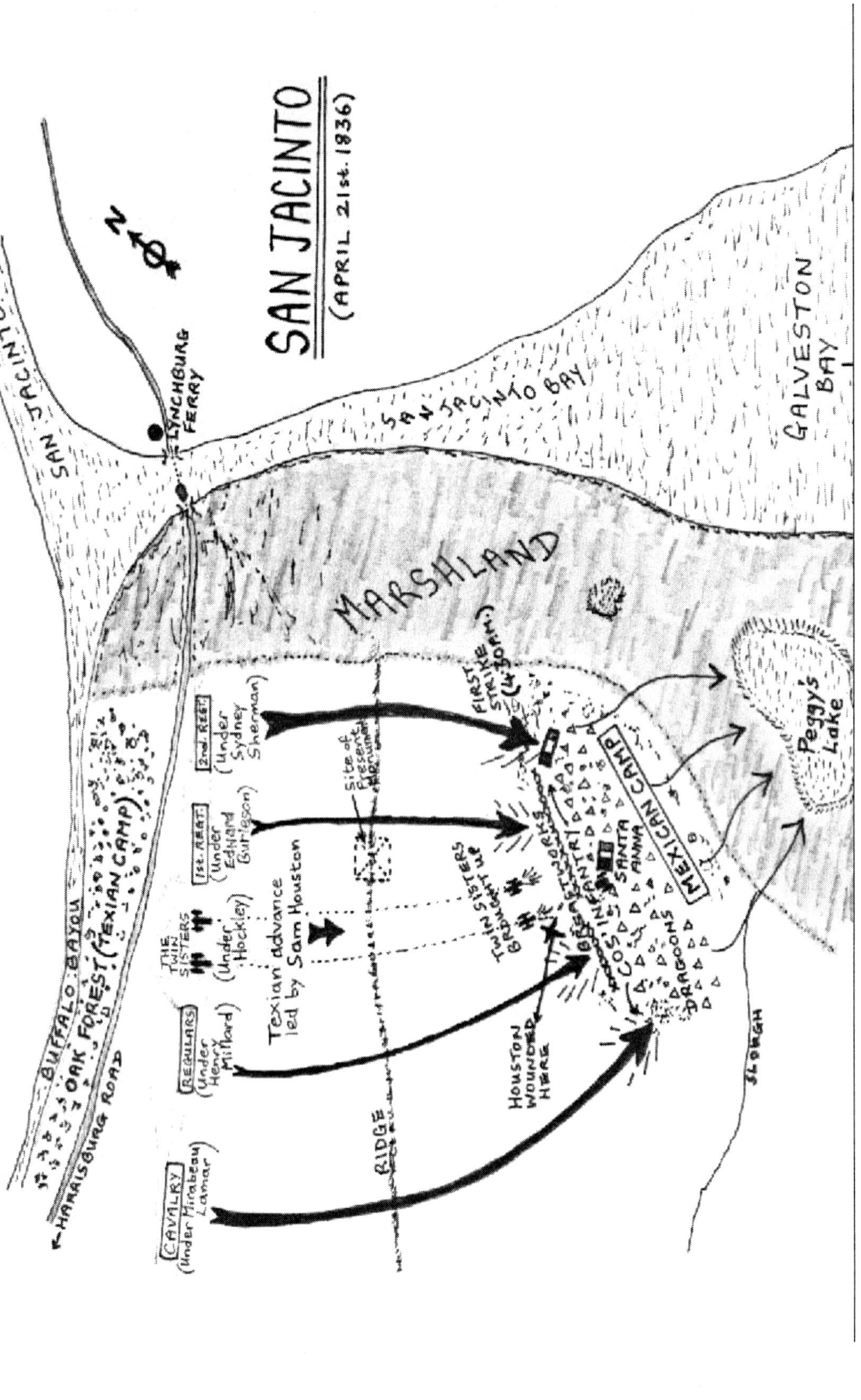
SAN JACINTO
(APRIL 21st. 1836)
N
SAN JACINTO RIVER
LYNCHBURG FERRY
SAN JACINTO BAY
GALVESTON BAY
MARSHLAND
BUFFALO BAYOU
OAK FOREST (TEXIAN CAMP)
HARRISBURG ROAD
CAVALRY (Under Mirabeau Lamar)
REGULARS (Under Henry Millard)
THE TWIN SISTERS (Under Hockley)
1st. REGT. (Under Edward Burleson)
2nd. REGT. (Under Sydney Sherman)
Texian advance led by Sam Houston
Site of Present Monument
Twin Sisters brought up
FIRST STRIKE
BREASTWORKS
INFANTRY
COS' INFANTRY
SANTA ANNA
MEXICAN CAMP
DRAGOONS
HOUSTON WOUNDED HERE
RIDGE
SLOUGH
Peggy's Lake

LIBERTY

In the confusion, Santa Anna and many of his men managed to escape from the bloodbath at San Jacinto; but not for long. They fled in disorder, scattering far and wide with the relentless Texians in pursuit. Over the next day or two, most of these Mexicans were captured.

Don Demonio lost his horse somehow several miles from the battlefield. Alone and powerless he ditched his fancy clothes and changed into the uniform of a common soldier. As the Texian scouts searched the countryside for fugitives, the president tried to hide in a thicket near the demolished Vince's Bridge but he was flushed out and interrogated, convincing his captors that he was nothing more than a humble aide.

He kept this charade going right up until he was taken back to the Texian camp, where, in a moment of comic relief amidst the tragedy, he was recognised by the other prisoners. How must he have felt when, attempting to disguise himself, his own men exposed him by rising to their feet and crying "Viva El Presidente!"? A great and pleasant surprise for the Texians who must have found it hilarious. This initial amusement quickly turned to anger as the Texians remembered what this arrogant Mexican aristocrat had been responsible for. Men crowded around the new prisoner demanding that he be strung up or shot without delay (or worse), and the more rational Texians guarding him had considerable difficulty protecting him from the mob. At last, with the situation calmed down, Santa Anna was taken to face Sam Houston. The Texian commander, lying down and resting his injured leg, met his arch enemy in the shade of a tree. Don Demonio looked anything but the sparkling despot he had been just two days before, but he did his best to retain his dignity, even congratulating Houston on his victory. There are many rumours about this historic meeting, including a story that the two commanders shared some opium together. It is also said that Santa Anna managed to avoid execution by displaying a secret sign of distress to Houston, who, like him, was a member of the craft of Freemasonry, but this is unlikely. Houston almost certainly spared Santa Anna because it made much more sense to keep him alive as a bargaining chip in the diplomatic wrangles which were to follow. The Mexican dead were neither buried or burned but were left to rot where they lay.

Don Demonio was kept captive for several weeks, no doubt grateful and surprised that he had been spared. Under the circumstances, he readily agreed to send orders to the scattered remains of his army to abort the campaign. This surprised several of his still active senior officers, especially the undefeated General Urrea who thought the war far from lost. Well over 4,000 Mexican troops were still active in Texas and, with good leadership, could still be effective, but the stuffing had been knocked out of them. They were hungry, tired and sick of this hostile country. Desperate for an excuse to return to Mexico, General Filisola, who had inherited command of the army from his president, gladly agreed to Santa Anna's orders, called an armistice and began to withdraw his troops.

Eventually, with the hostilities over, Santa Anna was allowed to return to Mexico unpunished, having promised that he would agree to recognise Texian independence. Of course, once safely back home, he betrayed this vow and continued to make trouble for many years to come, but, for now, he had lost favour with his people. Resilient as ever and wily as a fox, Don Demonio would eventually regain power, as we shall see.

Three months after San Jacinto, Sam Houston was elected President of the Republic of Texas, although the new province would not be admitted into the American Union as a State for nearly 10 years. Mexican claims on Texas would not cease until a war had been fought with the U.S.A. itself in 1846, securing the dreams of the War Dogs at last.

*   *   *

And what of The Alamo itself? Following the battle of March 6th., Santa Anna left General Andrade in charge of the garrison while the bulk of the Mexican army marched on into Texas. The fortifications were destroyed, all wooden structures were burned, the cannon were spiked and many of the walls were levelled. In May, as a result of Santa Anna's capture at San Jacinto, the Mexican occupation force withdrew.

Juan Seguin returned to Bexar with the rank of colonel and was given command of the entire area. In February 1837, a most poignant scene took place when he, and his cavalry company, officially examined the remains of his friends who had died at The Alamo, a fate which had so nearly befallen him personally. There was not much to see. Just three slight piles of dispersed ash and cinders with an odd, long charred bone here and there. Of course, it was impossible to identify any individual remains, but the loyal Tejano officer had them gathered up, placed in a coffin and carried to the San Fernando church. The bells of the church tower tolled all day as prayers were said and people wept, then a procession, led by Seguin, took the coffin back to a site close to The Alamo. Seguin then addressed the crowd with a heartfelt speech in which he honoured his "comrades in arms" before ordering several volleys fired over the coffin. It was then buried and within a few years a grove of peach trees had grown over the spot.

The town of San Antonio de Bexar gradually expanded over the years, swallowing the grounds of The Alamo within its precincts. In 1849 the old mission was rented by the United States army and they carried out the reconstruction work which gave the chapel its famous "humped" look which is so familiar today. During the American Civil War, in 1861, The Alamo was taken over by the Confederacy but it saw no action. After the war, returned to the Union, it served as a government depot until 1876. By now all that really remained was the Long Barracks building, courtyard and the chapel itself, the former two being bought privately and turned into a grocery and liquor store. This store became part of the Hugo and Schmeltzer Company in 1886. As for the revered chapel, battered and neglected, it was sold to the State of Texas but no one gave much thought to its preservation or historical significance until a hotel syndicate tried to buy it in 1903. This incensed the Daughters of the Republic of Texas, a group of patriotic ladies, who were determined to raise the necessary $75,000 to preserve this historic symbol for posterity. With great dedication, they managed to do this and they eventually obtained state funding to reimburse their costs. In 1905 The Alamo chapel, courtyard and Long Barracks building were actually conveyed, by state legislation, to the Daughters of the Republic of Texas and their successors are still responsible for its existence to this day. And a fine job they are doing too.

*   *   *

It is generally thought that The Alamo was a massacre which resulted in no survivors but this is not strictly true. Apart from the non-combatants in the sacristy, most of whom were spared and released by Santa Anna, there is evidence that more than a few actual defenders managed to escape in the last stages of the battle, probably during the mass breakout to the east and south. As we have seen, the vast majority of them were cut down by Sesma's waiting dragoons, but odd stories have emerged over the years of Texians who made it home. Most of their names are lost but perhaps this is not surprising. Passion about The Alamo always ran so high it would be a rare man who readily admitted to having fled while his brave comrades remained to die at their posts.

An exception is Henry Warnell, the 24 year old jockey from Bastrop who served as an artilleryman under Capt.Carey. According to convincing written records, Warnell did get away but was so severely wounded he died two months later. An interesting thought. Then there was Brigido Guerrero, the Mexican who managed to talk his way out of trouble by the skin of his teeth. He claimed to be a soldado prisoner, but maybe he was a defender who just used his head for self preservation. And we must not forget the six or so Texians who surrendered (possibly including Crockett) only to be ruthlessly put to death. Also, Joe, Travis' slave, who can be counted as a defender because he claimed to have continued firing upon the enemy after his master had been killed.

Louis Moses Rose, the old French soldier who allegedly took off from The Alamo just before the final assault (at Travis' invitation) is worthy of a little further examination. It seems he packed his gear quickly, shared a few last words with Bowie and Crockett, then disappeared over the wall into the darkness. Making his way across the prairie, avoiding the Mexican pickets, he tore his legs up badly in thorn thickets, resulting in infections which plagued him for a long time to come. He was an illiterate who was unable to write his story down and thus it was disputed for many years. It originally came to light through a family named Zuber, with whom he had sheltered, and was not made common knowledge until 1873. Since then, several pieces of evidence have emerged which seem to confirm that he was indeed present in The Alamo for most of the siege. When challenged about why he had deserted his comrades, he would usually only say, "I wasn't ready to die".

Sue Dickinson quickly became absorbed back into daily life in Texas, her historic role soon becoming a fading memory. Spending much of her time in the newly established town of Houston (near to San Jacinto), she worked her way through a trio of further husbands who subjected her to the trials of wife beating and alcoholism. Divorced for the third time, and with no state pension, she ended up earning her living as a prostitute. She did try hard to find a decent husband for her daughter, Angelina, but the "babe of The Alamo" (as she became known) was to inherit her mother's misfortune. Unlucky in love, she apparently abandoned her children, became a camp follower during the Civil War and died in Galveston of a uterine haemorrhage. Maybe they should have taken up Santa Anna's offer after all.

Enrique Esparza, the young son of the heroic gunner Gregorio, lived on in San Antonio until 1917, becoming the last surviving eye witness of the battle. It was only in his old age that people began taking an interest in his version of events but he did famously say, "You ask me, do I remember it? I tell you, yes. It is burned into my brain and indelibly seared there. Neither age nor infirmity could make me forget".

Madame Candelaria is another figure who became something of a tourist attraction around San Antonio until her death in 1899. I have not mentioned her until now because her actual presence in The Alamo during the battle is a subject of huge controversy. Living to be well over 100 years old, this colourful lady claimed to have actually nursed Jim Bowie during his final days and said she tried to save him from the soldados, even displaying the scars of bayonet wounds to prove it. Although much of what she said has an authentic ring to it, her claims are very doubtful.

Juana Alsbury's baby son, Alizo, grew to be a big, strapping fellow with an insatiable appetite for the ladies. He joined the San Antonio police force. As he died in 1918, this would, strictly speaking, make him the last survivor of The Alamo, but as he was under one year old during the battle his memories of it were somewhat non-existent.

John "El Colorado" Smith, the Bexar carpenter who became such a leading figure in The Alamo story, went on to become the first Texian mayor of Bexar, in 1837. He died of pneumonia in 1845 while serving as a senator for the Republic of Texas. His namesake, Erastus "Deaf" Smith, with whom he is often confused, is the Smith who really deserves the accolades of a true Texas hero, following his impressive achievements and battlefield bravery during the War for Independence. Unfortunately, he did not live for long to enjoy the fruits of the Republic. Serving as a Texas Ranger's commander his health deteriorated and he died without a cent to his name in 1837. Fortunately, the government showed their gratitude to his widow by awarding her a pension of $500 per year.

Juan Seguin's story leaves a bitter taste and poor legacy in the founding of the state of Texas. Having served the Texian cause so loyally, his treatment, and that of other Tejano volunteers, from certain quarters after the war was outrageous. Although he was elected to the Texas senate and served as mayor of San Antonio de Bexar, he was resented by the newly arrived American settlers who obviously did not appreciate the significance of his role in their presence. They saw him, and other Tejanos, as "mere Mexicans", all of whom were to be tarred with the same brush. Suffering abuse and eventual accusations of treasonous contact with the Mexican government, Seguin was forced out of office in 1842. Fleeing to Mexico, he and his family were arrested and he was forced to serve in the Mexican army against the U.S.A. in the War of 1846. After the way he had been treated, he can hardly be blamed for this. Eventually, he was able to return to the States after Texas had joined the Union, but he and his kind were made to feel unwelcome by many for the rest of their lives. He died in 1890 and was buried in Mexico but his body was returned to Texas decades later and lies at peace, finally, in the town that bears his name; Seguin, a few miles to the east of modern San Antonio. Now, at least, his name is revered again.

True to form, Santa Anna did not disappear after his humiliating defeat at San Jacinto. Although he was initially ousted from power, he regained influence several times during the ensuing years, demonstrating a unique ability to manipulate the Mexican people. Never was this more apparent than in 1842 when he lost his left leg fighting the French near Vera Cruz. The people paraded his dead limb through the city streets, worshipping it like some holy relic and turning it into a shrine. Don Demonio exploited this for all it was worth, imploring his adoring public to believe that he had sacrificed his leg out of love for them! Out of favour once more and in exile when the Mexican/American War erupted in 1846, he somehow became president again only to suffer further defeats, but even this did not finish him off. In 1853 he served his final term as Mexican president and got himself kicked out as always, only to be allowed back to idle away his dotage in his luxurious hacienda, close to where he had suffered the loss of his leg.

Stephen Austin, the long suffering idealist, who is fairly regarded as the real "Father of Texas" lost out to Sam Houston in the Texian presidential election immediately following San Jacinto, but he was granted the post of Secretary of State. Overworked and continually in ill health since his imprisonment in Mexico City, he died in December of that same year.

Sam Houston served two terms as President of the Republic of Texas (1836-38 and 1841-44) and he always fought hard during this period to annexe Texas into the United States of America. Unfortunately, it was a slow process which was largely blocked by anti-slavery sympathies in the northern states. As a matter of interest, Victorian Great Britain was one of the first to recognise Texas as a seperate entity and the office of the Texas legation was situated in the heart of London, just across the road from St. James' Palace (Prince Charles' ex-home). To this day you can see a plaque on the wall of Berry Brother's Wine Merchants, the old home of the legation, and a bust of Houston in Pickering Place, just behind the building. Texas finally became an American State in 1845 and the war of the following year eradicated all further Mexican claims.

Big Sam remarried, gave up his heavy drinking and became a stable, more mellow character. His wife Margaret presented him with eight children whom he adored. Although happy at home, his political life was entering its most turbulent phase for the Civil War was looming on the horizon. Serving as a United States senator, Houston was determined to preserve the Union, an issue which had always been close to his heart, therefore he opposed secession and the formation of the Confederacy. This made the old hero highly unpopular in Texas, even though he was Governor of the state, and there were even threats against his life. With war between north and south declared, he refused to sign the oath of allegiance to the Confederacy and was ousted from office in 1861, a sad end to the career of such a man. Retiring to his steamboat shaped house in Huntsville, he lived for two more years, sadly observing the war which raged around him, tearing his country apart. Another two years and he would have seen the Union victorious and the reformation of the nation. As it was, he died with these words on his lips, "Texas, Texas ..... Margaret ....."

*   *   *

And so we come to a conclusion of the story of The Alamo and its background. Note how I say *a* conclusion and not *the* conclusion, for I think we can be sure that there is still much to be said (and new light discovered) for the foreseeable future. Travis, Crockett, Bowie and their immortal brethren will continue to fascinate and inspire generations to come.

However you view it, it remains a classic tale, untouched by changing trends and tastes, with elements of the best and worst of human nature. We can all learn from it, in many different ways, even if it is only to experience appreciation of a time when values were simpler, ideals were grander and heroes, for all their ignorance, and probably because of it, existed in the truest sense of the word.

The San Jacinto Monument

Viewed from the top of the monument, the battlefield of San Jacinto.

At the site of Santa's Anna's camp, the author stands alongside the water into which the soldados were driven and slaughtered.

In the heart of London, England, opposite St. James' Palace, stands Berry Brother's Wine Merchants, which in the 1830s-40s operated as the Legation for the unfounded State of Texas. Behind the building, in the yard of Pickering Place, stands this emotive bust of Sam Houston.

TEXAS TODAY

The old Mexican woman was still there. I had first noticed her maybe an hour before when I had wandered past this spot and had not given her presence much thought, but she and I were virtually the only people around. What was she doing?

I stopped about 100 yards from her, screened by the trees, fascinated. This was far more than an ageing local lady out for a walk in the countryside. She was pretty ancient; eighty odd, maybe ninety, dressed in a plain dark dress, her white hair tied severely back in reverential style. Parched brown skin and classic Hispanic features, etched with the deep lines of a long, eventful life. In one hand she held a branch of leaves, in the other her rosary beads. She seemed to be concentrating very intently upon the ground, wandering in slow circles, occasionally crossing herself and muttering what I assumed were prayers. Every so often she would stoop down, a great effort for her, to brush the earth with her hand. It was intense, ritualistic and it brought a lump to my throat.

This was the field of San Jacinto, one week after the 165th. anniversary of the battle. Late afternoon with the sun shining warmly upon the gently waving long grass, sparkling water and pretty trees, very similar to the conditions which were enjoyed by Santa Anna's dozing army before the vengeful Texians rained death upon them so savagely. The aged senora was old enough to have had a great grandfather in the ranks of Don Demonio's soldados, so maybe that could be an explanation. Respect and reflection for a long dead relative. I desperately wanted to speak to her but decided that her private moment was far too personal to warrant a selfish intrusion from me. Reluctantly, I walked away and carried on down to the water's edge.

It was all so peaceful and emotive, reminding me of the way I had felt when wandering over a similar battlefield just a year before. The only sound came from the whisper of the breeze in the tree branches and lush green grass, complemented by the soft lapping of water from Galveston Bay. So easy to imagine the Mexican tents and camp fires, the stacked muskets and smug contentment of a victorious army, their lines stretching away from the trees and down towards the open plain. As I basked in the atmosphere, all alone, it suddenly became very oppressive. I had been lost in thought, my imagination in overdrive as I tried to transport myself back across the years. The comfort evaporated abruptly. I opened my eyes wide, my palms sweating. The buzz of the mosquitoes seemed much louder than before and I became overcome with the desire to get back nearer to the road where I had parked my car.

I walked quickly back through the trees, staring ahead at the same open ground across which Sherman and Burleson's regiments had swept over the Mexican breastworks. Every so often a marker informs you where those structures once stood. Looking down from the quiet road, which forms a circuit all the way around the battle site, you can still walk the routes taken by each of the Texian units. From these various places they drove the panicking soldados down across the marshes and into Peggy's Lake. Looking at it now, it resembles a naturalist's haven. Water birds and paradise; the scene of so much horror and carnage. Call me dramatic, but I swear I could almost hear the beat of Dick's drum and the distant notes of "Come to the Bower".

Today, all of this stands in the shadow of the massive 570' high San Jacinto monument which dominates the open landscape for miles around. Built between 1936-39 to commemorate the centenary of Texas Independence, this 35,000 ton concrete and Cordova shell stone tower is topped by a 34' high Lone Star. Thanks to the Daughters of the Republic, many acres have been turned into a beautiful and well preserved national park which can be explored at leisure. For a small fee you can take an express elevator ride to the observation tower of the monument, an absolutely essential thing to do to get an overview of the battleground. From up there you can really appreciate what happened as you look down onto the marshy landscape, so high up you are able to take it all in at a glance. If you focus onto the actual area of the conflict, it is virtually untouched by time, especially the clear ground off to the right by the slough where Mirabeau Lamar's cavalry trampled the dragoons. The only disappointment comes when you raise your head a little and your eyes are ravaged by the ugly distant skyline of modern day Houston with its skyscrapers, refineries, huge smoking industrial chimneys, spaghetti junctions of freeways and haze of pollution. How far things have come since 1836, when this sprawling, confusing metropolis was nothing more than a tiny, backwater trading post called Harrisburg.

Attached to the monument is an excellent museum, crammed full of mementoes from the Texian's struggle. Weapons from the battle, uniforms worn by participants, original diaries and personal items, even a musket ball taken from the head of a slain volunteer. There is a 35 minute long multi-screened film presentation too in a purpose built theatre, which is well worth seeing for an outline of the basic facts. The gigantic, multi-gunned World War Two Battleship Texas is moored nearby, close to the Lynchburg Ferry which still operates, taking cars now (instead of wagons, oxen and horses) across the mouth of the San Jacinto River.

I ended my day here watching the absurdly huge orange ball of the sun going down in a blazing sky over the Buffalo Bayou, the big container ships chugging darkly up the estuary. It was tranquil and therapeutic, but also starkly dramatic to absorb the contrast of history and nature against the harsh backdrop of a modern, brutish looking framework.

At last, I dragged myself away, walking past another militaristic memorial to the freemasons who fell for the Texian cause. Freemasonry is very big in Texas. Starting the car, I could not resist one final drive around the battlefield, the long shadows and dying sunlight stretching out like grasping fingers of destiny. More monuments and markers. Millard's advance, the first Mexican position, Sam Houston wounded here .....

As I drove slowly along the water line I spotted a lone figure in the trees. That old Mexican woman, swaying, praying and still making spiritual contact with her ancestors.

*   *   *

About fifty miles north of the coastal town of Corpus Christi, just off Highway 59, lies the historic town of Goliad. This is pure Americana, like a setting out of one of those old Judy Garland movies, with its white stone courthouse, drug stores and real cute, tree lined central square! One of these trees, long limbed and sturdy, is especially beautiful, until you become aware of its sinister history, for this is the Hanging Tree where swift "necktie" justice was meted out to many in the 1850s and 60s!

Goliad takes its name as an approximate anagram of Father Miguel Hidalgo, the patriotic priest who was highly active in Mexico's struggle for independence from Spain. Much happened here during the Alamo period and just a mile out of town you can find the Presidio la Bahia, or Fort Defiance, the stronghold of the ill fated Col. James Fannin. The original name translates as the fort of the bay, which may be confusing as the present structure does not appear to be anywhere near a bay. However, the original fort was built some miles away, in 1721, by the Spanish on Lavaca Bay, but the location was moved, twice, until it settled on its present spot in 1749. The nearby town, like so many settlements, grew up shadowed by the protection of the fort, a most sturdy structure which is still in an excellent state of preservation. You can see why Fannin was reluctant to leave it as it is much more compact and impregnable than The Alamo was.

The grounds are very neat and well maintained, the church still being in use. Our Lady of Loreto Chapel is where Fannin's men were held captive just before they were massacred. The old officer's barracks has its own museum and video presentations. Highly recommended for anyone with the slightest interest in the subject. Above it all flies the Texas Lone Star flag (which you see all over the State), but also a plain white banner embellished with the chilling image of a severed arm clutching a scimitar dripping with blood. In 1836, the colonists and volunteers flew this symbol to state "we would rather lose our right arms than live under the yoke of a tyrant".

Just behind the fort stands a mound which is crowned by a tall plinth, underneath which are buried the charred mortal remains of Fannin and his hundreds of executed men. The names of all those known are immortalized here in stone.

*   *   *

From an historical point of view, there are so many fascinating places to visit in modern day Texas, provided you have no fear of immense distances. The vastness of the State simply cannot be imagined until you experience it first hand, much of it being very flat and relentless. That said, Texas is also an area of enormous contrasts, from the mountains and prairies of the west to the almost tropical coastline and Gulf plains. There are also the stunning eastern Piney Woods, the southern canyons, sweeping rivers, escarpments and the beautiful, lush green Hill Country deep in the heart of the State, west of San Antonio. At Washington-on-the-Brazos you can visit a replica of the old Independence Hall, where the Declaration was signed, stand at Coleto Creek where Fannin fought his last battle and wander over significant places like San Felipe, Seguin and Gonzales, all of which are festooned with monuments, museums and historic trails. Texas really cherishes its history proudly, in fact many Texans see themselves as unique amongst Americans, perhaps with some justification.

Away from the War of Texian Independence, there is plenty of other history too. Check out Galveston Island where Jean Lafitte ran his pirate empire, the town which basked in high faluting glory until the gigantic hurricane of 1900 washed it from the face of the earth killing over 6,000 inhabitants. It re-invented itself as a popular seaside resort, millions having been invested in coastal defences to prevent a similar disaster. Swimming in the Gulf of Mexico, I could not help but think of Jim Bowie and Lafitte thrashing out their slave trading deals on the shoreline here.

Austin with its impressive Capitol building and monuments to the confederate war dead, the River Walk of San Antonio and crossing the border into Mexico where the atmosphere and feel of life changes in the blink of an eye. So many delights. And the little towns of the Hill Country, nestling amidst the greenery, bustling trees and blue bonnets, each one with its own individual charm. Like the German immigrant quaintness of Fredericksburg to the cowboy homeliness of Bandera where I met Clay, a true good ol' boy if ever there was one! Walking the boardwalks and visiting the eating houses and saloons of this terrific little town I experienced the warmth of America at its best. Great country bands (like "Dusty Britches") and open music sessions at the Forge, honky tonks, Lone Star beer and wonderful characters.

"Hey Harve!" cried a grizzled cowpoke as he staggered out of Arkey Blues, "That ain't ma truck!"

Harve stumbled back from the battered pick-up, a bewildered look on his whiskered, lived in face, "I wouldn't know," he mumbled, almost losing his soiled Stetson, "Ah bin drunk fer three weeks!"

"Mister Mike," grinned Clay, "you gotta meet ma brother. He talks shit like you. If you're writin' about The Alamo, you'd best not forget t' mention the Meskins who fought with the Texicans!"

Well, Clay, I hope I have done that to your satisfaction. You never did show me your gun collection!

At Seco Canyon Pass, 22 miles to the south west, a remote spot can be found where in 1876, Captain Jack Phillips of the Texas Rangers, riding alone, had his horse shot from under him by renegade Indians. He ran for his life for half a mile before being overtaken and killed. Ten miles to the north of town, at Bandera Pass, a whole company of Rangers were ambushed by hundreds of Comanches in 1841, much of the battle being hand to hand, Bowie knife against skinning blade. You can visualise it still happening.

Shame about the snakes and cockroaches but I guess you can't have everything!

Far to the west along Highway 90, nestled in the fork between the Rio Pecos and the Rio Grande, you will find (if you look hard enough!) the tiny border hamlet of Langtry, population thirty! Here, perfectly preserved, is the clapboard headquarters of Judge Roy Bean, emblazoned with his legendary "Law West of the Pecos". He was a self appointed Justice of the Peace who called his saloon come courthouse The Jersey Lilly, in honour of his unrequited love for an English actress who preferred the company of King Edward V11. Bean's colourful life story belongs in another book but I felt I had to mention him. The visitor centre is top notch and the surrounding wilderness stunning, but do not expect to experience much night life here.

Heading back along the Highway I got pulled over and interrogated by the gun toting border patrol. Yee ha!

*   *   *

Finally, a special mention for a place which, after all this history, has unique significance for me, taking me back to my childhood.

About twenty miles east of Del Rio, on the Mexican border, leave Highway 90 at Brackettville and travel north up the 674. Pretty soon you will reach a rough and ready gateway in the middle of nowhere which bears the legend "Alamo Village". Pay a nominal entrance fee to the cowboy here and you will be on your way through wild scrubland which seems to carry on endlessly, but, at last, a most familiar sight will loom ahead. The Alamo!

Well, not actually *The* Alamo, of course, because that (or what's left of it) is about eighty miles further on in the centre of San Antonio's bustling streets, as was explained at the beginning of this book. This is the movie set which was built for John Wayne's epic film version of the tale, and it is pretty much as it was when completed in 1959. The first thing to strike a scholar of the battle will be the care and attention which went into the construction of this replica fort, because the layout closely matches the dimensions of the original. The authenticity of the detail is quite impressive, the set designer obviously having done considerable research before he commenced work. As is usually the case in the world of film making, many liberties have been taken for the sake of artistic licence, but the general features are all there. The mission itself (the portals identically recreated), the south east palisade, the main gate, the corrals, the Long Barracks and the north wall are all in the right place and cover the correct size of area too. Inside the chapel, you can actually walk up the slope to Dickinson's gun emplacement and as you look back down to the church doorway, you can get an impression of how the real place must have looked in 1836.

It was a delight for me to walk around this place, absorbing the atmosphere, recalling various scenes from the film and recognising the angles from which they were shot. My wife and I were completely alone there, which pleased me no end, but the feel of the place actually became quite eerie after a while.

Just a few hundred yards away is the Western town which was built to simulate old San Antonio de Bexar. This time absolutely no effort at all was made to model the set on historical accuracy. The buildings are not even situated on the right side of the fort, but the place is still impressive and emotional in its own way. It is still used as a working movie location and numerous films, especially Westerns, have been shot there over the years. This has meant that the town has been re-modelled and added to considerably since John Wayne's day but the main feature of what is supposed to be the San Fernando church remains dominant. The town, as a general reconstruction of an old Western habitation has been beautifully done and even has its own herd of genuine Texas longhorn cattle which roam idly on the outskirts.

Then there is the Old West Museum which is filled with props, photographs and various artefacts from The Alamo movie. Memories galore and a wonderful wallow in nostalgia. The Cantina operates as a working cafeteria where the lady serving us was extremely friendly and full of information. I did not need to be told that the long bar was the same one where Big Duke met Laurence Harvey (as Travis), and the Tennesseans had their fist fight. We even ate at the same table used by Chill Wills (playing the fictional Beekeeper) as he sat with a senorita on his knee to sing *"Heres to the Ladies"*. Sorry to go on, but it meant a lot to me! Happy days .....

And Jimmy, our guide, a brilliant old character dressed in full western rig who oozed charm and warmth. I learned a lot about the film from him but I think I had the edge when it came to Texan history!

The Alamo chapel re-created for John Wayne's 1959 film and looking more like the 1836 version than the real one does today.

The author at the south east palisade. This film set was built at Happy Shahan's ranch.

Looking down from the chapel roof's gun battery towards the inside of the church door. Although this is the fake version, it does give an excellent impression of what faced Dickinson, Bonham, Esparza and the other last defenders in their final moments, although it would have been in early morning darkness.

A SEMI EPILOGUE

On June 22nd. 1876, in a cosy hacienda near Vera Cruz, Mexico, a tired, one legged old soldier reached the end of his life. At 82 years of age, he had once been a figure of huge importance but for a long time he had lived only with memories of past grandeur.

Antonio Lopez de Santa Anna would now, perhaps, have to answer to a higher authority at last.

That very same day at noon, many hundreds of miles to the north in the state of Montana, U.S.A., at the junction of the Yellowstone River and Rosebud Creek, Lieutenant Colonel George Armstrong Custer separated from the main column of the U.S. Army to lead his 7th. Cavalry to a date with destiny.

PART TWO

"…..TO CUSTER"

PART TWO: "….. TO CUSTER"

CONTENTS

CHAPTER	PAGE
25 Where Lies the Great Spirit?	137
26 The People	139
27 First Blood	142
28 Massacres, Red and White	147
29 The Boy General	153
30 A Rising Star on the Plains	158
31 Wichita	165
32 Onward the Seventh	169
33 Black Hills Gold	176
34 Ultimatum	182
35 Custer's Luck	186
36 The Way of the Warrior	189
37 Forward Ho!	193
38 Boots, Saddles and Autie's Boys	197
39 Campaign	202
40 The Battle of the Rosebud	206
41 Reno's Point	208
42 Pursuit	213
43 At the Crow's Nest	219
44 Peace on the Greasy Grass	224
45 Into the Valley	226
46 Reno's Charge and Defeat	232
47 "We've got 'em, Boys!"	236
48 "A Good Day to Die"	240
49 On Reno Hill	243
50 Last Stand	248
51 Besieged on the Bluffs	254
52 "A Scene of Sickening, Ghastly Horror"	257
53 Lakota Swan Song	263
54 For the Love of Libbie	268
55 The Survivors	270
56 Honouring the Dead	275
57 The Greasy Grass Today	279

WHERE LIES THE GREAT SPIRIT?

On ponies and horses they came, these young braves of the Oglala Sioux, galloping wildly along the valley of the Little Bighorn. As scores of hooves drummed on the parched ground, the group at the summit of the hill grew tense, watching apprehensively as this war party bore down upon them. With their blood curdling "Hi, hi!" and "Yip, yip!", these warriors meant business, the outriders yelling aggressively at all who drew near.

"No cameras!" they cried, for this was the morning of June 25th. 2001, the 125th. anniversary of a world famous battle, and the youthful bucks of the Oglala were in no mood for reconciliation.

Around the site they rode, their mounts prancing and rearing, dust rising. Woe betide any spectator who dared to attempt risking a sly snapshot, for the outriders were as vigilant as hungry hawks. One hint of a raised lens and they would sweep in, yanking on their bridles, gesturing, threatening, their faces ugly with resentment. Completing their consecration dance, two of the braves, war paint livid on their bodies, rushed to the crown of the hill, leaping onto the stone lip of the monument which commemorates the men of the 7th. Cavalry who died there. Lashing out at the carved names, the victorious pair "counted coup" on the vanquished slain before rejoining their group.

It was shocking, an affront to many of those present, but such was the intention. Thousands were attending the day's ceremonies on this normally bleak hillside; scholars, historians, veteran representatives of the modern day 7th. Cavalry, the president of the Northern Cheyenne Tribal Council, a former U.S. Congressman, mildly interested tourists, local ranchers, the media, even direct descendants of the battle's participants, including Ken and Chip Custer, relatives of "Long Hair" himself. Most were not expecting such aggression on a day which had been designated to honour the fallen of both sides, a time when it was hoped that bad blood between "red and white" had become a memory.

The armed Park Rangers and Crow Indian Police (whose reservation the land lies upon), had not moved a muscle to protect the usually well guarded monument. They, at least, were aware of the depth of bad feeling which unfortunately is still prevalent in certain areas of the Indian community and knew it was a day to let the hot heads have their moment. Reduced medical facilities, higher than average infant mortality, drugs, alcoholism, high unemployment and gross misrepresentation are all issues which plague the modern day native American. Today, at such a spotlighted event, an ideal opportunity could be grasped to make their point. (It had happened before, in 1976 at the 100th. anniversary, when militant Indians had hijacked the ceremony.) In addition, the main focus of such a display of emotion went much deeper than mere symbolic political protest. This was a day of celebration for the Sioux and Northern Cheyenne, the anniversary of their greatest ever victory over a mighty power which would eventually expel them from their land.

For many years after the battle, the world's attention and sympathy seemed to totally surround the tragedy of Custer and his men. The Indians were looked upon as the "bad guys", the 7th. Cavalry the noble heroes. In more recent times, this balance has shifted somewhat. The Custer Battlefield, as it was long known, has been re-named the Little Big Horn Battlefield National Monument, to reflect the non-bias of, hopefully, modern liberal attitudes. However, in 2001 there was still no monument honouring the Indian dead and that subject also was a reason for resentment. An Indian monument had been long planned, even a site set aside for it, just down the slope from the cavalry memorial, but the cost was enormous (over $2,000,000). A crusade in Congress achieved the necessary legislation but now it would need to be paid for. Donations and federal funds (they hoped) but also a percentage of visitor's fees and generous benefactors. One of these substantial donations had already come from the 7th. Cavalry Regiment's Association, food for thought indeed for the hostile Oglala.

When the dust had cleared and the angry Sioux had taken their leave, the atmosphere calmed down and the more reasoned business of the day continued. There were speeches from a variety of groups and individuals, with much emphasis laid upon the need for progress, reconciliation and understanding. A long gone conflict left many deep rooted scars which still required to be addressed. Comparisons were drawn with such ongoing world troubles as the Middle East and Northern Ireland. The children of the Cheyenne and Arapaho danced with their one time enemies the Crow and Arikara, whose scouts rode for Custer. There was also a lengthy but poignant reading of a roll call of those who fell that June afternoon, long ago, white and red (and, in one case, black), the Montana National Guard joining forces with the Indian Honour Guard to parade up Last Stand Hill. A further consecration, this time by Chief Many Bad Horses of the Northern Cheyenne, and the laying of a wreath by far travelled members of the Custer Association of Great Britain, present to pay homage to their countrymen who had ridden, and died, with the 7th. Cavalry.

As the sun began to edge towards the western horizon, to disappear behind the distant Rocky Mountains, gunfire echoed again across the ridges and gullies of the Greasy Grass. In 1876, men had fallen to that sound, but now a new generation stood in silent tribute as a volley of carbines crackled a solemn salute.

In some ways, the war goes on. Let us look at how it all began .....

THE PEOPLE

My first close encounter with a buffalo in the wild took place some miles west of the Shoshone River, Wyoming, along the Yellowstone Trail. An area of truly staggering beauty, described by President Teddy Roosevelt as the "most scenic stretch in America". He may have been right. Although the States are crowded with awe inspiring natural wonders, I cannot think of another region where stunning sights are so condensed in one relatively short passage. From pine clad slopes and majestic canyons, through tunnels cut into the mountain side and over glittering, royal blue lakes, it is hard to imagine how this paradise was once a source of great danger to lone pioneers.

After many miles of customary empty road, I was suddenly pleased to encounter a score or so of bison grazing contentedly in a clearing by a copse of cottonwoods. It looked like a scene from a Remington painting, so I pulled over, grabbed my camera and stepped out of my vehicle. The first thing to strike me was how big they are. Huge shaggy beasts with gigantic heads and stubby horns, the broad, towering hump appearing too absurdly large to be supported by those thin, hoofed legs. Some stand six foot high at the shoulder. As I cautiously approached, most of them turned and cantered away, surprising me how quickly such ungainly creatures can move. A half dozen remained where they were, raising their heads and glaring at me with their beady black eyes. They seemed defiant but I got within twenty feet before one vindictive bull began snorting and pawing the earth with his hoof. On the face of it they appear docile, until you are standing in their backyard, then suddenly the realisation floods into your mind that this thing could trample you into mincemeat without batting an eyelid! Later I met Park Rangers who were to tell me that you should never get too close to such an unpredictable animal as a buffalo. Apparently many greenhorn visitors to the wilds are gored, injured and even killed every year, so I guess I was lucky to get away with just a dirty look from *Mr.Tatanka!*

These buffalo are a fairly common sight around the wilderness of North America now, but it has taken a long time to re-populate the herds following the wholesale policy of mass slaughter by white hunters which almost made them extinct in the late 19th. century. In earlier times the buffalo roamed the prairies in their millions, the herds stretching as far as the eye could see. Back then their only worry was the odd four legged predator as even the native American Indians were not bothering them too much. Those were the days when the Indians hunted on foot with bow, arrow and lance, before the life changing horse and gun had been introduced into their communities. It was difficult and dangerous to prey on the swift, cantankerous buffalo back then, so the early Plains tribes existed mainly on a diet of small game, occasionally making a meal of the dogs which provided their main source of transport. By that, I mean that dogs were employed as draft animals to drag travois around.

In 1519, the Spanish explorer Cortes landed in Mexico with about fifteen stallions and mares, the first modern horses to be seen in the new world. The native Aztecs were in awe of them and they bred the terror which enabled such a small group of Spaniards to conquer the country. As more Europeans arrived, spreading mayhem and disease amongst the indigenous peoples as they pushed west and north, the horse population grew, some of these animals escaping from domestic herds and turning feral in the open country. Within a generation or two, huge groups of wild horses and ponies were galloping across the Plains, indulging in uncontrolled breeding which produced the mustang of popular folklore. Naturally, they became a target for the Indians who quickly realised the potential of such a fleet footed, hardy and tameable beast. The Plains Indians west of the Mississippi River struck up an instant rapport with the horse and it changed their lives forever. For the Indian to become mounted and mobile had immense impact on their development and culture. They now turned essentially nomadic, roamers who could follow the buffalo and hunt them with ease. The buffalo hunt was a key factor in the very existence of the tribes and they became reliant on the bison in all walks of life for food, shelter, clothing and numerous other uses. Raw liver and buffalo tongue were particular delicacies, the thick furry hides made excellent winter robes, battle shields and canoe linings too. Sinews were transformed into bow strings, shoulder blades made tools, dried dung could be burned as fuel, blood became dye and war paint, the woolly, long black hair ornamented clothes, thin bones made needles and even glue could be boiled up from hooves. Just a few examples of how the ability to suppress the buffalo became essential to the Plains Indians.

They were natural horsemen, in the same vein as Genghis Khan's Mongols and the Cossacks of the Russian Steppes. Riding bareback and with only a simple halter to control his mustang's head, the average Indian was like a gymnast when mounted, the horse itself becoming like an extension of his own body. White observers never failed to be impressed by the graceful skill of Indians as they hunted and made war. For these were the two prime motives which drove the Red Man in his quest to prove himself to his tribe. Skill as a hunter and courage as a warrior.

This role, the classic image of the proud mounted brave, feathered, painted and armed to the teeth came to fruition quite quickly and by the late 1700s had become the norm, at least for the Plains tribes. Other tribes who had been suppressed were, within a few years, relocated by white expansionism from their original eastern homelands to areas such as Indian Territory (modern Oklahoma) where they became domesticated, many of them turning to farming. These docile Indians were regarded contemptuously by their cousins across the untamed Plains who still revelled in living a free life, riding, hunting and making war on rival tribes largely unhindered by the white man; for now, at least.

It was around this time that a significant shift took place in the location of the various Indian tribes, whether voluntarily or by Government enforcement. Inspired by their new way of life, revolving around the horse and buffalo, a large confederation of warrior people moved west onto the Great Plains for the first time. One group were the Cheyenne, a handsome people who crossed the Missouri River in search of game on the southern expanses. More numerous, and simultaneously, the various tribal groups of the fiercely proud Teton Sioux left their ancestral homeland in Minnesota, making war upon any other tribes who stood in their way. Pushing across Dakota, and Wyoming, the Sioux became arch enemies of the Crow who fought back to preserve their land, but the invaders were too strong for them and succeeded in driving them out. The Black Hills of South Dakota became particularly sacred to the Sioux, a place they regarded as holy. Travelling across those beautiful and spiritually uplifting slopes today it is easy to appreciate why this was so.

The name Sioux is a direct reflection of how these people were viewed by other tribes for it derives from a rival Indian word meaning "enemy". So, to most native people, who had suffered from Sioux aggression, this is how they came to be regarded. To the Sioux themselves, they preferred to think of their being the Lakota, meaning "the People". They formed occasional loose alliances with the Cheyenne and Arapaho, even Southern Plains tribes such as the Kiowa and Comanche, but there was no real unity amongst these people. Looking after one's own was very much the order of the day, although the tribes did agree upon a mutual respect for a universal Great Spirit and the One-ness of nature.

There was a lot of inter-tribal warfare as Indians fought with each other to fulfil the urge to control the most prime land, the richest game, steal each other's ponies and win battle honours. Amongst the Sioux tribal groups, there were none more fierce than the Oglala who seemed to be hostile to all outsiders. Other groups within the Teton Sioux confederation included the Brule, Hunkpapa, Minneconjou, Sansarcs, Blackfeet and Two Kettle. Their first guns were acquired from French trappers, a great boost for hunting and fighting, and they did all they could to enhance their reputation as a nation of warriors. Therefore, the Great Plains were not reserved as an idyllic retreat for nature lovers. They ran red and echoed to the sounds of war long before any serious conflict arose with the white race.

And yet to the Sioux, the family unit came first, pampering their children and teaching by example rather than with chastisement. The Lakota were never able to understand the white settler's beating of their young. Although it was the man's role to make war and hunt, the woman's function was equally important on the domestic front, for she ruled the family, ran the tepee and was responsible for all the home comforts. Although the taking of several wives was accepted, monogamy was the norm. As long as they had family to care for them, the elderly of the tribe were highly respected. The Sioux also loved story telling and pipe smoking around the camp fire and were probably the most freedom loving of all the tribes. They were also very tolerant, accepting all kinds of diverse behaviour and eccentricities as long as they did not disrupt the well being of the overall group.

Prized eagle feathers which the men wore in their braided hair were not awarded easily. Each feather had to be won by the carrying out of a brave or worthy deed, therefore warriors with gigantic feathered war bonnets had proven themselves many times. Counting "coup" (the French word for "blow") was considered highly laudable in Indian society. Whacking the coup pole as he danced around proclaiming mighty deeds was a brave's prerogative, but in war this behaviour was even more respected. To get close enough to an enemy to count coup, without killing him, then get away unscathed was considered ultimately commendable.

Every year, the Sioux would indulge in their annual Sun Dance which had little to do directly with the sun. It was all about endurance, a plea for spiritual help to the Great Spirit. A post would be driven into the ground with cords attached and the young braves would gather around it. Two slits would be cut into each breast and sticks would be pushed into the incisions. The cords of the pole would then be attached to these sticks and the braves would jerk around, dancing and pulling on the cords with the weight of their bodies until their flesh ripped free. Enduring pain in this way proved personal courage and often brought about the creation of new tribal leaders. During these extremes of self torture, visions would often come to the participants as they danced for the preservation of the Lakota.

Fighting men who could put themselves through such agony for the sake of pride and honour? A formidable foe indeed.

FIRST BLOOD

So who in their right mind would actively seek out conflict with such a ferocious people who thrived on the idea of war?

The answer lies in progress and expansionism, as well as old fashioned greed, a policy vigorously and ruthlessly pursued by a succession of American government administrations. They would learn many lessons along the way but it would ultimately lead to the destruction of a whole race's way of life.

Following the American War of Independence and the creation of the United States in 1776, this brand new nation was based upon a strong principle of freedom, opportunity and the rights of the individual. That was the theory, anyway. The entire eastern seaboard, all along the coast and deeply inland, quickly became civilized with cities, ports, roads and settlements springing up at an alarming rate. Of course, this was a fertile land with seemingly endless space for everyone, rich in natural resources and crying out for settlement. Immigrants arrived by the boatload, fresh from the grime and restrictions of their old European world and anxious to become part of this promised land where they could make a new start and doubtless better their lot.

Some stayed in the cities of the east, creating the great melting pot of international humanity which has become the American people, while the more adventurous headed west into the vast unknown. Thousands of square miles of unexplored territory to be crossed before reaching the Rocky Mountains and the pacific coastline far beyond. From the white race, only trappers, Indian traders and the odd scientific expedition had ventured that way before, some of them never to return. The wagons rolled west along the Oregon and Santa Fe trails, sometimes in long, snaking columns and sometimes alone facing hardships that we, in the comfort of the 21st. century, can only shudder to think about. They were seeking their fortune but often they found only death from thirst, starvation, the savagery of the elements, outlaws or hostile Indians. In the early years of western migration, there was no unified effort by the tribes to attack the white settlers, but the wagons and isolated settlements were regularly raided by bands of marauding warriors who were just exercising their natural flair for horse stealing and killing. Most Indians initially welcomed the strange white people who were passing through their country, curious about them and behaving in a friendly fashion. However, after a few years, the tribes grew concerned that this flow of white people appeared to be never ending, in fact it was growing more intense by the day. No longer were they just odd groups passing through. They were beginning to encroach on land which the tribes felt belonged to them. The buffalo herds were being displaced by the un-natural movement of the wagon trains, temporary settlements were becoming permanent, the freedom of the Indian was being threatened. It was all very well to acknowledge these pale skinned folk but to stumble over them every day was a different matter. Not surprisingly, resentment began to rear its ugly head, especially with the introduction of white diseases such as cholera and smallpox which decimated the tribes.

In turn, the settlers took a dim view of the Indians, seeing them at best as scavengers and at worst as murdering thieves, a terrible nuisance to detract from the goal of creating a new life. They began to turn to their government, demanding that a solution be found to this Indian problem. Of course, it wasn't as simple as that. Realising the delicacy of the situation, the U.S. Army began tentatively establishing the odd outpost or two within the bounds of the "Permanent Indian Frontier" as it was known, so as to make pioneers feel a little more at ease. In reality, these few troops afforded practically no protection to their people in such a vast land, in fact they were ineffective, but their presence did succeed in inciting Indian sensitivity.

The government could not forbid the settlers to cross this land; the best they could do was try to offer some kind of security, a virtually impossible task. In the meantime, as Indian anger mounted, more and more wagons and cabins went up in flames and the prairie became littered with arrow bristled, scalped corpses. The Indians began to realise that their very way of life could be in serious danger. As for the U.S. Government, they simply did not know how best to deal with the Red Man's unpredictability and his violent nature, but the fact remained that something would have to be done, and soon.

To a Sioux warrior there could simply be no alternative to his life of roaming far and wide, following the buffalo from season to season, going where he wished and killing his enemies as he pleased. He could not understand that there could be no room for such behaviour in the so called civilized nation that men far away in big stone tepees were trying to establish. Take away a Lakota's freedom of choice and you would be stripping him of his dignity, his culture, his very reason for living. If anything was worth fighting for it would be that. At this stage, very few Indians realised what a hopeless struggle it would prove to be.

In 1851 a treaty was signed at Fort Laramie, sited on the Oregon Trail, just south west of the Black Hills. The U.S. Government was represented by officials of the Bureau of Indian Affairs and the Indians were partially spoken for by a selection of chiefs from the Sioux, Cheyenne, Arapaho and even the Sioux's mortal foe the Crow. It did not seem too bad a deal for the Indians (inexperienced as they were at treaty making at this time) for they were promised considerable benefits to merely keep their distance from the Oregon Trail itself, an arrangement which would still leave them free to roam across vast areas of prime hunting land. Unfortunately, as usually proved to be the case, the chiefs were unable to establish total control over the movement of their people, such being the Indian way. Although at this time there had still been no major clash between the U.S. Army and the Indians on the Great Plains, that situation was about to dramatically change, all because of an idiotic misunderstanding and the suicidal behaviour of a drunken lieutenant named Grattan.

In 1854, just prior to another gathering at Fort Laramie, a young Brule Sioux found a lame cow alone on the trail. Assuming it to be abandoned, he and his companions killed and ate it, thereby arousing the wrath of the Mormon settler who owned it. The fact that the settler had abandoned the animal was irrelevant. He was incensed at the idea of these savages having a meal at his expense and thereby demanded payment. Acting as spokesman for the frightened Brule youth, a Teton Sioux chief named Conquering Bear generously offered to pay $10 to the Mormon as recompense but this cow owner seemed to think that it was worth $25 and would accept no less. Conquering Bear thought this demand unreasonable and left the Mormon to take his case to the authorities. This, unfortunately for everyone as it turned out, happened to be Lt. Grattan who hit the whisky before heading for the Sioux camp with thirty men, two cannon and a one track mind. His belligerent attitude did nothing to salvage the situation, his demands being so unreasonable that Conquering Bear's braves became agitated. Probably panicking, Grattan ordered his men to open fire, killing the chief before being overwhelmed by the infuriated braves of the village. Only one soldier escaped alive to tell the tale.

Knowing that retribution would fall upon them, the Sioux wasted no time breaking camp and dispersing but, strangely, the army seemed in no hurry to track them down, waiting until the following summer before sending out a force of 1,300 troops. They attacked the first band of Sioux they encountered, a friendly camp which had not been involved at all with the previous year's incident. Never-the-less, the camp was wiped out, many braves were killed and the women and children taken captive.

In the meantime, a group of Conquering Bear's braves had avenged their chief's death by attacking a mail wagon and slaughtering the occupants, so the army demanded that these five warriors be immediately given up or the Sioux would pay another dreadful price. Fearing a further mass attack, and bowing to pressure from their chiefs, the braves surrendered chanting their death songs. Amazingly, in an uncharacteristic act of mercy, (but with great foresight) the U.S. President pardoned them and they went free. One of them was to become famous as that great peace negotiator Spotted Tail, a Lakota who obviously obtained wisdom the hard way.

This one incident did more harm than all the previous years of uncertainty. Now there existed a tangible atmosphere of distrust along the frontier between red and white. In neighbouring states clashes boiled up constantly. Texas had become a flashpoint of violence where Texas Rangers seemed to be in continual conflict with the Comanches and in Kansas the Cheyenne were on the warpath.

The next major blow would fall when the white authorities were otherwise distracted by one of the most significant events in American history. The Civil War.

*   *   *

Although there had been disharmony and conflict between the northern and southern American States for years, the first real shots of the Civil War were fired in 1861. From then on there existed a great divide in the nation, with many of the southern states seceding from the Union and defiantly forming the Confederate government under their own president Jefferson Davis. The Union held firm under their president, Abraham Lincoln, the issues fought over being complex but rooted in the difference of opinion concerning slavery, the south being in favour and the north against. It was never as simple as that, for many of those who fought for the north could hardly be called abolitionists. However, this book does not really concern the Civil War and is mentioned only because of the effect it had upon the situation on the Great Plains.

While the country's vast armies tore each other apart on the battlefields of the east and south, the Plains Indians noticed that the peace keeping forces of the U.S. Army were becoming somewhat depleted as most able bodied troops were being recalled for deployment in the war. Skeleton garrisons of lower quality fighting men were left in charge of those outposts which had not been closed down, but the Indians failed to exploit this sudden advantage. If they had united at this point, they could easily have overpowered the weakly guarded settlements but it seems they were unable to understand such an opportunity. Instead, they just welcomed the chance to return to their old ways for a while, raiding intermittently, enjoying undisturbed hunts and fighting each other, safe in the knowledge that the white soldiers were too busy elsewhere to worry too much about what was happening on the distant frontier.

In such a lawless land, chaos inevitably began to reign. East of the Rockies, in northern Colorado, the town of Denver was established as a base for fortune hunters who were seeking the gold that had been struck in the State. It was a rough and ready place, the saloons, gambling dens and streets echoing to the sound of gunfire and fighting. A man had to be pretty tough to make his mark here and most of them had little time for humanitarian concern for the Indians. Here, the Southern Cheyenne struck back against prospectors who were pillaging their land and the whites responded with revenge attacks of their own, both sides being aware that there was barely anyone around to restore law and order.

Unexpectedly, the first significant Sioux uprising did not occur on the Plains amongst the wild Teton but further east in Southern Minnesota, the Lakota's traditional homeland. Confined to a narrow strip of land, the Santee Sioux had more or less surrendered to the reservation system in return for promised awards of cash and supplies. Unfortunately, by the summer of 1862, administrative delays had resulted in hardship for these Indians, aggravated by crop failures. Justifiable complaints to the authorities were met with indifference, one white trader responding to Indian hunger with the remark "Let them eat grass".

With resentment simmering, it was inevitable that boiling point would be reached. It started with a small group of young warriors taunting each other's manhood following an incident where hen's eggs had been stolen from a white settler. This led on to a heated debate between the braves as to whether or not the Lakota should fear the white man. Four of them decided to prove they had no such fear by riding to the nearest homestead and promptly murdering the inhabitants. Back at the reservation, where the braves openly boasted about the killings, the chiefs called a tribal council to discuss how best to deal with the problem. The whites would doubtless punish the whole tribe for the deeds of a few, as they had done before, so would it not make sense to strike first while the army forces were still weak in the area? Did they not deserve it after the way they had cheated the Lakota?

Chief Little Crow tried to reason for peace, saying how the whites were too numerous to fight. Even if the Sioux could beat the whites here, more soldiers would come eventually so it would all end in disaster. Never-the-less, the council decided to wage war and Little Crow threw in his lot with them and agreed to lead the warriors.

The carnage was terrible. Santee war parties were merciless as they struck out at every white settlement within thirty miles, burning the buildings, slaughtering all the men (often after torture) and taking women and children captive. There were many reported cases of the latter being killed too, and of settler's wives and daughters being gang raped. By the end of the first day the white death toll ran into hundreds. The trader who had dismissed the Sioux's hunger so flippantly was later found dead with his mouth stuffed full of grass.

The terrified white survivors fled to the supposed sanctuary of the badly undermanned Fort Ridgely but by the next day, Little Crow and his horde were on their doorstep, having already routed the first detachment of soldiers which had been sent to oppose them. For three days the fort held out, inflicting heavy casualties on their attackers before the Sioux got tired of the siege and sought easier pickings. This they thought they had found in the small town of New Ulm which they fell upon with renewed savagery. Although much of this settlement went up in flames, the fugitive community here formed a stalwart resistance and after some hard fighting managed to drive Little Crow away.

The Santee continued their reign of terror for just over a month, carrying out atrocities and fighting skirmishes along the Minnesota River until a hastily mustered and trained force under Col. Sibley beat them in a decisive battle at Wood Lake. Sibley followed up his victory with a ruthless hunt for Little Crow's rebellious braves, who had scattered far and wide. As a result, something like 2,000 Indians were rounded up, the vast majority of whom had not taken part in the uprising.

The white authorities were determined to make an example of the perpetrators of these horrors against "peaceful, civilized folk" and therefore put hundreds of suspects through a rushed show trial. Little Crow himself had managed to get away, but over 300 of his warriors were sentenced to death. This somewhat extreme ruling was rethought, following an appeal for clemency to President Lincoln by a humanitarian bishop, and most of these braves were reprieved. Eventually, under forty of the most guilty (i.e. the proven rapists, torturers, etc.) went to the gallows, executed simultaneously on a giant scaffold which dropped them all in the same instant, much to the glee of the assembled, vengeful crowd. Little Crow remained on the run until the following year when he was spotted picking blackberries and shot dead. The Minnesota Sioux reservation ceased to exist and many of the Santee were driven west to join their Teton brethren.

This whole sorry episode was a turning point in relations between the Plains tribes and the white race. Bitterness, distrust and hatred took a quantum leap in the attitudes of both sides, sowing the seeds for the terrible, blood soaked years ahead.

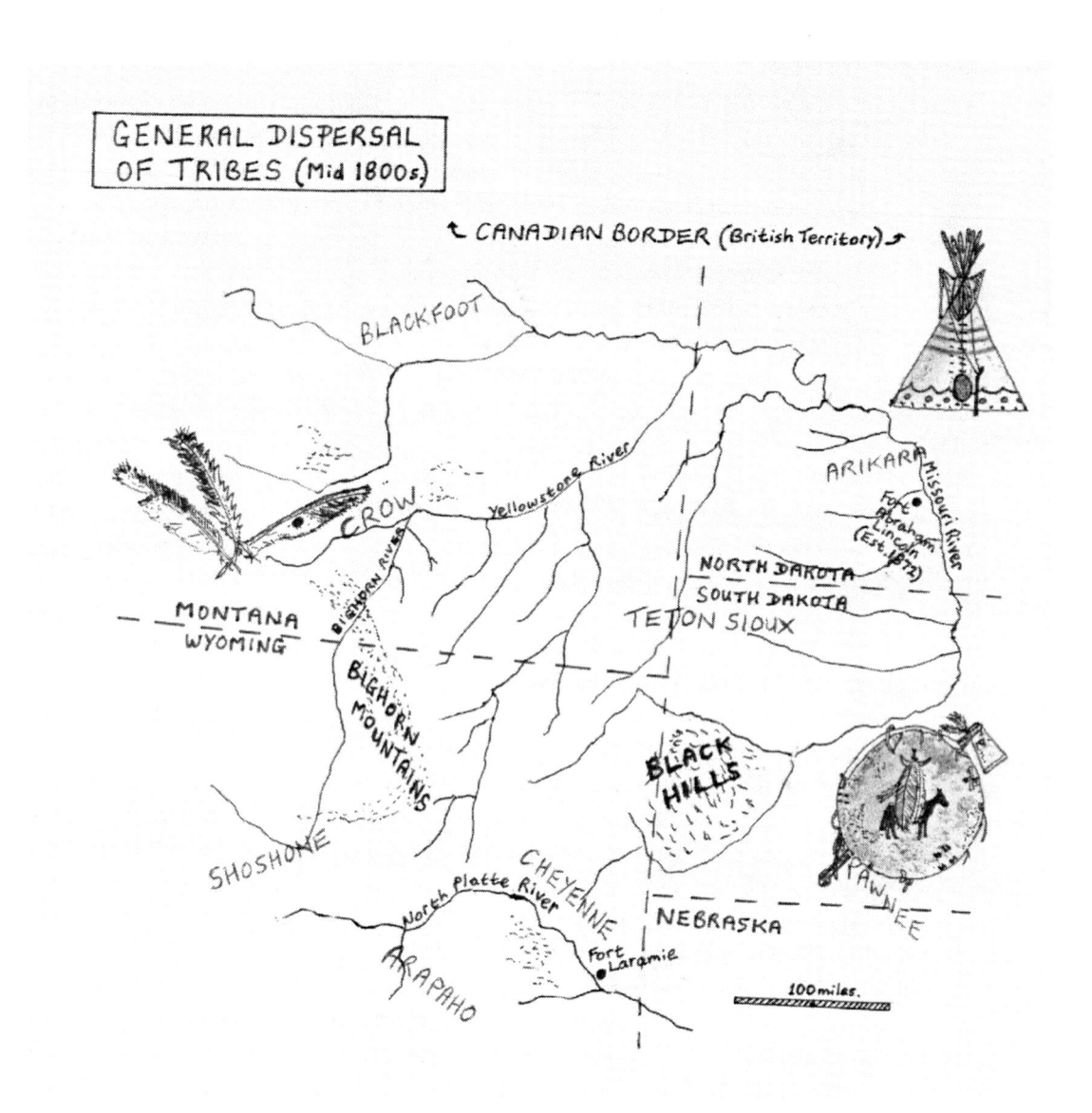

MASSACRES, RED AND WHITE

Between the Civil War and Custer's infamous demise at the Little Bighorn, the ebb and flow of incident on the Great Plains was highly eventful, but I will concentrate only on certain aspects to set the scene. It is a tale decorated with much horror which needs to be addressed before an understanding can be achieved of the depth of feeling which led to the savagery perpetrated by both sides.

No better example of this can be found than in Colorado in 1864. With the Civil War at its height, the Southern Cheyenne and other tribes in the area were raiding freely, although there were still chiefs who advocated peace. Black Kettle, for example, a Cheyenne who said "all we ask is peace with the whites". It is probable that he was sincere in this wish, but he had the usual Indian dilemma of extending full control over his individualistic braves.

The situation regarding U.S. Government response to the Indian problem in the region is complex, but the lack of available manpower led to the formation of some questionable units of militia, such as the 3rd. Colorado Cavalry. This unit was largely compiled from a variety of roughnecks who signed up for a 100 day period, hardly what you would call truly professional soldiers. They were itching for a fight, anxious to get their hands on some Indians, *any* Indians. Their period of enlistment was reaching its end and they had barely been in action, bringing them a reputation in Denver as the "Bloodless 3rd.". Led by Col. John Chivington, an ex-Methodist preacher whose hulking physique and wild eyes gave a clue to the fanatical hatred which dwelt within him, these militia men would find an outlet for their suppressed violence.

There had been no significant trouble with the Cheyenne for most of that autumn and Black Kettle's band were located along a dried up watercourse called Sand Creek, about forty miles from the nearest fort. Led to believe that they were under government assurance of protection, these Indians were settling in for the winter with their families, about 600 strong, maybe 200 of whom were warriors. Little did they know that Chivington was bearing down upon them with over 700 war hungry troopers, most of whom came from the "Bloodless 3rd.".

Chivington had his men in place at Sand Creek on a snow covered, late November dawn, advancing slowly from the bluffs, the sleeping village barely aware of their approach. The early risers amongst the Cheyenne lodges were merely curious at first, having no real reason to feel that they were about to be attacked. Black Kettle had been given a gift of an American flag by the Commissioner of Indian Affairs and it flew above his tepee as a symbol of his good intentions. Unfortunately, Chivington had already stirred his men's bloodlust, telling them to "kill and scalp all, big and little". "Nits" he said, "made lice", and he was also reported to have growled, "I long to wade in gore"! With a commander like this opposing them, what chance did the Cheyenne stand?

The mad preacher's four howitzers split the peace of the morning with their booming roar as shells rained down upon the lodges. Indians were sent spinning through the air by the blasts as others ran from their tepees, reaching for their weapons. Before most of the tribe realised what was happening, the Colorado cavalry were upon them, galloping and whooping through the camp, firing pistols and carbines and waving their sabres. Black Kettle's attempt to raise a white flag alongside his American standard was to no avail. These troopers were heeding nothing but their own savage instincts.

Although the braves resisted the attack as valiantly as they could, it was a one sided skirmish. Pretty soon all the Cheyenne fighting men had been wiped out and the women and children were at the mercy of Chivington's militia. Encouraged by Chivington himself, who snarled threats at those few of his officers who objected to the atrocities that followed, the "Bloodless 3rd." indulged in a day long orgy of the most despicable acts imaginable. Wholesale rape, torture and mutilation. Ears cut off and strung on necklaces as souvenirs, braves castrated, a pregnant squaw cut open and her unformed baby ripped from her body. One trooper was seen riding around with a bleeding heart on a stick. Several non-combatants were scalped whilst still alive, children were used for target practice by troopers who laughed like demons and women's removed private parts were stretched across saddle pommels or worn on the cavalrymen's hats as obscene decorations. The 3rd. were "bloodless" no longer.

A few Cheyenne managed to escape, including Black Kettle himself who would live to suffer a similar horror just four years later. Chivington's men were lauded by the populace of Colorado who placed them on a "pedestal of glory" for having supposedly given the "red devils" a taste of their own medicine. Such criticism as was levelled at the 3rd.'s barbarity was justified by the claim that white scalps were found in the Indian lodges. Within days of the Sand Creek massacre 100 Cheyenne scalps were said to have been displayed on the stage of Denver's Appollo theatre to a cheering audience.

*   *   *

The Civil War ended in victory for the Northern States in April 1865 and, amidst the post-battle chaos, the government began to turn its attention again to the western frontier. A new surge of settlers began streaming westwards, along with prospectors who were seeking to get rich quick in the newly discovered gold fields of south west Montana. During the war, a new route had been discovered to this area by an adventurer named John Bozeman, a route which would shorten the journey to the diggings by nearly 400 miles. The fact that this Bozeman Trail ran from Fort Laramie all the way through the Powder River country up to Virginia City, thereby contravening the conditions of the 1851 Treaty, did not seem to bother the thousands of rowdy white folk who commenced using it. Naturally, the Sioux were incensed by this blatant disrespect and disruption of their promised hunting lands and reacted accordingly by attacking wagon trains.

Although granting lip service to the Sioux by expressing a degree of sympathy for their grievances, the U.S. government also supported the illegal acts of the settlers and prospectors by sending troops into the area to protect them from attack. In 1866, while supposed further negotiations were taking place at Fort Laramie, the Sioux were infuriated to learn that a string of army forts were being built along the Bozeman Trail. Forts Reno, Phil Kearny and C.F. Smith were established in blatant disregard of Lakota sensibilities, strung out north to south along a 150 mile stretch running parallel to the Bighorn Mountains.

In charge of much of this building operation was Col. Henry Carrington, a methodical, scholarly and reasonable man, who had been a lawyer before becoming a professional soldier in the Civil War. He based himself at Fort Phil Kearny, the central outpost of the three, an 800' by 600' wooden stockade which was sited in a narrow valley with high ground on almost every side, a peculiar arrangement for the establishment of a stronghold. When hearing of these plans, Chief Red Cloud of the Oglala stormed away from the talks at Fort Laramie, apparently waving his rifle and vowing, by the Great Spirit, that he would make his mark. He certainly kept true to his word.

Enough chiefs had succumbed to pressure by signing a new treaty to make the government representatives feel they had achieved their aim, thereby justifying the building of the forts. The threats of Red Cloud and those who supported him did not worry the authorities at this stage, but the situation would change when the Sioux began to harass the newly established forts. Wagon trains continued to be attacked on a regular basis and any soldiers who ventured from their posts were likely to be ambushed in a series of hit and run operations. Wood cutting parties (which were sent out systematically from Kearny to obtain fuel and building materials) became a particular target. The policy of the fort became a defensive action under the watchful gaze of the Lakota from the surrounding hills.

Newly assigned to the fort was Capt. William Fetterman whose aggressive style immediately came into conflict with Carrington's ponderous caution. Fetterman was a fighting soldier who had seen much action in the Civil War and it seems he resented his colonel's lack of combat experience. (Carrington had been a staff officer during the war.) The freshly arrived captain was openly contemptuous of Indians and could not understand why well armed soldiers had shut themselves up in the fort in fear of what he saw as a bunch of savages. He also boasted that given eighty men he could blast a path through the whole Sioux nation.

On the freezing cold morning of December 21st. 1866, one of the fort's wood cutting details came under attack, a common occurrence, and Fetterman was ordered by Carrington to go to its aid. Venturing out across the snow covered hills, the captain led just under fifty infantrymen, accompanied by a smaller group of Lt. Grummond's cavalry. Fetterman was also joined by his good friend Capt. Frederick Brown (who tagged along without authority) and two civilians, Isaac Fisher and James Wheatley, who were keen to try out their brand new Henry repeating rifles. Altogether, and uncannily, considering Fetterman's boast, this company numbered just over eighty men. Carrington made it clear that their mission was only to relieve the wood cutting party and that they should not go beyond the Lodge Trail Ridge.

As it happened, Fetterman and his men became the victims of a beautifully laid trap. It seems that Red Cloud's braves were determined to inflict a heavy blow on the army that day and went to considerable trouble to bring it about. The beleaguered wood cutting party were left alone as Fetterman's troops approached, a small group of Sioux warriors riding just out of range to taunt the bluecoats. They then galloped away, infuriating Fetterman and causing him to give chase beyond the forbidden Lodge Trail Ridge. They were soon over the slopes and well out of sight of the fort.

Grummond's cavalry, filled with confidence at the sight of the Indians fleeing, cantered ahead, soon leaving Fetterman's foot soldiers several hundred yards behind. As these infantrymen reached the summit of a hill, they were able to look down upon their mounted comrades riding parallel to the Peno Creek on their left. Suddenly, the small party of retreating Sioux split into two groups, each one leaving the trail on either side. This was the signal that their fellow braves had been waiting for, for vast numbers of them (possibly in excess of 2,000) were hidden in the deep gullies all along the trail, many of them with their hands clamped over the noses of their ponies to keep them quiet. A blood curdling war whoop trilled from hundreds of Lakota throats as swarms of arrows darkened the sky, raining down upon the shocked troopers and their horses. Further back at the top of the hill, Fetterman must have felt a moment of sickening panic as he realised what he had gotten himself into.

There was no way out. Painted Sioux warriors, on foot as well as on horseback, were surging in on the two pitifully small groups of soldiers from every side. Already many of Fetterman's men had fallen, spitted with dozens of arrows. Grummond's surviving cavalrymen dismounted and attempted to form some kind of defence but their horses got away and they were hopelessly exposed. Cut off from their comrades, Fetterman, Brown and the infantry closed up in a tight group, standing back to back or huddling down in the snow. Just ahead of the cavalry, the civilians Fisher and Wheatley, both fine marksmen, crouched together and took a fearful toll with their sixteen shot repeating rifles but the final outcome of this mismatched battle was inevitable. One of the last to die was the bugler Adolph Metzger who was engulfed swinging his instrument like a club. A dog which had accompanied the troops from the fort was hit by several arrows as it ran yelping back along the trail. It appears that Fetterman and Brown had mutually agreed to place their revolvers at each other's temples to blow their brains out in unison. (This was a common final desperate act by soldiers fighting Indians when all hope was lost, preferable to the alternative of being taken alive and almost certainly tortured.)

The sound of the firing could be heard back at the fort only about a mile away and Carrington surmised that Fetterman must be in serious trouble. A relief force was sent out, with orders to exercise the utmost caution, and this left the fort so slimly defended that a concerted Sioux attack would have definitely overwhelmed the place. Fortunately, Red Cloud was not forward thinking enough for that and his braves contented themselves with chopping up what was left of Fetterman and his men. The relief column, under a sensible and courageous captain named Tenedor Ten Eyck, reached the sight of the massacre by taking a sweeping arc to the east. Ten Eyck observed the vast horde of braves in the valley who were obviously jubilant as they taunted and defied the distant soldiers, daring them to come down and fight. Waiting until the Sioux had tired of their celebrating, gradually withdrawing to the west, Ten Eyck finally reached the battle site as darkness was beginning to fall.

The horror of what greeted the relief force was extreme even by Indian standards. This time the Sioux had let loose with the full fury of the hatred and frustration they felt for the white man. The stripped corpses of Fetterman's command lay strewn across the slopes, naked and contorted in pools of frozen blood. Often it was hard to recognise the mangled shapes as having once been human beings. The trooper's faces had been pounded into jelly, their limbs had been cut off, private parts severed and their brains extracted from smashed skulls to be laid in almost ritualistic fashion on top of rocks, alongside extracted eyeballs. Some bodies had cross shapes carved into their chests and backs and Ten Eyck's men, making their way through the long snow covered grass, did not realise at first that they were walking on a carpet of human internal organs. Fisher and Wheatley were so mutilated that it was hard to tell one from the other. One of them resembled a pin cushion with 105 arrows protruding from virtually every part of his body. Strangely, one soldier's corpse remained almost intact save for the wounds which had caused his death, in fact, he had been treated with respect, his frozen body covered over with a buffalo robe. This was Bugler Metzger whose courage was apparently appreciated by the Lakota. (In the Jim Gatchell Museum at Buffalo, Wyoming, they actually have Metzger's bugle on display. Although it is heavily battered and squashed flat, the sight of the long dead trooper's improvised weapon is a most emotive experience.)

The dead were buried at Fort Phil Kearny on Christmas Day, but although the mourning was intense, the surviving inhabitants of the garrison knew that their own plight was desperate. With the fort in danger of attack at any time, Carrington knew that he must receive reinforcements if his command (along with their women and children) was to have any hope of further survival. A message would have to get through to Fort Laramie, 236 miles away to the south. In a gesture worthy of the most romantic images of the Old West, a scout named "Portugee" Phillips volunteered to try and get through and, amazingly, he succeeded. Mounted on Carrington's own horse, Phillips endured an epic ride in sub-zero temperatures, battling blizzards as he rode across hostile territory. Averaging sixty miles per day (double the expected rate for a horseman under *normal* conditions) the scout made it to Fort Laramie, bursting dramatically into the officer's festive ball and relating the dreadful news before collapsing. He spent months recovering from this ordeal and his horse died of exhaustion, but the monuments which stand today in the Powder River country pay homage to a true frontier hero.

*   *   *

Although Carrington was relieved and Fort Phil Kearny reinforced, all the forts that winter lay under a virtual state of siege by superior numbers of Indians who persisted in continuing with their attacks on travellers and harassment of army patrols. Following the Fetterman disaster, most troop commanders were extra cautious but no headway was being made by either side. The army had a couple of successes the following summer when small contingents of troopers, greatly assisted by their newly issued Springfield breech loading rifles, managed to beat off mass attacks of Red Cloud's braves inflicting heavy casualties at little cost to themselves. (The celebrated Hayfield and Wagon Box fights, excellent accounts of which can be found in numerous places.) These small victories helped to restore some of the army's pride which had been so violently lost the previous winter but the situation was still at stalemate. Finally, the U.S. government realised that the Bozeman Trail was simply not worth the trouble and in the Spring of 1868 they agreed to another treaty which promised the Sioux huge tracts of South Dakota, including the Black Hills, as well as exclusive hunting rights across the wilderness beyond the Republican and North Platte Rivers. In addition, the peace negotiators from Washington agreed to close the Bozeman Trail and abandon the hated forts. Red Cloud did not appear at Fort Laramie for these talks and said he would only sign the treaty once the trail forts were empty of white soldiers.

Fort Phil Kearny was at last closed down during that summer, the troops pulling out and leaving the ill fated stockade at the mercy of the Sioux. Whilst still in sight of their former garrison, the soldiers were able to look back on the wooden buildings, watchtowers and walls engulfed in flames as the jubilant Lakota warriors, whooping and dancing, applied the torch to this symbol of white aggression. That done, Red Cloud readily signed the treaty. He had won his war and vowed that he would not fight again. From then on he grew proud of his role as a man of peace.

However, Red Cloud, though a great chief, was far from being the only Sioux leader of influence. There would yet be much trouble on the Plains, much of it instigated by an ex-Union army cavalry officer who the Sioux and Cheyenne would come to know as Long Hair, Yellow Hair and Son-of-the-Morning-Star.

Captain Fetterman's troops over-run by the Lakota, December 21st. 1866.
(Painting by J.K.Ralston, reproduced by courtesy of Fort Phil Kearny/Bozeman Trail Association)

The battlefield in the 21st. Century, complete with monument.

THE BOY GENERAL

Clad in confederate grey, the officer was a big man, powerfully built, but his horse was a strong thoroughbred and carried its rider with swift ease. Hooves pounding the earth, they were leaving the battlefield at the gallop, no doubt determined to rally and fight another day. Here at White Oak Swamp, the Billy Yanks may have pulled off a small victory, breaking the rebel position, but the war was young; plenty of time yet to turn the tide.

Bent low over the saddle, the rebel officer glanced back over his shoulder as he rode, astounded to see that his relentless pursuer was still keeping pace with him. Ahead was a rail fence which his sturdy mount jumped effortlessly, but this was no obstacle to the dark uniformed Yankee whose own horse vaulted it without breaking step. A fine horseman, this Yankee. Long haired and determined, he called out to the retreating rebel, ordering him to halt but the big man galloped on. Maintaining his steady canter, the union officer raised his weapon and pulled the trigger but hitting a target on the move from a running horse was no easy feat. Still the Reb retreated.

Young Captain Custer gritted his teeth and refused to give up. This fleeing confederate was his quarry, to be hunted down like an animal. Concentrating hard and summoning up his deepest instinct and skills, Custer aimed again and let fly. This time the rebel jerked in the saddle, his horse broke step and stumbled and the big man fell. He hit the ground with a sickening thud but somehow managed to struggle to his feet, raising his hands before his legs buckled and he dropped again.

Custer galloped on by, chasing after the rider-less thoroughbred which he eventually caught and claimed as his own. It was a beautiful horse, saddled in expensive red and black morocco, the leather studded with silver trim. The previous owner had obviously been a man of means. Custer found his way back to the prone body of his victim who lay with blood trickling from his mouth. Bending down to pick up the dead rebel's sword, the youthful captain pondered for a moment over the Spanish inscription on the blade; "Draw me not without reason nor sheathe me without honour". This appealed to Custer's code. Considerably longer and wider than an average cavalry sabre, this sword was quite a prize, one of the spoils of war which Custer would treasure for the rest of his days.

War. It was the biggest love of his highly passionate and eventful life.

*   *   *

George Armstrong Custer began his earthly span modestly, born the first surviving child of a blacksmith/farmer's second marriage on December 5th. 1839 in the ground floor back bedroom of a simple log house in New Rumley, Ohio. This was an insular community and young George spent his early years taking on the mantle of a typical mid-West farm boy, roaming the hills and leading an active outdoor life. Early on, his childish mispronunciation of his middle name earned him the affectionate diminutive "Autie", a nickname which he would answer to in later life, but only from his closest family and friends. The Custer household was a full one, for Autie was soon joined by three younger brothers; Nevin, Thomas and Boston, and a sister, Margaret. (Along with offspring from his father's previous marriage.)

Although he was an impatient schoolboy who excelled in sports rather than academic pursuits, George was a popular figure whose sense of humour and love of practical jokes certainly got him noticed. Being the centre of attention was what drove him. He also quickly developed an abiding interest in all things military, attending drill meetings of the local militia with his father. Even as a small boy he was able to mimic soldierly movements with the aid of his wooden toy musket.

As a youth he was living in the town of Monroe, Michigan with his step sister, working for a while, aged sixteen, as a teacher before successfully applying to enter the famous military academy at West Point, an application significantly helped by the personal recommendation of a U.S. Congressman whom he had impressed. Becoming a cadet in July 1857, George Custer only took to certain areas of his intensive studies to become an officer and a gentleman. As a swordsman, marksman and horseman he could scarcely be bettered but, as at school, the academic side of things bored him, resulting in the accumulation of 726 demerits to his record. The archives of the academy show a long list of his numerous misdemeanours, including being late and boisterous, throwing bread in the mess hall, defacing walls, lounging about, having a long beard and hair at inspections, wearing un-authorized ornaments and so on. West Point's regime of rules was notoriously cloying and strict and many cadets were unable to stay the course, either being expelled or giving up, but Custer always had sense enough to keep himself just within the limits. Coming from simple stock, Autie made up for his shortcomings in the social elite with his bright, jokey personality and soon became a firm friend of most of his fellow cadets, many of whom were the sons of highly placed families within the upper strata of American society. These were connections which would serve him well in later life. He swore and drank outrageously as a student, (when he could get away with it) quite a contrast to his later life, but he always maintained his love for reading volumes of European military history and adventure tales of the distant frontier, a dreamlike place which he longed to visit. How apt that he would one day be more synonymous with the Wild West than just about anyone.

With the outbreak of the Civil War, the country naturally gave a great call to arms and the first to answer were those who had any kind of military experience. Cadets at West Point were faced with a dilemma, especially those who wished to join the Confederacy, for they had to leave their studies to join the secessionist South. Those who wished to join the Union were rushed through the final stages of their training, graduating and dashing off to war, thereby creating the poignant situation of friends facing each other across the battlefield. In June 1861, with the war only a few weeks old, Custer graduated 34th. in his class of 34, one year earlier than he, or the rest of his class, should have done, not exactly an auspicious start to his career, but the Union Army was desperate for properly trained officers and so he joined G Company of the 2nd. U.S. Cavalry as a 2nd. Lieutenant. One should not place too much emphasis on Custer's low grading in his class because he *did* graduate whereas many did not. Also, a note on his divided loyalty. Autie, like his father, was a Democrat through and through who actually was opposed to many aspects of President Lincoln's Republican administration. The young Custer was certainly no abolitionist and felt great sympathy for the Southern cause (indeed, many of his closest friends were Confederates) but his background was such that there was no way he could consider fighting against the Union.

Meeting his regiment on the very day that they played an active role in the first Battle of Bull Run (near Washington), Lt. Custer made an impression almost immediately and was cited for bravery in the field. From then on it was difficult to hold him back for he took to warfare with flair and enthusiasm and was always at the forefront of any engagement. Transferring to the 5th. Cavalry, he participated in the defence of the Union capital, Washington, fought in the Peninsular Campaign and joined the staff of General McClellan as his aide-de-camp, whereby he was promoted to captain. McClellan, who never saw eye to eye with Lincoln, was very fond of Autie who always seemed to be in the right place at the right time when the General needed impressing. (The volatile young officer may even have been involved in the rumblings of a plot to stage a treasonable *coup d'etat* to depose the president and replace him with McClellan.) When McClellan was dismissed by Lincoln, Custer was infuriated, especially as his rank was knocked back down to 1st. Lieutenant, but his star was still rising and he continued to impress a string of senior officers, becoming particular friends with the supreme cavalry commander General Phil Sheridan. At Williamsburg, Custer personally captured a confederate captain and five other rebels, along with a battle flag, all this during a daring daylight raid.

With the removal of McClellan, Custer was forced to take an extended leave and he kicked his heels in Monroe for a while, his frustration eased by the attention he lavished upon the second love of his life. This was the very pretty, demure, chestnut haired daughter of Judge Daniel Bacon, a girl who Autie had admired from afar for years. Her name was Elizabeth (although she was Libbie to him), and although she was highly flattered by the wooing of this dashing young cavalry officer, her father disapproved strongly of any kind of relationship, feeling that an army beau, especially the son of a humble blacksmith, was below his daughter. Judge Bacon actually forbade Elizabeth from contacting him but Custer, as in everything he did, was persistent.

Leaving his love life on hold, Custer was recalled into the Army of the Potomac, this time as aide-de-camp to General Pleasanton, who was a strong advocate of the use of cavalry, Custer's speciality. More battle honours followed and in July 1863, at the age of just 23, Autie was promoted again to the giddy heights of Brigadier General, one of the youngest ever to attain such a high rank in the U.S. Army. No sooner had he sewn on his General's stars than he was in action again, at the Battle of Gettysburg, the terrible struggle which turned the tide of the war against the Confederacy, paving the way to its eventual defeat. Custer, as usual, was prominent in the battle, helping to prevent the famous rebel General Jeb Stuart from attacking the Union rear.

Custer, as a newly appointed senior officer, was at first resented by many of the men under his command but, following his actions at Gettysburg, he quickly gained their respect. He had now been given command of the Michigan Cavalry Brigade (1st., 5th., 6th. and 7th. Regiments) and he called them his "Wolverines". Autie was becoming famous now for his exploits on the battlefield and he courted publicity wantonly. He was a born showman with a massive ego and loved to have himself photographed in an array of fancy uniforms. He actually designed his own military wear and favoured a black velveteen tunic, closely cut in Hussar style and decorated with huge swirls of gold braid. His broad collared shirts had a nautical look, his high rebel boots enhanced by golden Spanish spurs. As for his hats, they were always broad brimmed and sweeping, usually decorated with a garish plume. His real trademark, however, was the bright cherry red necktie he always wore, claiming that it made him easily recognisable to his men when in action. This soon became irrelevant when most of his Wolverines began wearing the same type of neckwear to show the admiration they felt for their courageous commander. "We swear by him," they would say, "his name is our battle cry". That name was a household word in the eastern cities where he was often featured in such prestigious publications as "Harper's Weekly". Whenever he was on leave, Custer was in constant demand as a guest at society functions and dinner parties. He loved every minute of it.

As a battlefield commander he always led from the front, usually bellowing out his war cry of, "Come on you Wolverines!" He seemed to lead a charmed life, for his men would fall in droves around him as he galloped through the shot and shell. Notorious for leading reckless, headlong sabre charges, his troops had one of the highest casualty rates in the Union Army, but still those men were proud to serve under him. He did not escape the war unscathed though, for he was wounded by shrapnel at Brandy Station and had several horses shot from under him. In the Shenandoah campaign he suffered a humiliating setback when his personal baggage train was captured and he lost virtually all his possessions save for the toothbrush he carried with him. The confederates delighted in poring through the letters they found, including copies of the sentimental love messages he had sent to Libbie. With cruel glee, the rebels had several of these mawkish letters printed in the Richmond newspapers to embarrass the Union's "Golden Boy" and take him down a peg or two. Unfazed, Custer was avenged some months later when he managed to capture the baggage train of rebel commander "Tex" Rosser, amusing his Wolverines by strutting around camp wearing the confederate's outsize uniform. Rosser was Custer's ex-room mate from West Point so Autie could not resist writing to him, saying, "instruct your tailor to cut the tails a little shorter next time"!

Nursing a leg wound back in Monroe, Custer was able to renew his pursuit of Libbie and this time Judge Bacon's attitude to the young hero Phil Sheridan was calling "the ablest man in the cavalry corps" had softened somewhat. Autie proposed, Libbie accepted and her father agreed, the marriage taking place in the bride's home town. It was a model wedding. February 9th. 1864 saw the couple hitched in the First Presbyterian Church, Monroe, with many important guests in attendance. Libbie looked gorgeous in a rich silk gown festooned with lace and flowers while her dashing new husband towered over her. Never did a man wear a dress uniform with more poise and style. Epaulettes and gold braid adorned his blue frock coat, well tailored to hug his tall, trim body. The effect was heightened by Custer's proud, handsome features, stalwart posture, piercing blue eyes, fashionable drooping moustache and thick, curly, reddish gold hair (treated with oil of cinnamon).

By now Custer had given up drinking (favouring milk at the dinner table) but he was still a social animal who lapped up the delights of their extended honeymoon. They travelled quite extensively; New York, Washington, Baltimore, and were feted wherever they showed up. Libbie was excited to meet Abraham Lincoln and various war heroes of her husband's acquaintance. The president made her smile when she expressed hope that her Autie would continue with his courageous exploits and he commented, "Then you want to be a widow, I see".

By nature, Custer was easily excitable, a man who would grow animated and passionate during heated conversations. His voice would gradually rise in pitch and he was known for his shrill laugh. In many ways he was larger than life, an image he strived to underline. His critics regarded him as absurd but they were far outnumbered by his numerous admirers. Even those who were not impressed by his flamboyance could not deny his undoubted courage. On the battlefield he was an inspiration to everyone, although his style of leadership was pure bravado depending greatly upon what came to be known as "Custer's Luck", a phenomenon which seemed to always carry him through. He trusted gut feeling all his life and used standard tactics only as a trimming for his unique style. Brave, yes; clever, no.

When in the cities of the east, the "Boy General" loved to visit the theatre and was an ideal member of any audience, for he would become wide eyed and openly emotional in all the right places. He would gasp and unashamedly weep, as well as laugh uproariously, especially at raucous comedians. After the war he would cultivate a close friendship with the renowned classical actor Lawrence Barrett. Autie was also greatly moved by music whether it be sentimental love ballads or stirring military marches.

However, at the root of all this showmanship and sensitivity, dwelt the heart of a ruthless disciplinarian and killer. When on campaign he drove his troops to the limits of endurance, but he was always there with them, leading by example, tireless and seemingly invincible. Although he was known to display dramatic sympathy at the side of dying soldiers, he did not hesitate when it came to crushing his adversaries, such as when he captured six of Col. John Mosby's confederate guerrilla fighters. Mosby, known as the "Grey Ghost", was a legendary figure who became a painful thorn in the side to the Union forces with his hit and run raids behind the lines, destroying communications, capturing supplies and generally causing havoc. Custer's answer to this was to create fear and shock by executing his prisoners. Infuriated, the normally humane Mosby ordered the execution of some of Custer's men in return.

And so the war raged on with Autie in the thick of it, until April 1865, when, after a final bloody struggle around Appomattox Courthouse, General Robert E. Lee surrendered the Confederate Army unconditionally. Sitting at a small, pinewood table, Lee and the Union commander, General Ulysses Grant, signed the necessary documents, putting to an end four years of horrific struggle which had torn the nation apart, leaving scars which would never heal.

As tensions eased and celebration coursed through the Union ranks, General Phil Sheridan purchased the table which had been used by Lee and Grant to sign the declaration of surrender, making a gift of this historic piece of furniture to his favourite young cavalry officer. This was a boy with a future, although what that might be was unclear at the present time. Sheridan dashed off a letter to Libbie in praise of her "very gallant husband".

As for Custer, he was heard to sigh, "war, glorious war".

A RISING STAR ON THE PLAINS

So, what now for the "Boy General" who had contributed so much to the winning of the war and now, it seemed, had no one left to fight? Initially, in the months following Appomattox, there were still a few cleaning up operations to be dealt with; odd renegade forces who refused to surrender or the general subjugation of resentful southerners as the victorious northern army occupied their homeland. However, this was small fry to the ambitious Custer who longed to see the continued ascendance of his acclaimed star.

Sheridan found a role for him quickly, despatching him to East Texas in command of 4,000 troops to keep the peace there. And so, Autie found himself stationed at Houston, close to San Jacinto where, just under thirty years before, General Sam had whipped Santa Anna and avenged The Alamo. There were still veteran Texians around who had fought there and doubtless Custer would have sought them out for their accounts of the famous fight. He always liked to hear the details of a good scrap. Libbie accompanied him and he did all he could to ensure the comfort of his wife, including supplying her with a curtained, sprung wagon.

By contrast, he was very hard on his men. They had a tough journey into Texas and were poorly supplied, but Custer strictly enforced his standards of discipline, insisting that they march in formation, fully equipped with their tunics buttoned to the neck. Many collapsed in the searing heat. Small misdemeanours were punished severely by with-holding pay, shaving heads and flogging, even though the use of the lash had been banned by Congress. As usual, Custer felt he was a law unto himself. Without combat to distract them, many of the rank and file under his command grew to hate him. Autie seemed indifferent to their griping, reserving all his concerns for Libbie or his pet dogs which he cherished as if they were children.

By the end of the year, the army of occupation was reduced considerably and most of the men were mustered out. For the majority this was hugely welcome, but not for Custer who had made the military his life. To make matters worse, his esteemed high rank as a Major-General had only been of Brevet status (meaning temporary) in the Volunteer Army. He was now forced to transfer to the Regular Army, losing his rank (plus having to accept a huge reduction in pay) and becoming a mere captain again. This was a devastating blow to Custer's ego, even though it was inevitable, and he left Texas, with his adoring Libbie in tow, to try and seek inspiration for his future in New York. Sending Libbie back to Monroe to await the announcement of his plans, Autie toyed with the idea of leaving the Army, but not for long. There were veiled promises of various jobs in the government but it was obvious where his heart lay.

A more interesting offer came from south of the border where Juarista rebels were fighting to rid their country of the Austrian puppet leader Maximillian who had been installed forcibly by the French as Emperor of Mexico. Impressed by Custer's glowing war record, the rebels offered to make him a Major-General again, commanding their forces in the struggle. Such an opportunity to fight as a mercenary was attractive to Custer. Adventure and action again, plus a handsome financial reward for his services, but it would mean permission for a year's leave of absence from the U.S. Army. Despite a recommendation from General Grant, President Johnson (Lincoln having been assassinated by a confederate sympathiser) would not let Custer go.

Custer's disappointment was short lived, for Sheridan had been campaigning on his behalf. At last, an outlet had been found for this restless soldier's talents, a role which he had been born to. He was to be sent out west, to that distant frontier he had dreamed of since a boy, re-instated as a senior officer to command a new horse regiment which was being formed to meet the only surviving threat to the fledgling U.S. government and their plans for expansion.

George Armstrong Custer was to lead the 7th. Cavalry.

*   *   *

Autie was delighted and headed west without delay. He was given field command of the 7th. on the day the regiment was formed; July 28th. 1866 at Fort Riley, Kansas, a distant outpost which bordered the relentless, dusty plains. The fort was a last ditch kicking off point before plunging into the dangers of Colorado and the unknown wastes which led to the West Coast. Coyotes howled in the darkness and hostile Indians were always looking for a chance to lift your hair but the 7th.'s new commander was more than ready to meet the challenge.

Having long agitated for an active service command, Custer's only concern was that he be given a white regiment. During and since the Civil War, several units of the U.S. Army had been formed exclusively from Negro recruits, and cavalry regiments like the 9th. and 10th. (all black save for the officers) were being sent to the frontier. The Indians called them "buffalo soldiers", probably because of their woolly black hair, similar to the bison's, and the fact that their black skin resembled the teat of a buffalo cow. Custer's attitude to race was not untypical of the times he lived in, in fact, he was more enlightened than most. He said, patronisingly by today's standards, of course, that he was in favour of the Negro improving his lot but not at the expense of the progress of the white race. Consequently, he only wished to ride at the head of white troops. That said, regardless of his devotion to Libbie, he was not averse, according to heavy rumour, to sleeping with his black cook.

The 7th. Cavalry contained no black skinned troopers but it was largely made up of mixed nationalities. Many newly arrived immigrants from Europe joined up, often out of desperation and using anglicised false names, therefore the ranks were filled with men from Ireland, Germany and numerous other countries, quite a few of whom could barely speak English. Others might be New York city toughs or shady characters on the run from the law, so they were a mixed bunch, not all of whom would be welcome at your grandmother's house for tea! A lot of them were battle hardened Civil War veterans, both Union and Confederate, who re-enlisted either in the hope of adventure or simply because they had nothing else to do. In return they were plunged into a hostile environment and allotted cramped, bare, draughty living quarters, atrocious, inadequate food and harsh discipline. With women in short supply and routine on the outpost being mind numbingly dull, it is little wonder that alcoholism became a major problem, for officers as well as enlisted men.

Custer immediately applied himself to knocking this motley crew into some kind of shape. He would not tolerate sloppiness and engaged his notorious iron hand without mercy. Not being a drinker himself, he tried to enforce prohibition but it was a hopeless task. If the men could not obtain conventional drinks they merely turned to distilling their own hair raising concoctions, raw alcohol flavoured with just about anything, the results of which were worse than plain whisky.

Custer drilled his men relentlessly, determined to make fine horse soldiers of them, and woe betide any recruit who failed to measure up to his expectations. His punishments were as harsh as ever, including outlawed flogging, branding and the wearing of a crippling ball and chain. Men were sometimes spread-eagled to the ground and left for hours, tormented by insects and begging for mercy. Others might be hung by the thumbs or "bucked and gagged" which involved trussing the victim's arms and legs together behind his back with a rough stick crammed between his teeth. Hardly surprisingly, the desertion rate from the 7th. Cavalry (and other frontier units) reached epidemic proportions with men disappearing in droves.

Although his rank was now officially that of Lieutenant Colonel, Custer was mostly still referred to as "General", a normal practice in respect of the highest rank he had achieved in a brevet capacity. His hard pressed cavalrymen, however, had several whispered names of their own for him, usually confined to the barrack room; "Hard Ass" being but one.

The wind whipped across the raw landscape but Libbie Custer was content enough, glad to be at her adored Autie's side and putting the finishing touches to the cosy house she shared with him. It had a large parlour and lots of rooms which she decorated with lace curtains, multi coloured carpets and cane furniture. A welcoming fire was usually flickering in the grate, creating a cheerful atmosphere for the long evenings when she, Autie, favoured officers and friends would indulge in civilized parlour games like table croquet or sang popular songs together. On quieter occasions, she might indulge in some needlework while the "General" worked at his desk, often poring over his books on British military history or Napoleon's campaigns. All this while the common troops drank themselves stupid or fought amongst themselves to alleviate the boredom.

It was not long before the famous factionalising of the regiment became evident, although it would be some time before definite sides were established. Owing to his methods, Custer was soon hated by many of his men but there were also quite a number who idolised him. He formed a strong base of loyal supporters which grew as the years progressed. For instance, he brought to Fort Riley his brother Tom, five years his junior, and they were particularly close. Tom was also a Civil War veteran, although he was not a West Pointer, instead having enlisted in the Ohio infantry as a private, working his way up through the ranks and becoming his brother George's aide-de-camp until the war ended. While not being quite as flamboyant as Autie, Tom made a considerable impression as a fighting soldier, brevetted a major in 1865 and being awarded the Medal of Honour twice for gallant conduct in separate engagements where he captured confederate battle flags. On the second occasion he boldly leaped his horse over the enemy breastworks and survived being shot in the face. Appointed 1st. Lieutenant in the 7th. Cavalry, Tom could obviously be relied upon by Autie. The younger brother even had his own room at the top of the stairs in the Custer household.

Another officer who joined the regiment on the day it was formed and quickly became a close Custer confidante was William Cooke. Cooke was a Canadian by birth, hailing from Ontario, and he was twenty years of age when he arrived at Fort Riley with the rank of 2nd. Lieutenant. He had served in the war between the States in the New York Volunteer Cavalry and was wounded at Petersburg where he distinguished himself. This young Canadian, tall, well built and athletic made himself popular at his frontier posting with his sporting prowess. He was apparently a very fast runner and a crack shot, one of the best in the regiment. These talents would be of use in the various competitions which were often staged to pass the time. Cooke was also famed for his splendid whiskers which fell luxuriantly from his cheeks to his chest leaving only his chin bare.

By contrast, Capt. Frederick Benteen was far from being an admirer of the Boy General, in fact he became one of Custer's most ardent critics. And yet he was in a position of greater authority than most because he rode with the 7th. Cavalry from its earliest days through to its great disaster at the Little Bighorn and beyond. He, therefore, would be in an undisputed position to form a well observed opinion of his commanding officer. It was not a glowing one, as we shall see. Benteen was a mature officer of considerable experience by the time he joined the 7th. in 1866, in fact at 31 he was five years older than George Custer. A Virginian, Fred Benteen was working as a house painter in St. Louis when the Civil War broke out, consequently enraging his father's Southern sympathies by enlisting in a Union Volunteer Cavalry unit. He came up the hard way, his battle honours proving to be excessive and impressive and he ended the war with the rank of colonel, briefly commanding the 138th. Coloured Infantry. Time and again he proved himself to be a most capable officer and a fine leader of men. Assigned to Custer's brand new 7th. Cavalry as a captain the two men's personalities clashed almost immediately. Benteen had a deep distrust and dislike of Autie which went back to when he had known him during the war. Custer responded by treating him with caution. Physically, Benteen's appearance was deceiving. He was quite a thick set man whose pleasant, jovial features gave an impression of boyishness, for he looked younger than his years. Clean shaven with a heavy thatch of prematurely white hair, only his eyes seemed to occasionally betray a harder side to his character. Popular with the troops, who saw him as steady, fair, reliable and a trusted leader, Benteen enjoyed his pipe, gambling and only indulged in occasional heavy drinking bouts. That said, there is much evidence of his jealous nature and his ability to whip up a storm. He was to become a leading player in the saga of the Little Bighorn.

Also pro-Custer was Capt. Myles Keogh, a rough, tough Irishman whose dark, macho sexuality made the lady's heart's flutter. Keogh had lived a colourful life even before he arrived in the U.S.A., having been born in 1840 in County Carlow, Southern Ireland. As a teenager his adventurous spirit inspired him to roam the world as a soldier of fortune and he found his way, via Africa, to Italy where he was appointed a 2nd. Lieutenant in the Battalion of St. Patrick of the Papal Guard. He spent several months as part of the Vatican's army in Rome and was personally awarded a Pro Petri Sede medal by the Pope. He proudly wore this award around his neck on a thong for the rest of his life. Also in recognition of his services he received the Cross of the Order of St. Gregory. Eventually he went to England, boarding a ship in Liverpool with three Irish companions before arriving in New York, U.S.A., in April 1862. Keogh had been drawn there by the thrill of action in the Civil War and as an experienced soldier he was quickly utilised by the Union army. Soon he was serving on the staff of cavalry brigade commander General Buford and spent the remainder of the war in the thick of the fighting, battling his way through over thirty engagements and being brevetted a Lieutenant Colonel. The war over, he spent a brief period in the 4th. Cavalry before being assigned to the 7th. Cavalry upon its formation in 1866. As already inclinated, he was a handsome devil with animal magnetism and piercing eyes, although his broad Irish brogue and sometimes abusive manners could be alarming. Commanding Company I, he drank hard and treated his men roughly, often lashing out at them with his silver handled, stout swagger stick if they displeased him. These troopers developed accordingly so it is perhaps appropriate that they came to be known as the "Wild I".

It is quite likely that Keogh made the original suggestion for the stirring Irish jig *Garry Owen* to be the 7th.'s official regimental tune although Custer himself may have been familiar with it already as it was a popular piece generally with troops during the Civil War. The song itself dated back to the previous century, originating in the town of Garry Owen in the suburb of Limerick, Ireland, where it was taken up by the Royal Irish Regiment and became their marching tune during the Napoleonic War. Being a highly infectious snatch of music, *Garry Owen* with its jolly bounce and lyrics about drinking and running wild, became known to soldiers everywhere, notably in the Crimea. Custer grew particularly fond of it and to this day it seems its familiar notes will be forever associated with the 7th. Cavalry riding off to do battle with the Redskins.

*   *   *

Custer had been sent to mould his 7th. Cavalry in direct response to the Indian problems which were simmering steadily all over the Southern Plains. Regardless of an eventual new agreement, the Medicine Lodge Treaty, which gave the usual assurances of reservation land and supplies, this time specifically for the Southern tribes (i.e. the

Kiowa, Arapaho, Comanche and Southern Cheyenne), the young bucks were often out of control. Pioneers were being attacked, white women and children taken hostage, homesteads and stagecoach stations burned. Work on the progress of the Kansas-Pacific Railroad was being delayed by constant harassment of surveyors and line layers and it was not unknown for the hostiles to have succeeded in derailing trains.

Further north Red Cloud's Sioux had won their temporary victory and the U.S. Government was content to let them be for now, but official policy in Kansas was being disrupted to such an extent that Washington decided that something must be done. Still smarting from the shock of the previous year's Fetterman massacre, and just prior to the Medicine Lodge Treaty, the U.S. Army took to the field under the command of Major General Winfield Hancock with the intention of subjugating the Lakota's allies before any large scale uprising could take place.

In the spring of 1867, Hancock set off on a punitive expedition leading some 1,400 troops which included infantry, artillery and Custer's 7th. Cavalry, along with a couple of journalists for good measure. With their clattering, creaking wagons and general demeanour of chaos, this lumbering army made an awful commotion as it blundered across the prairie seeking an elusive foe. The problem was that neither Hancock nor hardly any of his men had any real experience of dealing with Indians. This was a new kind of enemy and could hardly be compared to the sweeping battle formations of the recently ended Civil war, the kind of conflict most of these troops were used to. Indians rarely faced their opponents in open battle order. Their methods involved swift hit and run raids, flurries of action, "cut and slash" before melting away into the depths of the wilderness.

To the likes of Custer this was immensely frustrating but he soon learned the ways of the frontier. He realised that success against these hostiles would depend upon changing methods accordingly, largely by playing them at their own game. Tireless as ever, Autie seemed to thrive on barely any sleep, always pushing to the front and never sitting back on his laurels. Often he would ride far ahead of the column, putting himself at great risk but seemingly oblivious to danger. He even adopted a new mode of dress to suit his latest role, taking to wearing a heavily fringed buckskin jacket, although he still kept his trademark cherry-red neck tie. Bounding along beside him, as he cantered through the sage brush, came five of his favourite hounds. On one such jaunt, when he recklessly left the column to single-handedly chase a buffalo, he accidentally shot his own horse and found himself lost, alone and afoot on the open prairie. Only a huge dose of "Custer's Luck" enabled him to be rescued!

On this expedition, Custer found a kindred spirit who would drift in and out of his life to the end. The famed "Wild Bill" Hickok, working as a deputy marshal at Fort Riley, was assigned to Hancock as a civilian scout. This notorious frontier legend had already gained quite a reputation for himself as a Union guide during the war, hunter, gambler, tracker and Indian fighter but, most of all, as a deadly shootist. Hickok's prowess with a revolver had been earned genuinely and he was probably one of the few Western household names who truly deserved his renown. He had often worked for the army, retrieving stolen horses for them as well as tracking down deserters, which in itself could be a full time job. Custer was impressed by Wild Bill's style and was, perhaps, influenced by him, for the scout was tall and slender with shoulder length, well groomed hair and a flowing moustache. He also favoured broad brimmed hats and flamboyant dress and seems to have shared more than a hint of Custer's ego. That said, Hickok was said to be calm and collected unless riled. Autie described him as " ...a plainsman in every sense of the word, yet unlike any other of his class". Libbie, spoiled for choice in a man's world, went further for she was to later describe this gun fighting cavalier thus; "Physically he was a delight to look upon ... fantastically clad ... his word was law ..." and so on. One can imagine her swooning over him!

Hickok spent most of that summer's campaign riding back and forth with dispatches, whilst he and his fellow scouts tracking efforts were frustrated by Hancock's slow moving army. Hancock met with some chiefs, offending them with his officious, unbending warnings and they fled, leaving him to burn a deserted village. For several weeks, he sent Custer and the 7th. on a series of wild goose chases, for the nimble Cheyenne were always one step ahead of them, dispersing and reforming, almost making a mockery of the army's efforts to pin them down. Custer had a parley or two with a Sioux chief named Pawnee Killer who had allied himself with the Cheyenne, but the words were empty. Pawnee Killer showed his true colours by ambushing and wiping out a ten man detail of the 2nd. Cavalry who were carrying new orders to Custer. On the face of it, the 7th. had failed, but in actual fact they kept the hostiles on the move and Autie was learning all the time.

As a result of this hopeless expedition, Hancock was humiliated, withdrawing from the frontier and leaving Custer to hold general sway over the western outposts. Hancock was replaced by Phil Sheridan, Custer's mentor, who became Commander of the Department of the Missouri, meaning that he was now responsible for the Indian situation on the Plains. Sheridan was a "no nonsense" member of the top brass. Although physically small with a strangely shaped head and stumpy legs, "Little Phil" (as he was known) was intense, short tempered and authoritative, believing in solving the Indian problem by ruthless subjugation of the tribes. He had come straight from his post in charge of reconstruction in Texas and Louisiana where he had dealt with ex-confederates and their sympathisers just as harshly. The expression "The only good Indian is a dead Indian" is attributed to Little Phil although that is not strictly what he said when facetiously responding to a Comanche chief's claim to be good. He actually said, "The only good Indians I ever saw were dead", and even that was a derivation of a statement previously made by a U.S. Congressman. However, he did grumpily agree that the Plains Indians were proving to be the "finest light cavalry in the world".

The Medicine Lodge Treaty solved next to nothing and Custer resolved to continue his fruitless pursuit of phantom-like war parties. He tried hard to catch his prey, desperate for a showdown so that he could come into his own, but the light and agile Indian ponies could easily outrun those heavy cavalry mounts. In the meantime, unfortunate white folk caught in the open carried on losing their hair. Public opinion seethed against the Indians and uninformed agitators were demanding to know why these "heathen savages" were being permitted to carry on with their atrocities. The supreme Commander of the Army, ex-Civil War giant General William Tecumseh Sherman, was already hinting to the Secretary of War in Washington that the solution could only lie in the total extermination of the Indian's way of life.

That summer, Custer's rising star was stopped abruptly, if temporarily, by a couple of incidents which were a direct result of his impetuous and arrogant nature. Leaving Libbie at Fort Hays, he set off on another foray against the Southern Cheyenne, this time chasing them around western Kansas and down the Republican River into Colorado. Pushed as hard as ever by their golden haired "General", the cavalrymen responded with their customary grumbling. Some of them decided they had suffered enough, deciding instead to take their chances on the open prairie, preferring to face hostile scalping knives than another day under "Hard Ass". Although the rate of desertion in the 7th. was shockingly high (about 500 men in a single year), this campaign actually saw the disappearance of 10% of Custer's column. Out of 350 men, this was an unacceptable figure, especially on active service, and so an infuriated Custer came down on them harder than ever. Determined to make an example of one particular group (about a dozen strong) who deserted camp en-masse, Autie sent a squad in pursuit with orders to bring them back "dead or alive".

Leading this vengeful troop was one Maj. Joel Elliott, a senior officer and Custer favourite, who the "General" knew would carry out his task satisfactorily. Elliott was an aggressive officer who tracked his prey to the Platte River where six of them were caught on foot, the rest managing to escape. According to Capt. Benteen, who witnessed the incident, three of these men resisted arrest and were shot down by Elliott, Custer's little brother Tom and Lt. Cooke. Apparently, one of them was fired upon while pleading for his life. Brought back to camp, these wounded troopers were crying out so much that Custer himself threatened them with his revolver, saying he would shoot any man who did not cease his noise immediately. "Hard Ass" indeed! It had the desired result though, because there were no further desertions on that particular expedition.

This caused considerable murmurings of disapproval in the ranks, even amongst some of the officers, but Custer was unperturbed and continued with his Indian hunting. Depositing his wounded prisoners at Fort Wallace, where one of them died, he was given a message from Fort Hays which had suffered a flash flood, the normally dry creek having a risen level of over thirty feet of raging water. There were rumours of cholera too and apparently there had been fatalities. Custer was horrified and concerned for Libbie's safety. Unable to contact her, he straightaway left his command and galloped off with an escort of 75 men to find out what had happened. Of course, this was a severe abuse of his authority, and in many ways was similar to desertion, but it was typical of Custer's attitude that he was a law unto himself.

If the men felt they had been pushed hard before, it was nothing compared to this. With his beloved wife's life in jeopardy, Autie was making allowances for no one. Taking army provisions, he rode like the wind, commandeering two mail coaches he met on the trail and illegally searching the post bags in case they contained a letter from Libbie. Exhausted troopers began to lag behind and the renegade column was stretched out for miles. A sergeant was sent back with a squad to gee up these stragglers and found itself attacked by a large Cheyenne war party, but Custer seemed indifferent to everything except getting back to Fort Hays with brother Tom and the faithful Canadian Cooke at his side.

Reaching Hays he was distressed to find Libbie absent so, desperate, he carried on to Fort Harker and then by train to Fort Riley where the loving couple were finally reunited. Relieved to find her safe, along with her dramatic account of surviving the flood, Custer no doubt spent some blissful time with his Libbie but he was to get a rude awakening. Even Sheridan would not come to his rescue this time. He was guilty of flagrant dereliction of duty, a most serious offence.

Arrested on several charges including "absenting himself from his command without proper authority" and ordering the shooting of deserters without trial, the authorities knew that, regardless of his past glowing record, no ranking officer could be allowed to behave in such a manner and get away with it. Benteen, no doubt gleefully, was amongst those who testified at the court martial hearing, the result of which was that Lt. Col. George Armstrong Custer was sentenced to be suspended from his rank and command for a period of one year without pay.

Many, including General Ulysses Grant, thought this penalty to be surprisingly lenient but, typically, Custer himself was indignant, insisting that the charges were unjustified and that he should have been acquitted.

WASHITA

There followed a frustrating period for Custer but he decided to make the best of it. He must have known in his heart that they could not do without him on the frontier for long and so he bided his time, resting up back in Monroe leading a leisurely social life with Libbie. He was so famous by now the Custers were never short of party invitations. Holding court to an adoring audience was still a favourite past time and Autie enjoyed regaling his many admirers with colourful tales of adventure fighting rebels and savages. He also began making notes for his memoirs. This was a little premature perhaps, as he was still only 28 years old, but it had been an eventful life, to date, and, in any case, he had plenty to say in the magazine articles he was constantly being commissioned to write.

The months passed swiftly. Early in 1868 Custer received a telegram from Sheridan which made it clear that the 7th. Cavalry would be spearheading a major campaign against the hostiles by the autumn. Little Phil also stressed that it was his intention that Custer, by then, should be back at the head of his regiment. Feeling that enough time had elapsed for Autie to have been forgiven his misdemeanours, Sheridan issued official orders for the volatile "General" to rejoin the 7th. and whip them back into shape for a showdown with the Indians.

Determined to redeem himself, Custer hurried back to Fort Hays where he took over from Maj. Elliott who had been given temporary command. Standards in the 7th. had slackened somewhat during Custer's absence, but he wasted no time in re-stamping his authority and troopers were soon jumping to and fro. This re-awakened old resentments and grudges. Benteen, in particular, must have cursed openly on Custer's return, but Autie was pleased to find that another old friend had joined the regiment. Capt. George Yates, commanding the 7th.'s Co. F, who, like his C.O., had fought at Bull Run and Gettysburg and had been attached to General Pleasanton's Staff. Yates had been one of the first to congratulate Custer on his appointment to Major General. More power to the "Custer Club".

Throughout the year, the Southern Cheyenne and Kiowa had been making a thorough nuisance of themselves with their perpetual raiding and the Army high command was heartily sick of it. They were under constant pressure to solve the problem and Sherman and Sheridan decided a decisive blow must be struck. As their instrument of destruction they chose Custer. They made it clear that the southern tribes needed a lesson. Peace efforts had been exhausted and annihilation of the hostiles and total suppression of reservation Indians was the only course left open. Sherman said that he would do nothing to restrain the troops from doing whatever they deemed necessary and would defend their actions with his whole authority. Sheridan agreed, so this, in effect, was giving Custer a totally free hand to mount an assault however he saw fit. This suited his style perfectly.

Winter was approaching, a time when activity usually grew quiet on the frontier. As a rule, the Indians would settle down in their camps, battening down the tepee flaps. It was a time for reflection, the warriors wrapping themselves in buffalo robes, surviving on pemmican, telling tales and looking forward to the springtime when they could resume hunting and raiding. A great concentration of these Indians had gathered to make their winter camp on the banks of the Washita River in the Indian Territory (modern day Oklahoma), thousands of braves, old men, squaws and children with all their animals and paraphernalia, stretching for over ten miles along the water's edge. Several tribes had come together here but they were well spread out; Arapaho, Comanche, Kiowa, some Apache, and, of course, the mischievous Southern Cheyenne, all largely minding their own business. It was time to take the war to the hostile's doorstep.

Custer's specific target was the Southern Cheyenne, and the group he found happened to be under Black Kettle. There was a great irony in this for the old chief was the same tribal leader whose village had suffered that horrific attack by the "Bloodless 3rd." at Sand Creek. Black Kettle had narrowly escaped with his life that fateful day, the experience of which you would think may have eliminated any hopes he had of peace with the white race. Strangely, he still retained optimism regarding bloodless settlements which means he was either naive or a philanthropist. Whatever, he had no reason to suspect that his band would be attacked again that winter.

The snow lay thick on the ground as Custer's troops approached in the early morning darkness. It was November 27th., almost exactly four years since Sand Creek (which had taken place on November 29th.) in virtually the same snow bound conditions. The troopers of the 7th. shivered in their saddles as they watched a bright morning star herald the dawn. A cloying ground fog obscured their vision, but they knew the Cheyenne lodges lay before them, quiet and peaceful. Custer had demanded total silence during the approach, even ordering the execution of the various dogs which had accompanied the regiment all the way from the fort. To Autie this was a deadly serious business for he found it in his heart to spare just one of his own beloved hounds, his favourite, Blucher, named after Wellington's Prussian ally at Waterloo. Throat cutting and strangling would ensure that no barking or whining would alert these sleeping Indians.

Ignoring the other Indian villages, most of which he was unaware of, the "General" split his command of over 700 men, directing them to various points so that the lodges were totally surrounded. There could have been no more than 150 Cheyenne warriors in the camp and Custer probably knew this, acting on information received from his scouts, men like sombrero wearing California Joe and a dozen friendly Osages. As the first grey light fell upon the lodge poles, Autie gave the command to attack. The 7th.'s buglers sounded the charge and the long lines of cavalrymen surged forward. Yelling triumphantly they bore down upon the tepees, riddling them with bullets while above it all came an incongruous sound, the jolly strains of *Garry Owen*, played as if on a parade ground by the regiment's own brass band. Only for few minutes, though, for the instruments soon froze up.

67 year old Black Kettle must have thought it was deja-vu. Along with the rest of his people he stumbled blearily from his lodge into a panorama of death and destruction. Caught completely by surprise the Cheyenne braves attempted to resist as best they could but the battle was already won. A few troopers were shot or dragged from their saddles (including a young captain who was the grandson of U.S. statesman Alexander Hamilton) and Custer's dog, Blucher, running along with the troops was skewered by an arrow, but none of this hindered the charge of the 7th. Cavalry. Lt. Cooke commanded a team of specially selected sharpshooters who positioned themselves on the north bank of the river to fire upon any fugitives. Capt. Benteen, at the head of his company, had his horse shot from under him. Struggling to his feet out of the blood stained snow, the white haired officer took aim and dropped the retreating Indian who had laid him low. Later it was discovered that this youthful Cheyenne marksman was one of Black Kettle's nephews.

Black Kettle himself attempted to escape again. Leaping onto his pony, he dragged his wife up in front of him and tried to make it across the river but they were hit by a fusillade of shots which peppered their backs. After the battle the old chief and his woman were found lying together beneath the icy water.

The main part of the fight was over in minutes but shots continued to be heard for a long time afterwards. Warriors were still sniping from cover as troopers fanned out to hunt them down. Maj. Elliott, as reckless as ever, took off with just under a score of men in pursuit of some fleeing Indians and was soon out of sight, an act of ill conceived madness which would prove to be his undoing.

The soldiers were now working their way through the devastated village, exploiting the spoils of war. Over a hundred Cheyenne had been slain but the vast majority of them were non-combatants. Although the level of atrocity was nowhere near as bad as that carried out at Sand Creek, the churned up, reddened slush was still littered with the corpses of infants, women and the elderly. Many weapons were found, hundreds of buffalo robes, finely crafted native artefacts and sacks of flour carrying government stamps. Custer selected a beautifully crafted white tepee as a personal souvenir. Some of the officers and a few men managed to conceal a selection of prime pieces but the "General" gave the command that all Indian property was to be burned. The Osage scouts were allowed to take their pick of this crop and their ponies were soon draped with ornaments and the fresh scalps of the Cheyenne dead.

A huge herd of hundreds of Cheyenne ponies (and some mules) had been secured. Custer allowed his officers and scouts to choose any they wanted to keep, plus about fifty more were set aside to transport the captured women and children, then Autie assigned a grim task to 1st. Lt. Edward Godfrey. This amount of frisky Indian animals would prove too hard to handle and nobody wanted them to fall back into enemy hands. A Plains Indian without his mount was a fraction of the man he could be. Moreover, Custer, following Sheridan's directive, was determined to teach these "upstart Redskins" a lesson and so he ordered Godfrey to supervise the slaughter of the entire herd. Even following in the wake of the massacre of the Cheyenne themselves, there is something particularly chilling and ghastly about the spectacle of so many dumb beasts being methodically killed. Apparently it was no easy task. At first, the troopers set about them with axes and knives, but the terrified ponies and mules reared and kicked, letting out terrible brays and whinnies of distress. Exasperated, his men blood spattered and exhausted, Godfrey brought in reinforcements to shoot the remainder of these poor creatures.

Once again, justification for such an attack on a sleeping village was found by the production of hostile evidence. Soldiers said they had discovered white scalps and clothing. It was not good enough for Black Kettle to advocate peace whilst harbouring braves who went raiding when it suited them. Also, a captive white woman and her little son, who were the subject of ongoing negotiations, were found that day freshly murdered, apparently struck down out of spite as the 7th. Cavalry advanced. However, it was never made exactly clear where these unfortunate civilians were found and it is possible that they were killed by the Kiowa some miles away.

Those lodges not already burning were dragged down, the poles being used as the kindling for large bonfires, into the flames of which were thrown numerous articles of Cheyenne origin. Robes, delicately woven beaded clothing, artwork, shields, bows, quivers, lances, leggings and food ..... it was soon all reduced to smouldering ash. Terrible wanton destruction which saddened more than one of the watching troopers, but "war is hell" and "Hard Ass" had to have his way. As the flames raged around him, Custer amused himself by taking pot-shots at the unfortunate captured ponies or any whimpering Indian dog which happened to scurry by.

In all the confusion, it seems no one paid much attention to the whereabouts of Maj. Elliott and his small command. Several hours had now elapsed since they had disappeared, whooping and galloping along the river bank, and no sign of them had been seen since. Eventually, various officers began to voice some concern and the pre-occupied Custer finally sent out a search party. When this squad failed to find anything, Autie gave orders to leave the area. In his defence, it was later said that increased Indian activity in the vicinity prevented any further search, but the rank and file of the 7th. felt differently. As the troops pulled out, there was a great rumbling of discontentment at the notion that Elliott and his men had been left to their fate.

Sheridan was jubilant about Custer's success at the Washita and told him so, emphasising that it reflected the "highest credit" on the regiment. Within two weeks, Little Phil himself had joined Custer's column so that he could see firsthand how things were shaping up. Autie took him on a personal tour of the now deserted Washita battleground, explaining his strategy in great detail. Sheridan appeared suitably impressed, then word came that one of the search parties had found something just east of the river.

Elliott's men lay in a tight circle, naked, frozen and abused in the usual way. Beheaded, sliced, dismembered. The major himself had been shot three times in the head and his right hand and genitals were missing. It seems that their wild chase had ended abruptly with more than they had bargained for. Alerted by the attack on the Cheyenne village, many warriors from the other Indian settlements along the Washita had rushed to the sound of the firing and Elliott had run smack into them. Largely consisting of enraged Arapahos, these newly arrived braves swiftly enveloped a score of troopers.

This unfortunate episode was to become an ugly blot on Custer's glittering career, much worse than his court martial, for it was felt by many that he had not done anything like enough for Elliott. Bad reconnaissance, indifference, self indulgence, glory hunting; Autie would have all these accusations levelled at him, but he parried them in his usual way. If he felt any guilt at all, he never openly showed it.

ONWARD THE SEVENTH

Although there were many chases, skirmishes and isolated incidents, the Washita attack was the only significant armed clash Custer ever had with Indians until his final fatal encounter at Little Bighorn, a fact which may seem surprising. This was quite a contrast to his eventful Civil War career and might make the casual observer wonder why he earned such a reputation as a seasoned Indian fighter. Well, from 1866 he certainly gained a great deal of experience on the frontier and personally found himself in regular close contact with the various tribes. He was keenly interested in their ways and, regardless of his ruthlessness, appears to have possessed respect for their culture. More than once he stated that if he were born a Sioux or Cheyenne, he would resist and fight for his traditional way of life as they were doing. As a fine horseman himself, Autie admired the Plains Indian's mounted skills and became quite adept at communicating by sign language. He would have loved to have had the opportunity to face his colourful foe in open battle more often but they were generally too elusive for him, as we have already seen.

Immediately following Washita, Sheridan stressed that the army must press home its advantage. A couple more heavy strikes on villages should do the trick, he said, and succeed in terminating the problem of hostiles under his jurisdiction. As it happened, this did not prove to be necessary. Custer showed a more diplomatic side to his volatile nature by making peaceful overtures to the scattered tribal groups.

Locating some other Cheyenne villages, Autie managed to negotiate a meeting with a few of the chiefs. Incredibly, he agreed to attend this "pow wow" accompanied only by Lt. Cooke (who by now had been appointed Custer's adjutant), which was highly courageous of him considering the destruction and death he had just meted out at Black Kettle's camp. What a picture this conjures up. The two brash cavalry officers riding jauntily through the teeming lodges, surrounded on every side by malevolent warriors who would gladly hack them down at the slightest provocation. I think we can assume that the steely Custer would not have betrayed the slightest hint of apprehension, aloof in his saddle as he looked down his nose at the morose braves and their squaws. The Cheyenne may have been intrigued by Cooke's especially fine flowing whiskers which he was so proud of, but was he aware that this image had gained white soldiers the Indian name "Dog Faces"?

Custer smoked a ceremonial pipe with the chiefs and indicated that further bloodshed would not take place, provided the tribes ceased all hostility and returned to their allotted reservations in the Indian Territory. The chiefs mumbled, showing their distrust. In sign language they made it clear that if "Long Hair" broke his word they would kill him and all his other "Dog Face" soldiers. One of them symbolically emptied the ashes from the peace pipe over Custer's boot to curse him with ill fortune.

This insult and warning cut little ice with the "General", but his brave foray into the inner sanctum of the hostiles seemed to bear results. For the remainder of the Winter and throughout 1869, Indian trouble across the southern plains was at a minimum and the 7th. Cavalry's duties consisted mainly of routine patrols. Stationed at Fort Hays, the regiment found itself with much time on its hands and Custer himself began to grow restless. Garrison life was generally a tedious business and for a live wire like Autie it proved to be especially irksome. True, he was surrounded by his clique of admiring officers, including brother Tom (now recovered from a wound he had received at the Washita) and, of course, doe eyed Libbie was always on hand to soothe his troubled brow, but none of this helped to advance his ambitions. He occupied himself by writing and studying, hosting parties, entertaining visiting dignitaries and riding out onto the prairie to indulge in some buffalo hunting. Also, he may have found comfort in the arms of an especially beautiful Cheyenne teenager, the daughter of a chief killed at the Washita. Her name, by popular translation, was Monahsetah and Custer wrote of her as being "exceedingly comely". The depth of his relationship with this girl has never been proven, but rumours abounded and Benteen, for one, spoke openly, in later years, about his commanding officer's infidelity, saying that Libbie was aware but chose to ignore it. Monahsetah is even said to have given birth to "Long Hair's" baby, but she was several months pregnant when he first met her so I think we can discount *that*! She certainly accompanied him, along with other Cheyenne female prisoners, ostensibly as a guide as the 7th. trotted around Indian Territory.

Benteen continued to be a thorn in Custer's side. Having unashamedly criticized the handling of events which led to the massacre of Maj. Elliott's troop, the mischievous captain's opinions found their way into the pages of a St. Louis newspaper. When Custer saw it he was infuriated, saying that if he found out who was responsible for such a slur on the regiment he would administer a beating. Cool as a cucumber, Benteen stepped forward and, looking the "General" straight in the eye, admitted responsibility, adding that he was "ready for the whipping". This was a tense moment for Autie, for he stood to lose face in front of his assembled officers. His temper had spoken rashly and he could hardly be seen to attempt to thrash one of his senior officers. Benteen knew this, of course, and no doubt revelled in the discomfort suffered by the commander he hated. In the end, much out of character, Custer backed down for the good of the 7th.. It could have got nasty. No way would a tough character like Benteen have meekly subjected himself to a beating, regardless of rank. The whole sorry episode just became another piece of fuel for the simmering resentment within the regiment.

*   *   *

At around this time, another officer joined the 7th. who would be added to the ranks of those who did not approve of the "General". This was Major Marcus Reno, a serious, dark faced individual whose unfortunate life seemed to furnish him with a permanent "chip on the shoulder". Brought in to replace Maj. Elliott, Reno was Custer's second-in-command, but the two men never saw eye to eye. Things seldom seemed to run smoothly for Reno. Scraping through West Point he had a wife whose rich relatives detested him, so none of their wealth ever came his way. Although he proved to be a steady, though unexciting, officer during the Civil War, he was, never-the-less, cited for gallantry and was wounded in action. On one occasion he led his men straight into a trap set by the rebels which resulted in high casualties, a misfortune he never lived down. As a trained and experienced cavalryman he resented his appointment back to West Point, after the war, as an infantry instructor and his official protests gained him a reputation for disobedience. Further assignments to far flung, remote postings brought similar protests and consequent disapproval from his superiors. In the end he was sent to the frontier. Although he and Benteen had a mutual dislike of their C.O. in common, that was where their parity ended. The white haired captain and the surly, hard done by major did not get on.

Close to the fort stood Hays City, the only real source of recreation for the troopers. Whenever they were off duty, the cavalrymen would descend in droves upon the gambling dens, saloons, dance halls and whore houses of the town where they let off steam with abandon. Perhaps they could not be blamed, when one reflects on their hard life, but the civilian population of Hays suffered for it. It must be remembered that although the eventual decimation of the regiment at Little Bighorn transformed them all, in many eyes, into heroic saints, the reality was that the 7th.'s rank and file were a rough lot. Hard drinkers, sex starved, desperate loners, fugitives hiding in uniform, men who fought each other and the locals with fists, feet, teeth, knives, coshes and sharpened knuckle dusters. Indeed, those smoke filled dens of iniquity, where bellowing blue clad troopers jostled against the bar alongside foul smelling buffalo hunters, bull whackers, mule skinners, railroad builders, professional gamblers and women of ill repute, were hardly places where law and order may be respected. Even so, somebody had to represent authority and in Hays, in late '69, the responsibility fell upon Sheriff "Wild Bill" Hickok.

"Wild Bill" was already known to the veteran members of the 7th. for he had scouted for them during the early Kansas campaigns. Also, he had represented the law at Fort Riley where he had earned the respect, and fear, of many troopers by the way he enforced his rules, "pistol whipping" being one of his favourite methods of subduing rowdy soldiers. In Hays City Hickok patrolled the streets, ivory handled Colt pistols protruding butts forward from his belt, a Bowie knife tucked in a bright sash wrapped around the waist of his embroidered frock coat and a sawn off scatter gun cradled in his arms. He meant business. On the whole, even the roughest characters quietened down when "Wild Bill" was around and he did succeed in making Hays a slightly safer place. That said, he had recently found it necessary to shoot dead a character named Jack Strawhan who had confronted him in Drum's Saloon.

With the "General" away on army business at Fort Leavenworth, it was rumoured that Hickok had made an enemy of Tom Custer. Tom did not share his older brother's aversion to the bottle and drunken incidents in town had led to a confrontation between "Wild Bill" and a handful of troopers who were determined to take the long haired lawman down a peg or two. Cornering him in a saloon, they jumped him and this led to a fearsome brawl which practically wrecked the place. Disarmed, Hickok kept them at bay bare handed until a friend threw him a pistol and bullets began to fly resulting in the death of at least one trooper and the wounding of others. Sheriff or not, Hickok knew he could not take on the whole 7th. Cavalry and so he left Hays, keeping out of the regiment's way for some time to come.

To Custer, such incidents served as a mere irritant. He wanted his regiment back in the field. Attending army conferences back east, Autie was forever pushing for a significant role in the re-shaping of the frontier but, at present, there was little for him to do. Alone in New York (with Libbie keeping the home fires burning in Kansas), Autie amused himself in his usual way. Although he did not smoke or drink, the "General" certainly enjoyed gambling in-between his visits to influential dignitaries, theatre going and streetwalking. As a handsome and dashing war hero, he was also a target for the flirtatious city ladies and it is probable that he responded to many of these advances. Libbie received regular letters from him in which he reported in detail on the latest female fashions. How she felt about the interest he was openly showing for the opposite sex is an intriguing slice of speculation, but it seems, as a couple, they had an understanding. There is little doubt that Autie and Libbie were a secure unit, both strong individuals who needed each other. As Capt. Benteen said, it was in Mrs. Custer's interests to ignore his possible infidelities, as long as he always returned to her. That said, Libbie herself may not have been the complete paragon of virtue she liked to be portrayed as, but we shall get to that later.

Time dragged on and Custer indulged in various pursuits including expeditions to purchase suitable horses for the army. In 1871 he was commanding a post in Kentucky but activities like policing hillbilly society and keeping the fledgling Ku Klux Klan in order hardly taxed his talents. He kept a huge pack of hounds which often brought him trouble with his neighbours. Autie's personal orderly, Private John Burkman, had his work cut out keeping these lively dogs under control and more than once they savaged local pets and livestock which led to petitions of complaint. Autie was bored and Libbie grew to hate tedious small town life.

A pleasant distraction arrived in early 1872 in the form of a most important visitor from overseas. The Russian Grand Duke Alexis Romanov had arrived in America on a state visit and having spent several weeks being wined and dined in style by the cream of Yankee society in the eastern cities, the young nobleman had now expressed a wish to see the Wild West. With General Phil Sheridan as his host, the Duke would experience his desire but not in the full savage splendour of its brutal reality. Little Phil wanted to impress his V.I.P. guest, but not to the extent of putting him in any possible danger. Consequently, orders were issued to find a suitable location for Alexis to indulge his fantasies safely, an area of the wilds which would deliver scenery, wild life and sport without the hazards of hostile Indians. A full scale operation began which tied up a vast array of government resources. It was decided to transport the Duke to a hastily assembled site, dubbed "Camp Alexis", in Nebraska, about fifty miles to the south of North Platte. This was close to the railroad so the young Russian could be taken almost all the way by train, reducing the necessity of him having to endure the rigours of the trail. He arrived at the Omaha rail stop in a specially commissioned luxury Pullman car, Sheridan greeting him in the grandest style, with a guard of honour and hundreds of townsfolk cheering him through the streets. From here the distinguished party was to continue on to North Platte where they would be transported, by a fleet of specially adapted ambulance wagons, to Camp Alexis.

Sheridan had planned this trip meticulously. The object of the exercise was for the Duke to experience an authentic buffalo hunt and scouts had located a convenient herd in the vicinity. To add flavour to the effect, Little Phil had even relieved the renowned buffalo hunter and scout Buffalo Bill Cody from his guiding duties with the army so that he could join the group. Realising the advantage of having such colourful characters along, Sheridan also telegraphed George Custer.

Autie did not need to be told twice and rushed from Kentucky in almost record time. He joined the Imperial Train, draped with its Russian and American flags, at Omaha, immediately hitting it off with Alexis who was struck by the "General's" flamboyance and reputation. This pleased Sheridan no end and as the locomotive puffed its way westwards, the jolly band of dignitaries partied through the night.

In the early hours of a grey, chilly morning, the train pulled into the tiny settlement at North Platte, a place which had never experienced such activity. With curious frontier folk gaping at their illustrious visitor, the group was met by Buffalo Bill and a company of the 2nd. Cavalry. Travelling on, by wagon and horseback, to Camp Alexis, the Duke was installed in a converted hospital tent which had been sumptuously decorated, floor boarded and carpeted. Authentic frontier conditions indeed! The camp was stocked with the finest food and wines, even crates of champagne. Surrounded by his Russian entourage, and the accompaniment of the 2nd. Cavalry's band, Alexis was delighted to view his first Indians but there would be no hostility from these docile tribesmen. Sheridan had arranged to persuade a bunch of reservation Sioux to journey up from the Brule agency in return for extra blankets and food. All they were asked to do was set up camp and look suitably ethnic. Ironically, the chief of this group was the famed Spotted Tail who, nearly twenty years before, had been a fearsome warrior with white blood on his hands. Now he was content to play the fool for foreign royalty.

The Duke was anxious to kill his first buffalo and so a hunt was arranged, scouts reporting that plenty of the shaggy beasts had been seen within a few miles of camp. Young Alexis Romanov mounted up and set off armed to the teeth, suitably clad in frontier garb and flanked by Custer and Buffalo Bill, their fringed buckskins wafting in the breeze. What a splendid sight they must have made; romantic Western imagery personified! Autie and Cody were under strict instructions from Sheridan to ensure that their honoured guest got just what he wanted, so when they encountered their first herd, the intrepid duo manoeuvred the Russian into just the right position to make an easy kill. This he achieved, clumsily by all accounts, but the accompanying newspapermen were able to report that the Duke celebrated by cutting off his slain bison's tail, whirling the bloody souvenir around his head with howls of delight. Within moments, champagne corks were popping again.

The fun continued with displays of Indian dancing, feasting and drinking copious amounts of liquor. Over the next day or two, Alexis improved his hunting skills and became extra friendly with Custer. The pair of them even competed for the affections of Spotted Tail's pretty daughter and the young squaw basked and giggled in the attention afforded her by these important palefaces. Custer's experience of dealing with Indians naturally gave him an unfair advantage.

When the Camp Alexis jaunt was over, Custer continued with his pleasant duties as the Duke's not quite official host, leading him on a tour through some of the southern States. Autie introduced Alexis to Libbie, who was charmed by his Russian posturing; partying and sightseeing and ending up sharing adjoining suites in New Orleans. The Duke had obviously had a wonderful time, returning to Russia and a life which never quite matched up to his American celebrity status. His family influence would be savagely erased forever in the 1918 Bolshevik Revolution.

As for Buffalo Bill, he used the publicity for the basis of his soon to be world famous touring Wild West Show.

*   *   *

The Custers were sorry to see the back of Alexis Romanov, but that winter they were able to experience a further addition to their social calendar before having to return to the tedium of Kentucky. George and Tom's little sister, Maggie, was getting married to an officer from the 7th..

Her husband to be was James Calhoun, a merchant's son from Cincinnati. Calhoun had been too young to obtain a commission in the Civil War but since 1864 he had been working his way up through the ranks of various infantry regiments before being appointed a 1st. Lieutenant in the 7th. cavalry in early 1871. George and Tom liked him and he quickly became a member of the Custer clique. This new officer was grateful to his new friends, swearing that he would prove himself ".....if the time comes". One day, on a bleak hillside in Montana, he would fulfil his promise.

Autie, Tom and Libbie were especially pleased to welcome Calhoun into the family fold and the wedding took place in Monroe in March 1872. The "General" now had a brother-in-law in his regiment.

Worth mentioning here is the fact that Custer was not the overall commander of the 7th. Cavalry. True, he was the field commander, responsible for all the front line decisions and day to day overseeing of the troops, but the actual C.O. was Col. Samuel Sturgis who seemed to spend most of his time on detached service, largely behind a desk in St. Louis. For all intents and purposes though, Autie *was* the 7th.. It was his baby, without a doubt.

However, regardless of "Custer's Luck", it could hardly be said that all ran smoothly, even on the personal front. One would think that the "General" and his wife had a solid relationship and, generally speaking, they probably did, even though Autie may have occasionally strayed. As previously indicated, Libbie's concern for self preservation (i.e. as the wife of a V.I.P.) was probably sufficient to keep her tolerant of such behaviour and one must also remember that she was very much a product of her times when women were not quite so prominent in society. Interesting then, that rumours abounded of a possible infidelity on her side.

　Benteen, always keen to stir things up for Custer, milked this scandal for all it was worth, but, even so, we are left with precious little to go on. It seems that Libbie, during the 1860's Kansas period at Fort Riley, became fond of Capt. Thomas Weir. Weir was an old comrade of Custer's, slightly older than him, whose army experience was impressive. A university graduate, he had served in the Michigan Cavalry alongside Autie during the Civil War, fighting many battles and becoming a prisoner of the confederates. After the war, he served on Custer's staff in Texas during the reconstruction period, consequently joining the 7th. Cavalry as a 1st. Lieutenant when the regiment first formed in 1866. The two men went back a long way. Weir's relationship with Libbie, which no doubt stemmed from those numerous garrison social gatherings, apparently grew from courteous chit chat to outright flirtatiousness. There is no real evidence that their friendship became any more intense than that, but it was enough to concern Custer himself, making him increasingly suspicious. There is reason to believe, despite the excuses of flooding and cholera, that Autie's deepest motive for deserting his command in 1867 (which led to his court martial) was because of tales he had heard about Weir and Libbie alone together at Fort Hays. Whatever, Libbie was lectured and Weir reprimanded. Following this, Weir became exceptionally loyal to Custer, as if he was trying to make amends to him. This loyalty would follow right through to the Little Bighorn where the guilty officer would eventually disobey orders and risk his life attempting to rescue his commander.

Some officers of the 7th. Cavalry.

BLACK HILLS GOLD

Stern faced Sioux warriors watched from rocky outcrops in resentful silence. Snaking out below them, for as far as the eye could see, were white man's wagons, big guns and countless mounted soldiers, wending their way steadily into the heart of the sacred Black Hills.

This was nothing less than a betrayal of all that been promised in the hard won treaty of 1868, an insult to the Lakota. How dare the white man go back on his vow that the Hills belonged to the Sioux for as long as the grass should grow and the buffalo roam. What were they doing here?

Following Red Cloud's war when the great chief had succeeded in convincing the U.S. Government to leave his people in peace (at the expense of Captain Fetterman and numerous others), the Sioux had continued to control vast tracts of land in Wyoming and Montana. In Dakota a reservation had been established giving these Plains Indians solemn rights of ownership, promising them that no whites would ever again be permitted to pass over or settle that land. The Black Hills, the dwelling place of Wakan Tanka, the Great Spirit, was particularly significant to the Lakota, the burial site of their ancestors and the scene of enormous spiritual enlightenment for the entire race. This area lay very much in agreed Sioux territory and as such should never be disturbed. In addition, to the west, bordered by the Bighorn Mountains lay what was called the Unceded Territory. This was prime hunting land, rich with buffalo, timber and water, which the Sioux roamed over unhindered. Although this was an area which had not been officially designated to the Indians, the government did not question the Sioux's right to exploit it and the Lakota themselves did not feel they had any reason to see the situation change. How wrong they were.

Over a few short years much had changed. For a while, the U.S. government was content to let the Sioux hold sway in the north western territory but expansion from the east was growing by the day, the hunger for land and settlement reaching boiling point. Of course, there was much land to be had in this vast, fertile country and for a while the Sioux could be left in peace, but rumours were growing of gold in these forbidden areas. There was no way any Washington agreement was going to keep its subjects from trying to get their hands on the precious yellow metal.

By this time Ulysses Grant had become president, many of his old Civil War cronies being given prime positions in his administration, especially within the armed forces. The Indian question was a real predicament for him for the Sioux and their "primitive" ways were standing in the way of progress. Yet how could they be removed without raising humanitarian, moral and honourable dilemmas which would reflect badly, perhaps disastrously, upon the government? After all, the 1868 treaty *did* make an undeniable promise which could not be bypassed with legal jargon.

Grant thought he could get around this by allowing an expedition to enter the Black Hills, ostensibly for scientific research. Although this was not strictly legal, he decided to take a chance, trusting that the Sioux may turn a blind eye and not attack, provided the expedition was well enough protected. It was also said that the expedition was charting the area for national geographic purposes and to log possible sites for the building of forts. Unofficially, one of the main purposes of this enterprise was to scour the sacred hills for traces of gold. The Sioux were not fooled. At the first sight of the wagons they were infuriated.

Chosen to lead this expedition was none other than Lt.Col. George Armstrong Custer. Who else? Since his Kentucky posting, Autie had been pretty active again. In 1873 he was prominent in the Yellowstone expedition, the purpose of which was to protect surveyors working for the Northern Pacific Railroad, but there were only sporadic clashes with the Sioux. Although he had not been in command of this particular venture, Custer utilized the experience to his advantage, taking the opportunity to collect fossils and capture a wide variety of exotic creatures to add to his ever growing menagerie at home. Long suffering Libbie often had to endure such regular occurrences as porcupines padding through her house! The "General" also took up a new hobby, acquiring lessons in the stuffing of animals from a taxidermist who was along for the ride. By all accounts, this latest interest absorbed him for hours at a time. Full of tireless energy, he would sit up for long into the night, working by lamplight in his tent. He even stuffed an entire elk he had shot on the trail, shipping the inanimate beast to Detroit for display in a club he frequented. Libbie had the dubious pleasure of receiving the head of a buffalo!

The commander of this expedition, one General Stanley, who was often drunk, openly disliked Custer, telling him that he was troublesome but Autie shrugged off such criticism with an air of superiority. This attitude merely succeeded in enraging Stanley even more.

Why should Custer worry? Straight from this trip he took command of a new post, this time up north, deep in the Dakota territory near the town of Bismarck at the railhead of the Northern Pacific. This was Fort Abraham Lincoln, a frontier garrison which stood right on the edge of sweeping, hostile plains, the homeland of all those potentially savage Sioux whose Black Hills lay a couple of hundred miles south west.

Fort Lincoln was situated on the banks of the big, muddy Missouri River and the Custers made this remote wilderness as comfortable as they possibly could, which was not always easy in a place which boiled in the summer and suffered temperatures up to 45 degrees below freezing point in the winter. Their first house burned down but George and Libbie had a big replacement dwelling built alongside the parade ground which included a billiard room and a ballroom, Autie's stuffed trophies adorning the walls. A granary was converted into a small theatre where amateur theatricals and lectures were staged. Each company would compete by throwing its own regular ball, although the shortage of women was such that the men often had to dance with each other! On each side of the Custer house stood the quarters of his favoured officers, men like his brother Tom, Calhoun, Cooke, Weir, Yates, Keogh and other sycophants. Standing beneath a much admired chandelier, to the tinkling of an imported grand piano, no doubt many a happy evening was spent with these men and their wives (if they had them), laughing, drinking and playing games. One can imagine characters like Myles Keogh rattling on about the "awld country", athletic Cooke twiddling his amazing whiskers and Tom Custer drinking himself into blissful oblivion, the women tut-tutting in ladylike fashion yet enjoying the fun of it all. And the songs ..... they always loved their musical interludes, whether it be regimental favourites like the jaunty "Captain Jinks of the Horse Marines" or maudlin ballads such as "Little Footsteps" or "Annie Laurie". Disapproving officers were notably absent from these happy gatherings. Benteen, for instance, was shipped off to another posting. In fact, it is worth noting here that the 7th. Cavalry were somewhat dispersed during this period, with several companies being sent to other garrisons along the Missouri River. Three companies were even sent to faraway Louisiana to carry out policing operations for the Department of the Gulf. Five companies remained under Autie's direct command at Fort Lincoln.

Libbie encouraged her husband to write about his experiences and just before the Black Hills expedition took place, he completed his book "My Life on the Plains" in which he gave a somewhat biased and sanitized account of his campaigns in Kansas and the Indian Territory. Benteen was to dub this well received tome "My *Lie* on the Plains".

The expedition set out from Fort Lincoln on July 2nd. 1874 and twenty days later the columns were creaking across the prairie just west of the sacred Black Hills. Custer must have contemplated the task which lay ahead of him with relish. This was an historic moment and Autie was an avid history maker. Never before had an organized white expedition entered the area, with the exception of occasional individual trappers or rogue miners. Apart from the highest peaks, none of this vast expanse had been charted. Up to now there existed no written accounts of exploration within the Hills. They were a mystery to just about everyone but the Lakota, a situation which was about to change dramatically.

Custer's expedition was hardly a low key affair. With him came approximately 1,200 souls including ten companies of cavalry and two of infantry, supplied by 110 wagons, each of which was pulled by six mules. There was also an artillery detachment, three Gatling guns and the entire sixteen piece 7th. Cavalry band, all splendidly mounted on pretty white horses and led by the Italian Chief Musician Felix Vinatieri. Autie did not like to go anywhere without his *Garry Owen*, nor his hounds, a dozen of which loped along beside the horses and 300 head of cattle. Also with the columns were about eighty civilians who served various functions. A pair of newspaper reporters, a geologist, a naturalist, an engineer and two mining specialists whose presence was probably more vital than any. To record it all for posterity came the photographer, William Illingworth, whose wonderful, informal pictures taken during the trip have left us with some of the finest and most interesting images ever to emerge from the frontier period.

Custer was totally in the hands of his Indian scouts, for he had little idea of what he might find. Prominent amongst these scouts was Bloody Knife, a mature and cynical individual who had worked for Autie the year before in the Yellowstone expedition. Bloody Knife aligned himself with the Arikara tribe (also known as Rees), Indians who had thrown in their lot with the whites and regularly scouted for them, his mother being of their blood. However, Bloody Knife's father had been Hunkpapa Sioux and although the boy spent his formative years with the Lakota it seems they did not accept him. He grew up being made to feel inferior because of his mixed blood and was often taunted and humiliated until his mother took him away to live with her own tribe. As a young man he tried to return to the Lakota but was violently rejected by them, shortly after which his two brothers were killed by a Sioux war party. This was the final straw for Bloody Knife. His father's people had given him plenty of reason to hate them and so he chose to serve the invading whites. In return, the Sioux observed him scouting for the hated *wasichus* and thus detested him even more. If there was one thing the Lakota hated more than white soldiers it had to be an Indian who rode with them.

Although Bloody Knife was impertinent to his employers and critical of their ways, Custer liked him. The "General" and the "Savage" formed an unlikely bond of mutual respect even though they were poles apart in many ways. Autie was entertained by this scout's eccentricities and admired his tracking skills, even tolerating his love of whisky which often left him reeling drunk, such a contrast to Custer's own tee-total and controlled lifestyle. But Bloody Knife's loyalty to the whites was commendable, a track record which stretched back to early days when he had carried mail through hostile Sioux country. Just before the Little Bighorn debacle, Custer had a special silver medal engraved with Bloody Knife's name on it, a gift which the scout wore with enormous pride. He regarded Autie as a "great chief".

The route they took into the Black Hills was meticulously plotted, longitude and latitude readings being taken at regular points. Crossing the prairie, the expedition had travelled in four columns abreast of one another, but now that it had entered the narrow confines of the valleys and hills, it condensed into single file. One of Illingworth's photographs, taken from a high peak, demonstrates this powerfully for you can clearly see the long line of wagons winding away into the distance, a column which stretched for over two miles.

From the first cautious advance, the expedition soon relaxed into a pleasurable jaunt.

The surrounding countryside was stunningly beautiful, the air rich with the sweet aroma of wild flowers which the troopers were able to reach down and pick from their saddles as they made their way through meadows of lush, knee high grass. Rough and tough soldiers, packers and mule skinners were seen delicately threading posies and bouquets, a sight which amused the scouts and intrigued Custer. All around grew gooseberries, blueberries, cherries and colourful plants of numerous variety. The sky was blue, birds sang from the pines and the temperature was lusciously warm, each day ending with a spectacular sunset over the hilltops and distant mountains. By night the stars would beam brightly like celestial campfires from a jet black sky, Vinatieri's musicians playing impromptu concerts in the wilderness which stamped a bizarre yet fitting mark of perfection upon such a paradise. One night they were treated to the sight of a comet blazing its way across the heavens. The men played baseball and ate well, for game was in such abundance that they hardly had to touch the beef herd they had driven with them.

It was a leisurely time for most enlisted men, exploring caves and ridges and carving their names in rocks, but there was also work to be done. The scientific team were busy with their experiments and record keeping and the two miners were carrying out their surveys, as ordered. Custer, as usual, was often far ahead of the column, energetic and enthusiastic, indulging in his much loved past time of hunting whenever the opportunity allowed. Killing helpless creatures was a source of great amusement to the "General" and one day he blasted a majestic pure white crane just so that he could measure its seven foot wing span. Another victim was a very old but enormous bear and Illingworth photographed buckskin clad Autie proudly posing beside its lifeless carcass, peering over the top of its huge, shaggy back as he clutches his rifle. Squatting just behind him, also cradling a rifle, is the haughty figure of Bloody Knife. He seems to be regarding his "great chief" with affection and pride. Custer also spent a day climbing almost to the summit of Harney Peak which stands in the present day Custer State Park.

Even with business pending, Custer had a fine old time surrounded by most of his clique, except for Capt. Myles Keogh who was on an extended leave of absence. Brother-in-law Calhoun detailed the natural splendour in his diary and wrote grandly of his desire that one day the "superiority" of the white race should rise high above the deprivations of the savage! Ever present Benteen was along for the ride but Maj. Reno had command of another survey commission further north. His wife had recently died and he was to be granted a long leave which would take him to Europe. Tom Custer passed the time idling in the sunshine and snaring snakes, occasionally joining his big brother George to play practical jokes on their youngest sibling, Boston, who was enjoying his first adventure in the wilds. 24 years old, Boston Custer was not in the military like his brothers but had been employed as a civilian forage master. Another Illingworth group photograph shows about forty individuals from the expedition lounging in front of their tents. Autie is there, stretched out on the grass with Bloody Knife standing behind him. Brother Tom too, sitting cross legged and happy surrounded by various familiar faces, officers, scouts, experts; many of them crowned by the strangely shaped campaign slouch hat which was the issue of the period. And then the miners confirmed what had long been rumoured. The presence of gold.

The first traces were panned from a streambed but the experts were soon able to state that the area was rich with the precious yellow metal. Custer was delighted and immediately sent one of his white scouts, "Lonesome" Charley Reynolds, south to Fort Laramie with the news. As for the Sioux they kept their distance, although Custer did parley with one small band of lodges he encountered, assuring the chief that his intentions were friendly. Despite the gifts they received, these Indians were not wholly convinced. Bloody Knife and his fellow Ree scouts, who had dressed themselves in preparation for a spot of Sioux killing, were held in check and forced to withdraw, disappointed.

In all, the Black Hills expedition served as a pleasant interlude to break up the monotony of garrison life on the bleak plains around Fort Lincoln, but it was to have serious repercussions. The expedition lasted sixty days and covered 880 miles. A handful of men died during the trip, all from illness and accident, for there was no violent confrontation between soldiers and Indians. This time the Sioux just watched, but the discovery of gold in their sacred heartland was to herald the end of their way of life. It would be a while yet and much blood would be spilt in what was to be the final struggle of the Lakota.

Officers and wives of the 7th. Cavalry pose on the porch of the Custer home at Fort Abraham Lincoln, 1873. Those named were present at the Little Bighorn three years later. KIA indicates "killed in action".
1. Lt. George Wallace   2. Lt. Col. George Custer (KIA)   3. Lt. Benny Hodgson (KIA)
4. Capt. George Yates (KIA)   5. Lt. Charles Varnum   6. Capt. Tom Custer (KIA)
7. Lt. James Calhoun (KIA)   8. Capt. Myles Moylan   9. Lt. Donald McIntosh (KIA)

(Photograph courtesy of the Little Bighorn Battlefield National Monument, National Park Service)

ULTIMATUM

Inevitably, news of the Black Hills gold strike spread like wildfire and the result was predictable. Prospectors swarmed into the sacred area in their thousands, professionals and amateurs alike, all keen to "get rich quick". It was an epidemic which proved impossible to control, even though the government's Indian Bureau did at first feel duty bound to stand by the terms of the 1868 treaty. A few half hearted efforts were made by the army to stem the tide, but little could be done. Grant and his administration knew that public opinion would not allow an old agreement with savages hinder the nation's progress. A rich resource like gold could not be left untouched because of some painted red man's heathen beliefs!

Soon the beautiful Black Hills were scarred by the workings of numerous mining operations, the streams dammed and the previously peaceful trails clogged with mule trains and wagons. Filthy smoke spewing shanty towns and tent cities sprang up all over the place and by the summer of 1875, in Deadwood Gulch, the settlement had become so large that it was estimated some 25,000 people dwelt there. It was a rough place, not strictly official, of course, where the only law was a man's ability to fight his way out of trouble. Clapboard stores were established alongside plank and barrel saloon bars. When not working their claims, the inhabitants spent their time drinking, fighting, gambling and generally "cutting loose", many fortunes being made and lost. Such women as were present mostly found themselves employed by the highly popular brothels. Some of these "ladies" were as tough as their clients and hardly any prettier!

The Sioux observed all this darkly and could see through the flimsy excuses of government representatives. Acting after the event, the Indian Bureau did try and make overtures to suggest the purchase of mineral rights from the Sioux, the idea being that the Black Hills would still lie within the reservation, but this was swiftly rejected. The Lakota wanted their homeland to themselves and did not wish to share it with raucous, bearded, pale faced profiteers who possessed not one ounce of respect for Indian culture.

There were other grievances too. For some years now, the Plains tribes had been growing increasingly disturbed about the ongoing decimation of the buffalo. Until just after the Civil War, the land north and south of the Platte had swarmed with vast herds of bison. Early white explorers spoke of ambling buffalo darkening the prairie for as far as the eye could see, and this was no exaggeration. There were literally millions of the shaggy beasts and the Indians had no reason to believe that their numbers would ever dwindle. The buffalo, after all, was essential to their way of life but the herds were large enough to absorb any Indian level of hunting.

White men with their guns were a different matter. Armed with heavy calibre, highly accurate Sharps rifles, the invading white hunters commenced an open season on the buffalo to supply the blossoming frontier towns and the eastern cities with resources and trinkets. These animals were notoriously stupid and easy to kill. Set yourself up in a cosy position on the right side of the wind above a grazing herd, your rifle cradled in a stand, and, as a lone hunter, you could drop scores of buffalo in a day. They would just stand there, munching and waiting to be shot. There were so many of them and such easy sport that the whole business of buffalo killing became a huge industry. Soon the Plains were littered with rotting carcasses, for it was not uncommon for a bison to be shot just for its tongue, a delicacy for white folks too. The Indians were particularly enraged by the wastage of the rest of the animal for they knew how to use every part.

That said, there was also money to be made out of buffalo bones and men would scour the prairie for skeletons to be collected, ground up and sold as fertilizer for $5 per ton. Buffalo hunting also became a national sport which was advertised overseas. The Grand

Duke Alexis' expedition with Custer had not been a unique event, for many dignitaries arrived from Europe to indulge in a spot of slaughter, the beasts still being so numerous that these lords and ladies could be driven right up to the herds in comfortable wagons or railroad carriages to open fire at point blank range.

Literally millions of buffalo were slain in just a few years, a situation which could not last forever. At this rate they would simply disappear. By 1900 the entire species was in danger of extinction.

The Plains tribes began to feel cornered and angrier than ever before. They could sense the net of the white man closing in on them and, for the first time, they understood the true crisis which was facing their dubious future as a separate entity. Some of the wise Sioux leaders, like Red Cloud and Spotted Tail, who had visited the great cities of the east, such as Washington and New York, already realised that resisting white expansion was futile. They had chosen to settle down on the allotted reservations and make the best of it, but there were still many warrior chiefs and young braves who clung to the old ways and were determined to do all they could to preserve them or die trying.

War parties again took up arms against settlers in and around the Black Hills. Isolated miners and homesteaders felt the brunt of Sioux and Cheyenne resentment and soon fresh stories of outrage and atrocity were permeating the pages of eastern newspapers. President Grant saw this as his solution.

Under pressure to solve the Indian question, Grant ordered his Bureau of Indian Affairs to compile a report about the volatile situation out west, the result of which was an excuse being found to wage outright war against the hostiles. Grant's target was not the reservation Indians who remained within their boundaries but those who insisted upon roaming across the Unceded Territory. They were under suspicion of carrying out attacks against U.S. citizens who had not trespassed upon their official land. Deciding to take a hard line, the government issued a directive, in early December 1875, that all the roaming Indians must make their way back onto the Dakota reservation. Any who had not returned by the end of January 1876 would be considered hostile and treated accordingly by military force.

Well, this was clear enough, if somewhat harsh on a race which had roamed free since time immemorial. Grant and his team knew that they had insisted on an unreasonable directive which the Indians, even if they were compliant, would have no chance of achieving. The winter was at its height and the weather and communication problems made it all but impossible to get news of this ultimatum to the numerous scattered tribal groups within the allotted time. Consequently, most Sioux and Cheyenne would not even be aware of what was being demanded of them. Not that the government cared. They knew that this would be the preliminary stage of the war they were trying to manufacture, a war which would settle the matter once and for all and give them a bonafide reason to seize the Black Hills as spoils of the conflict.

By the time the deadline was reached, when it was obvious (and a foregone conclusion) that most of the hostile winter roamers were not intending to comply with the demand, preparations were already well in hand to mount a massive military campaign against them, the intention being to crush their spirit of resistance forever.

*   *   *

The discovery of gold in the Black Hills by Custer's expedition put the "General" back in the public spotlight again, a consequence which pleased him no end. He returned to his command at Fort Lincoln and later that year, 1874, found himself on detached service in Chicago for a few weeks enjoying the comforts of city life. Regardless of his frontier reputation, Autie was never averse to a little civilized luxury.

He observed the results of his expedition with interest, noting the rape of the Lakota heartland and no doubt pondering on his future. It was apparent now that the days of his current adversaries were numbered and then, just like his situation after the Civil War, he would be left with no one to fight. For a feisty soldier like Custer that would be intolerable, on the face of it, but he was older now and perhaps looking ahead in a way that he would not have done as a redundant young Major General. With the hostile Indians finally subdued, which could not lie far ahead, he would be facing the prospect of dull service with a peace time army, looking forward only to retirement and obscurity. For G.A.C. this would simply not do. He would have to find a new direction. Outside of the army, what could that be for a man of Custer's talents? The answer had to lie in politics. He was well known and a champion of the people and certainly had a platform of success on which to base any future campaign. Perhaps he could go all the way to the top. The gruff and ponderous Grant had done it, after all.

With this in mind, there were things which had to be achieved first and maybe this coming campaign against the hostiles would suit Autie's purposes. The Sioux and Cheyenne could not win a war against the might of the U.S. Army obviously, but they were determined to go down fighting. Custer had enough experience and respect for the Plains Indians to know that this final showdown with them would be no push over. They would fight back bravely before being destroyed and the "General" was determined to be in at the kill. A last great battle was what he needed before embarking on a serious political career, something which would cement his reputation as the nation's great hero and the subjugator of her final enemy.

In the meantime, life went on at Fort Lincoln with routine patrols and occasional call outs to Indian incidents. In January 1875 an Hunkpapa Sioux warrior named Rain-in-the-Face suddenly turned up at the Standing Rock Agency on the Dakota reservation, a fact which interested the authorities at Fort Lincoln. This particular Indian was wanted on suspicion of having led a war party which murdered two civilians (a sutler and a vet) who had wandered away from safety during the Yellowstone expedition of 1873. Receiving orders to apprehend the suspect, Custer gave the job to his friend Capt. George Yates.

Yates took along two companies of cavalry troopers, plus the scout "Lonesome" Charley Reynolds who knew Rain-in-the-Face by sight. Tom Custer joined them too. This strong force was a little over the top for the arrest of one Indian on a peaceful reservation and when they arrived at Standing Rock their presence caused considerable consternation. It was a freezing day with thick snow hemming everyone in. Word came that the suspect was inside a storehouse, unaware that he was being hunted. The soldiers made their way to the building and entered quietly. Once "Lonesome" Charley had positively identified their prey, a group of troopers positioned themselves around the warrior, who was still blissfully ignorant of his predicament. Suddenly, Tom Custer launched himself at Rain-in-the-Face, clamping his arms tightly around him. Rain-in-the-Face struggled, the pair of them whirling around until they lost their balance and fell heavily to the floor, so the story goes, wrestling in the dust as the troopers closed in to assist. Held immobile, the Indian was forced into handcuffs and one unsubstantiated tale tells of him being kicked and beaten by Tom. Whatever, the totally stunned Rain-in-the-Face was thrown into the Fort Lincoln guardhouse where he remained for four months before managing to escape. This time, completely alienated from the reservation system, the miffed warrior made his way straight to the Unceded Territory to join up with fellow Sioux who spurned contact with the whites. His treatment by Tom Custer no doubt got to him, for he harboured a great lasting hatred for Autie's brother which possibly manifested itself at the Little Bighorn battlefield just over a year later. For now he apparently sent Tom a ragged piece of buffalo hide upon which he had drawn a heart dripping with blood, the significance of which was obvious to everyone.

* * *

As for Autie, he was to get himself in further trouble by upsetting no lesser mortal than the president, Ulysses Grant. Unfortunately, it could not have come at a worse time for the "General", especially in view of his ambitions, but "Custer's Luck" would prove triumphant one final time.

Lt. Col. Custer took a long leave from duty which lasted from the end of September 1875 until mid February 1876. He was not idle during this period and spent much time in the east building the foundations of his future, making no secret of his Democratic leanings whilst openly criticizing Grant's Republican administration. When the deadline for the Indian's return to their reservation had passed, Custer was an obvious choice to play a prominent part in the campaign against them and he returned to Fort Lincoln to prepare. Then came a complication, for Custer was recalled to Washington to testify before the Clymer Committee at the House of Representatives. This was a great nuisance to Autie, in the middle of his arrangements to take to the field, and his sense of irritation probably contributed to what happened next. He was asked to give evidence against the Secretary of War, William Belknap, who was undergoing investigation regarding alleged mishandling of government funds. Custer, open as always and speaking straight, told the hearing publicly what he thought about corruption in the government agencies which spread from the frontier to Washington itself. To make matters worse, he even implicated Orville Grant, the president's brother, portraying him as little more than a cheat.

President Grant was embarrassed and infuriated by Custer's behaviour, regarding him as an ungrateful jumped up arrogant cavalier with delusions of grandeur. He immediately decided to cut him down to size. Autie was unrepentant, no doubt regarding himself as far too important in the forthcoming campaign to suffer repercussions. How wrong he was. Grant knew just how to strike Custer where it hurt most. Not only did he deny the "General" the high command he had been earmarked for, he went the whole hog and removed him from the campaign completely.

With no role to play in what would undoubtedly be his last chance to distinguish himself on the battlefield, Autie was like a ship without a course. His career would be over and he would be doomed to face the ultimate horror of obscurity.

Of course, he was devastated. Even in view of what eventually happened to him, this current crisis, which in his eyes was nothing short of emasculation, was the nightmare which threatened to destroy his very being.

CUSTER'S LUCK

Little Phil Sheridan's plan to subjugate the hostiles would involve a three pronged advance by separate strong forces into the Unceded Territory. The philosophy behind the coming campaign was based on long held beliefs, honed from general experience, about the way Indians would react when under threat. It was universally thought that the tribes would not stand and fight when faced with a large, organized army, the biggest fear being that they would scatter in their usual elusive way. (i.e. The frustrating problem faced by Hancock and Custer years before in Kansas.) To overcome this, Sheridan decided that it would be important to strike when the Indians were at their least mobile, restricted by harsh weather conditions, therefore a winter campaign was essential. The Washita had proved this. If they could be caught in their villages, hampered by their dependants, the warriors would be forced to fight open battles they could not win. Such was the theory, but first they had to be found.

It was believed that the defiant winter roamers were scattered far and wide across the Powder River country, north west of the Black Hills, and it was estimated that altogether their fighting strength could not exceed 800 warriors. Rather than chasing them, it was thought that this triple pincer movement could crush them from every side, blocking their flight whichever way they ran. And so it was arranged that three independent columns would muster at various outposts before converging upon the common foe.

From the west, Col. John Gibbon would strike out from Fort Ellis, Montana, while from the south, based at Fort Fetterman, Wyoming, would come Brigadier General George Crook. Crook was a highly experienced senior commander who had recently taken charge of the Department of the Platte. Apart from a considerable Civil War record, this eccentric, grizzled, fork bearded officer had been fighting Indians, with much success, for many years, particularly down south in Arizona where he had opposed the fearsome Apaches. Here he had developed the use of Indian scouts to a fine art, a policy which was soon duplicated throughout the frontier garrisons. Indians respected him as a worthy adversary and powerful chief and in return he regarded them with more credence than would the average white officer.

The third column would advance west from Fort Abraham Lincoln, Dakota, this being the force which would include, naturally, the famed 7th. Cavalry. As such, and as commander of the fort, George Custer had originally been selected to lead the whole column, but following his unfortunate run in with the president, this was not to be. Instead, Grant gave command to Brigadier General Alfred Terry, a senior officer who headed the Department of Dakota.

Throughout January 1876, even before the deadline had passed, moves were being made to prepare the ground for the coming conflict. On the Great Sioux Reservation, an embargo was enforced to impede the sale of weapons and ammunition. Also, there was a famine which caused considerable hardship. This bred further resentment because the Indians were aware that the situation was un-necessary and had been caused by corruption within the system. Reservation life was supposed to solve their problems so what was the point of these proud people allowing themselves to be humiliated and exploited? Knowing that the government was preparing to move against them, many Indians drifted away to join their kinfolk in the Unceded Territory. Consequently, these scattered groups began to band together for protection.

As it turned out, owing to logistical problems with Terry and Gibbon's columns, complicated by atrocious weather, the only force to take to the field that winter was Crook's. However, it would prove to be a false start. Some would say an omen for worse things to follow.

Crook's column left Fort Fetterman on March 1st. driving blindly north through freezing blizzards. Frank Grouard, Crook's highly capable chief scout, did an amazing job leading the troops through such appalling conditions and it says much for his skill that he was able to locate a sizeable Indian encampment sheltering in the Powder River valley. These were mostly Cheyenne, aligned with some fugitive bands of Sioux, but the attitude of these particular Indians, at present, was not outwardly hostile. They were just minding their own business whilst trying to survive the winter but Crook decided to strike the first blow of the campaign against them. Crook himself took a back seat for this one, giving field command to his subordinate Col. Joseph Reynolds; not a good choice as it turned out. Reynolds, at 54, was old before his time, suffering from ill health and lacking the required stamina for chasing Indians. The attack began well enough with the Indians fleeing to the surrounding bluffs and losing their pony herd, but then things started to go wrong. Lack of communication resulted in chaos for Reynold's units, each one unsure what the other was doing. Exploiting this, the Indians returned fire from the bluffs and counter attacked, Reynolds losing his nerve and ordering a premature withdrawal. In the ensuing haste little was achieved and the Indians succeeded in retrieving most of their herd.

Stunned by this early setback, Crook decided to pull back all the way to Fort Fetterman to re-evaluate his strategy. Reynolds, shamefaced, beaten and sick of it all would later face a court martial for his mishandling of the action. All his attack had achieved was to force more Indians to throw in their lot with the hostiles. Word quickly spread throughout the scattered bands. The white soldiers were coming and they meant business.

*   *   *

Custer smarted for a while, watching the campaign preparations with increasing envy. On hearing Grant's decree that he would not be allowed to accompany his regiment into action, Autie tried to appeal but the president refused to even see him. Distraught, the "General" left Washington and returned to Fort Lincoln where, robbed of a role, his frustrations grew. It is said that the highly dramatic Custer even dropped to his knees in front of General Terry, imploring his embarrassed superior to intercede on his behalf.

Fortunately, Autie still had friends in high places. General Sherman, supreme commander of the U.S. Army, whispered in Grant's ear and Little Phil was very much on the case. Terry was sympathetic too, as well as practical. Despite his long service, he was inexperienced as an Indian fighter and knew that Custer's frontier abilities would be of benefit to the campaign. With this in mind, he wrote a tactful letter to the president, stressing that he would not question orders but subtly pointing out that "Lt. Col. Custer's services would be very valuable ..... " Custer too added his own part, with an impassioned plea to Grant in writing, this time appealing to the old soldier and Civil War comrade on sentimental grounds. He wrote, *"I respectfully but most earnestly request that while not permitted to go in command of the expedition, I may be allowed to serve with my regiment in the field. I appeal to you as a soldier to spare me the humiliation of seeing my regiment march to meet the enemy, and I not to share its dangers."*

This seemed to do the trick. Bombarded by Custer sympathisers and no doubt touched by the "Boy General's" plea, Grant's attitude softened. He had known Autie for a long time and had to admire the man's courage and spirit, even though he did not like him. For Grant, Custer was too reckless a commander to trust with a delicate operation, on that his opinion had not changed, but it was true that it made no sense to exclude the army's most famous Indian fighter from what would probably be the last big frontier campaign. How would he explain *that* to the American people?

At last the president relented and sent word that although Terry would retain command of the Dakota Column, George Custer could accompany him at the head of his precious 7th. Cavalry.

Sitting Bull, some years after the Little Bighorn.

(Photograph courtesy of the Little Bighorn Battlefield National Monument, National Parks Service)

THE WAY OF THE WARRIOR

One day a huge monument is destined to stand in the heart of the Black Hills, a gigantic sculpture blasted and hewn out of a mountain which will dwarf the famous faces of U.S. presidents carved at nearby Mount Rushmore. The plan is that it will depict a mounted Indian warrior, his outstretched arm pointing out across the sacred homeland of his people. It was begun way back in 1939, instigated by the Sioux themselves to honour the spirit of their most symbolic leader, the legendary Crazy Horse. After many years work, and the removal of nearly 8,000,000 tons of granite, the monument, at the dawn of the 21st. Century, was still far from completion. The original sculptors are dead and it is estimated that the project will take perhaps another two lifetimes to complete. Eventually, this awe inspiring structure should be 173 metres high and 197 metres long.

Why such regard for a distant ancestor? One would really need to be of Lakota blood, I guess, to understand that fully.

Crazy Horse was an Oglala Sioux who by the time of the Little Bighorn was in his late thirties. (In fact, it is estimated that he was born around the same year as Custer.) By the 1870s he had become a revered figure on the Great Plains, renowned for his courage and intelligence in battle. And yet, physically he was not the muscular, bronzed Adonis of popular folklore. He was actually only of average height with a slim, sinewy build and did not have the look of a typical Indian at all. His skin was strangely light and his hair fair, almost sandy. He had survived being shot in the face by a fellow Sioux in a dispute over a woman and this had left his narrow features with a livid scar.

Crazy Horse had been around many of the major incidents on the Plains since his earliest days. As a boy he had witnessed the spectacle of Lt. Grattan's men being massacred near Fort Laramie and he is said to have been part of the decoy party which led Fetterman to his doom. He was prominent in intertribal warfare and personally slew several Crow and Arapaho adversaries but he never boasted about his achievements. By nature he was quiet and a good listener although his general behaviour was considered odd, especially following the death of his young daughter when he seemed to become completely carefree about his own safety. That said, he was not reckless in battle like so many other braves who sought to prove themselves. Crazy Horse always appeared to think things through before he acted but even so, like his adversary "Long Hair" Custer, he still had several mounts killed beneath him in combat whilst preserving his own well being.

Crazy Horse was a loner in many ways. He would disappear from his village without explanation for long periods and would not take part in the Sun Dance, but he was intensely spiritual and lived his life according to what he had learned from his many visions. He wore his hair unbound, crowning his head with the petrified carcass of a hawk or single feather instead of the expected ostentatious feathered war bonnet. In battle he wore only a breech clout, moccasins and his various spiritual charms, his body being painted with white spots and his face streaked with a single jagged line of red. Apart from violent encounters, he avoided contact with the white race and, unlike many of his contemporaries, refused to be photographed because he believed it would shorten his life. More than anything he possessed a charismatic quality which seemed to draw others to him and thus he became one of the leading lights of the Sioux people.

Sitting Bull was similar in that respect but by 1876, well into his forties, he was not expected to fight anymore. Not openly on the battlefield, anyway. His fighting would be carried out in a more subtle fashion.

An Hunkpapa, Sitting Bull looked more like a stereo-typical Indian than Crazy Horse. He was a large man, brown skinned, big nosed, bow legged with a pock marked face, who had gained a fierce reputation as a warrior in his youth. A wound received during his fighting days had left him with a pronounced limp, but he could be a cheerful soul with a considerate nature. Except for white folk, that is, whom he detested with an intense passion because of the inroads they were making into his country and way of life. Refusing to accept the terms of the 1868 Treaty, Sitting Bull carried on with his free life and was soon recognised as a significant religious and cultural leader. He was a holy man whose prophecies were greatly respected but, unlike Crazy Horse, he took an active part in day to day village life and was thus not such a remote figure. Other Indians enjoyed his rich singing voice and the pictures he drew, along with the poetry he composed. His following became immense, especially during that fateful winter of 1875-76 as the white soldiers closed in.

Allied with Sitting Bull in the Hunkpapa circle was the mighty Chief Gall, a magnificent specimen of the warrior code if ever there was one. He *was* photographed several times and his proud bearing, handsome haughtiness and physical power are most apparent. His very presence was said to be intimidating and he had plenty of reason to oppose the *wasichus,* for at one time he had been repeatedly bayoneted whilst resisting arrest, kicked and left for dead. He had then staggered twenty miles through a snow storm before reaching safety.

Other Hunkpapas included Rain-in-the-Face (he who had escaped from Fort Lincoln and sent Tom Custer that picture of a bloody heart) and Crow King, as well as Oglala chiefs like Comes Out Holy, American Horse and Low Dog. Sansarcs too, such as the majestic Spotted Eagle and hawk nosed Minneconjou leader Red Horse. These and many others began to congregate under the collective leadership of Sitting Bull and Crazy Horse, the various tribal groups developing a tendency to be drawn to each other for the sake of self preservation. As the weather improved and the spring grass provided grazing for the pony herds, the tribes became mobile again, their numbers swollen by large groups who were moving out of the Great Sioux Reservation to support them. This, of course, was grossly defiant of the government's directive but it seemed that more Indians were in a hostile frame of mind than ever before. They were desperate now and knew that their time had come. Hope, if any, could only lie with their great spiritual leaders.

This led to a fatal miscalculation by Washington's Indian Bureau of just how many fighting warriors would be facing the invading armies of Gibbon, Crook and Terry. The figure of 800 braves had been a reasonable estimate of those with the winter roamers but had not allowed for the numerous disparate tribal groups who were flocking to the area, along with all those summer roamers off the reservation. The actual figure would exceed 2,000 well armed hostiles, their blood lust up and prepared to do all they could to save themselves, their families and, most importantly, their race.

* * *

At this point, it is appropriate to detail just what opposition the U.S. Army would be up against as it made its way into the heart of hostile territory.

The most important thing to appreciate in the Plains Indian Wars is the huge contrast in the combat attitudes of the opposing forces. As explained earlier, the government soldiers came very much from the European tradition of tactical fighting, discipline, uniform and unquestioning obedience when given orders by superiors. The Plains Indian had no concept of this way of thinking. He was a free spirit who did as he pleased within the deep rooted tribal laws which were based on spirituality and the overall good of the tribe.

To the average Sioux or Cheyenne brave, his entire being revolved around the hunt and personal combat. Society, religion and culture depended upon it. It was all about individuality with warriors doing their utmost to win honours for themselves by acting recklessly, such as counting coup on living and dead enemies. The ultimate coup would be to snatch an enemy's weapon from out of his hands and get away with it; far more important than actually killing him. So, bravado reigned with discipline being barely considered. The leadership of chiefs existed not so much in their ability to issue orders (which no warrior was compelled to obey) but more in the respect they could manufacture which would lead to a personal following. Chiefs in battle acted as rallying points whose job it was to inspire their followers, a talent which the likes of Crazy Horse and Gall managed perfectly. So an Indian charge would be a "cut and thrust" free for all, with braves weaving in and out of the melee, showing off and shrieking. That said, warriors would instinctively know where they might be needed for the good of all and would usually react accordingly.

The horse or pony was immensely important, of course, and mounted skills were a standard feature of the Plains tribes. No brave would survive for long without his legendary agility on horseback. One skill involved shooting from under the shelter of a pony's neck whilst at the gallop.

Tribes were made up of warrior societies or *akicitas*. Membership was earned by the winning of various honours or feats of endurance and each had its own badges of rank and prestige, very much a pecking order. The Cheyenne, for instance had their Dog-Soldiers, tenacious fighters who sometimes served as a kind of tribal police force. Sitting Bull apparently belonged to the Kit-Fox society although there were others like the Brave Hearts and Whitemarks. There was a great deal of competition between these societies.

Dressing for war was also a priority and, if a warrior had time, he would spend hours painting and preening himself, decorating his hair, body and pony before picking up his weapons. These decorations meant far more than pure vanity, for each design denoted recognisable traits, from society membership and visionary experience to battle honours and personal "medicine" (i.e. power). Leaders wore "scalp shirts" as a badge of office, decorated with beadwork, pendants and hair, all of which meant something. War paint was highly personal but there were certain standard markings like a hand print on a pony's flank which would indicate the killing of an enemy in hand-to-hand combat.

A wide variety of weapons were carried. The traditional bow and arrow had been in constant use since earliest times and became shorter for easier handling when the tribes adopted the horse. Arrows were personalised with intricate markings, the heads of bone or flint being gradually replaced by metal as business with white traders increased. These shafts, in the hands of a skilled bowman, could be fired with great force and could penetrate deeply into a human skull at close range. Stone headed war clubs were also carried, along with metal bladed hatchets and tomahawks. Knives, often of the Bowie and Butcher variety, were usually obtained from the whites, while long lances were most often carried by the Cheyenne. Small round shields added to a warrior's protection although they would not stop a bullet. They looked pretty, though, being lavishly decorated and imbued with apparent spiritual power. A coup stick might very well complete a brave's armoury.

As for firearms, ever since the first guns had been traded or taken from the early white explorers, they were considered objects of enormous prestige. The better the gun, the better the man. That fateful Summer of 1876, Sitting Bull's followers would carry into battle a mind boggling variety of rifles, muskets, pistols and revolvers. There were at least 200 modern repeaters of the highest quality and numerous other cartridge fired weapons, and that was even before the Indians managed to capture large numbers of army weapons from the battlefield. Most of these had been obtained from conscience free white entrepreneurs, although most of them denied it, hence the embargo on the arms trade. Indians were particularly fond of hand guns, like the six shot Remington or Colt, when they could get them, for it was an ideal weapon for close up fighting on horseback.

They also liked to customise their rifles by brass studding the stocks and keeping them in embroidered buckskin scabbards.

This time, much to the surprise of the army, the Indians were not going to run.

Sioux and Cheyenne warriors gather before the battle. The Cheyenne brave in the foreground is armed with a Winchester repeating rifle. Behind him a mounted Lakota chief clutches his war club and coup stick.

FORWARD HO!

Lt. Col. George Armstrong Custer must have been in his element. Always energetic, forever keen and optimistic, here was a man who made huge assumptions about his destiny. His eventual immortality would no doubt have pleased him but he could not have expected for one moment that it would take such a tragic course.

Defeat could not have been further from his mind than on that early misty morning of May 17th. 1876 when General Terry ordered the Dakota Column to strike out west from Fort Abraham Lincoln. The array of troops and strong support was impressive. Terry was leading five companies of infantry, 150 mule drawn supply wagons, 200 civilian employees (teamsters, etc.) and about forty Arikara (Ree) Indian scouts. He also brought along three Gatling guns, those devastating multi-barrelled weapons which were so effective against a massed enemy but which proved to be far too cumbersome for a campaign such as this. However, the pride of the force had to be Custer's dashing 7th. Cavalry, all twelve companies reunited at last.

Wheeling and prancing his horse at the head of his column, Autie can well be imagined basking in the glory of the moment. Re-instated to his rightful position at the final hour, the "General" would have been feeling particularly pleased with himself as he looked ahead to his golden opportunity. Mounted on Dandy, his perfectly groomed favourite horse, Custer led his troops on a final trot around the parade ground. Wives and other assorted women had turned out in droves to watch this glorious departure, none of them entirely sure if they would see their menfolk again. Waving men away to war has always historically been a poignantly stirring moment. Some of the women wept as they embraced their partners, others kept their dignity and hid their feelings, wafting little white handkerchiefs in the breeze. As the soldiers rode by their quarters a few ladies dashed forward, reaching up to clasp hands, pass farewell gifts or force their men to lean down out of the saddles for a last snatched kiss. The families of the Ree scouts were demonstrative in their own customary manner, wailing despondently and pulling at their hair.

Custer looked every inch the cavalier, controlling his mount with effortless skill, those piercing blue eyes acknowledging familiar faces in the crowd with a superior air. He oozed authority and confidence. Those women must have felt slightly comforted by the knowledge that their men were going into battle under the command of a man whose luck was legendary and who had never faced defeat. Autie was dressed in a crisp, blue nautical style blouse, decorated with rows of gleaming buttons and white piping on the chest and collar, from beneath which fluttered the vivid scarlet slash of his trademark scarf. His knee length, black cavalry boots were of the finest leather into which were tucked fringed buckskin trousers. He also had long white gauntlets and a cream coloured hat, the broad brim of which was pinned to the crown to give a sweeping, jaunty effect. On this campaign he was wearing a new buckskin jacket which had been specially made for him by one of his men, who was a tailor by trade. This was Tipperary Irishman Jeremiah Finley, a sergeant in Tom Custer's Co. C. Finley had been with the 7th. since the Washita. This kind of display of devotion was not unusual from the men who rode with Autie. He still carried the finely crafted pocket watch which had been presented to him by his troopers during the Civil War, the back inscribed with the message *"To General Custer from the Michigan Brigade. 'RIDE YOU WOLVERINES'"*.

The "General", like many of his officers, had armed himself with his own personal choice of weapons. Autie favoured a pair of British made, snub nosed, self cocking Bulldog pistols which he wore in flapped holsters, butts forward, on either side of his waist. His rifle was a Remington, sporting model. Close behind him rode the bearer of his battle flag, another Irish sergeant named Robert Hughes. This flag was of swallow tail design, red and blue and emblazoned with white crossed sabres.

George Custer was now 36 years old and although he still cut a dash, as they say, he was not quite the "Prince Rupert" figure of a dozen years before. He had not exactly mellowed, but he was wiser and perhaps slightly more cautious. Experience and the stress of frontier command (as well as concern for his future) had resulted in a certain strain becoming evident in those haughty features. His body was still lean and active but those famous long golden locks were not as luxuriant as they had once been and he was showing signs of early balding. Although he generally continued to wear his hair long, for this campaign he had dramatically changed his appearance and had it shorn off and cropped close to his head. Even so, he still retained his huge moustache which bulged bushily away from his lips and swept almost down to his chin. Bloody Knife and the other Rees referred to him, reverentially, as "Son-of-the-Morning-Star", in homage to his victory at the Washita when that bright star had preceded the attack.

The 7th. Cavalry was considerably under strength the day they left Fort Lincoln, for quite a few officers and enlisted men were absent on detached service. That said, Custer was pleased to be able to number most of his favoured clique as he rode out west. Brother Tom had been promoted to captain just six months before and now commanded C Co.. Brother-in-Law James Calhoun rode with Tom as C's 1st. Lieutenant and young brother Boston had been found a position (on the insistence of the "General") as a civilian quartermaster and "guide", although he was not really qualified for the post. Completing this jolly family group came the Custer brother's eighteen year old civilian nephew, Harry Armstrong Reed (also known as "Autie"), who joined the column devoid of any specific role (arguably, he was a herder) and was merely along for the ride.

Custer's immediate staff included Maj. Marcus Reno, now back from his European leave and with his nose somewhat out of joint. Thinking that Custer had been removed from the equation, he had been petitioning Terry for full command of the 7th. in the field and was brooding about having been knocked back to this secondary role. Canadian Adjutant Cooke, his whiskers still as magnificent as ever, was Autie's trusted right hand man, an officer who had proved himself efficient time and again during his long service with the regiment. The chief trumpeter, assigned to the staff in that capacity, was a German who originally hailed from Hanover, one Henry Voss. Voss had been recently promoted from a private in Capt. Thomas McDougall's B Co. to this exalted position at the head of the regiment with his C.O.. Quite a surprising move when considering that just a few months previously Voss had been in serious trouble for assaulting a sergeant. Now he was proudly doing his best to make up for that shortfall. Custer's Sergeant Major was an Englishman, born in Yorkshire, who for some reason liked to state that he was born at sea. His name was William Sharrow and having transferred from the 2nd. Cavalry, he had been with the 7th. since 1869.

Commanding the scouts was 2nd. Lt. Charles Varnum. White civilian scouts, contracted to the army, included characters like Fred Girard, who had been engaged expressly as an interpreter for the Indian scouts. The only black man on the campaign was big Isaiah Dorman, a mysterious figure who had lived an active life on the frontier intermittently working for the whites and living with the Sioux. He was well known to the tribes who called him by several names, including Black Hawk and Teat. Described by Fred Girard as "... a man of considerable intelligence who enjoyed the respect and confidence of the soldiers ...", Isaiah married a Santee squaw and fathered two sons. Custer made a point of requesting his engagement as an interpreter for the Sioux so he was obviously considered an asset to the expedition. He was popular with the Lakota but was destined to suffer badly at their hands because they considered him a traitor for having helped the *wasichus*.

And then, of course, there was "Lonesome" Charley Reynolds who Custer had held in high esteem as an advisor and scout since first meeting him during frontier engagements in 1869. Reynolds was not outwardly typical of his breed for he came from a respectable background in Kentucky where his father was an eminent physician. Charley even attended college for three years before heading west for adventure. First he tried digging for gold in Colorado, got involved in Indian fights and worked as an escort on the Santa Fe trail. During the Civil War he fought as a volunteer along the Kansas-Missouri border before trying various trading ventures in New Mexico. He then became a professional buffalo hunter along the Republican River as well as a trapper, the experience furnishing him with the necessary skills which would eventually be so valuable to Custer. By nature he was quietly spoken with darting blue eyes which never seemed to miss a trick. Stocky in build, he did not seem to abide by swearing, drinking or smoking, which was most unlike his fellow scouts. His reserved manner could easily be misconstrued however, for he was a formidable fighter, when necessary, and once even crippled an army officer who pushed him too far. As a rule, he kept very much to himself but was glad to take Custer's offer to work as a guide in the Sioux campaign of 1876.

Contemptuous, but useful, Capt. Benteen commanded H Co.. By contrast, hanging on Custer's every word and, nowadays, keeping a respectful distance from Libbie, rode Capt. Tom Weir at the head of D Co.. Custer's close friend George Yates was still the captain in charge of F Co., along with the devilish Myles Keogh and his "Wild I" Co., Capt. Myles Moylan's A Co. and Co. M under Capt. Thomas French. 1st. Lt. Donald McIntosh, another Canadian, who had Scottish and Indian blood in his veins, rode with Co. G and would eventually lead them. His mother was a direct descendant of an important Indian chief of the Six Nations but his father was actually killed by red men when Donald was only fourteen years old. Judging by his photographs, McIntosh, with his cleft chin and sharp nose, resembled a young Kirk Douglas, but he was said to have a slow, "pokey" manner which engaged the wrath of the 7th.'s overall commander, Col. Sturgis, who rebuked him for being an inefficient malingerer. Custer, however, did not seem to have a problem with him. His friends called him "Tosh".

1st. Lt. Edward Godfrey was to lead K Co.. He had twin mustachios which almost (but not quite!) challenged the splendid set of Adjutant Cooke. Godfrey had been placed in charge of the infamous pony slaughtering squad by Custer at the Washita in 1868. Since then he had served in every major action with the 7th. Cavalry, including the Yellowstone and Black Hills expeditions (in which he had acted as assistant engineering officer). In late 1875 he had been given the task of disarming agency Indians in the build up to the Sioux campaign. As such he was a highly experienced and valued officer. Finally, making up the total complement of Custer's company commanders, came 1st. Lt. Algernon "Fresh" Smith (Co. A), another Washita veteran, who would eventually find himself transferred to the head of E Co., a unique troop because they alone were mounted on light grey horses. They were therefore unanimously known as the "Grey Horse Troop". These, then, were the twelve companies of the 7th. Cavalry in the summer of 1876. Note the absence of a J Co. to avoid confusion, because J, when spoken, can sound like A, and when written can look like I.

Little Phil Sheridan had made a point that he did not want any newspapermen tagging along on this expedition, but Custer had other ideas and wanted to make sure that his exploits were related in full to the outside world. True to form, he arranged for a reporter from the Bismarck Tribune to accompany his column in the field. This would ensure that all reports would also find their way into the widely read and influential New York Herald. Assigned to the task was an editorial assistant named Mark Kellogg, a 43 year old, grey haired, bespectacled studious type who rode a mule laden down with bulging canvas saddle bags.

How stirring it must have been, regardless of the early hour, to watch the long column moving over the hills of the western horizon, saddles creaking, horse bits jangling, wagon wheels turning, flags and pennants fluttering, sheathed sabres and other weapons glinting in the watery sunlight, Custer with his staghounds lolloping along beside him as they tried to keep pace with Dandy. All this to the strains of Vinatieri's excellent brass band as they played *Garry Owen* (naturally!) and that other anthem of the cavalry, immortalized in those John Ford Western films, "The Girl I Left Behind Me".

How eerie that the meteorological conditions were just right to create a most peculiar but stunning effect, for the whole column was reflected high above in the sky, giving the impression that the soldiers were spookily, but gloriously, making their way to Heaven! The Fort Lincoln populace gasped at the spectacle but it was all too much for Libbie Custer. She bit her lip and placed her hand against her mouth, trembling from the sheer drama of the moment. Autie's goodbye had been wonderfully romantic, Victorian melodrama at its best, as he embraced his wife from the saddle and whispered for her to look out for his return. Unable to watch him go, Libbie, along with the similarly affected Maggie Calhoun, mounted up and took off after the vanishing troops, catching up with her "darling boy" along the trail.

And so it was that Autie and Libbie were able to spend a final blissful night together beneath the stars, but, in the cold light of the following morning on the banks of the appropriately named Little Heart River, their loving goodbyes had to be final.

It was the last time she would ever see him.

BOOTS, SADDLES AND AUTIE'S BOYS

It may have been a euphoric departure for Custer, but many of his men were not quite so keen as they made their way deep into this largely uncharted wilderness. Private Jim Troy of I Company was not untypical of the way the rank and file felt and had seen enough already. The landscape was windswept and bleak, broken only by the odd ravine, and they had made painfully slow progress in the seventeen days since leaving Fort Lincoln. Although it was early summer, the column had been held up for two days by a harsh and most unseasonal blizzard which had swept the plains with driving snow. Only now, June 3rd., had they been able to get under way again. With the Little Missouri River at their backs, the troops and their support had covered 25 miles that day across the soggy, thawing ground, destined to camp that evening on Beaver Creek. Fort Lincoln was still only 200 miles behind them and they had a long way to go in their hunt for old Sitting Bull.

Private Troy hunched in his saddle and looked around at his comrades as they plodded along the trail. He was pleased to feel a little mild warmth creeping back into the atmosphere at last but the men were morose and resentful. Old "Hard Ass" hadn't helped by withholding their pay until they were well clear of anywhere where they might be able to cut loose and spend it. Autie was no fool. He knew the reputation of his troops and did not wish to take to the field with a hung over regiment. Consequently, the 7th. were riding into hostile territory with their pockets bulging with cash. Only the regular gambling games in the nightly camps could relieve them of any of it.

Troy was glad to be part of the "Wild I" and, like the rest of his company, felt respect (and some trepidation) for their troop commander, Keogh, who rode point on his big bay horse, "Comanche", head bent against the wind. Keogh, with his dark eyes that blazed like embers, was not greatly liked by most of his subordinates because of his drunken temper but they looked up to him as a combat leader and fighter of admirable spirit. A true Irish brawler. More than a few of his troop shared his far away heritage; men like Sergeant James Bustard from Donegal, Private Pat Kelly from County Mayo and Private Archie McIlhargey from Antrim. In this they had much in common, the universal bond of sentimental, hard drinking Irishmen far from home, but Myles Keogh never let them forget that he was their captain. Even that horse of his was tough, reputably receiving the name Comanche during a scrap with that tribe down near the Cimarron Strip a few years back when he was hit in the rump by an arrow.

Jim Troy was 27 years old, had grey eyes, brown hair and a dark complexion. At 5'5" tall he was not uncommonly short for a trooper in the 7th. for the company rosters show that the average height was between 5'4" to 5'9", with most of them being at the lower end of the scale. In civilian life he had been a shoemaker who had enlisted in Boston at the end of 1871, but his army career had been stormy, making him an appropriate candidate for the "Wild I". More than once he had faced dishonourable discharge for such offences as abusive language on duty, drunken-ness and theft. Like Chief Trumpeter Voss (on Custer's staff), he too had assaulted a sergeant, a past-time which seems to have been popular in the 7th. Cavalry. Just seven months ago, Private Adam Hetesimer (also from the "Wild I") had seized an axe, whilst confined for other offences, and hurled it at one of his company sergeants, Milton de Lacy. This missile had fortunately missed its target, for all of these men now rode together in a single unit, doubtless nursing their various grievances.

Troy had only recently completed his sentence of confinement and hard labour, along with enforced loss of pay, and would have been dressed in typical campaign attire. His sky blue, kersey wool trousers, with inside legs and seat heavily reinforced with canvas to relieve all that saddle friction, would be worn either over or tucked inside his knee high, black leather boots. His much darker blue over blouse, single breasted with a row of brass buttons, was made of coarse material and the standard issue grey flannel under shirt may have been replaced by a garment of his own choice. Not a few of the troopers preferred to wear more comfortable privately purchased shirts which were often of the popular, frontier chequered variety. Bandanas were personal items and could be of numerous patterns and shades. The 7th.'s headwear would officially have been the previously mentioned black felt slouch hat, a strange looking *chapeau* which could be bent into odd shapes. More often than not, the troopers wore it with the brim flopped down. They were also issued with an overcoat, a rainproof poncho, haversack, tin cup and canteen for water (although these were often topped up with hard liquor). Mounted on what was known as the McClellan saddle (made of beech wood and leather), Custer's men also carried a rope and picket pin for securing their horses and a rough blanket would be rolled up and strung across the saddle's pommel. Slung alongside this would be a canvas bag of oats to keep the horse nourished whilst on the trail.

Cavalry weapons included two standard firearms, a carbine held by an adjustable leather sling, and a revolver. The former was the 1873 model .45/.55 calibre Springfield Carbine, a single shot weapon which was breech loaded through a trap door mechanism. Despite a reputation it gained for unreliability, the Springfield was, in fact, a rugged piece which usually performed well provided it was kept maintained. It has often been asked why the army issued its soldiers with single shot weapons when so many of the enemy possessed repeating rifles, but there are several reasons for this. Primarily it was because the Springfield's design was simple (a repeater being quite complex) therefore making it much more economical to produce in large numbers. Without intricate mechanisms, it reduced the chances of parts failing and made the weapon less susceptible to damage or climatical deterioration. A slower rate of fire would enable officers to exercise more control over their men when in combat and would encourage accuracy rather than rapidity. This would also result in a more efficient use of ammunition, i.e. much less waste of cartridges. Even so, a competent trooper would still be able to snap off at least six well aimed shots in a minute. In addition, the Springfield had an effective range of 250 yards, double that of a rapid firing repeater, so the logic behind the decision was sound. That decision had been arrived at by a specially appointed board of officers, chosen by the Congressional Appropriation's Act. Coincidentally, as it turned out, the president of this board was Brigadier General Alfred Terry (eventual commander of the Dakota Column) and one of his team was Maj. Marcus Reno. Strange that Reno should have been one of those responsible for the choice of a weapon upon which his life would one day depend. The carbine went into production in 1873, acquiring its name from the armoury where it was manufactured in Springfield, Missouri, but the 7th. Cavalry were not issued with it until mid 1875.

The 7th.'s side arm was the radical newly designed Colt single action revolver (1873 pattern), or "Peacemaker", which was made famous to modern eyes by its regular appearances in countless Western movies. It carried six shells in its chamber and had been in use by Custer's boys since early '74, so they had plenty of opportunity to try out their target practice in the sacred Black Hills (although use of ammunition was strictly limited). Issued with leather pouches to carry their ammunition, most cavalrymen preferred to store their shells in looped cartridge belts around their waists, one thick leather band for carbine rounds and a thinner one for the "Peacemaker"'s bullets. On the trail, mounted troopers were issued with 100 rounds of carbine ammunition (half of which would be carried in their saddle bags) and 24 rounds of revolver ammunition. As a rule, on a big campaign, they were able to rely upon the nearby support of a pack train for reserves. The majority of men also liked to carry a sturdy knife too, not only as a back-up weapon but because of its myriad other uses. Naturally, as cavalrymen, the 7th.

had curved sabres kept in scabbards, but these "long knives", as the Indians called them, were to play virtually no part at all at the Little Bighorn, as we shall see.

Several of the regiment's officers had copied their C.O. by adopting the wearing of fringed buckskin jackets (notably brother Tom, Adjutant Cooke and George Yates), along with fancy (although military or naval style) shirts, giving them an even more emphasised appearance as some kind of elite club. Officers, as well as sergeants and corporals, were authorised to sport bright yellow stripes down the outside seams of their sky blue trousers. Indian scouts were issued with standard U.S. Army uniforms although, as a rule, they tended to wear a mixture of these items and their traditional tribal apparel. Contracted to the army as civilians, white scouts could wear what they pleased. (The role of all scouts was to provide terrain knowledge, navigation and intelligence about enemy movements.) It was, therefore, a most colourful and mixed bag of heavily armed individuals who pursued Sitting Bull that summer. (Godfrey's K Co. were even known as the "Dude Troop" because they had taken their white canvas stable duty trousers and had them tailored into tight fitting britches.)

*   *   *

So how detailed was this campaign plan designed to destroy the spirit of the hostiles forever? The answer is, not very. Little Phil Sheridan had come up with an overall scheme which, despite his long experience of frontier command, seems to have severely under rated the fighting capability of his adversaries.

Lack of co-ordination was the main problem. Sheridan did not specify one overall commander of the three pronged advance against the hostiles and Terry, Gibbon and Crook acted independently of each other with only a most basic single objective to go on. It was all very well to speak of crushing the enemy in this triple vice, but communication between the columns was dependent upon mounted couriers who sometimes mis-interpreted information and, naturally, took considerable time relaying messages.

Sitting Bull and the bulk of the hostiles were thought to be congregating in the country south of the Yellowstone River. This was the northern Powder River territory which was criss crossed by numerous tributaries of the Yellowstone, such as the Rosebud, Tongue, Tullock and Mizpah Creeks, as well as the larger, far western Bighorn River (which flowed through the Bighorn Mountains) and the Powder itself. It was a massive area in which to pin down elusive Indians and the main fear of the army commanders was that their prey would manage to slip through the net. That was why it was imperative that the scouts must quickly locate the main bands and then keep close tabs on them until the main bodies of troops could begin their assault. The army columns were powerful but slow moving, no match in speed for the nomadic, nimble tribesmen and their families who could dash away swiftly, once warned, as they had done so often before. Units like Custer's highly mobile 7th. Cavalry would therefore be invaluable in such a campaign.

The regiment's twelve companies were grouped into battalions of variable sizes, between two and seven companies in each, depending upon the circumstances. Each company comprised 60 to 75 men, approximately, although, as previously mentioned, by the time the 7th. got to the Little Bighorn it was well under strength, owing to various reasons. Technically, each company should be led by a captain but situations sometimes changed this. For instance, by late June, 1st. Lt. Godfrey was in command of his "Dude Troop" K because their captain was on detached service. For the same reason, 1st. Lt. "Tosh" McIntosh was to lead Co. G. Co. L's officers were all absent, so 1st. Lt. Calhoun would end up transferred from Tom Custer's Co. C to take command. All a bit complicated, but officers and enlisted men often found themselves assigned to different companies. Each company was also supposed to have a 1st. and 2nd. lieutenant, one 1st. sergeant, four or five subordinate sergeants, three or four corporals, at least one trumpeter, probably two farriers to care for the horses, a saddler and a few dozen privates. Battalion commanders were Maj. Reno and senior captains Yates, Keogh and Benteen. Counting Vinatieri's band and Custer's staff, this sent the 7th. Cavalry out into the field with the Dakota Column numbering under 800 men.

However, although Custer and most of his regimental officers were long serving, experienced campaigners, that was not the case with the bulk of his men. Quite a few of the 7th.'s rank and file had been with the "General" since the beginning, and these men were worth their weight in Black Hill's gold, but in 1876 the regiment had a large percentage of raw recruits who had barely learned to control their mounts properly by the time they left Fort Lincoln on this urgent campaign. Even the majority of those who had enlisted some time ago had never fired their weapons in combat for it had been some time since there had been a significant action against Indians. Many of Autie's boys were riding into their first and last battle.

And, similar to the situation at The Alamo forty years before, not all of them could claim to be "All American Boys". Like any frontier regiment (and less than some) the 7th. Cavalry's company rosters could boast immigrant recruits from all over the globe. Not surprisingly, the largest contingent were Irish; over 130 of them, then came almost the same amount from Germany or its provinces, forty Englishmen, twelve Scots and a couple from the Welsh valleys. Then there were those from Poland, Norway, Sweden, Switzerland, Italy, Spain and Hungary, for example, and even one from Australia.

Apart from alcoholism, which was rife, not a few of these troopers suffered from chronic back problems and poor dental hygiene. (Although Autie himself was meticulous about the care of his own teeth.) Dysentery appears to have been a common occupational hazard.

Not exactly the crisp looking, chisel jawed, tanned and healthy uniform bunch who rode to the rescue across Hollywood's silver screen for decades, but, on the whole, they would prove themselves tough in the hard times that lay just ahead. As for George Custer, regardless of their imperfections, he had total confidence that his men could take on the entire Sioux Nation.

At least, he was about to try.

7th. Cavalry weaponry (not to scale). Standard issue to troopers, 1876.

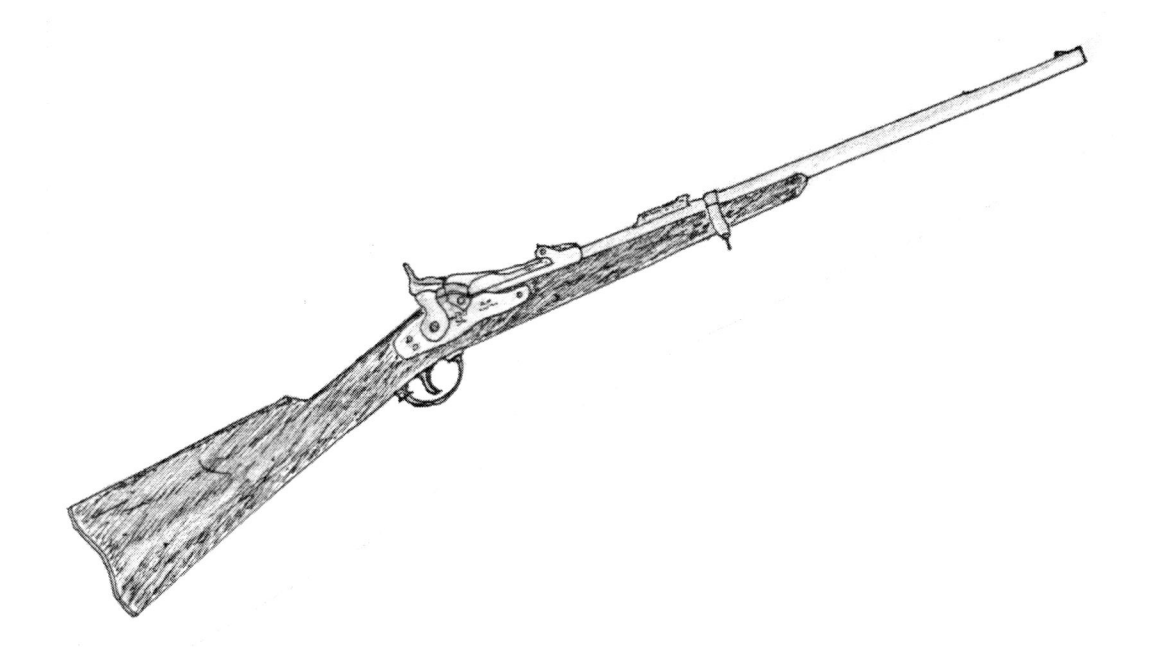

Springfield carbine.

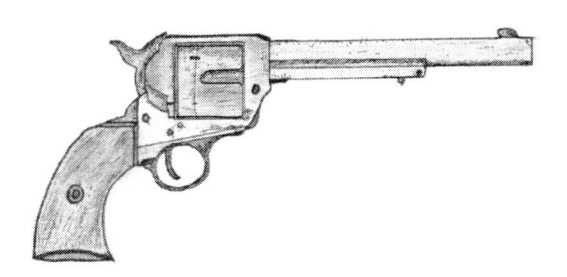

Colt revolver.

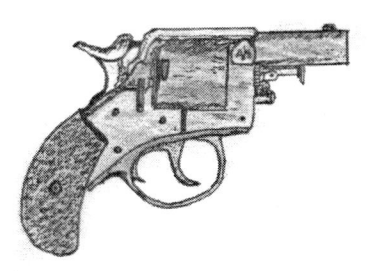

Lt. Col. Custer's personal choice. Two of these British made Webley "Bulldog" revolvers. He also carried a long range Remington Creedmore sporting rifle.

CAMPAIGN

By the time Terry's Dakota Column left Fort Lincoln, Col. John Gibbon's Montana Column had been in the field for over six weeks. It had left Fort Ellis, which was sited on the old Bozeman Trail, on April 1st. heading east along the Yellowstone River before consolidating a camp at the mouth of Tullock Creek. Here Gibbon received orders from Terry's couriers to wait until the movements of all the columns could be co-ordinated.

Gibbon was an infantry officer whose column comprised not only six companies of the 7th. Infantry but also four companies of Maj. James Brisbin's 2nd. Cavalry, about 450 men in all. He had employed 25 Crow Indian scouts who were under the command of a particularly skilled officer who understood his charges well and acted with great initiative. This was 1st. Lieutenant James Bradley, a man who would prove extremely valuable. As chief interpreter for the Crow scouts, Gibbon had chosen a half breed named Mitch Bouyer, a character who the colonel described as being, ".....next to Jim Bridger, the best guide in the country". Bouyer's father was a French trapper who was killed by Indians, but his mother was a full blood Santee Sioux which gave him his broad face, large nose and dark looks. Mitch's relationship with the frontier became second nature to him and he learned his trade by working with the likes of the great scout Bridger himself, who became his mentor. He spent his whole life as a guide and interpreter in and around the Powder River country and therefore knew it like the back of his hand, associating freely with the Sioux, Bannacks, Snakes and Crows. Naturally, he spoke Indian languages fluently and forged an especially close relationship with the Crow tribe which led to his decision to take the white man's side. That said, he had many contacts amongst the Sioux, who knew him as "Two Bodies", but, never-the-less, helped the soldiers fight them. Bouyer, like "Lonesome" Charley, was apparently softly spoken but he was also affable, intelligent and courageous. More than anything, he was known to be loyal to those he served with and would eventually make the ultimate sacrifice.

Idling his time on the river, Gibbon sent his scouts out on a series of patrols to scour the area for Indian sign. At first they found nothing, but Bradley eventually located a hostile village on the Tongue. Gibbon's attempts to attack it were thwarted by his failure to transport his troops safely across to the south bank of the Yellowstone, although the nimble Sioux retaliated by spending the next couple of weeks harassing the army camp. Abruptly, this contact with the enemy ceased on May 23rd. and they melted away again.

In the meantime, Terry's column was pushing west. Impatient as ever, Custer took the initiative to lead a limited scouting expedition of four companies on May 29th., without Terry's authority, but returned on the 31st. having found nothing. Mild mannered Terry scolded the errant "General" for having deserted the main command but Custer took it in his stride. It was then that the unexpected blizzard set in, delaying the whole column for two days before they managed to push on to Beaver Creek where a messenger arrived from Gibbon with a dispatch dated May 27th.. The message downplayed what had been happening to the Montana Column and spoke only of Indians in the area with no significant activity. Gibbon did, however, ask for the use of a boat to enable his men to cross the river. This last request could be granted, for Terry had arranged for the expedition to be supported by steamboats which had travelled up the Missouri River, turning south-west along the Yellowstone. They were now at the Glendive Depot, just to the north of Beaver Creek, so Terry sent orders to the steamer *Far West* to carry on along the river to establish a base at the mouth of the Powder.

Terry was anxious for the two converging columns to link up. The Powder River confluence with the Yellowstone was still a ninety mile ride away so the Dakota Column was ordered to move on with all haste. This time Terry personally went ahead, leaving an envious Custer in charge of the column, and when the Brigadier-General arrived at the

Powder, on June 8th., he found advance elements of Gibbon's 2nd. Cavalry waiting for him. Meeting up with Maj. Brisbin, and later with Gibbon himself, Terry was given a full update on Indian activity in the area. With the supply laden *Far West* docked on the shoreline and Custer riding in with the remaining troops, this meant that matters were nicely consolidated and the campaign could move into its next phase.

As Gibbon's superior in rank, Terry now had full command of both columns. The officers and scouts conferred about the most probable movements of the hostiles and it was decided that the main body of the troops should carry on west along the Yellowstone while a reconnaissance force was sent south. The command of this mobile foray was given to Maj. Reno, a decision which satisfied him no end, for it incensed the jealous Custer who felt he should have the monopoly on this kind of thing. Perhaps Terry kept Custer in check on this occasion to teach him a lesson although Autie himself felt that it was an un-necessary scout which would only delay the campaign. After all, the known Indian activity was much further west than the area which Reno had been told to explore.

Reno's orders were specific. He was to take six companies of the 7th. Cavalry (Troops B, C, E, F, I and L) and ride in a clockwise loop, first south along the Powder and then back north across the Mizpah and Pumpkin Creeks before reuniting with the column at the mouth of the Tongue, hopefully having gathered fresh information. Terry was definite in his instructions that on no account was Reno to venture west across the Tongue, for it was feared that his presence might forewarn the largest groups of Indians who it was suspected had gathered along the Rosebud.

Initially delayed by a heavy downpour of rain, Reno smugly set off at the head of the troops on the afternoon of June 10th., taking with him a Gatling gun and the knowledgeable Mitch Bouyer as his guide. Their discoveries were to prove much more significant than anticipated.

* * *

Much further south, at Fort Fetterman, Brigadier General George Crook had been re-assembling his force and was now ready, and determined, to make amends for the humiliating debacle brought on by Col. Reynolds' inefficient offensive back in March. Crook was to ride out on May 29th. at the head of the largest of the three columns, pushing north towards the advancing armies of Gibbon and Terry. Supported by the usual huge supply train and civilian contingent, Crook's column included fifteen companies of the 2nd. and 3rd. Cavalry and five companies of the 4th. and 9th. Infantry. Crook made it clear that he was now very much at the helm, for he had every intention of preserving his hard earned reputation. His appearance may have been eccentric and slightly alarming, with his wild beard, cork sun helmet and double barrelled shotgun across his shoulder, but this old soldier had proved himself to be an Indian fighter par-excellence.

Taking an uncertain, roundabout route (because his chief scout Frank Grouard was absent on a recruiting assignment), Crook's men finally bivouacked some dozen miles south of the Tongue where, on June 14th., Grouard rode into camp with over 250 Crow and Shoshone warriors who had agreed to help oust their hated enemies, the Sioux. Unlike Terry and Gibbon's Indian scouts, who were present merely to *find* the enemy, these native allies of Crook's *were* expected to fight. This brought the strength of the Wyoming column up to over 1,300 men. Little wonder that they felt confident.

* * *

As for Sitting Bull and his followers, since late April they had been moving steadily south west from the Powder, a vast, ponderous trail of warriors, women, children, old folk, dogs, travois and a gigantic herd of ponies. With each passing day additional nomadic groups joined this throng and the mood of these so called fugitives was growing increasingly confident as their numbers swelled. Crossing the Tongue, pausing only to take a few stabs at Gibbon's troops, the Indian exodus made its way to the Rosebud and ambled south down the Creek in leisurely pursuit of a particularly large buffalo herd. In early June they camped on the bank to indulge in their annual Sun Dance ceremony.

This year the Dance would be especially significant. The Lakota and their allies knew they were being pursued but they felt their medicine was strong. Sitting Bull had inspired his people, imploring them to appeal for help to the Great Spirit. The revered holy man was personally prominent in the coming ritual, symbolically painting his body all over and having fifty chunks of flesh cut from each of his arms as an offering to Wakan Tanka. Along with others, he was then hooked by his chest muscles to the ceremonial pole, pouring with blood as he commenced to dance. Face turned upwards to the sun, Sitting Bull bore this ordeal for two days and nights before finally sinking into a trance. Anxiously his followers waited for him to revive and when he did so, he spoke of a vision which had shown the Lakota winning a big fight against the white soldiers. Afterwards he had visualized these *wasichus* tumbling headfirst into the Sioux camp.

This was excellent medicine indeed, although some said that the second part of the prophecy warned that spoils must not be taken from the dead soldiers. "Take things of the white man," said Sitting Bull, gravely, "and it will prove to be the curse of the nation". The Sioux heard but their mood was too jubilant for dark thoughts.

Let the Long Knives come. The Lakota were ready for them.

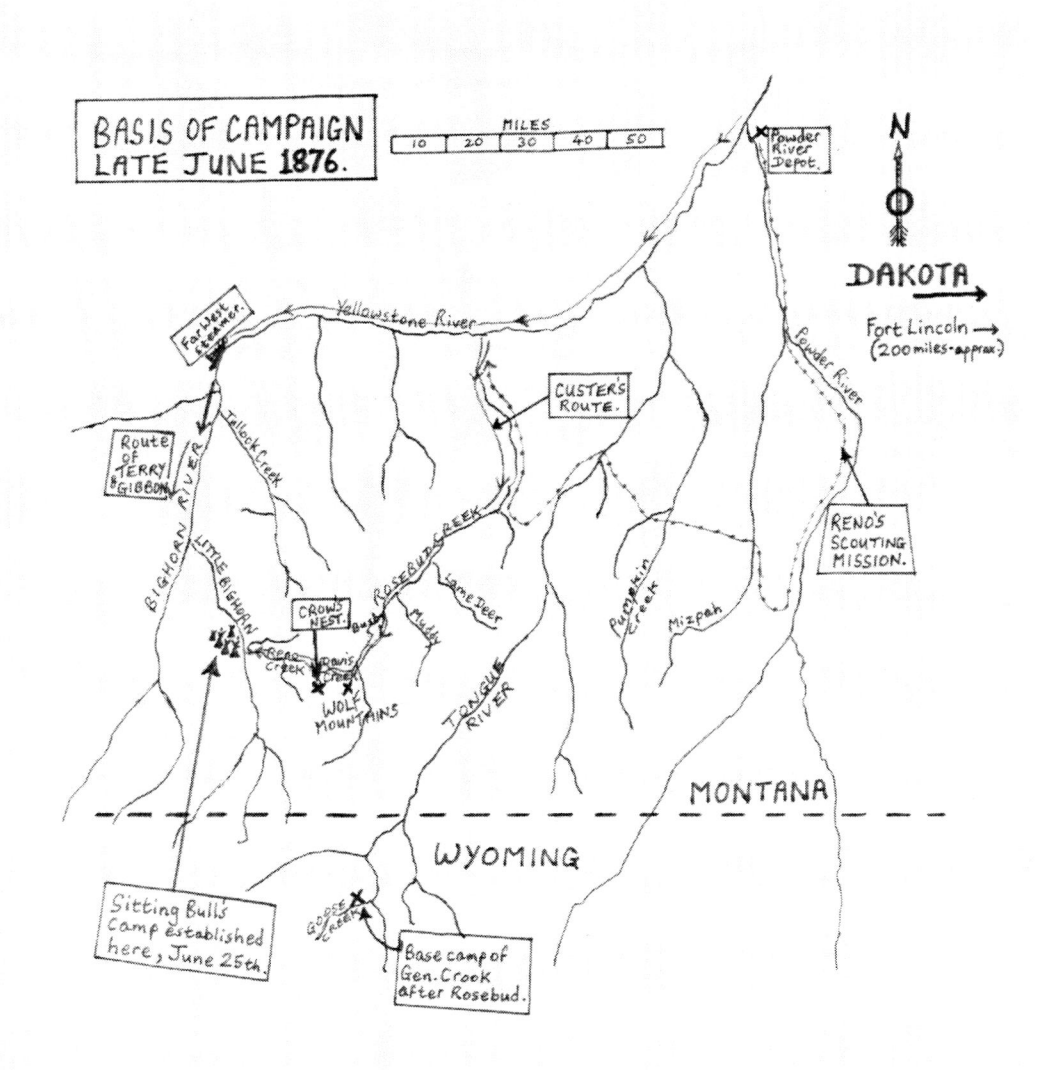

THE BATTLE OF THE ROSEBUD

New information on hostile movements via Grouard inspired Crook to get moving without further delay. Leaving his base camp at Goose Creek, the old Indian fighter ordered his men to prepare themselves for a speedy advance, travelling light with meagre rations. Even the infantrymen were to be mounted ..... on the pack mules! Many of these foot soldiers experienced great difficulty with their single day's riding training and it brought much hilarity to the watching cavalrymen who ribbed the clumsy novices mercilessly.

The whole column moved out at dawn on June 16th., trailing downriver before turning northwest along Spring Creek, a tributary of the Tongue. Early that evening, following a tiring 35 mile march (particularly for the mule riding infantrymen), they made camp in a swampy area close to the source of Rosebud Creek. Crook did not allow them to rest for long, however, for he had reveille sounded at 3.00am to prepare for another dawn start. Pushing on along the south fork of the Rosebud, the atmosphere grew tense. The rocky walled canyon was fringed with the blossom of roses and wild plums, the petals drifting gently down through the early morning sunlight; a tranquil scene which heralded the calm before the storm. Cautiously, the Crow and Shoshone scouts probed ahead, failing to find any definite sign of enemy presence yet instinctively sensing that the hated Lakota were nearby.

It was 8.00am. on June 17th.. The troops were looking fatigued already so Crook allowed them to stop and rest; no proper camp, as such, just a halt in marching order but the men were glad of it after their early start. Suddenly, rapid bursts of gunfire roared from the direction of the northern bluffs followed shortly after by a frantic scout who rode amongst the soldiers crying out that the Sioux were upon them.

Moments later, Crook and his officers were startled to see the unexpected spectacle of his Crow and Shoshone scouts galloping over the skyline, falling back and firing over their shoulders, hotly pursued by hundreds of shrieking Sioux and Cheyenne mounted warriors. These hostiles were taking the offensive in no half-hearted fashion and it was a ploy no one in Crook's column had allowed for. Sitting Bull's band were supposed to be fleeing but there was nothing craven about this screaming mob of savages. They were all fully adorned in war bonnets, scalp shirts, and buffalo horned helmets and had obviously taken plenty of time to prepare themselves for this moment. This kind of open aggression against a powerful army column was virtually unknown and said much about the hostile's confidence in their ability and willingness to resist.

The valiant fighting efforts of the scouts had slowed the Indian attack just enough to allow Crook to deploy his forces, otherwise the warriors would have been amongst the troops before they had a chance to throw aside their coffee cups. For the rest of the morning and well into the afternoon, both sides hurled themselves at each other in a series of attacks and counter-attacks, swooping in bold charges which more than once ended in savage hand to hand combat. At one point the battalion under the command of Lt.Col. Royall seemed in danger of being cut off and it was only a bout of particularly bold fighting which saved them. The Indians were acting with such aggression that Crook was convinced they must be desperately defending a nearby camp filled with their women and children, but this was not the case. This attack was the deliberate result of a recent tribal council meeting in which it had been decided to take the fight to the *wasichus*, whose progress had been monitored for days. It was the last thing they would be expecting and was a completely new tactic for the Sioux and Cheyenne, especially as they had acted with such uncharacteristic discipline in approaching Crook's column undetected. Although the great Chief Gall was not with them on this occasion, they were led by the mighty Crazy Horse.

It had been a long battle in which the hostiles had fought the U.S. Army to a standstill. Although Crazy Horse's braves eventually withdrew, the Indians considered it a victory. They had certainly exasperated, stunned and humiliated the great soldier chief "Grey Fox" Crook who had never before suffered such a setback. 1876 was not proving to be the General's year.

Even so, despite the hard fighting, the casualties were surprisingly light. Ten troopers and a Shoshone scout dead, with about twenty more wounded. One army casualty is worth detailing because he proved to be such a wonderful example of tenacious, frontier grit. Col. Guy Henry, who led the rear battalion which included the civilian contingent of packers, etc., was in the thick of the fighting when a hostile bullet smashed through his face, taking out one eye and demolishing his nose. Incredibly, he remained in his saddle, spitting out orders through mouthfuls of blood, urging on his men until he finally passed out and tumbled to the ground. Had it not been for a group of Shoshones who surrounded his body and fought hard to rescue him, that would have been the end of the tough colonel, but he was dragged to safety where he reportedly snapped, "It is nothing. For this we are soldiers!" Later he told a captain that despite what the surgeon had told him, he had no intention of dying just yet. Amazingly, this indestructible officer survived an extremely rough journey back to civilization where he recovered and eventually found himself back on active service!

The Sioux and Cheyenne suffered an estimated 100 dead and wounded, but their unusual willingness to accept such casualties during an extended battle, along with their staggering ferocity, had reaped rewards. Crook found it hard to believe the evidence of what he had just faced. Clearly shaken and realising that the Indian strength, not only in attitude but also in numbers, was far greater than anticipated, the "Grey Fox" decided to withdraw again. Taking his strong force back to the Goose Creek base camp, Crook entrenched himself there to lick his wounds and try to work out what went wrong. This effectively removed the entire Wyoming Column from the campaign for several weeks, a fact which would have severe repercussions for Terry and Gibbon further north.

The Sioux and Cheyenne were rightly overjoyed by what they had achieved although they realised that the fight was far from over. Crook's repulse at the Rosebud had been significant for them, but it did not fulfil Sitting Bull's prophecy of white soldiers falling headfirst into the Lakota camp.

That was yet to come.

RENO'S POINT

Several miles to the north, down the Rosebud, as Crook's men battled for their lives, six companies of the 7th.Cavalry were enjoying a leisurely, though cautious, halt on the banks of the Creek. The troopers were watering their horses and making the most of this unexpected and extended respite having endured the rigours of a night march. Their commander, Maj. Reno, had driven them hard over the last few days, reminiscent of the way they were used to being treated by their "Hard Ass General". The atmosphere was one of nervous anticipation, for the whole of this scouting column now knew that they were hot on the heels of their prey. Reno was taking no chances though. Pickets were posted around the camp and orders given that there were to be no bugle calls or other loud noises made.

Reno had been on his separate trail for a week and had initially followed his orders from General Terry closely. However, his scouts had found precious little sign of hostile activity so there would be nothing of significance worth reporting to the main column. It seems that Reno, anxious to assert himself, decided to take a chance and thereby take it upon himself to over-ride his orders, using the excuse that circumstances had led to a situation which inspired him to act independently for the over-all good of the campaign.

Having carried out about half of his intended mission, proceeding south up the Powder as ordered, then north down the Mizpah Creek, Reno consulted his scouts on their opinion as to the most likely route of the hostiles. Worldly wise Mitch Bouyer put forward his experienced viewpoint and this led to the column veering west beyond the Tongue, directly convening Terry's instructions. Bouyer and the Indian scouts (who numbered four Rees and four friendly Sioux) had found the abandoned site of the large hostile camp which Lt.Bradley had discovered a month before. Here was evidence of some 400 lodges and 300 campfires arranged in nine circles, a formidable gathering of Indians indeed. The half breed Bouyer was then able to report to Reno that a very large trail of hoof prints and dragged lodge poles (travois) could be seen stretching away along the Rosebud valley. This news was received late in the evening of June 16th. which led to Reno ordering a night march, the troops striking the Rosebud in darkness as they followed the trail.

At about 10.00am. the following morning, a halt was called on the banks of the Creek where the troops idled away most of the day while Bouyer and the other scouts rode ahead to investigate. Mitch led his Rees up the Rosebud, tracking the obvious signs for a further twelve miles until they came across the deserted site where Sitting Bull had held his Sun Dance at the beginning of the month. From here the scouts pushed on for a further seven miles to an oblique bend in the Rosebud called Lame Deer Creek. Now they were only a few miles north of the spot where, at that very moment, Crook and Crazy Horse were hacking away at each other but they were just too far away to be aware of it. Instead, the scouts wheeled their ponies and hastened back to Reno where Bouyer was able to report that the hostile camp's progress had three possibilities. It would probably continue to Busby Bend where it might carry on southwest up the Rosebud, north down Tullock's Fork or maybe west towards that tributary of the Bighorn River, the Little Bighorn. Whatever, Bouyer stated that a forced march would enable Reno's men to overtake the hostiles within 24 hours.

What to do? The troopers and their mounts were tired following the pressure of the last few days and provisions were stretching thin. Reno was tempted to press on and maybe win a little glory for himself, but common sense prevailed and he decided to abort his mission and pass on what he had learned to the main column. This information would be valuable indeed for it would necessitate the cancellation of Terry's original strategy. The intention had been to send two columns south, Gibbon up the Rosebud and Custer along the Tongue, with Autie's swift moving cavalry cutting west towards the Rosebud so as to, theoretically, catch the hostiles in a pincer movement. Mitch Bouyer's intelligence gathering had now rendered this plan obsolete as it was now obvious that Sitting Bull had travelled much further west than anticipated.

By the following day, Reno's column had linked up again with Terry, Gibbon and Custer, making contact at the mouth of the Tongue where it converged with the Yellowstone. Terry was angered by Reno's flagrant disregard for his orders but, privately, he could not deny that in doing so, the errant major had saved the whole expedition from an embarrassing blunder which would doubtless have led to the enemy's escape and dispersal. Custer officially called Reno's behaviour "inexcusable" and "inexplicable", characteristically putting more emphasis on the major's failure to overtake the village than on actually disobeying Terry's orders. Autie even stated that he thought a court martial could be pending. However, most of this outraged posturing by the high command was just a ploy to cover up their own errors. In reality they must have felt an enormous sense of relief that they had been presented with this unexpected opportunity to re-think their strategy.

* * *

There followed a day of rapid and chaotic re-organization as the various units consolidated their positions on the banks of the Yellowstone. Steaming down from the mouth of the Tongue came the *Far West*, laden with supplies which were well received by Reno's fatigued companies. However, there would be precious little rest for them since Autie had taken full command of the entire regiment once more. By 4.00pm. on June 20th. the re-united 7th. Cavalry was making its way west along the south bank of the Yellowstone to link up at the mouth of the Rosebud, some 25 miles away, with Gibbon's troops.

Early the next morning, the *Far West* tied up close to Gibbon's camp where the remainder of the men were re-supplied. On board was General Terry who wasted no time in putting into operation the next phase of his new plan. Having spoken at length with Mitch Bouyer, Terry held a conference below decks that afternoon with his highest ranking officers; Gibbon, Custer and Maj. Brisbin of the 2nd. Cavalry.

It was decided that the basis of the original plan was still sound, just the location and timings would need to be adapted. With hindsight, it is now easy to criticize this strategy but it must be remembered that Terry was operating with limited information based largely upon guesswork, the best that he had available. Also, he had no way of knowing that Crook's column had been removed from the equation, depriving him of expected support from the south. Amazingly, no news would arrive from Crook for some time to come. Also, at this stage there was no solid reason to believe that the army would be facing many more than the expected 800 warriors. Crook knew different by now, of course, but for some strange reason did not apparently feel it necessary to send word to his fellow commanders who would obviously soon be facing the onslaught he had just suffered.

So now it was vaguely known where the main body of Sitting Bull's hostiles were most likely located although the danger still remained that they could scatter at any time. It was very important that they must be trapped in one place and dealt with by a single blow. Everyone knew that Indians never bunched together like this for long. At least, they never had until now, but times were changing. The essence of Terry's operation must now be speed.

The idea centred upon Custer's fast moving 7th. Cavalry operating as a mobile strike force. Autie was to be sent with his regiment south up the Rosebud while Gibbon's slower moving infantry, supported by the 2nd. Cavalry, should march west along the Yellowstone to the mouth of the Bighorn River where they would then push south down into the valley of the Little Bighorn. In the meantime, the 7th. should have swept around below the hostiles, forcing them north where their escape would be blocked by Gibbon. In this way Sitting Bull would be forced to fight or submit. It was estimated that the two columns should be able to link up for this strike on June 26th..

Terry gave Custer written orders which have since been subject to much scrutiny and varied interpretation. The simple truth is that they were composed in such a way as to give Custer the opportunity to use his renowned flair and judgement as he saw fit, depending upon the circumstances he found. In essence it said, "…..proceed up the Rosebud in pursuit of the Indians….. turn towards the Little Horn feeling constantly to your left so as to preclude the possibility of their escape to the south or south east by passing around your left flank….." along with this lengthy phrase which more or less gave Custer *carte blanche* to do as he pleased; "The Department Commander places too much confidence in your zeal, energy and ability to wish to impose upon you precise orders which might hamper your action when nearly in contact with the enemy….." So, did Autie disobey orders at the Little Bighorn? Read on and judge for yourself.

This was exactly the type of assignment Custer had been longing for. To be given free reign to tackle the enemy on his own terms was a dream come true. He must have felt, at this time, that Custer's Luck was riding high. Oh, the opportunity which surely lay ahead of him!

The 7th. were expected to get moving without delay. Highly impressed by the intelligence and cool resolve of Mitch Bouyer, Custer managed to negotiate the half breed's transfer to act as a scout for the 7th.. Bloody Knife and the Rees were an asset but their knowledge of this country, which Bouyer knew intimately, was very limited. To support Bouyer, Custer also managed to obtain six of Lt. Bradley's Crows, who were called Half Yellow Face, Hairy Moccasin, Goes Ahead, White Swan, White Man Runs Him and Curley, a teenaged youth whose role in the coming battle was to be significant. Also from Gibbon's column came a white scout, George Herendeen. Losing these valuable scouts did not go down too well with Bradley, but Custer usually got what he wanted.

Autie made a point of personally acquainting himself with these Crows which, following a spirited pep talk, resulted in considerable mutual admiration. The "General" had always felt an affinity with Indians and enjoyed a good relationship with his native scouts. Treating them fairly and with respect they responded by serving him loyally. That evening he was to write his last ever letter to Libbie in which he described his newly acquired Crows as "jolly….. sportive….." and the handsomest Indians he had ever seen. Not wishing to make the favoured Bloody Knife jealous, he repeated his oft spoken promise that one day, when he became the Great Father in Washington, he would make his Arikara brother into a mighty leader who would live in a fine house with riches and plenty to eat. Beaming proudly, Bloody Knife puffed out his chest and showed off his medal again.

On the face of it, all was well, but, regardless of Custer's confidence and optimism, the fact remained that there was a great deal of uncertainty in the plan. The regiment would be riding largely into the unknown, towards a vague location where the enemy's strength was merely being assumed. And, as mentioned earlier, the 7th. Cavalry, which had been under strength when it left Fort Lincoln, was now even more sorely depleted. Many troopers, including the bulk of the fresh recruits, had been placed on detached service far behind at the Powder River Depot. More were detached at the Yellowstone, making it necessary to transfer several officers between companies. This included Bandmaster

Vinatieri and Custer's prized musicians, so Autie must have really meant business to have made the decision to leave his precious band behind. There would be no stirring rendition of *Garry Owen* on *this* ride, such was the desire to move with speed. This was also behind the decision to deprive the men of their sabres, therefore all of the 7th.'s "Long Knives" were packed up in cases and left behind. (All that is except for the sabre of M Co.'s 1st.Lt. Edward Mathey, commanding the pack train, who kept it packed away until it was needed to kill snakes. Apparently Co. E's 1st.Lt. Charles De Rudio, an Austrian, also kept his sabre with him, because he liked the weapon, and somehow managed to smuggle it into the Little Bighorn valley.) Many of the men even left their overcoats behind, anything to make their load a few pounds lighter. Custer was offered the Gatling guns but he turned them down saying they would impede the speed of his march. Likewise he said no to Terry and Brisbin's suggestion that he should take some companies of the 2nd. Cavalry with him, boasting that the 7th. could handle anything that was thrown against it. Autie was determined to be a lone hero in this one.

The last muster revealed that the regiment numbered just 566 enlisted men led by 29 officers. Added to this were quite a few quartermaster employees, two non-military doctors and other civilians like Bouyer, Herendeen, Bloody Knife, "Lonesome" Charley and the Custer's kid brother Boston. Their nephew Autie Reed was also present along with newspaperman Mark Kellogg, interpreters Isaiah Dorman and Fred Girard, half a dozen packers, twenty odd Ree scouts (including the young half breed Jackson brothers, Bob and Billy), four Sioux and the six Crows; 647 men in all.

By midday on June 22nd., as Generalissamo Antonio Lopez de Santa Anna breathed his last in far off Mexico, the 7th. Cavalry were mounted and ready to pass in a final parade ground style review in front of Terry, Gibbon and the remaining troops. Many said afterwards that they appeared a fine body of men as they rode by in their columns, pennants and standards fluttering, Custer and his clique of officers in their buckskin, the Indian scouts whooping and chanting their death songs, the colour of horses carefully matched to each company (the Grey Horse Troop of Smith's E Co. looking particularly impressive) and the bugles blaring.

As a parting shot, Autie cantered back through the dust, reining his horse in before Terry and Gibbon with an expert flick of the halter. Exchanging goodbyes and good luck wishes, Gibbon cautiously added, "Now then, Custer, don't be greedy, but wait for us."

The "General" smiled and tipped the brim of his big cream hat. Turning his horse's head towards the departing regiment he waved and, it is said, chirpily called out, "I won't!" before galloping away to join his men.

It could have meant anything.

The 7th. Cavalry en-route to the Little Bighorn. Custer observes the terrain ahead while one of his Crow scouts looks for signs.

PURSUIT

As they headed south up the Rosebud, the general mood of the 7th. Cavalry was jubilant. They had been chosen to strike the initial blow. Proud and refreshed, fully supplied with fifteen days rations and supported by a 175 mule pack train, the positive aura of the column survived throughout the afternoon's ride.

The "General" himself rode in advance of the troops, as usual, accompanied by some of his staff but paying particular attention to the observations of Mitch Bouyer and Bloody Knife. Not expecting to find too much hostile Indian sign at this stage, the Crows only scouted a short distance ahead, while the Rees, unfamiliar with this country, trotted along on either flank.

The appearance of the troops, by now, after more than a month on campaign, would not impressively grace a parade ground. Their clothing was worn, patched and grimy, supplemented by the many non-issue personal items which were always favoured by frontier cavalrymen of this period. Many of the men had discarded their floppy slouch hats ("A useless rag…." as described by one officer) or peaked kepis (a Civil War vintage cap known as the "bummer") and were wearing a wide variety of headgear. Troopers seemed to particularly like the idea of expressing their individuality through what they placed on their heads. Because of the increasing summer temperatures, quite a few of them, especially the officers, had purchased light, broad brimmed straw hats from traders at the Powder River depot. Beards had grown long and bushy, and as they rode through the clouds of dust thrown up along the trail, every man found himself coated with a grey, clinging film of gritty powder.

As stated before, the 7th. Cavalry were a highly mixed bunch who represented many nations across the globe. Take Private Ygnatz Stungewitz of Tom Custer's C Troop, for example, whose mother Russia must have seemed a distant memory to him, or Private George Horn (an assumed name, no doubt) of Co. D who came from Andalusia, Spain. The Grey Horse Troop, E, had Greek Private Alexander Stella (who had been born in Athens) and English born Private John Hiley. Hiley was a keen gambler who possessed his own faro bank, but his real name was, grandly, John Stuart Stuart Forbes, his mother being a lady of Scottish nobility. It seems that Hiley had been forced to leave his native land because of some undisclosed trouble he had gotten himself into. He possessed a recent letter from his mother which informed him that this trouble would soon be resolved and he could return home safely, but, alas, coming events would make that impossible. Unlike most of his comrades, however, who were to die with him, Hiley/Forbes is not forgotten. In Edinburgh, Scotland, in St. John's Episcopal Church, a brass plaque, complete with coat of arms, displays his name and describes his fate fighting in a foreign land.

Custer's striker, Private John Burkman (Co. L) had other things to occupy him, apart from the proximity of unfriendly Indians. His hero worship of the "General" knew no bounds and he would not hear a word said against him. Having served in the 7th. for nearly six years, Burkman had been at Autie's side throughout all the major events of the regiment's history since 1870, attending to his every need. He was only slightly older than his hero and spent much of his time caring for the "General's" staghounds, two of which, Bleuch and Tuck, had loped along on this campaign. Apart from his horse Dandy, Custer had also brought along his Kentucky thoroughbred, Vic, a blaze faced sorrel with three white stockings which he had chosen to ride this day. Dandy had been entrusted to Burkman's care, for Autie was already planning to enter this fine steed in a race when they returned from whipping Sitting Bull.

Regardless of the keen start, the column only travelled about a dozen miles up the Rosebud that day, making camp well before sunset. Custer seemed pre-occupied and called his officers to a conference in his tent. Almost immediately, Autie's subordinates were struck by his uncharacteristic behaviour. The "General", usually so confident, brash, in control, arrogant even, seemed very thoughtful as if doubts had revealed themselves to him during the few hours since leaving Terry and Gibbon. Calmly he explained his reasons for declining the offer of support from Brisbin's 2nd. Cavalry and the Gatling guns. The officers nodded in sombre fashion, except for Benteen who had doubts, as usual, expressing his wish that they should have at least taken the offer of additional troops. "We will regret not having them," he said, sternly, as he met his C.O.'s withering stare. Custer, surprisingly, did not rise to the bait but took this criticism in his stride. Instead he looked around at the familiar faces of his officers, most of whom knew him well, having ridden at his side for years, (since the formation of the 7th. in many cases) his attitude almost apologetic. He went on to give details of the latest information and theories received from the scouts, saying how the regiment could now well be facing as many as 1,500 warriors, taking into account the summer roamers who would be leaving the reservations to join Sitting Bull. Even so, Autie emphasised his confidence that the 7th. alone would be more than a match for them. Yet again it was stated that these Indians would never stand and fight unless cornered. The biggest problem would be containing them before they had the opportunity to scatter. To ensure that, it was important that the column must maintain the element of surprise. From now on, everyone would have to be extra vigilant, the troops must keep together, sleeping with their weapons and making a minimum of noise whilst on the move. Except in an emergency, there were to be no bugle calls. Although still putting on a bold front, it was obvious to everyone that their "General" was depressed. They were all surprised when he actually asked for suggestions and advice, something which was virtually unknown.

With the atmosphere heavy and sullen, Custer terminated the meeting and dismissed his officers ruefully, and as they wandered away in the dark, they muttered with apprehension. Lt. Godfrey walked alongside "Tosh" McIntosh and 2nd.Lt. George Wallace (both of Co. G) and they all commented on Custer's strange demeanour. Wallace, long necked, tall and gangly, was serving as acting engineer officer and knew the "General" as well as most, having served with him in the Yellowstone and Black Hills expeditions. He seemed greatly disturbed by the meeting, prompting him to say, "I have never heard him talk this way before ….. I believe General Custer is going to be killed". Sobering stuff but food for thought indeed.

Godfrey carried on alone to make his rounds, checking on the security of his "Dude" Troop's horses. Coming across the camp of the Indian scouts, he stopped to speak with Mitch Bouyer who had been indulging in heavy debate with Bloody Knife and the Crows. Bloody Knife had been hitting the bottle and was obviously drunk but all the scouts seemed troubled. Bouyer asked Godfrey if he had fought the Sioux before and if he thought the lone column could beat such a large band. Godfrey, an experienced Indian fighter whose memory preceded the Washita, answered that he knew the Lakota, and feeling that he should express confidence, added that he thought the 7th. could whip them, as they had done before. Translating his words to the Indian scouts and noting their negative reaction, Bouyer turned back to Godfrey and stressed, "Well, I can tell you we are going to have a damned big fight".

In an attempt to lighten the darkening mood, a number of officers gathered together in a tent to sing a few of their favourite songs. It probably helped, for a while at least, as the strains of such ditties as "Little Brown Jug", "Man on the Flying Trapeze" and, of course, "Captain Jinks", floated across the wide Montana sky, but, for several of those officers, it would be the last party they would ever see.

* * *

By dawn the following morning, June 23rd., Lt.Col. Custer had pulled himself together and seemed fully in control again. In less than two weeks, the cream of the nation's society would be gathering back east in the fancy city of Philadelphia to celebrate July 4th., Independence Day. Yes, the United States was having its Centennial, a new country, just 100 years old. It was going to be a huge occasion, full of positivism and prestige, and Autie was determined to be there with Libbie at his side. Firstly, however, he needed to subdue the Sioux and Cheyenne nation so that he could return a hero. Time was running out.

With pressure mounting, Custer chivvied his company commanders to get the men into their saddles as quickly as possible. Breakfast was rushed and the column was on the move again by 5.00am. Bloody Knife had disappeared during the night but turned up in time for the departure, sober now but moody. Autie did his best to reassure him and made sure he kept his favourite Indian close at hand. The other scouts were very busy now and took trails far in advance of the column which travelled a total of 33 miles that day, pushing south up the Rosebud. On the way they passed the deserted sites of hostile encampments, most of which had already been discovered during Reno's earlier mission. There was, however, evidence of additional bands trailing the large camp, doubtless summer roamers intent on joining Sitting Bull. The abandoned wickiups and lodge circles were numerous, the acres of cropped grass and pony droppings bearing witness to a vast herd. All this was increasingly worrying, for it was now growing obvious that the 7th. could well be facing more than it could comfortably handle. Custer must have realised this but refused to let it openly dent his confidence. In any case, he determined to follow this drama through to its conclusion, whatever that may be.

Calling a halt to camp in the late afternoon, having ridden almost non-stop for eleven hours, Custer received the returning Crow scouts in his tent that evening to hear the latest news. They had some grisly discoveries to show him. Scalps and beards cut from white men, some of them almost certainly victims from Crook's Rosebud battle, although Custer still had no way of knowing that this fight had taken place. Autie's men had grown grimly used to finding such horrific trophies. Recently at the mouth of the Tongue, for example, they had found the scant remains of a fellow trooper (probably from Gibbon's column) who had apparently been beaten and burned to death by vindictive Sioux warriors. The soldiers growled vengefully at this, but were not entirely innocent of outrage themselves. Just days before they had come across a Lakota burial ground which they had gleefully desecrated. Items were taken as souvenirs, scaffolds were pulled down and decaying corpses were flung into the river. Custer's young nephew Autie Reed was especially pleased to acquire a dead warrior's bow, arrows and moccasins, seemingly unconcerned by such blatant grave robbing. This was proving to be a harsh conflict with little quarter or respect shown by either side.

June 24th. dawned with another early start, but within two hours the column had reached the previously scouted site of Sitting Bull's Sun Dance. Although the day was still young, the "General" considered the site so significant that he ordered a halt which lasted about an hour whilst investigations were carried out. The Crows were far ahead, as usual, having left camp before the troops had risen from their blankets, but the Rees took a thorough look around. Spread all over the area were religious symbols, sand pictographs, stones arranged in patterns and other clues which represented the mood of the hostiles. Custer asked the Rees what it all meant and their reply did nothing to reassure him. The Lakota were expressing their new found faith for all to see. Here was an enemy that did not intend to run. They were fired with enthusiasm and confidence, certain of victory over the hated *wasichus*. Autie swallowed the news soberly, refusing to accept the notion that these hostiles would behave any differently to the way he had always known.

Whilst still exploring the site, Custer welcomed the return of the Crows who had ventured ten miles ahead to Lame Deer Creek where they had discovered fresh trails of summer roamers. Following a swiftly addressed officer's call, Autie mounted up and led two of his companies out at 7.30am., leaving orders for the remainder to follow at a half mile interval, thereby reducing the density of rising dust clouds. Progress was considerably slower than before, as the regiment made its cautious way up the right bank of the Rosebud. The scouts were busier than ever and Custer kept on their backs relentlessly, demanding to receive reports of every little detail. Lt. Varnum, the scout's military commander, was assigned a young 2nd.Lt. from Godfrey's "Dude" troop K to assist him, one Luther Hare, and these two officers had their work cut out riding back and forth along the trail keeping tabs on things. Bouyer, Herendeen and "Lonesome" Charley Reynolds were active too, all with strict orders to particularly scout for any sign of diverging trails, the appearance of which were to be reported to the "General" without delay. One such trail was found by Herendeen which prompted Custer to call a long halt at East Muddy Creek while Varnum and some of the Rees were sent off to investigate it. This halt lasted about four hours and the men took advantage of the opportunity to brew coffee and prepare a meal, for they knew that with "Hard Ass" in charge there was no way of knowing when they would next get such a chance. Varnum eventually returned only to report that the diverging trail merely rejoined the main one, but Mitch Bouyer and his Crows were able to reveal that signs of a fresh camp had been found about fourteen miles ahead just beyond Busby Bend, where the Davis Creek forked away south west from the Rosebud. This indicated that the hostiles were dangerously close. Now it was just a question of ensuring which direction they were travelling in.

It was time to push on, to close the gap between the 7th. Cavalry and their prey. The troopers were riding along a valley scored by countless trailing lodge poles and the debris of thousands of Indians on the move. Signs of new and old camps lay everywhere and by early evening the trail had become so fresh that Custer grew outwardly anxious. He ordered flankers far out to the right and left. "I want to catch the whole village," he said, the pitch of his voice rising as it always did when he became excited, "keep a sharp lookout, for nothing must leave this trail without my knowing of it". However, the hostiles appeared to be well consolidated by now and no further branching off was reported. This, at least, seemed to please the "General".

Approaching sunset, Custer ordered a halt a couple of miles below the mouth of Davis Creek. The column had travelled about 27 miles that day, making slow but informative progress, and the men had every reason to believe that they would now be bivouacked for the night. Gladly they dropped from their saddles, stretching their aching limbs. It had been a long day and they were exhausted, but for Autie himself there was no time for rest. Seemingly inexhaustible, the "General" squatted on the ground, alternately deep in thought and consulting his officers and scouts. Four of the Crows were absent again, searching for the information the Son-of-the-Morning-Star craved. Imperative now was the answer to a simple question. Which way was Sitting Bull headed? North down Tullock's Fork, south up the Rosebud or west to the Little Bighorn?

An air of glum foreboding had settled over the camp and many of the men sat or lay morosely absorbed in their private thoughts. Not that many of them would have fully understood the implications of what they were facing but more than a few retained total faith in their "Hard Ass" commander. Odd hushed whispers and horse whinnies permeated the silent, dark atmosphere. Some troopers speculated about what lay ahead but most were taking advantage of the chance to grab a little well earned sleep. The remaining scouts sat together, the white contingent distressed to witness "Lonesome"

Charley offering his personal belongings to any takers. He didn't possess much in his bag; just a small darning set, a nub of tobacco, a shirt or two, Indian trinkets and so on, but he wanted to pass them on. As they averted those poignant, darting, big blue eyes, Charley's compadres knew this could only mean one thing on the frontier. Custer's favourite white scout had a sense that his end was drawing near and nobody would be able to dissuade him from thinking otherwise. He was in pain too, suffering from a swollen and badly infected thumb which he was attempting to treat by wrapping it in a bulky hardtack poultice supplied to him by Custer's striker, Burkman. Reynolds had already expressed reservations about this enterprise but went along with it all the same. In that he was not alone.

Around 9.00pm. the Crows returned and Bouyer quickly, but clearly, interpreted what they had to say. They now knew that the hostiles, and their entire entourage, had crossed the divide to the Little Bighorn, probably on the lower reaches rather than the upper section as expected. This meant that Sitting Bull and his followers were much closer than anticipated. The Crows added that, come morning light, they would be able to scan the valley from a high point they knew (called the Crow's Nest) and thereby confirm the necessary information. Without delay, Custer decided to send them straight out again, but this time he insisted that Lt. Varnum go with them for he wanted an "intelligent white man" to be present. In addition, Bouyer was to accompany them to interpret all information (so that there would be no misunderstanding), along with a few of the Rees to act as messengers. "Lonesome" Charley also tagged along to contribute his valued viewpoint. One of the Crows, Half Yellow Face, and most of the Rees, were to remain with Custer. The "General" promised Varnum that the column would follow at a safe distance, expecting news at any time.

Custer then sent word out for his subordinates to attend yet another officer's call. Groping their way through the dark but finally gathering around Autie's tent, the officers listened intently as their "General" explained that owing to the latest intelligence, a radical change of plan would be needed. With the hostiles so close, it meant that the 7th. Cavalry had reached their objective at least a day ahead of schedule. Up to this point, Custer had obeyed his orders implicitly. Following the trail of the hostiles up the Rosebud, checking on diverging trails, locating Sitting Bull's presence; but it had all been achieved too quickly. Custer estimated, correctly, that Terry and Gibbon, at the mouth of the Bighorn far to the north, would still be a good thirty miles from their intended blocking position. There would be no point in Custer trying to drive the hostiles up the valley into a trap which was not yet there, or in continuing to push south, as ordered, just to kill time. However, if he delayed any longer he ran a strong risk of his men being discovered and the hostiles scattering. Terry's orders had been flexible, remember, saying how he did not wish to impose precise instructions upon Custer's "zeal, energy and ability" which might *"hamper your action when nearly in contact with the enemy"*. This was good enough for Autie. He had an alternative plan. With a forced night march, the 7th. could position themselves much closer to the divide by morning and thereby lie concealed for the day in the labyrinth of hills. That night, under cover of darkness, they could complete their approach to Sitting Bull's village, additional information being supplied by the scouts along the way, and position themselves for a dawn attack on June 26th.. Taken by surprise, the hostiles would be forced to flee to the north, as per plan, straight into the clutches of Terry and Gibbon. Still plenty of opportunity for Autie to emerge as the hero of the hour! It would be the Washita all over again. Oh, how warmly he would be received in Philadelphia. The Boy General, Scourge of the Rebs would now be the Buckskin Cavalier, Scourge of the Redskins!

The plan was generally well received by the officers and Custer told them to assemble their companies within the hour. Just before he dismissed them, the Custer clique paused pensively to regale their C.O. with a little maudlin serenade. This time the songs were not of the enforced jovial variety which had been sung at camp just two nights before. The mood was now reflective and genteel, tinged with the sentiment of men who had come a long way together across the years. "Little Footsteps", "Annie Laurie", "Doxology", "Goodbye at the Door"; lovely lilting ballads, all troop favourites, which were no doubt appreciated by the surrounding soldiers who lay scattered in the darkness, wrapped in their blankets. The baritone and tenor strains of the 7th.'s tough officer brotherhood must have echoed through the night, so it was odd that such a noisy concert was allowed by the "General" when in such close proximity to the enemy. True to form, he must have been overcome by the emotion of the moment, for he was always a theatrical at heart! No doubt he was especially moved when this be-whiskered, dusty choir honoured him with a chorus of "For he's a jolly good fellow….." to reprise their concert.

The impromptu party over, it was back to business as the officers went their separate ways. 1st. Sergeants and other N.C.O.s from all the companies were soon roused, indulging in the unenviable task of getting the grumbling troopers back onto their feet.

Capt. Myles Keogh probably muttered a curse or two for he had been planning to share a frugal meal of beans, hardtack, coffee and, most likely, a drop of liquor, with some of his commissioned friends. The last supper he was never to have. Instead they would be spending an uncomfortable night in the saddle. No doubt he absorbed it philosophically. He was a professional fighting soldier, after all, and this was the sort of circumstance he knew he had to accept. Keogh was not the kind of man to become easily fazed, but even he had uncharacteristically taken the trouble, within the last few days, to draw up his last will and testament.

During the day, at one of the halts, Sgt. Robert Hughes, of Custer's staff, had taken the trouble to plant the "General's" battle flag firmly in the ground, but as he had walked away, it was blown over by a gust of wind, its spike pointing back along the trail towards the Yellowstone. Immediately this swallow tailed guidon was picked up by Lt. Godfrey who bored it more firmly into the hard earth, but moments later it fell again into the same position, as if mocking the regiment. The superstitious Lt. George Wallace shook his head, un-nerved by such a bad omen. Against his better nature, he felt sure that the 7th. was heading towards disaster.

AT THE CROW'S NEST

In pitch blackness, the 7th. Cavalry hit the trail once more, shortly after midnight. It was not an easy ride as they groped blindly along, guided only by the cacophony of sound from those who rode ahead. The noise of this moving column reached levels of grand farce, what with the snorting and stumbling of horses, the jangling of equipment, curses of fatigued, ill tempered troopers and the braying of pack mules. Quite a few men lost the trail in the dark and were forced to call out to find their way back to their companies, all of which was a huge potential advertisement of the approach of what was supposed to be a clandestine force. Right out front, as always, feeling the way, was the "General" himself, fresh as ever, riding alongside Bloody Knife, Half Yellow Face and the interpreter, Fred Girard.

Benteen chewed on his pipe, concentrating on the clattering all around him as he rode doggedly on. He had known worse conditions during his long action filled career. What troubled him, as usual, was having to bend to Custer's will. The regiment's veterans, like Benteen, had mixed opinions and concerns about their commander, but none could deny his energy and courage. Whatever anyone said, the "General's" spirit had never let them down yet. That said, the sad memory of the fate of Maj. Elliott and his men at the Washita still rankled deeply.

Tall and burly Frank Varden, the 1st. Sergeant of Keogh's "Wild I" was typical of the kind of man who made up the sturdy backbone of the regiment. Square jawed and blue eyed, his big moustache drooping over firmly set lips, Varden kept a close watch on his grizzled troopers. They were a rowdy, hard drinking bunch; tough, grouchy and ready for trouble, just the kind of boys you would want alongside you in a scrap. Varden was well qualified in his position as their senior N.C.O., for he was no angel himself. Originally an infantryman for the Union in the Civil War, he eventually deserted to enlist in the 2nd. Cavalry under an assumed name. Apprehended in 1872, it seems he avoided severe punishment by personally impressing Keogh who had him assigned to the 7th.. Working his way up through the ranks, he was now a valued member of the command who could be relied on to keep the "Wild I" under control. A similar stalwart soldier acted as 1st. Sergeant for L Co.. Although slighter in build and shorter than Varden, Sgt. James Butler was steady, true and highly respected for his courage and long experience in the field.

Another veteran who could boast experience of a unique kind within the regiment was 1st. Lt. Charles De Rudio, he who carried his sabre into the Little Bighorn valley. Born Carlo Camilio di Rudio in Venetia Province Austria, some 43 years prior to this arduous night ride he was enduring, De Rudio was apparently a rather smooth character with his sunken dark eyes, waxed moustache and devilish forked chin beard. Although he was part of the Grey Horse Troop, E, this interesting officer was to be attached to Co. A, a fortunate move for him, as it turned out. In fact, throughout his life fate seemed to play a series of games with his fortunes which usually resulted in his salvation. As a young man, he had travelled to England where he found work as a dockyard labourer in the East End of London, marrying his pregnant girlfriend in the leafy Surrey suburb of Godalming, of all places. Aged 25, he got himself involved with a group of terrorists in Paris, assisting them in their attempt to assassinate the Emperor Louis Napoleon III with bombs as he arrived at the Opera House. They succeeded only in killing a couple of the Emperor's escort and were subsequently arrested. Although two of De Rudio's three accomplices lost their heads on the guillotine, Charles himself managed to get his death sentence reduced to life imprisonment, whereby he was sent far away to the dreaded Devil's Island penal colony in French Guiana. Within a year, he had managed to escape to sea in a hollowed out log, and after various other scrapes, found his way back to England. From there, following several failed career moves, he carried on to the U.S.A.

arriving just in time to catch the tail end of the Civil War serving as a private in the 79th. New York Infantry. A commission followed but only because he was willing to serve as a 2nd. Lt. commanding black troops, this being a stepping stone to his transfer as an officer in a regular regiment. Pretty soon, however, his dark past was discovered by the War Department and they cancelled his appointment, although not for long. It seems even terrorists were welcome in the 7th. Cavalry for he was re-assigned, this time to join Custer's boys at Fort Hays, Kansas. By late December 1875, he had been promoted to 1st. Lt., adding to the regiment's highly colourful roster.

Not all the officers (or troopers) of the 7th. could speak of such varied experience. Young 2nd. Lt. James Sturgis was 22 years old and had been a 7th. Cavalry officer for just a year, fresh out of West Point. Some might say he was favoured, for his father was the actual commander of the regiment, Col. Samuel Sturgis, the officer who reigned over the 7th. in absentia while Autie took effective field command. Young Sturgis was assigned to Capt. French's Co. M, although on the day of the Little Bighorn he was detached to serve with Smith's Grey Horse Troop, a most unfortunate, and fatal, transfer.

2nd. Lt. John Crittenden, turned 22 just two weeks ago, was not even a cavalryman but had been detached from his infantry regiment by special order to serve with the 7th. Cavalry just five days before they left Fort Lincoln on this campaign. Now he rode alongside Autie's brother-in-law, James Calhoun, who had just taken charge of L Co.. Crittenden had a nasty disability for one so young. During a hunting trip the previous October, he had attempted to prise a cartridge with a knife which caused a mini explosion, resulting in a piece of the casing being blown into his eye. Taken to Cincinnati for proper medical care, the surgeon had been unable to save the eye and it had to be removed. Lt. Crittenden now had a glass one to replace it. Like Sturgis, his father was also a high ranking army officer.

At about 3.15am., the column was relieved to hear Custer call a halt on the edge of Davis Creek. The men were so tired that most of them did not even unsaddle their mounts before taking a nap. About one hour later, as the sun rose, a more ordered camp was evident as the troops settled themselves and began to light breakfast fires. Strange that Custer should have allowed such smoke, but following the officer's concert and the noise of the troops on the move, perhaps he thought the damage was already done.

During the night, far ahead of the column, Lt. Varnum, Mitch Bouyer, "Lonesome" Charley, the Crows and the Ree couriers had made progress along the Creek, turning south and making their way up into the lower reaches of the Wolf Mountains. Apart from a few stops when Varnum allowed the vigilant Crows to smoke, they covered a lot of ground quickly, finally arriving at a small timbered pocket below the Crow's Nest just before 3.00am. while it was still dark. Not being able to see into the valley before the sun rose, most of Varnum's party lay down to sleep, although two of the Crows could not contain their patience and climbed to the highest point ahead of the others.

Within an hour, Varnum was being shaken out of his fitful slumber by one of the Crows who said he must come to the high point immediately. The first streaks of daylight were starting to lighten the sky by now, so Varnum shook off his fatigue and steeled himself to ascend the slope. By 4.00am., he and all the other scouts were on the peak peering hard into the valley which lay to the west. The Crows were pointing to the far distant Little Bighorn River about fifteen miles away where they could see signs of a large village beyond the bluff. Many white tepees were there, they said, and smoke was rising above black specks which could only indicate a huge pony herd. Like worms crawling across the grass, said Hairy Moccasin, and "Lonesome" Charley nodded sombrely as he studied the horizon through his field glasses. Varnum rubbed his sore eyes, which were inflamed from dust and lack of sleep, but could see nothing.

Beside him, Bouyer and the Crows spoke their native tongue, exchanging views, and they all stood there for quite some time, waiting for the growing light to reveal more. At last, still blind to what the seasoned eyes of his Indian companions were seeing, Varnum decided that their word was good enough and sat down to write a note to Custer. It was 5.00am. by now and other lines of smoke could be seen, this time in the opposite direction to the north east, rising up above Davis Creek. The Crows mumbled angrily, annoyed that the Son-of-the-Morning-Star should be so foolish as to allow his men to make signs in the sky for the Sioux to see, but Varnum was satisfied that the troops had followed closely, as promised. His note was brief, but he knew it would tell the "General" what he wanted to hear.

It took the Ree couriers about two hours to reach Custer who had been anxiously awaiting news as the troops relaxed around him. The Ree scout Red Star was squatting down drinking coffee when Autie approached, asking him in sign language if he had seen the Lakota. Red Star made sign that he had, handing Custer Varnum's note as he did so. Autie read it, nodding excitedly before explaining to those around him that the village had been spotted and could be viewed from a butte just a few miles ahead. Waking Girard, Custer expressed a wish that he intended to join Varnum at the Crow's Nest so that he could see his prey for himself. It would also be an ideal opportunity to take in the lay of the land before deciding on his next move. As the scouts mounted up, Autie may have sought out Maj. Reno (even though Reno later denied it), leaving him orders to follow on with the troops in due course to a point near the divide where he would join them shortly.

Custer mounted Vic and rode out with Bloody Knife, Girard and a trio of Rees, Red Star leading the way. Tom Custer was there to see his brother off, having been told to remain with the troops, but as Autie's party disappeared in a cloud of dust, a bugle call, probably blown by Chief Trumpeter Voss of Custer's staff, broke the still of the morning. It was the first reveille heard for a while so Custer was obviously growing confident again. (Regardless of Reno's evasive remarks, the whole regiment would be on the move within 45 minutes, although there is some controversy about who actually ordered them forward.) Just before Custer's group left for the Crow's Nest, word came of a pack of hardtack which had been lost during the night march, it having come loose from a mule belonging to Capt. Yates' F Company. Not having been missed in the darkness, this discovery was regarded as serious enough to send a small squad back along the trail, led by one Sgt. Curtis, to try and pick it up before any Sioux or Cheyenne wanderers found it.

By the time Autie arrived at the Crow's Nest (about 9.00am.), there had been further developments. A couple of small groups of Sioux had been spotted separately, both riding close enough to cause concern that they would discover the advancing regiment. Varnum led the scouts in a sortie with the intention of ambushing one of these enemy groups but lost contact with their prey whilst struggling through hard country. Returning to the Crow's Nest, Varnum could only assume that the alarm would be raised, grim news which he had to relate to Custer as soon as he arrived. Autie listened to this report before beginning his ascent to find a spot to view the valley, but at first he refused to accept that the column had been discovered, although this may have been a touch of "burying head in the sand" syndrome. He did not climb to the very top of the Crow's Nest but halted part way up at a point which would show him all he needed to see.

Custer stared into the valley for a long time with "Lonesome" Charley Reynolds at his side. After a while, they were joined by Fred Girard who heard the "General" say that he could see no Indian camp. Reynolds quietly explained what he should be looking for, lending Custer his field glasses so that he could take a more detailed look. At first, Autie was sure that the scouts were mistaking pale buttes for white tepees but as time went on he slowly became convinced that they may be right. He crouched down to steady his vision.

The air was growing clearer by the moment and although the interpreter Girard could see no tepees, he did recognise evidence of a gigantic pony herd, appearing from this distance as an ominous, black mass from which dust arose. Varnum was going into detail about all he had seen over the last few hours while Custer occasionally addressed Bouyer for his opinion.

Sighing, the "General" lowered the glasses and said, "Well, I would say I've got about as good eyes as anybody, but I can't see any village, Indians or anything else."

Bouyer drew a breath in his cool collected way. "Well, General," he said, narrowing his dark eyes, "if you don't find more Indians in that valley than you ever saw together, why, you can hang me!"

Autie looked at the half breed with a wry smile before springing to his feet like a man half his age. "It would do a damned sight of good to hang you, Mitch, wouldn't it?" he chuckled before calling on Varnum to accompany him down the slope towards the tethered horses.

It was mid-morning now. Custer had spent more than an hour studying the valley and as he descended the hill he could see large clouds of dust rising about two miles to the north at the divide. Reno had brought the regiment forward. As Custer prepared to ride down to join them, he became embroiled in a vigorous argument with the Crows for he was still insisting that the village would be unaware of the soldier's approach. He intended, he said, to place his troops around the Sioux camp under cover of darkness as originally plotted but the Crows wailed that it was a bad plan. Some said that any attack must be made immediately so that the Sioux's pony herd could be captured, thus immobilising the warriors. They kept saying that the Lakota would soon know all about the Long Knives at their door and, slowly, Custer seemed to see sense in their logic.

The long columns of the 7th. Cavalry could now clearly be seen reining to a halt in the near distance and as Custer's party cantered towards them the familiar mounted figures of Tom Custer and Jimmy Calhoun were recognised spurring their horses up the slope.

Autie frowned, and before his brother or brother-in-law could speak, the "General" was verbally lambasting them for leaving the column contrary to orders. Tom raised his hand, calming his big brother's anger as he explained why he and Calhoun had been so anxious to meet him. They told of Sgt. Curtis who had just rejoined the main column having returned from his mission to retrieve the lost pack. Along the trail, Curtis and his tiny squad had come across a party of hostiles sifting through the broken packages and had immediately opened fire on them. These scavenging Indians fled without delay, but all the white officers were convinced that the village ahead must surely now know of the trooper's approach and hostile intentions.

Time for yet another officer's call. Custer explained that there was no point in further attempts to conceal the column as all this Indian activity must mean that they had been discovered. All that mattered now was speed of reaction to these new circumstances. Delaying any longer would be disastrous, for the Indian village would be scattering and on the move within hours. This fear of losing the enemy rather than fighting it was still the over-riding concern, even though the Crows and Rees had repeatedly warned Autie about the sheer size of the camp and of how this huge assembly of warriors would fight desperately to protect their women and children. Custer brushed such cautiousness aside. The only possible option now to ensure success for the campaign would be to attack at once, in broad daylight. That, at least, the hostiles would never expect.

With the 7th. Cavalry committed to such vigorous action, the company commanders commenced final inspections of the troops as all was made ready for a major assault. Weapons were checked, saddle girths tightened and probably the odd prayer was muttered. Each leading officer was authorized to assign six troopers and one N.C.O.

from each company to accompany the pack train.

Herendeen approached Custer to remind him that Tullock's Fork lay just to the north, the area which Herendeen had originally been earmarked to scout and thus report his findings to General Terry. Testily, Autie replied that such a mission was now redundant as the hostiles were obviously just ahead. Custer added that it would make sense for Herendeen to remain with the column where he would be of much more use.

With the hubbub of arrangements clattering all around him, the "General" took a moment to address his scouts again. Through sign language and the interpretation of Bouyer, Girard and the big black man, Isaiah Dorman, Autie inspired the Rees and Crows with talk of courage through a hard day in which great honours could be won. He told them that there would be many Sioux ponies for the taking and that he would expect them to do it. The scouts listened, impressed by the Son-of-the-Morning-Star's bravery in the face of such odds, although they still thought such an attack to be madness. Death songs were sung and the Rees rubbed their chests with sacred clay which had been brought from their home village.

Mitch Bouyer took Custer aside to say, "General, I have been around Indians for thirty years and this is the largest village I have ever seen."

He should not have bothered. Autie's mind was made up. Shortly before noon, the entire assemblage of the present 7th. Cavalry were ready to move into the valley of the Little Bighorn. It was a boiling hot day and most of the men had removed their blue blouses, tying them to the backs of their saddles as they rode into battle in shirt sleeve order.

Sunday, June 25th. 1876. A date which the Lakota would forever revere. Perhaps the reporter Mark Kellogg had expressed it best in the prophetic closing sentence of the last dispatch he had sent by courier to his editor, when he wrote, *"I go with Custer and will be at the death"*.

PEACE ON THE GREASY GRASS

Hunkpapa war chief Gall was a happy man. The hunting was good, spiritual medicine was strong and there was enough grazing here on the Greasy Grass (the name the Lakota gave to the Little Bighorn) to support this gigantic village for several more days. A big, powerful warrior whose following was impressive, Gall himself was staggered by the sheer size of the camp which had grown around him, especially over the last few days since the young bloods had beaten the "Grey Fox" Crook and his Long Knives in open battle. Gall was sorry to have missed that grand fight, for the returning warriors had been full of glorious tales of combat and honours won. His Oglala "cousin" Crazy Horse could take the credit for that one, but everyone knew that another clash with the *wasichus* was imminent and then there would be enough honour to be had for all. However, Gall had no pressing need to prove himself as his fighting pedigree already stretched back over twenty odd years of adult life when many a foe, red *and* white had fallen beneath his hatchet. Had not the great medicine man Sitting Bull himself adopted Gall as a brother? Gall nodded contentedly at this thought, sitting cross legged in his lodge as he cast his wild, black eyes over the faces of his myriad wives and children as they gathered around him. Life was good.

Indeed, there had been much celebration in the tribal circles since the battle on the Rosebud. For six days now, the warriors had danced and rejoiced, although there had been sadness too as the squaws mourned the deaths of their men folk. However, these warriors had died gloriously, battling against the hated *wasichus* who were trying to take their land. Word spread quickly of Sitting Bull's prophecies and ever growing medicine, and when this was qualified by tales of the Rosebud clash, Indians began to pour out of the agencies in epidemic proportions to join and become part of this great movement of power. By June 24th., the huge village had moved again, north down the Greasy Grass, in pursuit of reported antelope herds. By this time, so many summer roamers had tagged along that in the last week Sitting Bull's following had swollen to more than double its previous size. As they settled on the south western banks of the Little Bighorn River, flanked by steeply rising, rugged bluffs on the eastern shore, the number of Indians had risen to approximately 7,000, some 2,000 of whom were undoubtedly warriors of various fighting ages. The river itself wound drunkenly like a stricken snake through thickets of cottonwood trees which cast welcome, dappled shade upon naked, dark children as they swam in the swiftly flowing stream. Having sprung from the peaks of the icy, far off Bighorn mountains, the water was cold but refreshing in the savage heat of the Montana sun. To the south east lay a wide grassy plain of unbroken land while beyond the bluffs the terrain was rippled by rolling hills and treacherous ravines, spiked with coarse vegetation and dust. The valley along the river, however, was a pleasant place where the tepees and wickiups stretched for close on three miles, complemented by a nearby grazing pony herd which numbered several thousand. It was a staggering sight, and one which neither Custer, nor any of his men, could have foreseen, although most of his scouts had already begun to anticipate it. If not the biggest gathering of Indians ever known, it was certainly the largest concentration of hostiles on the continent at that particular time.

Laying furthest to the south east, acting as a kind of anchor to the magnificent encampment, stood the largest circle made up of 260 lodges under Sitting Bull and Gall's Hunkpapas, including some Yanktonnais and Santee Sioux. Concentrated nearby, in a rough circular formation, lay several other Lakota groups; Crazy Horse's Oglalas (240 lodges), a combined 120 lodges of Brule, Blackfeet and Two Kettle, Minneconjous under Chief Red Horse (150 lodges) and Chief Spotted Eagle's Sansarcs (110 lodges). There were even some Arapaho led by a chief called Little Powder, Indians who would not normally ally themselves with the Lakota but who had recently been ill treated, disarmed and detained by white soldiers and had therefore decided to throw in their lot with the charismatic Sitting Bull. In the lead position, to the north, came the 120 lodges of the Northern Cheyenne circle led by such chiefs as Dull Knife, Old Bear and Lame White Man. Visiting them were some of their Southern Cheyenne cousins, probably the only Indians present who, as a group, may have known "Long Hair" Custer by sight. They would never forget the soldier chief who had destroyed their kinfolk at the Washita. However, even they did not know, at this stage, that the hated "Long Hair" was in such close proximity.

Word had been arriving for some time of Long Knives closing in on the village, but no one seemed unduly worried. This was a case of safety in numbers. Would the *wasichus* really risk attacking such a large camp? Surely not. Certainly not in broad daylight anyway. All the assembled Indians felt safe for now. They knew they were strong enough to meet the threat. The Rosebud had proved that they could match the might of the Long Knives, and had not Sitting Bull's vision of soldiers falling upside down into camp ensured the strength of their medicine?

Scouts had indeed observed the approach of Custer's column but the general feeling was that these soldiers must belong to "Grey Fox" Crook, returning to try and avenge their defeat at the Rosebud. Ironically, virtually all the groups of Sioux and Cheyenne who Custer and his men had observed close to the column within the last hours of their approach to the valley, hostiles whom it was assumed would carry word of the advancing 7th. Cavalry to their brethren, were not even bound for the village. Instead, they were actually leaving it. The Indians fired upon by Sgt. Curtis and his men after they had been caught rifling the lost pack, were in fact a group of Cheyenne who *were* making their way to join the camp but would not reach it until after the battle was over. The same applied to other groups seen and yet Custer based his entire last minute strategy upon these assumptions. (To be fair, in retrospect, they were reasonable assumptions to make.)

As dawn broke on Sunday June 25th., there were surprises ahead for everyone.

INTO THE VALLEY

Riding determinedly across the divide, Custer led his regiment to the bank of another creek which would later bear Reno's name. Here, Autie raised his hand and the weary columns halted again. Sitting Bull's village lay about twelve miles to the north west but although the soldiers knew it was there, somewhere, they could not see it from their present position.

The "General" had been doing some heavy thinking during the short trot from Davis Creek and exactly what was on his mind we shall probably never know. As far as facts go, it is known that this is the point where he hastily made the decision which undoubtedly sealed the fate of his men. He split his command.

Not knowing exactly what he was facing ahead, Autie was probably acting cautiously, even though he has been accused of wanton abandon. All knew that the hostiles must be contained and that would mean encompassing their village as much as possible. To approach *en masse* would no doubt enable the Indians to slip away around the regiment's flanks. To counter this, Custer decided to fragment his companies into three separate battalions, each with a mission of its own. Benteen was given command of D and K companies (led by Tom Weir and Edward Godfrey respectively), to add to his own company, H, 125 men approximately. Dumbfounded, (he later claimed) the white haired, cynical officer listened as his C.O. ordered him to take these men on an oblique scouting foray to the left, the object being to scour the valley for any hostiles attempting to escape in that direction. If none were found, he was to make his way back to the main body of troops ahead as soon as he felt it prudent. Maj. Reno was told to lead a further three companies (Moylan's A, "Tosh" McKintosh's G and French's M) and scouts along the left bank of the creek in the assumed direction of the enemy. Custer himself would take the largest group, five companies (C, E, F, I and L), perhaps 225 men, to ride parallel with Reno on the right bank. (These companies, with the addition of B, were the ones taken by Reno on his recent controversial scouting mission.) Bringing up the rear, would come the heavily guarded pack train, commanded by French born 1st. Lt. Mathey. As the three lead battalions would be pushing swiftly ahead, this exposed pack train would need to be protected by a whole company, the job going to Capt. McDougall's B Co., in all numbering about 130 souls. The idea, it seemed, was to sweep the valley for all eventualities.

This dispersal was to prove fatal for many individuals on that hot Sunday. Small, rotund and jovial 2nd. Lt. Benny Hodgson was to act as Reno's adjutant that day, one of the few men in the regiment who the dark faced major could call a friend. The Rees were to go with Reno also, so that meant Bloody Knife would be separated from his blue eyed chief, Son-of-the-Morning Star. The moody, half blood Sioux, wearing a black bandana decorated with blue stars around his throat, seemed unhappy still and was observed looking up at the sun, signalling to it with his hands, the meaning being, "I shall not see you go down behind the hills tonight". His morbid demeanour was not unique. "Lonesome" Charley was not saying much either as he slouched morosely in the saddle, massaging his swollen thumb.

Not everyone was quite so downhearted. The troops were generally good spirited again, laughing, joking and exchanging bets now that they knew something was happening, at last. The civilian Autie Reed acted like he was about to attend a student party. This was a big adventure for him; his first Indian fight with his heroic uncles at his side. Custer's striker, Burkman, did not share their mood, however. Glum faced, he held Custer's horse Vic by the bridle as the "General" nimbly placed a foot in the stirrup before swinging into the saddle like the veteran horseman he was. Ordered to the rear with the pack train, Burkman mumbled that his place was alongside the regiment's commander, but Custer just grinned, patted his faithful servant's shoulder and assured him that all would be well. Acting as Autie's orderly that day would be a young Italian immigrant named Giovanni Martini, a trumpeter from H Company. Able to speak only limited English, this trooper had tried to help his case by anglicising his name to John Martin.

Lt. George Wallace was to have a lucky escape that afternoon. Although he belonged to Co.G which rode with Reno's battalion, he was the regiment's engineer officer and therefore should take his place with Custer's immediate staff. When they were all mounted up and ready to resume their advance, Lt. Varnum, the chief of scouts who led the Rees with Reno, rode alongside his friend, shouting good naturedly, "Come on with the fighting men ….. don't stay with the coffee coolers1"

Wallace glanced uncertainly at Custer who laughed and waved his hat in Varnum's direction, saying something to the effect, "Away you go then, Wallace", and that is how the lanky, superstitious officer lived to fight another day.

For this campaign, a trio of senior medical men had been assigned to the 7th. Cavalry. Two civilian doctors were employed by the army, attached to the regiment as acting asst. surgeons. These were doctors James DeWolf and Henry Porter, both of whom were sent with Reno. With Custer's battalion rode Asst. Surgeon George Lord, with the rank of 1st. Lt.. He had assisted Custer's troops on a few occasions in the last year or so and was now Chief Medical Officer with the regiment. Thirty years old, bespectacled and not overly in love with frontier life, Lord had been unwell himself since setting out on the last stretch of this rigorous mission. Here on Reno Creek, he seemed exhausted and had been unable to eat or drink for some time. Custer had little patience for this but suggested that Dr. Lord be sent to the rear, his place to be taken by one of the other doctors, but the redoubtable surgeon refused to give up his post. Assisted by his orderly, Corporal John Callahan, Lord insisted on carrying on, as long as he was able to ride. Autie tersely agreed, perhaps admiring the man's mettle.

As the men went about their tasks and dispositions took place, it was down to Benteen, as usual, to voice doubts. "Hadn't we better keep the regiment together, General?" he queried, with more than a hint of sarcasm. "If this is as big a camp as they say, we'll need every man we have."

Custer shot his old adversary a withering look. "You have your orders, Captain Benteen," he snapped, his blue eyes flaring in a challenging manner. Benteen stiffened and shook his head barely perceptibly, then turned away to join his men. He always swore that he could not see the point of this strategy.

Mitch Bouyer was also still trying to get the "General" to reconsider. "There will be more Indians there than we can handle," he was insisting, but Autie had run out of patience with those who dared to question his tactical decisions. He replied sharply, using the same glare he had used on Benteen. "If you are afraid, you could always remain behind."

These were strong words, insulting and unjust, but the worldly wise scout kept his cool. He understood that Custer was under a great deal of pressure and thus made allowances. "No, General, I'll go wherever you," he said, nodding his head gently towards the north west, "but if we enter that valley, neither of us will come out alive." This cautious attitude was echoed by the Crow leader, Half Yellow Face, who it is said confronted Custer, either in sign language, or by interpretation through Bouyer, saying, "You and I are both going home today by a road we do not know."

How many more warnings would it take? A thousand more would probably not have made any difference. Custer was determined that these hostiles must not be allowed to slip through his grasp. They were so close and their loss would be his disgrace. Although the camp was obviously huge with many warriors, Autie would have been following his instinct, based on years of frontier experience. True, there had been massacres of white troops before, but this had always been owing to situations where the victims had been led into a trap, vastly outnumbered and caught in the open. The "General" obviously felt that there was no reason to concern himself with such an eventuality here. He had a very strong force, albeit fragmented and preparing to attack in daylight. Remember, he would have still been totally unaware of the shocking and daring assault inflicted upon Crook at the Rosebud and of how ultra confident Sitting Bull's followers had become. More than anything, one must consider Custer's own confidence. "Custer's Luck". Up to now, his dashing and brazen gambles in battle had always paid off. As long as he led from the front, as he always had since the days at the head of his Wolverines, he must have thought that sheer guts, determination and a sense of divine justice would reap the usual rewards for him. And, there was always that gnawing thought that his actions here on the Little Bighorn would be his final stab at military glory, the result of which would shape the course of the rest of his life.

Whatever, there was no way he was going to be dissuaded. The five companies accompanying him and his staff included most of his clique. Autie forever maintained that element of nepotism within his command structure. Tom Custer relinquished command of his Co. C to the capable 2nd.Lt. Henry Harrington, because Tom had been assigned to act as his big brother's aide-de-camp. With Calhoun leading L Co., Keogh with his Wild I, Yates at the head of F and "Fresh" Smith with E, this made for a jolly gathering of old friends and comrades. Mounted on a pure white horse, Lt. Cooke maintained his long held position as the "General's" Adjutant, Sgt. Hughes still clutched Autie's personal battle flag and Sgt.Maj. Sharrow, Trumpeter Voss and the ailing Dr. Lord completed the rest of Custer's staff.

The "General" also insisted on keeping Mitch Bouyer and the Crows with him, for he had grown somewhat dependent upon the information supplied by these highly competent scouts. In addition, he was taking his nephew, Autie Reed, along, and Kellogg, the newspaper reporter, although brother Boston had to carry out his duties following up behind with the pack train.

Lts. Varnum and Hare were sent ahead with the majority of the scouts but they were soon followed by the divided columns of cavalry, Benteen veering off to the left while Reno's men took a slow canter down the left bank of the creek, Custer's companies lagging slightly behind on the right bank. For the first few miles, the detachments were all within sight of each other, but eventually the slow moving pack train was left far behind.

Descending down a long, gradual incline, and passing a swampy morass, Custer's column covered about eight miles before catching up with a number of the Ree scouts at the site of a recently deserted Sioux camp. Fire embers were still warm here and there was evidence that the inhabitants had packed up and left in a hurry. It was shortly after 2.00pm and Autie was angered to find the scouts wasting time. There was a single white tepee remaining which the Rees had slit open to discover inside the corpse of a finely clad, dead Sansarc warrior laid out in the customary ceremonial manner, a casualty from the Rosebud fight. The Rees seemed intrigued by this, lashing out at the tepee with their quirts, ransacking the dead Sioux's belongings and generally discussing the matter. Custer demanded to know why they were still here when he had ordered them to push on with all haste to supply him with information and run off the Sioux ponies. He said they had disobeyed him and that they must stand aside and let the soldiers pass. "If any man of you is not brave," he added, furiously, "I will take away his weapons and make a woman of him!"

Custer was further angered by the scout's reaction, for they laughed, one of them responding by relating to the interpreter Girard insolently. "Tell the Son-of-the-Morning-

Star that if he does the same to all who are not as brave as we are, it will take him a long time". However, they did redeem themselves by adding that they were hungry for battle. As for the 7th.'s troopers, they amused themselves by setting the burial lodge on fire, something else to trouble the scouts who could not understand why these soldiers were so keen to advertise their approach.

In the meantime, Varnum, Bouyer, Herendeen and the Crows had been acting conscientiously, bypassing the Lone Tepee and riding up to some high ground where they had been observing signs of the main Indian village. In the distance they could now clearly see the Sioux's gigantic pony herd, along with a number of warriors who appeared to be in a state of agitation; running away, it seemed. This was news which needed to be relayed to Custer immediately so Lt. Hare was sent galloping down to meet him.

Autie was in the process of settling matters with the argumentative Rees when Hare arrived with his dreaded tidings. The "General" instantly turned his attention to this pressing problem for the enemy were now apparently doing what had long been feared. The Little Bighorn river still lay a further five miles to the west and the village another two miles north west of that, along its banks. If the Indians had indeed been alerted to danger, as now seemed the case, they would have plenty of time to escape.

Autie had already been anxiously awaiting news from Benteen but had heard nothing. With battle imminent, those three companies would be urgently needed, but Custer could not delay any longer. Benteen could be anywhere, scouting the land to the south, so the "General" would have to pursue his plan with what resources he had available in the hope that Benteen and the pack train would catch up shortly. Reno, who was close by, was summoned and ordered to lead his battalion "out at a trot" in the direction of the village, taking the Rees with him. With this new sense of urgency, the 7th. took to their saddles again, Reno's companies in the lead with Custer following closely behind. At this point, Autie was doing his utmost to keep his available troops together and desperately needed to make contact with Benteen. Adequate information was still sadly lacking upon which to base a sound battle plan, so Custer would have been "coasting with the flow" whilst keeping an eye on developments.

From the Lone Tepee, the battalions, raising lots of dust, trotted uneventfully for a couple of miles down onto some level ground near to where the north and south forks of the Creek converged with the Little Bighorn. At the upper end of the flat, the Crows ascended a small butte where they spotted a pair of mounted Sioux warriors riding towards them from the village. At the same time, the interpreter Fred Girard, looking down into the valley from a nearby ridge, saw much activity as Indians milled around raising the alarm. Turning in his saddle, he faced the troops and waved his hat, yelling excitedly, "There are your Injuns, Gen'l, running like devils!"

Now was the time to act. Custer made a snap decision which he must have known would be hugely reliant upon his famous "Luck". Barking out orders, Autie sent Adjutant Cooke galloping across to Reno where the be-whiskered Canadian relayed his instructions to the dark faced major.

"The village is very close and running away", said Cooke, as he controlled his prancing mount, "move forward as at rapid a pace as prudent, then charge afterwards. The whole outfit will support you."

It was a vague order which would, in effect, be sending Reno's battalion into the unknown, but the feeling was that something had to be done in haste. At least, if the enemy were running away, they had been caught at a disadvantage.

Reno ordered his men forward and they cantered down to the mouth of the North Fork and then on to a suitable ford where they prepared to cross to the west bank of the Little Bighorn. Cooke and Capt. Keogh accompanied Reno this far, discussing the situation in earnest as they rode, before turning back to report to Custer. At the ford,

Reno halted the troops for a few minutes to water the horses and gather the battalion into some semblance of order.

Indian sightings were now abundant for Reno's men. The two Sansarc warriors spotted by the Crows had been riding around in circles to signal danger to the village but the scouts had opened fire on them, killing one while the other fled. Groups of Indians were seen in the distance and the edge of the village could now clearly be seen a couple of miles away across a wide open plain. It was now evident that the enemy was ahead in great force and not fleeing as anticipated. Custer would need to know.

As Cooke and Keogh had already turned back with their observations, Reno decided to send another courier to underline the graveness of the situation. He chose his striker, Pvt. Archibald McIlhargey, who was galloping back over the river before all the battalion had crossed it. Within minutes, Reno was sufficiently concerned to send a second messenger, this time his cook, Pvt. John Mitchell. Both veterans of the 7th., each of them serving their second term in the regiment after nearly ten years with Custer, McIlhargey and Mitchell were married men with children. Tough Irishmen, they were typical members of Keogh's "Wild I", although that particular morning they had been detached from their usual company to serve with Reno. Now they were being sent back to join their friends in their own unit. In this way, fate was to deal these two troopers a cruel hand.

With excitable warriors massing in their hundreds ahead of him, Reno was growing increasingly nervous, but he had his orders. He was committed to attack.

*   *   *

It was just after 3.00pm. when Cooke reported back to Custer the disturbing news that the Indians were present in force and seemingly not intending to leave, tidings which were confirmed moments later by the arrival of Reno's other two messengers. By this time, Custer was on the move himself, having followed Reno's trail for a short distance before turning sharply right towards higher ground. Before this he had ordered his men to water their horses at the North Fork with the words, "Do not let them drink too much because they have to travel a good deal today".

Leaving the flat at a reduced pace, while Reno cantered on in haste, Autie ordered two of the Crows, Half Yellow Face and White Swan, to go ahead to a ridge and report back what they could see. However, through some misunderstanding, Varnum, who rode on to join Reno, somehow managed to gather them into his own group of scouts leaving Custer with a reduced complement. This still included four of the Crows and the stalwart Mitch Bouyer, all of the other scouts having gone with Varnum. Bouyer therefore carried out Custer's order and came back with valuable intelligence about developments in the valley.

The "General" had been lagging behind in the hope that Benteen would catch up with him at any moment, but no amount of wishful scouring of the back trail would make the white haired captain appear. Now there could be no further delay. This latest, unexpected news would require an immediate response. Autie had indeed been intending to support Reno, probably by following him, but now something radical would have to be done. From Custer's subsequent movements, it seems likely that his intention was to rethink his strategy by supporting Reno with a flank attack on the right side of the village. With the major's battalion coping with far more resistance than expected, Custer could lend more effective support by taking pressure away with a surprise assault further down the valley. Firstly, however, a suitable crossing place over the river would need to be found.

Even at this stage, the "General" must have been brimming with confidence.

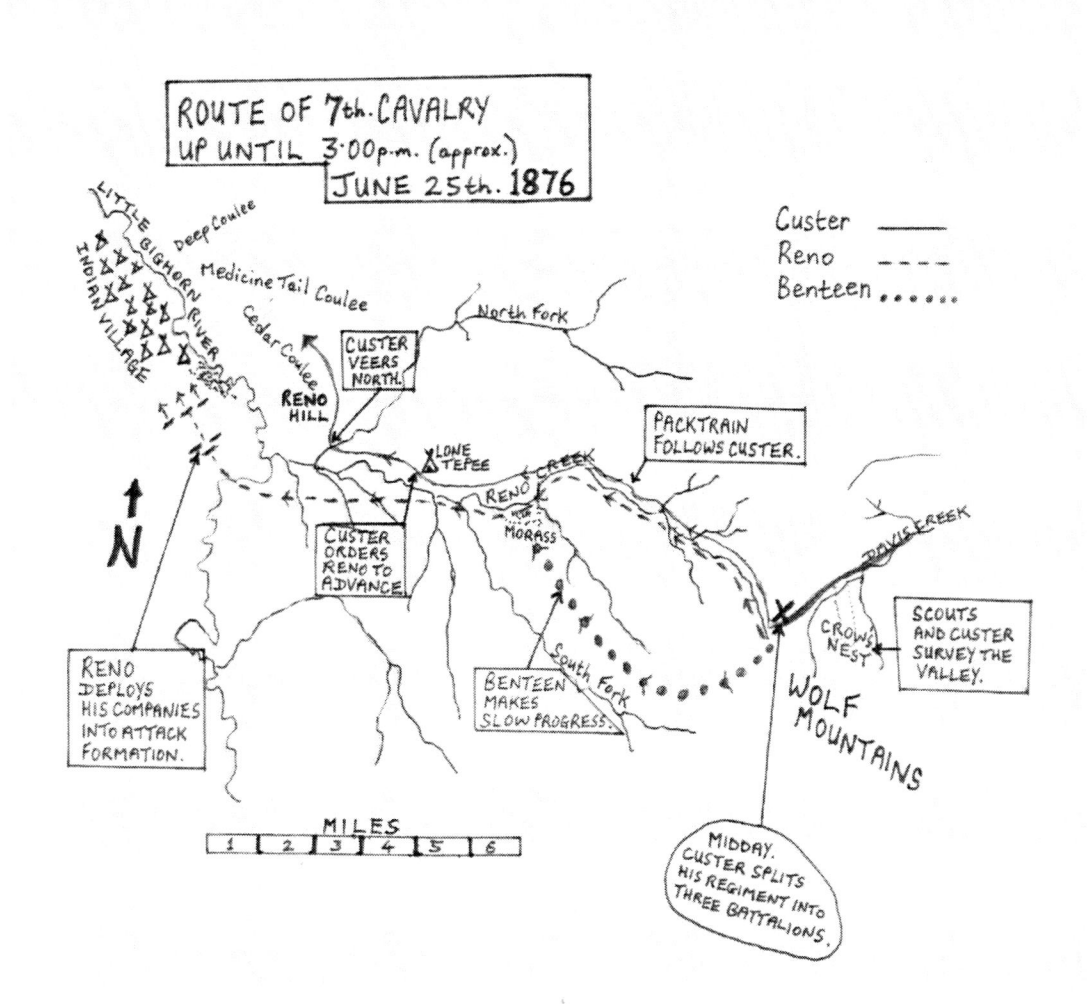

RENO'S CHARGE AND RETREAT

Down at the ford, an uncertain Reno assembled his three companies to commence an advance towards the village. The cavalry horses were tired, having been driven relentlessly for days, but a swift pace was ordered with two companies (A and M) in line and the third (G) following in reserve. As the lines accelerated from a trot to a gait and, finally, to a gallop, several of Reno's men saw part of Custer's battalion a mile or so away across the river, observing the advance from the high ground. Some said the "General" was waving his hat enthusiastically.

The charge pressed on with nothing to stand in its way except those ominous and ever growing clusters of warriors who were emerging aggressively from the village. Spotting some Sioux women and children fleeing across the river towards the timber and a tempting herd of ponies, some of the Ree scouts broke away from the column in pursuit. The remainder of the Rees diverged to the left, galloping hungrily towards the huge main herd which was grazing on the southern edge of the camp.

Reno was concentrating his attack upon the Hunkpapa circle, Sitting Bull's own people, whose name actually translates as "those who camp at the end", therefore it was the Hunkpapa warriors who were the first to react. Boys guarding the pony herd were already attempting to drive it towards the village and warriors were rushing forward to mount up, grabbing any available weapon as they ran.

By now the cavalrymen were in full charge across the plain and Reno yelled at Lt. "Tosh" McIntosh to bring G Co. into line with the others. However, the warriors were still showing no sign of crumbling beneath this attack and were actually riding out to meet it, whooping and firing as they came, their numbers increasing by the moment. They were confident, outraged and determined to defend their families.

The troops under Reno's command numbered less than 140 and it was soon apparent that they were facing at least four times that amount. Reno suddenly realised, with sickening dread, that to press onward with so few men through such odds would be tantamount to suicide. Some 400 yards short of his target, the major ordered an abrupt halt, the troopers pulling hard on their bridles and reining in around him in confusion, although a couple of men lost control of their excited mounts and galloped helplessly on to be swallowed up in the advancing enemy horde. As Sioux bullets and arrows whistled around their heads, Reno's men were then ordered to dismount and form a skirmish line, a standard manoeuvre in Indian warfare. This meant that one in four of the men would be designated as horse holders while the others, now numbering less than 100 combatants, could take up position in a long line to open fire upon the enemy. Their only cover consisted of a small forest of calf high prairie dog mounds but they commenced firing at will towards the village as the warriors pressed home their advantage.

Reno's right flank was protected by a thick brush of timber but his left was hopelessly exposed as hundreds of Indians swarmed around it and began to threaten the line from the rear. A detail from French's M Co. plunged into the trees, clearing the way for the horses to be secured there in safety, although a few mounts were shot down during this operation. The skirmish line had been holding off the Sioux for nearly fifteen minutes now but the situation had grown desperate. Reno had no choice but to order the whole command into the comparative safety of the trees, although everyone knew that such sanctuary would be only temporary. The Sioux closed in, screaming their war cries and blowing on their ear piercing eagle bone war whistles as Reno's men began to fall. Most of the Ree scouts had given up by now, retreating back along the valley at full pelt, driving what few Sioux ponies they had managed to seize, although the faithful Bloody

Knife volunteered to remain at Reno's side.

Within the natural defences of the cottonwoods, with the river behind them, the cavalrymen were able to consolidate some form of order, but already the Sioux were beginning to infiltrate the trees, assisted by war parties who boldly hurled themselves at the thin blue line. Although a mature officer with much combat experience, Reno was fazed by such unexpected aggression and was beginning to lose control. As the men looked to him for instructions, the major dithered, looking this way and that as panic began to take a hold of him. More than once he illogically gave the order to mount up and then dismount again. Everything finally disintegrated when Bloody Knife tried to reason with him. A Sioux volley came as a blast from the bushes and Custer's favourite Indian was struck in the head, spraying brains and blood into Reno's face. As Bloody Knife dropped lifeless to the ground, it was the final straw for the hard pressed major. Shocked, his eyes bulging, it seems that at this point Reno lost his nerve completely. He had lost his straw hat, replacing it with a red bandana which he wrapped Indian style around his head. With Ree grey matter still dripping from his face, Reno yelled to those within earshot, "Any of you men who wish to live and make your escape, follow me!" He then spurred his horse towards the river and galloped off alone.

It was a poor display of leadership. No bugle call had been ordered and only a few troopers had heard their fleeing commander. Some immediately leapt into their saddles and followed him but many others were oblivious to what was happening, confused and frightened as they blundered through the woods. Quite a few had lost their horses during the upheaval of retreat and either attempted to hide in the brush or surrendered to their fate. As the soldier's defences collapsed, the Indians howled triumphantly, bearing down hard on their heels and quickly dispatching any stragglers.

Reno would one day claim that he led a charge of retreat, a situation which could not have been improved upon, but in fact the breakout from the cottonwoods was nothing more than a rout which the Sioux exploited gleefully. It was a case of every man for himself, a total breakdown of order. Their only hope was to make it to the high bluffs across the river but that was at least a mile away.

Warriors had already made their way to the river bank to try and cut off any line of retreat and were massing there in such numbers that Reno and his fleeing men were forced to the left. They reached the river at a point which could hardly be called a ford, but the pressure behind and alongside them was so fierce that the soldiers on their big horses had no choice but to plunge blindly ahead. It was a steep drop down into deep, fast flowing water, creating a scene of sheer chaos as horses whinnied and splashed about in terror, throwing their riders into the white cascading foam. Troopers were separated from their mounts, losing their weapons as they struggled helplessly in the water, fighting to reach the opposite bank.

Reaching the river had been a hellish experience too. With their retreat completely exposed, no consideration having been given to a rearguard, the cavalrymen galloped along almost totally at the mercy of the Sioux who rode alongside them, picking them off at leisure. Some were shot and others knocked out of their saddles with war clubs. One warrior told the tale of a soldier he unhorsed then beat to death with his bow. Another was wounded and held struggling beneath the Little Bighorn's surface until he stopped moving. Some troopers were caught in the undergrowth, desperately trying to evade young Indian boys who were shooting arrows at them.

That said, there were still incidents where the 7th. redeemed itself. Lt. Godfrey reported how he had observed a trooper slay a warrior in hand to hand combat, before taking the Indian's pony to ride across the river. The Crow scout White Swan fought on with most of his right hand shot away. A corporal from McIntosh's G Co. even stopped to take the scalp of a Sioux he had killed, waving it around for his comrades to see. As for "Tosh" himself, he did not fare so well. The half breed officer was last seen galloping through the woods on a borrowed horse, a long lariat dragging behind him. He suddenly found himself cut off and alone, surrounded by about thirty mounted Sioux who closed in on him mercilessly, dragging him from the saddle. Just like his father before him, killed by Indians.

Nearby, "Lonesome Charley" Reynolds nearly made it to the river. When the action started he had torn the poultice off his infected thumb to enable him to handle his rifle more effectively, but now he was riding "hell for leather", weaving in and out of the screaming warriors until a bullet brought him down, pinning the scout beneath his wounded horse. He probably fought hard from where he lay but stood no chance.

Lt. Benny Hodgson, Reno's adjutant and friend, also had his horse brought down right by the river's west bank. Shot through the leg, Hodgson dragged himself to the water's edge, calling out for assistance. A passing mounted trooper paused, removing his foot from a stirrup so that the lieutenant could grab it. In this way, Hodgson was dragged across the river, probably relieved as he gasped his way up the east bank only to be struck a further three times by bullets and an arrow.

The big, black interpreter, Isaiah Dorman was seen alongside his dead horse, kneeling down and calmly firing upon the advancing Sioux with his rifle. As a well known and popular figure with the Lakota, Dorman was in an odd predicament, but his old friends were not in a forgiving mood. He killed at least one of them before they laid him low with shots to his legs. Perhaps they intended to catch him alive for he was beaten with stone hammers and slashed with knives. The Sioux also shot about a dozen arrows into his chest and pinned him to the ground with a picket pin through his privates. For some reason they even collected some of his blood in his metal coffee cup which they left beside his body. "With friends like that, who needs enemies?" one might ask.

Several men made it to the opposite bank but found themselves surrounded by warriors who were lying in wait for them. One was the surgeon, Dr. James de Wolf, who was killed and scalped in full view of other fugitives who were splashing across the river. Those who reached the far bank intact then faced a further ordeal, for the summit of the bluffs they were trying to reach still seemed a long way off, perhaps another half mile climb up a steep, craggy slope, under fire all the way. Many of those on foot were so spent that they had to hold onto the tails of passing horses to assist their climb. A few troopers, Lt. Hare amongst them, turned to fire across the river at their pursuers in an attempt to give a little cover and relief for those trying to escape.

Reno made it to the summit of the bluffs, with the bulk of his shattered command, by 4.10pm. but they had been lucky. If the Sioux had pressed a bit harder and not been distracted by another development, probably all three companies would have been wiped out. Between thirty to forty of Reno's command had been killed outright during the retreat with about fifteen more wounded. Nearly twenty were missing, most of whom had been trapped in the trees and forced to hide. This last group included the scout Herendeen and the ex-terrorist Lt. De Rudio.

It had been a humiliating and disastrous defeat for the 7th. Cavalry, but there was worse to come.

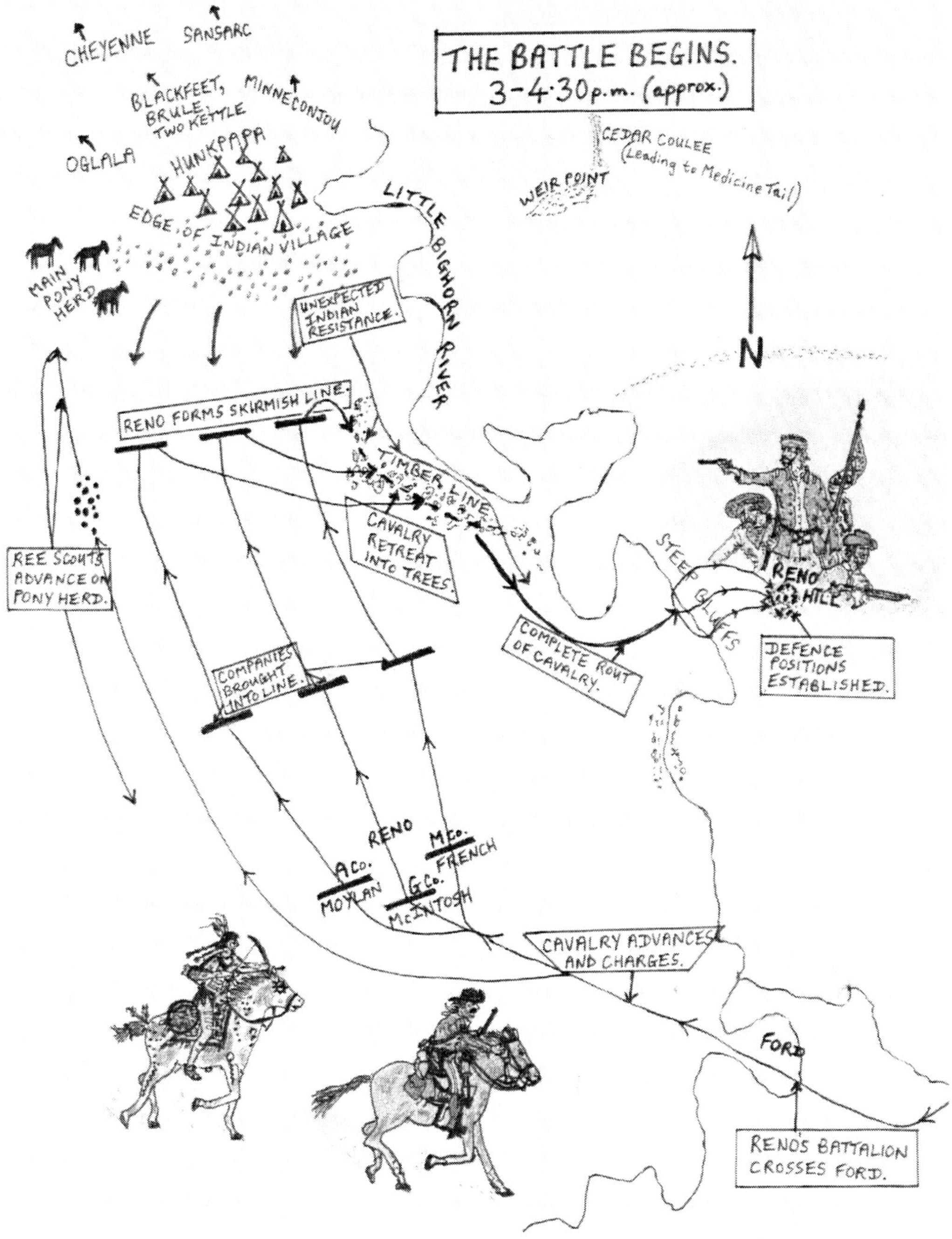
THE BATTLE BEGINS.
3-4·30p.m. (approx.)
CHEYENNE
SANSARC
BLACKFEET, BRULE, TWO KETTLE
MINNECONJOU
OGLALA
HUNKPAPA
EDGE OF INDIAN VILLAGE
MAIN PONY HERD
CEDAR COULEE (Leading to Medicine Tail)
WEIR POINT
LITTLE BIGHORN RIVER
UNEXPECTED INDIAN RESISTANCE.
N
RENO FORMS SKIRMISH LINE.
TIMBER LINE
CAVALRY RETREAT INTO TREES.
REE SCOUTS ADVANCE ON PONY HERD.
STEEP CLIFFS
RENO HILL
DEFENCE POSITIONS ESTABLISHED.
COMPLETE ROUT OF CAVALRY.
COMPANIES BROUGHT INTO LINE.
RENO
A Co. MOYLAN
G Co. McINTOSH
M Co. FRENCH
CAVALRY ADVANCES AND CHARGES.
FORD
RENO'S BATTALION CROSSES FORD.

"WE'VE GOT 'EM, BOYS!"

Custer, at the head of his five companies, now urged on the advance, keen to reach the high ground so that he could get a better view of the valley. Within minutes, the troops had made it to the summit of the bluffs, reining their lathered horses in behind their commander. Before the hour was out, Reno's routed command would be burrowing for cover on this very spot, immortalizing it in history as Reno Hill. For now, however, circumstances were not quite so desperate and Autie's men were delighted to be able to get their first proper sight of the hostile village they had sought for so long.

Obscured by trees along the river bank, Custer could only look down upon the southern end of the camp (mainly the Hunkpapa lodges), but plenty of activity was evident. Over to the left, Reno's companies could be seen charging towards the enemy in good order.

The "General" was elated as he watched his loose strategy unfold. He had removed his buckskin jacket, his sweat stained blue shirt still fastened at the neck where it was clamped by the inevitable red necktie. The brim of his big cream hat was clipped to the right side of the crown to enable him to sight his rifle more easily. After weeks on the trail, the crisp appearance of Fort Lincoln was somewhat jaded, but Autie still sat erect in the saddle, regardless of his dusty, grimy clothes and heavy beard.

"Courage ... we've got them!" he cried, pulling off his hat and waving it. The men responded enthusiastically and began cheering, some of them losing control of their mounts which skittered out of rank.

"Hold your horses in, boys," continued Custer firmly, "there are plenty of them down there for all of us."

The next pressing concern would be the assurance of ample ammunition to cope with what was surely shaping up as the big fight Bouyer had foreseen. Turning to his brother Tom, Autie ordered word to be sent back to the pack train immediately. Tom chose one of his company sergeants, Daniel Kanipe, to relay this message. "Find McDougall," Kanipe was told, "and tell him to hasten on cross-country without delay. If the packs get loose, don't stop to fix them; cut them off and leave them on the trail." Kanipe was also instructed to look out for the elusive Benteen and hurry him on as well.

As the sergeant galloped away, Custer ordered the advance to continue north in columns of fours, some of the men passing along either side of the ridge and the remainder cantering along its summit. Soon they had descended towards Cedar Coulee and lost sight of the valley, thus also concealing them from Indian sight. The plan was almost certainly to find an access point to take them down to the river where the supporting assault could be made. From here the pace was so urgent, across difficult terrain, that several of Custer's troopers simply could not keep up and their exhausted horses began to lag behind. They did not know it then, but this was to save their lives.

About a mile into the ravine, Custer ordered another halt where the natural course began to bend to the right. Here, Autie gathered his remaining scouts together, thanked them, then told them that they would no longer be needed and could seek safety in the rear with the advancing pack train. Three of the Crows, White Man Runs Him, Hairy Moccasin and Goes Ahead accepted this offer and turned back, but young Curley and Mitch Bouyer demonstrated their loyalty (and courage) by choosing to remain with the column. Bouyer, particularly, knew that they were heading for big trouble, but it seems that he simply could not bring himself to abandon Custer.

Leaving the column at rest for a moment, the "General" took a small party, which included Adjutant Cooke, Bouyer and Curley, and rode to the crest of a nearby high ridge. (This would later be named Weir Point for reasons which will become apparent.)

From there, they had their first truly enlightening view of the valley, including the shock of appreciating just how large the village really was. They could also now see that Reno's charge had been stopped in its tracks and the men were forming a skirmish line to hold off hordes of Sioux who were pressing them hard. This must have been Autie's first sobering moment, but, typically, he was not visibly downcast and his mind was soon racing ahead. If Reno could keep the hostiles occupied, Custer's command could still make a surprise attack by smashing through the centre of the village. Scouring the terrain, Custer's sharp eyes quickly fell upon the land ahead where Cedar Coulee led into Medicine Tail Coulee, a long, wide chasm which led down to the river where the tepees stretched right up to, and along, its western bank. A perfect crossing place.

Leaving Bouyer and Curley on the ridge to observe and report on Reno's progress, Custer rode back to his men. It was now more urgent than ever for Autie's companies to receive support from the remainder of the regiment who were stretched back along the trail. Where *was* Benteen? Another message would have to be sent.

The Italian trumpeter Martini (alias Martin) was summoned and told to ride like the wind to bring this much needed help. Martin was young but quite experienced in military matters, for he had even served in his native Italy as a drummer boy in action under Garibaldi. The main concern lay in his limited knowledge of the English language. To ensure that there would be no confusion, Cooke scribbled a note in his pocket book, tore out the page and thrust it at the orderly. It read …

Benteen,

Come on, big
village   be quick
bring packs.

W.W.Cooke

P. bring pacs

The sense of urgency is evident in the last line. Martin dug in his spurs and took off at the gallop, turning back to see the column on the move again, down into the depths of Cedar Coulee towards Medicine Tail. He noted that Smith's Grey Horse Troop (E) rode in the centre with the light sorrels of Co. C and the bays of Co.'s F, I and L on either side.

*   *   *

Frederick Benteen was not a happy man. Riding at the head of his battalion, he slouched in the saddle, his mind enveloped in dark thoughts about his commanding officer. It might even be said that he was sulking. His protests about what he saw as this pointless scouting foray had fallen on deaf ears, and now he felt relegated to a secondary role as if he was being deliberately excluded from the coming action. Could Custer really be so childishly vindictive as to exclude three whole companies from the fight? Was his arrogance so pronounced that he would put his entire command at risk just to score points against a bitter rival who hated him? It seems that Benteen suspected that such was the case, but he was almost certainly wrong.

For all his faults, Custer was not a fool. Sometimes daring to the point of recklessness, yes, but he was far too professional to let personal problems get in the way of his military strategy. Benteen's mission did have a purpose, for it made sense to ensure that there was no sign of Indians escaping to the south. Such an assignment need not have taken long, for we can safely assume that it was never Custer's intention for Benteen to be absent for an extended period. After the separation of the battalions at the divide, just after noon, Custer had quickly ridden on to a position where he was able to ascertain valuable information about the distant terrain which would be of value to Benteen. Acting on this, he sent two couriers, (his chief trumpeter, Voss, and Sergeant Major Sharrow) at short intervals, back to the bitter captain to tell him to hurry on to particular ridges which seemed to promise vantage points for observation. Voss and Sharrow delivered their information efficiently then wasted no time in galloping back to Custer, but Benteen did not hurry himself.

Benteen had no scouts with him, but his battalion did include some fine officers, including Godfrey, Edgerly, Gibson and Tom Weir. Apparently, Weir, as a Custer sycophant, grew increasingly impatient at the slow pace of the column. Heading west into an area of sagebrush hills, Benteen led his men across the ridges and over small branches of Reno Creek, sending Gibson ahead with a detail to see if anything of interest could be found. Having covered a few miles at a leisurely amble, sweating in the heat of the afternoon and feeling isolated, Benteen testily decided that he had gone far enough. Nothing could be seen but miles of empty country, but that in itself was news, for it meant that the hostiles were not heading that way. At this point, Benteen should really have sent a messenger galloping ahead at speed to inform Custer of this intelligence, but he neglected to do so, choosing instead to just slowly alter his course, turning north towards the main trail where he assumed he would eventually link up with the rest of the regiment. A little after 2.30pm., the wandering battalion reached the morass on Reno Creek where an official halt was called to water the horses, but before long other officers, apart from Weir, were beginning to grow restless about the delay. Benteen appeared to be acting as if he was on a Sunday outing.

At about this time, Custer's young brother Boston came riding up alone. Anxious to be part of the action, he had left his post with the pack train and, at great risk, was pushing ahead to join his brothers. Benteen's men remembered him smiling and waving cheerfully as he cantered past them. When the battalion finally got moving again, following Custer's trail, McDougall and the pack train could be seen plodding along to the rear.

Soon after this, Benteen reached the Lone Tepee which was still burning since Custer's men had set it on fire almost an hour before. This time the troops did not halt but carried on at the trot, for things were beginning to happen. First of all, they were met by Reno's Ree scouts who were charging towards them, whooping excitedly and driving the ponies they had captured from the Sioux herd, then came Sgt. Kanipe bearing the first message from Custer. Benteen told Kanipe that the pack train was only about a mile to the rear, so the sergeant rode on, calling out to the troops as he rode past them with a cheery, "We've got 'em, boys!"

Within minutes, the newly inspired battalion saw Custer's second messenger, Trumpeter Martin, galloping across the flats from the direction of Reno Hill. Martin was agitated as he drew to a halt in front of Benteen, greeting the captain with a crisp salute. His horse was bleeding from a gunshot wound in the withers, proving that he had experienced a rough time getting through. Handing over Cooke's note, Martin gabbled on, in his thick Italian accent, that the Indians were "skedaddling". Benteen read the note, showed it to Weir, then put it away in his breast pocket. Cooke had ordered Martin to return to Custer, if possible, but the young immigrant had been through enough and decided to remain where he was, making him the last white survivor of the battle to see the "General" alive.

Rapid and continuous gunfire could now be heard ahead beyond the bluffs to the north, so at last Benteen had no choice but to take drastic action. Forming his men in line and ordering them to draw pistols, the troops spurred on at a gait towards the sound of the guns. A dramatic moment which could have leapt from the silver screen. At the North Fork they reached the spot where Custer's and Reno's battalions diverged (which Benteen said was "the horns of a dilemma",) but the bulk of the column followed the right hand (Custer's) trail. Topping a rise, Benteen was then met by the alarming sight of sheer pandemonium in the valley below and on the slopes ahead. Here lay a smoke ridden scene of galloping Indians and fleeing cavalrymen, many of them unhorsed as they scrambled desperately across the river and up the bluffs. It was Reno and he was obviously in big trouble.

No more time could be wasted. Benteen urged his men onward, for Reno was in dire need of all the help he could get. On the way, this relieving force was joined by the three Crow scouts who had been released by Custer. Although they tried to explain by sign language the situation faced by the "General" ahead, circumstances on the spot appeared to require more urgent attention.

At this time, Autie would have been relying upon the arrival of Benteen but there was no way he could know that the cynical captain was otherwise engaged and would not be coming.

George Armstrong Custer would have to fight his final battle against impossible odds.

"A GOOD DAY TO DIE"

Curbing his growing impatience, Custer, contrary to his thrusting instinct, slowed the pace of the column as they approached the opening of Cedar Coulee. There were two reasons for this; the need to allow Benteen time to catch up and a desire to reduce any giveaway dust cloud. A little after 3.30pm. the entire battalion halted as they reached the coulee's mouth. Here the men adjusted their saddles as they observed a lone rider approaching from the south. Could this be a courier from Benteen, at last?

In a way it was, for this rider was Boston Custer who had rendezvoused with Benteen less than an hour before near the Lone Tepee. Autie and Tom were pleased to see their little brother and anxiously pumped him for news. The young quartermaster was able to give them optimistic tidings, for if Benteen was following at the trot, with the pack train in tow, they should be in sight any minute. As for Reno's command, Boston's last sighting of them, as he rode along the high ridge, was similar to Custer's, which merely confirmed that they were holding their ground, as hoped. Encouraged by this, Autie decided to carry on moving slowly down to the river, taking a sharp turn left into Medicine Tail Coulee. As they were leaving, the scouts Bouyer and Curley could be seen in the distance on the summit of Weir Point, attempting to signal the column. Thinking these to be positive signs, Autie and Tom waved back as the men cheered again.

However, from their vantage point, what the scouts had seen was far from encouraging. Having failed to get their point across visually, Bouyer and Curley spurred their horses towards the advancing column, catching up with it a little way into the coulee. The news they brought was enough for a shocked Custer to halt his troops again. Mitch informed the "General" that Reno's men were no longer holding their defensive position but had been broken by the intensity of the Indian attack. Now they had fallen back in disorder into the timber line, effectively removing them from any attack plan.

This gut wrenching news must have hit Custer hard, although he would characteristically have ridden the blow within sight of his men. It was just after 4.00pm.. Once more, the "General's" strategy would need a radical rethink and now *every* minute would count. Certain priorities had changed. Reno was actually in danger of being overwhelmed and Custer could not ignore that. He would need to do something immediately to relieve the pressure whilst still maintaining the possibility of turning the day in his favour. The plan he came up with, according to strong surviving evidence, was daring, desperate and fraught with risk, but under the circumstances was his only chance of success.

He could, of course, have aborted the mission, turning back at speed to reunite with Benteen and together they could have ridden to Reno's rescue. This would make the command strong enough to repel such a horde of Indians but only as a defensive action which was totally alien to Autie's nature. The 7th. Cavalry forced to dig in, fighting for their lives against savages and dependent upon the arrival of Terry and Gibbon? Unthinkable. Even in the heat of the moment Custer must have known his career and reputation would never survive such a scenario. Life would not be worth living. This was a case of glory or the grave.

With the river and the centre edge of the hostile camp less than a mile away, Autie split his command yet again. Madness, some might say, but there was method in it. Yates was to take command of a battalion consisting of his own Co. F and Smith's Grey Horse Troop, E. The trusted captain, so long part of Autie's clique, was saddled with the huge responsibility of leading his small command (just 76 men) in an attack against the village by carrying on down Medicine Tail Coulee. At least that was the impression they were hoping to give. Such a feint would cause much commotion in the centre of the camp thereby hopefully drawing away most of the warriors who were attacking Reno. Custer had already given command of the remaining three companies, C, I and L, (135 men) to his senior captain, Keogh, but this was the battalion that the "General" and his scouts would remain with. Their part in the initial plan would be to ride on up to the north rim of the coulee, maintaining a position there to observe events in the valley and support Yates as and when he should need it. Yates would not press home his "attack" (which would be sheer suicide), but was intended to disengage and draw the hostiles away. Depending upon the Indian's reaction, Custer's battalion would respond accordingly whilst covering the hoped for imminent approach of Benteen and the pack train of ammunition. Autie was also probably thinking that he could reunite his companies further down the river, by which time Reno, hopefully with the foresight and gumption of a good officer, should have been able to restore his force and bring them up to rejoin the fight. In this way, with aggression and Custer's Luck, the 7th. Cavalry could still maintain the offensive and emerge victorious.

Such was the theory, but at that time there was no way Autie could know that Reno had lost his nerve and Benteen, for reasons best known to himself, had decided to dawdle.

So, Custer and the Right Wing battalion turned north up the slopes as Yates, Smith and the Left Wing descended at the gallop down into Medicine Tail Coulee. They were making no effort to conceal their approach now for they threw up a lot of dust and noise, the company guidons fluttering above their heads. By this time those Indians who were in the vicinity were well aware of the advancing Long Knives. At first there were very few warriors around to resist this attack, just a handful who had been delayed from harrying Reno and were supervising the withdrawal of the village's women and children. Reports of just how many combatants came out to face Yates are confused and unreliable, but they were certainly a small bunch initially. Courageous too, for they came boldly to the water's edge and commenced firing upon the advancing column. Just how far Yates intended to press home his advance will probably never be known, but it has been confirmed that the troops halted abruptly on the river's eastern bank as the bullets began to fly. (All except for one unfortunate non-com of Co. E whose horse panicked and carried him across the river to his doom.) It was at this juncture that some research in the past has pointed to the possibility that Custer himself was hit here at the very beginning of the action, but more recent discoveries have made it much more likely that he was with the Right Wing as previously described. This belief largely came from Indian tales that a soldier chief at the head of the column, with a fair beard and dressed in buckskins, was shot by the river's edge. The Indians knew he was important because the other *wasichus* seemed alarmed and gathered around him, but this description could easily have matched Yates too. So, possibly the battalion commander became an early casualty, although perhaps only wounded for his body was later found some distance away. If he *was* killed here then his men took the trouble to carry his body with them when they withdrew.

Whatever, with the firing relatively light, Yates' battalion did not attempt to cross the river but turned right, carrying on along the bank with no sense of urgency before reaching the cutbank of another ravine, Deep Coulee, which ascended steeply north. The troops climbed the west rim of this coulee while behind them warriors crossed the ford, their numbers increasing by the moment. Many of these Indians were on horseback by now, growing bolder as they trailed Yates or entered Medicine Tail Coulee in an attempt to outflank him. Pretty soon they were beginning to achieve this and E and F companies were forced to dismount and form skirmish lines, opening fire on the encroaching warriors to keep them at bay. At the same time, the Left Wing battalion pressed on with the intention of rejoining the Right Wing on the heights.

From his position on the high ridge, Custer was able to observe the opposition faced by Yates at the ford, also the progress of the Left Wing as it meandered along the river bank and into Deep Coulee. At about this time, 4.25pm. approximately, Custer and the Right Wing began to face pressure from warriors who were emerging from Medicine Tail Coulee and fanning out amongst the gullies and ravines. Autie straightaway ordered a heavy fire to be directed at these hostiles which succeeded in keeping them pinned down. The Indians were not too numerous at this time, for the majority were still occupied with Reno, but this is the point where the emphasis of the battle changed. Custer's heavy volleys were heard up the valley both by Reno and the warriors attacking him, achieving the desired effect. Hundreds of braves lost interest in harassing Reno's routed force, turning their attention instead to this new threat as they screamed their war cries and directed their pony's snouts to the north west.

Custer knew he could not tarry any longer. Still no sign of Benteen on the horizon and Yates looked in danger of being cut off unless the "General" acted swiftly. Another courier was apparently sent, this time, it is said, to the north, which may seem strange as the rest of the force were to the south. However, this messenger was probably being sent with news of the unfolding catastrophe to Terry and Gibbon. We shall never know, for the trooper assigned this mission, mounted on a sorrel/roan horse, never made it.

Ordering the men to remount, Custer led an orderly withdrawal towards the top end of Deep Coulee where he hoped to achieve a reunion with Yates. Facing little opposition at first, within a mile his men had to reactivate a brisk fire to hold off more Indians who were beginning to mass on his left flank. For the first time, Custer's battalion was beginning to suffer noticeable casualties as hostile bullets and arrows found their targets. Firing on the move, the Right Wing at last negotiated a crossing of the upper Deep Coulee where Yates' men were beginning to emerge, largely on foot and dragging their spooked horses behind them.

This reunion must have brought a brief sense of relief. It was 4.45pm..

*   *   *

At the far end of the village, in the heart of the Hunkpapa circle, there was much activity. The Long Knives who dared to attack the village had been driven away, running like women to hide on a hilltop while the young men laughed at them, taking the scalps and guns of their dead. Sitting Bull would not fight this day, but he was as powerful a force as ever, encouraging his warriors and reminding them of his prophecy which spoke of white soldiers falling upside down into the Lakota camp.

Many warriors delayed joining the fight to dress themselves in their finery and put on their war paint. Crazy Horse was one of this group and by the time he rode up with his Oglalas, the old men were telling him that he had missed the battle. That was before heavy firing was heard to the north, informing the bloodthirsty warriors that the combat on the Greasy Grass was far from over.

The bullets of the white soldiers and their hated Ree scouts had inflicted a heavy toll on the village as they charged upon it. Lead slugs had torn through the flimsy hide coverings of the tepees, striking the innocent within before the warriors had rallied to turn the tide.

It is said that Chief Gall stood trembling with rage, letting out a great howl of anguish as he took in the terrible carnage. Two of his wives and three of his children, cut down by the *wasichus* murderous fire. Yet again the white devils had given him cause to follow the warpath. Grim faced, he grasped his terrible hatchet and leapt up upon his pony's back. The Long Knives were going to pay their debt to him in blood.

As the Lakota said, it would be a good day to die.

ON RENO HILL

Exhausted and in a state of complete disorder, the dishevelled survivors of Reno's command reached the top of the bluffs, with no doubt many a prayer and expletive to accompany their salvation. The men threw themselves down on the ground, gasping and reaching for their canteens as Indian bullets tore up the earth around them. At this time there was still no cohesive command structure and there remained very much an atmosphere of "every man for himself", a situation which could not reign for long if these troops were to have any hope of further survival.

For now, at least, Reno was in no fit state to command. He was no stranger to combat but the unified, civilized conflicts of the Civil War could hardly be compared to this primitive hell. It did not bear thinking about the fate of these troopers if such a merciless foe should overwhelm them. Such a doom would almost certainly have befallen them had not Benteen come riding to the rescue.

At the sight of three new cavalry companies, advancing in good order with pistols drawn, most of the Indians began to fall back, relieving the pressure on Reno's men. When he reached the bluff, Benteen ordered a skirmish line thrown out which commenced a heavy fire. This kept the hostiles at a distance although they remained defiant and spoiling for a fight.

Reno staggered up to Benteen, his face still smeared with bits of Bloody Knife, his pistol in his hand. Shortly before this he was reportedly seen discharging this pistol at Indians who were a good 900 yards out of range. Benteen peered at the major disdainfully as the fazed officer blurted out what had happened. As they spoke, heavy organized firing was heard from the north as Custer engaged the enemy. The bulk of the Indians immediately turned away from Reno and began to head up the valley.

Although this would have been an immense relief to the troops besieged on the bluffs, it was obvious to everyone that Custer's companies would now be facing a sticky situation. The "General" would need immediate support, including the extra ammunition he had requested urgently via two couriers. Although these requests had been direct orders, Benteen was still doing nothing about it and the pack train was nowhere in sight. As for Reno, as senior officer present it was his duty to take the initiative and reform his command. Potentially, these six companies (albeit three of them severely mauled) should make a formidable force but nobody seemed capable, at this time, of acting responsibly.

Instead, Reno seemed far more concerned about the loss of his adjutant, Benny Hodgson. Leaving his troops bewildered, the major began to descend the slope saying that he was going to try and find Hodgson in the hope that he was still alive. Incredibly, he was absent from his command for half an hour as scores of troopers idled away their time on top of the hill. Whether or not a rapid advance towards the gunfire would have saved Custer has been a matter of debate ever since, but many of the officers involved were harshly criticised in the coming years and actually created questionable alibis to try and cover up their actions.

To balance this, one does have to appreciate that we can now speak from a position of hindsight, for *we* were not on that hill having just faced hordes of shrieking warriors who longed for our scalps. The men, it seems, needed time to collect themselves and basically did very little except speculate about their C.O.'s movements along the valley. In the meantime, the distant firing continued, sometimes slackening and occasionally building to a crescendo. When Reno finally returned he was clearly upset, having found Hodgson's body and relieved it of some of its personal effects, but everyone was now looking to him for a decision about what to do. Still he failed to act, merely ordering Lt. Varnum to take a detail down into the valley to bury Hodgson, a noble gesture but hardly a priority at this time. However, on a positive note, Reno did at least order Lt. Hare to gallop back along the trail to hurry up the pack train.

As Reno and Benteen continued to dither, a particularly fierce series of co-ordinated volleys were heard from Custer's direction, prompting Capt. Tom Weir to approach his superior officers and demand to know what they intended doing about it. Reno replied that nothing could be done until the reserve ammunition arrived but Weir grew impatient, suggesting that the volleys sounded like distress signals, as if the "General" was calling for help. The argument grew quite heated with Weir's insistence on a move downstream bordering upon insubordination, but Reno would not budge. Disgusted, Weir turned away, strode to his horse and mounted up. Within moments he was riding away alone towards the firing. Caught unawares, Weir's company lieutenant, Winfield Edgerly, thought that his captain's move must be an order to advance so he quickly ushered his men into their saddles. Minutes later, Co. D was trotting away following Weir's dust trail as Reno and Benteen looked on. Afterwards, Reno would claim that Weir was acting as an "advance guard", as if he had ordered the move himself; an obvious cover up.

Another fifteen minutes were to pass before Benteen finally took his own initiative (probably inspired by a nagging feeling of guilt) and led companies H, K and M in the same direction as Weir. By this time, (about 5.20pm.) the gunfire down the valley had slackened to almost nothing, so what Benteen hoped to achieve is open to question. Had Custer disengaged the enemy, maybe retiring to the north? It was anyone's guess.

Shortly after this, the long awaited pack train, escorted by McDougall's Co. B, finally hove into sight. This raised the remaining men's spirits a little but there was still an uncomfortable feeling of doubt and confusion regarding Custer's whereabouts. A handful of men from the "General's" column had been straggling in, victims of Custer's swift advance when their horses had given out. Left behind on the trail in hostile territory, unable to keep up, these scattered, frightened troopers had decided to make their way to the rear. One of them was Pvt. Gustave Korn, a Silesian from Keogh's "Wild I" who claimed his horse had bolted, but this did not go down too well with his unconvinced company sergeant, Milton de Lacy, who was on detached service with the pack train.

Other men were beginning to reach the bluff too, including a party of about a dozen troopers on foot who had been hiding in the heavy foliage by the river before being led to safety under the cool leadership of the seasoned frontiersman George Herendeen. Although this was good news, there were still plenty of men missing. Feeling somewhat calmer now, Reno himself decided to follow the example of Benteen and rode out with his orderly to find out what was happening. Companies A, B and G went with him.

*   *   *

Keenly but cautiously, Weir made his way to the top of the ridge which would from now on be called Weir Point, the very spot from where Custer and his scouts had taken their first enlightened look at the size of the Indian village below them in the valley. Weir was now gazing at that same sight as his company trotted up behind him. Lt. Hare was with them, having completed his mission to find the pack train. The shock of the hostile camp was soon overshadowed by another sight which loomed ahead about two miles to the north, for there on the slopes was evidence of a dramatic struggle. Huge clouds of dust and smoke boiled above scurrying, tiny figures, many of them mounted. At this distance it was difficult to identify them, but one or two military guidons could be seen, prompting Weir to hopefully suggest, "That is Custer over there".

Nearby, one of the company sergeants handed the captain a pair of field glasses saying, "Here, sir, you had better take a look through these. I think those are Indians."

Weir looked, his face a grim mask. He could now see that those distant, mobile figures were definitely Indians and the guidons were in *their* hands as they rode about the field waving them like coup sticks. Such firing as could now be heard was sporadic and appeared to be coming from individual warriors who were shooting at objects on the ground. Indian women could also be identified in the chaos which did not bode well, for it meant that any engagement that had taken place there must now be over. Could this mean that Custer had been driven off?

Weir had now lost his enthusiasm for riding to Custer's relief for it looked like a hornet's nest ahead. Lt. Edgerly had led Co. D onto the north slope of the ridge putting them in clear view of many of the distant Indians who began to yell and spur their ponies towards them. Weir straightaway signalled for Edgerly to take the company back behind the ridge to a less exposed position. As Edgerly completed this circling manoeuvre, he was met by Benteen, Godfrey and French coming up from Reno Hill with their companies, just as Hare commenced to return to report to Reno with this latest grim news.

Benteen took one look at the advancing hordes and said, " This is a hell of a place to fight Indians. I am going to see Reno and propose that we go back….."

He then promptly turned his horse's head and galloped back along the trail taking his Co. H with him. This left companies D, K and M exposed on the high ground without clear orders, for Benteen had neglected to issue any. Before long, however, the ever active Lt. Hare had returned with instructions from Reno to withdraw back to Reno Hill. With the hostiles pressing menacingly close and bullets zipping through the air, the companies commenced an orderly retreat while the competent Godfrey, assisted by Hare, deployed men from Co. K as foot skirmishers to cover the withdrawal. This was text book stuff and proved successful, for only one man was lost in the retreat, a farrier from Co. D named Vincent Charley who took a bullet in the right hip which exited through the left side of his abdomen. Such a crippling wound rendered him unable to ride and the unfortunate trooper tried to drag himself along after his comrades on his knees with the aid of one arm. The hostiles were now nearly upon them so no one dared to go back and help the stricken man. Instead, Edgerly, and others, called out to him to conceal himself in a nearby ravine from where he could be picked up later. Most of his company must have known he did not stand a chance. Indeed, the Sioux caught him. How much they made him suffer before he died can only be guessed at but his body was later found with a stick jammed down its throat.

Back at Reno Hill, the major was beginning to apply himself to the idea of forming a proper defensive perimeter. By just after 6.00pm., all the companies had returned and work commenced on throwing up breastworks, largely constructed from packs taken from the mules. The men also attempted to dig in, but the hard earth and lack of tools made this difficult, although they did the best they could using knives and tin cups. Eventually they succeeded in creating a circular network of crude, shallow rifle pits. Three sides of this elevated position were screened by high ridges but the exposed side was blocked by picketing hundreds of mules and horses there. A field hospital was established in a broad depression at the centre of this improvised fortress, and Dr. Porter, the surviving surgeon, was soon hard at work tending to the wounded.

The Indians were returning in large numbers, apparently having completed whatever nasty business they had been dealing with up the valley. Now they could concentrate on Reno. Pretty soon hundreds of warriors had spread out all around Reno Hill, not making any concerted attacks, as such, but choosing instead to take up sniping positions from where they began to pour a withering fire upon the trapped soldiers. Reno's men were particularly distressed as they recognised the familiar crack of cavalry issue Springfield carbines being used against them, evidence of the recent loss of many of their comrades.

The firing tailed off as darkness fell but not before the 7th. had suffered quite a few more casualties. Out of sheer devilment, the hostiles also amused themselves by firing into the horse/mule herd, killing dozens of animals.

Troopers were beginning to mumble resentfully about Custer. Where was he? Very few, if any, would have harboured any thoughts about the possibility of "Hard Ass's" column being annihilated. The "General" had obviously seen some action somewhere ahead, but the most likely scenario seemed to be that those five companies had met more than they could handle. Custer would have put up a stiff fight, probably suffering heavy casualties (the captured guidons were evidence of that) but, knowing him, he would have withdrawn from the field honourably, doubtless frustrated and angry with himself. Never before had he been forced to retreat. The question now was where could he be? Why had he not ridden back to support the rest of his command, trapped helplessly on this hilltop? A united regiment could still reverse such a setback. Men were now saying that the "General" had abandoned them, taking his surviving companies north to link up with the approaching troops of Terry and Gibbon. More than a few of the veterans cast their minds back to the Washita and the fate of Maj. Elliott.

The truth would prove to be almost too painful to bear and would change the course of history.

The next chapter is devoted to the key phase of the Battle of the Little Bighorn, Custer's "Last Stand", as it is popularly known. Because there were no survivors amongst the men who were with Custer in his final moments, this obviously means that we cannot be sure exactly what happened. The Indian accounts which were given in the years following the battle cannot always be relied upon because the hostile participants were often misunderstood or understandably reluctant to say too much about their part in the slaying of Long Hair. Also, they had a tendency to tell white interviewers what they felt they wanted to hear. Therefore, this is where a lot of the myths surrounding the battle originated. That said, many Sioux and Cheyenne warriors, who were in the thick of the fighting, did eventually speak honestly and we have been left with reams of material which appears convincing. One must remember that an Indian's perception of such an incident was usually different to that of a white person, relying much more upon personal, local experience rather than a general overview. A lot of it has an allegorical quality too which needs to be seen through.

My interpretation is based upon a huge amount of research and thought. In recent years, new archaeological finds on the battlefield, including human remains which have identified individuals, have led to enlightening ideas about the battle's course which had not previously been considered. There has also been much painstaking work which included locating and logging cartridge cases and bullets. Incredibly, using state of the art technology, researchers have even been able to trace the course of individual weapons across the terrain. This kind of thing has helped enormously when it comes to the location of Custer's companies as they deployed during the final stages of the fight. The positions and condition of the army dead were reasonably well recorded by those who first came upon the scene, evidence which has been largely verified using modern methods.

So, what follows is, I believe, an accurate account of the most likely train of events which led to Custer's defeat and death, the foundation being the wealth of knowledge available at the time of writing. Any speculation is made clear and comes, at the very least, from informed analysis of the known facts.

LAST STAND

Re-uniting the Left and Right Wing battalions, Custer was now facing increasing pressure from swarms of Indians who were approaching from the west and south, fanning out, largely on foot, into the network of gullies, ravines and clumps of sagebrush which dotted the terrain. Cover was excellent for the advancing Indians as they crept up close to the cavalry columns, harassing them with a deadly fusillade of bullets and arrows. By contrast the "General" must have quickly realised that he was caught at a huge disadvantage, this being terrible country for the manoeuvre of cavalry. As he made some snap decisions about what to do, Autie told Tom to release the last of the scouts, thoughtfully giving them a final chance to save themselves. Mitch Bouyer had lost his horse during the confusion and had been wounded but he decided to stay. Turning to the young Crow Curley, the faithful half breed told him to leave and make his way to Terry. "Tell them that we are all killed," he said resignedly, then pointing to Custer he added, "that man will stop at nothing". Curley shook hands with the older scout, then turned his pony's head to the east, disappearing into the further reaches of Deep Coulee. Skilled in the use of cover and veering to the north he eventually emerged, unmolested by Sioux, on a high knoll where, at a safe distance, about a mile and a half, he observed the progress of the battle through field glasses. In this way Curley became the last man of Custer's immediate and ill fated command to survive and tell the tale.

Autie probably called his officers together for a hurried conference and we can imagine the optimism in his spirited pep talk. They were in a fix, true, but this was the 7th. Cavalry! If any soldiers could fight their way out of such a trap Custer's boys were the ones. At least, that is what he most likely tried to tell them and he would have received much support from the faithful clique of brother Tom, Cooke, Calhoun, Keogh, Smith and Yates (if he was still alive). The immediate problem would be to hold back the hordes coming from the direction of Deep Coulee and Medicine Tail Coulee and this task was given to Calhoun. Spreading the men of Co. L out in standard military fashion, the troopers five yards apart as the horse holders stood to the rear, Calhoun took up this position on a flat hill facing south east (later called Calhoun Hill) as companies I and C, under Keogh and Harrington, held back in reserve.

Custer and his staff, along with companies F and E, rode on north west along what became known as Battle Ridge, heading towards a prominent knoll of high ground (immortalised this day as Custer Hill). They were perhaps intending to seize this as a defensive position although Custer's intention might have been to carry on beyond it and down the slopes on the other side, perhaps all the way to the river. To the north of the Indian village he would have surmised that the squaws and their children might be sheltering, or fleeing to other sites of refuge. Although they would number thousands, if he could capture even a few of them perhaps they could be held hostage. This would buy him time, for the warriors would hold back in fear of harming their families. It was a desperate gamble but in any case, at present, he had far too few men to successfully carry out such a plan. Benteen was now needed more than ever.

If Autie did proceed beyond Custer Hill, he soon turned around, probably driven back by more massing warriors, and returned to the high ground where he would have been able to observe, with growing alarm, the harrowing events which were beginning to unfold below. Calhoun's Co. L had, at first, been successful in keeping their attackers at bay with a steady, disciplined fire but vastly superior numbers (fast approaching eight to one) were beginning to take their toll. Arrows fell in dense showers upon the troopers as constant salvos of gunfire from all manner of firearms ripped into the blue clad ranks. Many of the Indians were armed with repeaters and it was becoming evident that the 7th. Cavalry were being literally outgunned. Co. L's horses were getting very jittery and the holders were having trouble controlling them, their predicament not helped by the fact that they were under heavy fire from a party of hostiles in a nearby gully.

Seeing this, Keogh, positioned with the reserves, probably ordered Harrington to lead Co. C in a sortie against these sniping warriors to dislodge them, but the rescue bid failed when they came under intense fire from more warriors who had come up from the west. Co.C was decimated by this, the survivors falling back, pursued by mounted Cheyenne braves under the leadership of Chief Lame White Man. Calhoun tried to help them, it seems, by redeploying his skirmish line to the right in an attempt to cover Harrington's retreat, but within moments this proved to be a big mistake. As Co. L's rate of fire slackened during this movement, Chief Gall, leading the attack from the south, took advantage of the lull by goading his braves into a headlong assault. Shrieking and intensifying their rifle fire, the Lakota surged up the slope of Calhoun Hill. It all happened so swiftly, Calhoun's troops barely had time to react before the warriors were upon them. The combat was bloody and hand to hand, but it was a one sided affair and Calhoun and his men soon fell beneath the onslaught. Gall rode amongst the Long Knives, cleaving their skulls with his hatchet to avenge the deaths of his family. As he said years later, "My heart was turned bad". At the same time, more warriors had circled east of the line, falling upon its rear and killing the horse holders, the mounts being driven down into Deep Coulee where they were captured by Cheyenne squaws. From participant accounts, it seems that Co. L sold its life dearly, for Indian casualties were heavy here, including the death of Lame White Man. As for Jimmy Calhoun, he fulfilled the promise he had made on joining the Custer family back in '71 when he vowed that he would prove himself "when the time came".

This left Keogh and his "Wild I" hopelessly exposed and alone on Battle Ridge. More warriors had come up from the east led by Crazy Horse, the sight of whom inspired the Lakota to greater heights of confidence. One can imagine Keogh, his dark eyes blazing as he rode Comanche along I's skirmish line, swearing at his countrymen as he tried to maintain order in the face of impossible odds. Crazy Horse, newly empowered by a spiritual ritual he had just undergone, spurred his pony towards these *wasichus*, daring Sitting Bull's nephew, White Bull, to join him in a daring exploit. Together, these two Sioux leaders demonstrated their bravery by riding at the gallop right through the centre of Keogh's line, seemingly immune to the many shots which were fired at them. The watching warriors were hugely impressed by this and renewed their attack with extra vigour.

Keogh had deployed his men to try and assist Calhoun but he was now beyond help himself. As hundreds of warriors surged in, the dashing Irish captain ordered a final volley fired from the Springfields. With no time to reload their single shot carbines, the troopers bunched together near a cluster of wild cherry bushes, drawing their Colt revolvers as Keogh took a bullet which shattered his left knee and passed through Comanche's flank. The captain then dropped from the saddle still holding his horse's reins, kneeling and firing his pistol and, we can assume, still snarling Irish curses. Burly 1st. Sgt. Frank Varden was at his side and there they died, surrounded by the assembled roughnecks of the "Wild I" who probably fought as savagely with empty pistols, knives, feet and fists as they would have done in a Hays City saloon when the whisky ran dry. Indian descriptions of a particularly fierce fighter who fell courageously seem to match Keogh.

Just a half mile away to the north, on the south slope of Custer Hill, Autie, his staff and companies E and F were rooted to the spot in horror as they watched the annihilation of their comrades. It was happening so quickly and savagely, but who could have foreseen such an outcome? Maybe Mitch Bouyer, but it was pointless now for him to express any more warnings. Custer's legendary bravado and self confidence must have reached rock bottom at this point, for even he could not deny the terrible predicament they were in. For the first time he must have accepted that he was no longer on the offensive and that trying to save the lives of his remaining men should be his immediate concern.

Looking again to the north, the "General" could only see more Indians in overwhelming numbers infiltrating the broken ground there. To the east it was a similar story as Crazy Horse led his mounted Oglala towards the hill. A few handfuls of men, who had managed to survive the onslaught on Calhoun Hill and Battle Ridge, were desperately trying to reach temporary refuge with Custer and the Left Wing battalion where, for now, there was still some semblance of order. Some of these men were cut off, singly and in groups, and were soon overwhelmed, while others were cut down as they fled. The survivors (one can hardly call them "lucky"), mostly mounted and including no officers, made it to the hill where, breathless and bloodied, they were absorbed into the remaining ranks.

Custer was left with less than half of his column, perhaps one hundred men in all. They were in a hopeless position, totally surrounded on a bleak hillside which offered no potential for a realistic defence. The hostiles were pushing in from every side, fired up by success and blood lust as they waved bloody trophies which included the guidons of C, I and L. Now armed with the carbines and pistols of the slaughtered Right Wing battalion, Indian firepower increased considerably as they began to concentrate on the remaining Long Knives.

With no realistic prospect of breaking through the massed hordes, the troopers dismounted and grouped together, making them easy targets. Confusion, desperation and lack of time resulted in a sudden breakdown in order and there was almost certainly no proper formation of new skirmish lines. It was fast becoming a case of self preservation although Autie would have been doing everything he could to maintain control, even under these impossible circumstances. Men were holding the reins of their own horses in one hand whilst trying to aim and fire with the other, but the animals were so frightened that they reared and whinnied, pulling the men around and causing them to fire uselessly into the air. Arrows continued to fall amongst them and the men dropped in heaps, spitted and bullet torn.

One group did try to break out, it seems, but whether it was a cohesive order or a desperate escape attempt we shall probably never know. Perhaps Autie commanded them to stage a feint, or maybe they were trying to drive away some of their attackers to clear a path. Who knows? Whatever, a mounted group of maybe twenty men (on the grey horses of Co. E, apparently) suddenly surged out of Custer's diminishing circle in a sortie to the west but the gamble quickly failed. The Indians were simply too numerous and these riders were forced south towards a deep ravine. Isolated and exposed, they did not last for long.

It is not difficult to imagine the "General" at this stage, standing in the middle of his men, doing his utmost to instil hope in his command, barking out orders to the end. Did he instruct Trumpeter Voss to blow a call for support? If so it was not heard by Benteen and Weir far away as they approached Weir Point. From a small central group of about forty men surrounding Custer near the summit of the hill, the remainder of the command were stretched in a thin line south west down the slope. Here Dr. Lord would have been doing all he could for the ever growing numbers of wounded, but it was a thankless and ultimately pointless task. The few horses that were left were shot so that the men could use them as breastworks, a poor reward for these exhausted beasts which had carried their riders faithfully over hundreds of miles these last six weeks. At least a couple of cavalrymen somehow broke through the cordon and were chased from the field of slaughter by whooping red men. One of them was shot in the back as he galloped away but another, with "stripes on his sleeves" according to the Lakota, could have become the only white survivor but for a strange reaction from him. This sergeant/corporal, whoever he was, rode hard for several miles forcing his pursuers to give up one by one until only a lone, persistent warrior remained on his trail. Even this Indian was about to turn back when the soldier suddenly reined in and inexplicably put a pistol to his head to blow his own brains out. Obviously, it all became too much for his shredded nerves.

Autie was methodically firing his Remington sporting rifle, but the dust and smoke was so thick and black by now it would have been difficult to make out any targets in the choking gloom. He was probably comforted, slightly, by the close proximity of most of his favoured clan who gathered all around him, blasting away at the enemy. Brother Tom, Adjutant Cooke, Yates, "Fresh" Smith and his lieutenant, William Van Reily, as well as Sgt. Maj. Sharrow and Colour Sgt. Hughes who still brandished the battle flag. Brother Boston and nephew Autie Reed were nearby but a little further down the slope, while the newspaperman Mark Kellogg, who could never have imagined such a scoop, had probably already fallen west of Custer Hill, his plodding mule unable to keep up when the troops withdrew from the river. Mitch Bouyer chose his ground on the south skirmish line. He had once said, "If the Sioux kill me, I have the satisfaction of knowing I popped many of them over, and they can't get even now." It was a finale which Custer would have ultimately approved of. A disaster, yes, but one which furnished him with the immortality he always craved. Even if he had defeated the Sioux and become president, he would never have achieved the giddy heights of fame an early death in battle gave him. In a way then perhaps he, personally, won.

In the final moments, the last of Custer's 7th. died in a scene of horrific chaos. Burrowing down behind their dead horses, the soldiers made their choices about how they would bid farewell to life. By now it must have been obvious to all that they had no hope of survival. They were up against a merciless foe to whom surrender was not an option. Never-the-less, some of them apparently tried, handing their weapons over to bewildered warriors and raising their hands, pleading for their lives, but it was to no avail. Others lost their minds, blubbering and weeping like babies as panic and despair set in, but the Sioux killed them all the same. Then there were those who saved the Lakota the trouble by turning their guns upon themselves. That said, most Indian accounts seem to confirm that the majority of the 7th. Cavalry died fighting.

Indians and soldiers alike were firing their weapons blindly into the billowing black and grey clouds. It reached the stage where the Lakota were only catching occasional glimpses of the hated Long Knives as thin patches appeared in the dust and powder smoke. Legend has it that the trooper's carbines began to jam from overheating and verdigris build-up, but in truth little evidence was found of this. Whenever a movement was seen, the braves would concentrate their fire there until, suddenly, there was another development. In desperation, another group of troopers, at least a dozen strong and all on foot, abruptly leapt up from behind the dead horses and began running down the hill. Trapped and mad with fear, these men were left with no choice but to hurtle wildly towards the Deep Ravine where the mounted troopers of E Co. had last been seen being driven to their doom. Initially startled by this movement, the warriors at first did not react to these soldiers who ran insanely into their midst, but soon they swarmed in again. Only a few of these fugitives made it to the ravine, jumping down into it where they were caught like rats in a trap. Some of them squatted down, huddling into the corners behind rocks or foliage as their pursuers stood on the lip, hurling rocks down upon them or firing arrows. Realising their plight, others tried scrambling back up again, their hands clawing at the soil but the Lakota toyed with them before dealing out merciful death.

Back near the top of the hill, probably none of the surviving members of the column remained on their feet. If Custer was still alive at this stage, had he thrown aside his rifle to draw his twin Bulldog revolvers, portraying the image which has stirred many a romantic and heroic notion? Knowing his character, such a scenario is possible, even likely, if he was at all physically capable by now. His whole world had collapsed around him. Libbie, *Garry Owen*, the girls they left behind them ….

At last, Crazy Horse and Gall rallied enough warriors to consolidate a mounted charge which swept over the brow of the hill, trampling the last remnants of the 7th. beneath their pony's hooves. Then the others surged in for the final kill with whoops and cries of "Hoka hey!", hacking, stabbing and clubbing the wounded until all signs of life had been rubbed out. All that could be heard now was the firing of guns in Indian hands, as they discharged them into the air or into mangled corpses, along with the fearful shrieks of victorious warriors as they counted coup on the slain. Cheyenne braves rode around, thrusting their lances into the trooper's bodies. Out came the scalping knives as bloody trophies were taken ….

Then came the women, children and old folk from the village, venturing back from refuge now that the threat had been removed. These non-combatants set about the dead soldiers with a furious passion based upon frustration, hatred and the sheer elation of victory. Never could the Lakota have conceived such success over the *wasichus* who had dared to try and drive them from their homeland. How they had shown them! The squaws commenced stripping the bodies, gazing in wonder at the whiteness of the flesh before carving into it, slicing off genitals and severing limbs. A Cheyenne brave named Wooden Leg tore off one of Adjutant Cooke's luxurious, sweeping whiskers to brandish as a unique scalp-like souvenir.

Laughing, the Indian boys positioned some of the dead troopers onto all fours so that they could fire arrows into their upturned buttocks. Others amused themselves by pounding the faces of the slain into unrecognisable jelly. The white soldier's belongings were in great demand, of course, weapons being the first prizes to be claimed. Bloody uniforms were soon being worn on the backs of triumphant, proud warriors, although they often cut the seats out of the kirsey wool trousers for extra comfort. Boots were sliced into pieces to be utilised as soles for moccasins, and pocket watches were a novelty, although many were thrown away once they had stopped their funny ticking. Having been paid whilst on the trail, the troopers were not short of cash and the Indians hungrily seized up the pretty coins to string them on necklaces or use them as charms. The paper bills they had no use for and so thousands of dollars in greenbacks were soon blowing aimlessly across the hillside and down into the valley.

The Cheyenne were those who had most reason to feel particularly vindictive against the 7th. Cavalry, for some of them had actually been present at the Washita. However, probably few, if any, realised that they had actually defeated Long Hair himself, for not many knew him by sight and those who did may have had trouble recognising him with his short hair and tattered, trail worn condition. At least one Lakota may have taken note of the Custer brothers in the heat of battle for he had experienced many opportunities to view them at close quarters just a year before when he had been their prisoner at Fort Lincoln. Rain-in-the-Face had been interviewed by Autie several times during that period, but the chief's real malevolence was directed against the man who had arrested him so roughly. Capt. Tom Custer.

It was said that Rain-in-the-Face had vowed to cut out Tom's heart and carry it away in his mouth.

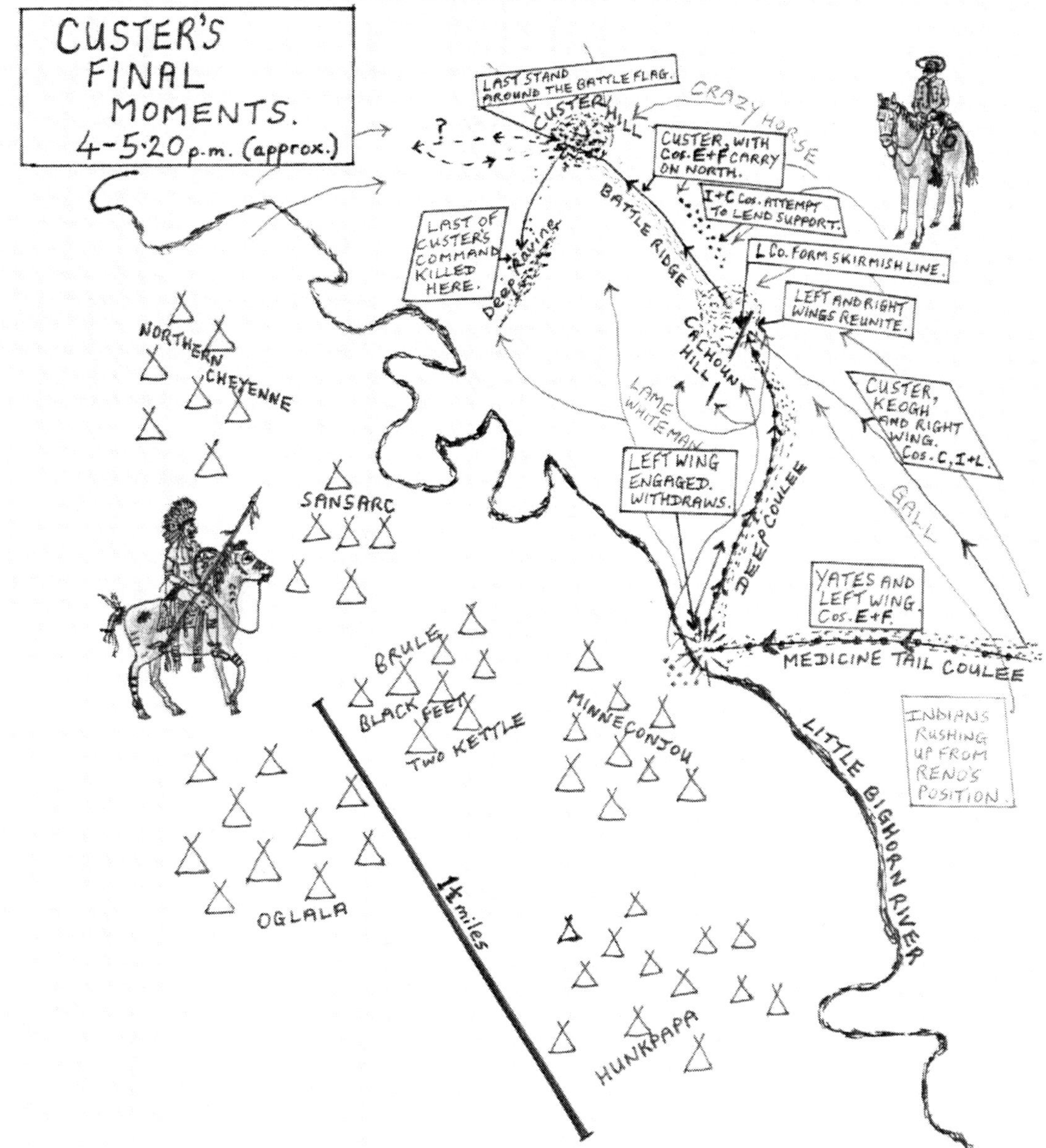
CUSTER'S FINAL MOMENTS. 4-5.20 p.m. (approx.)
LAST STAND AROUND THE BATTLE FLAG.
CUSTER HILL
CRAZY HORSE
CUSTER, WITH Cos. E+F CARRY ON NORTH.
I+C Cos. ATTEMPT TO LEND SUPPORT.
BATTLE RIDGE
LAST OF CUSTER'S COMMAND KILLED HERE.
DEEP RAVINE
L Co. FORM SKIRMISH LINE.
LEFT AND RIGHT WINGS REUNITE.
CALHOUN HILL
CUSTER, KEOGH AND RIGHT WING. Cos. C, I+L.
LAME WHITEMAN
LEFT WING ENGAGED. WITHDRAWS.
DEEP COULEE
GALL
YATES AND LEFT WING. Cos. E+F.
MEDICINE TAIL COULEE
INDIANS RUSHING UP FROM RENO'S POSITION.
NORTHERN CHEYENNE
SANSARC
BRULE
BLACK FEET
TWO KETTLE
MINNECONJOU
LITTLE BIGHORN RIVER
OGLALA
1¼ miles
HUNKPAPA

BESIEGED ON THE BLUFFS

With Custer's five companies wiped out, the Indians turned their attention in earnest upon the soldiers who battled for survival on top of Reno Hill. Ignorant of their commanding officer's fate, Reno's men fought hard to defend themselves.

The blackness of night brought sweet relief to the besieged troopers for their attackers ceased firing, having already added to Reno's casualty list. It was obvious that there were still warriors out there keeping watch, but most of them returned to the village, anxious to gloat over their spoils and dance the night away. Not all Indians, however, saw their victory as a symbol of great success. They had won a battle but hardly a war. The *wasichus* would no doubt come down extra hard upon the tribes to avenge the deaths of their soldiers and wipe out the stain of humiliation. Sitting Bull, who had spent much of the battle praying in camp, was cautious. After all, had he not warned his people to not take spoils from the white man or it would prove to be the "curse of the nation"?

Throughout the long night, the 7th.'s survivors dozed as best they could, carbines cradled in their arms whilst still manning their firing positions. Distant flashes of lightning could be seen, accompanied by feint rolls of thunder, but a light shower of rain did little to relieve the trooper's discomfort. Down in the valley, the glow of scores of camp fires was evident, complemented by the constant throb of drums, wailing and singing. Lakota and Cheyenne women could be heard mourning their dead, mutilating themselves in their grief by cutting off fingers and scarring their bodies. The Indians had not triumphed without losses.

At first light on Monday June 26th., the Indian snipers commenced firing again. During the night, many warriors had crept much closer to the soldier's entrenchments and were even mockingly throwing clods of dirt into the defence lines. One Sansarc brave had even attempted to count coup on a dead soldier with a long stick but had been shot dead for his trouble and now lay within feet of the defenders. Benteen, who had transformed from a grumpy sluggard into a pillar of strength since the siege began, cornered Reno, demanding that something must be done to drive the enemy back. It was unsettling to see the warriors so close for it was felt that a sudden rush by them might succeed in breaking the perimeter.

Although Reno still technically held command, Benteen was proving to be a much more capable leader. Already he had risen several notches in the troop's estimation by supervising the defence structures, encouraging the men with stirring phrases and an affable, unfazed manner. Eyes automatically turned to Benteen now for guidance rather than Reno, so the major had little choice but to give the captain permission to act as he saw fit.

Gathering together his Co. H, supported by a few men from M, Benteen squatted down in front of them, treating the beleaguered volunteers to a spirited talk. Checking their weapons, they followed the captain to the brow of the south western slope, looking down towards the river. "Give them hell!" growled the white haired officer, as he rushed over the lip, his men yelling madly, as instructed. Charging down the hill, eyes wild with excitement, Benteen's volunteers hurtled straight towards the startled Indians who reacted accordingly by leaping to their feet and taking off in the other direction, stumbling over each other in their panic to escape. The psychological effect of Benteen's dramatic manoeuvre proved highly effective and the squad returned to their positions elated, although they lost a couple of men to Indian fire as they retired.

As the morning wore on, the scattered clouds dispersed and the sun grew unbearably hot, scorching the defenders where they lay on the unsheltered hill. Conditions worsened from uncomfortable to torturous as the men writhed in the heat, frightened to move in case they made themselves better targets for the Indian sharpshooters whose rate of fire seldom slackened. Men from French's Co. M were pinned down by a murderously accurate fire from a particular Indian who proved himself to be an excellent shot. He killed one trooper and wounded two more before French directed a group of his men to fire a volley towards the source which seemed to succeed in silencing the sniper. Even so, men continued to be picked off, including the civilian packer Frank Mann who was shot through the temple as he sighted his rifle. Others had narrow escapes, like the trooper who had his rifle stock shattered in his hands. Pvt. Slaper of Co. M had been temporarily blinded by dirt that had been thrown up in his eyes by an Indian bullet striking the improvised mound he had built to protect himself. As he lay face down trying to clear his vision, a second hostile bullet tore the heel from his left boot.

Benteen continued his rounds of the defences, barking at the men to keep their heads down whilst seemingly immune to bullets himself. A sergeant begged him to take more care but the captain replied jovially, "Oh, I'm alright ..... they won't get me". Looking towards the village with his cold, pale eyes, he continued, "This is a ground hog case, men ..... live or die. We must fight it out".

By mid-morning, the shortage of water had grown critical and some soldiers were making offers of ludicrous amounts of money to anyone who would give them a drink. Sucking on pebbles or chewing grass did not seem to help much. A few men even started to go crazy, but it was the wounded who suffered the most. Dr. Porter, prominent in his long, white duster coat, sought out Reno and Benteen to express his concern that some of his patients were in danger of dying unless they got a drink.

Once again Benteen called for volunteers. This time a party was required to face heavy Indian fire to reach the river. Laden with canteens and kettles, fourteen men from various companies, led by two sergeants, made their way into a deep ravine (now called Water Carrier's Ravine) to sneak down to the Little Bighorn. Their route was covered by four riflemen from Co. H who positioned themselves on the high bluff, keeping the encroaching Indians at bay with accurate shooting. It was a well executed action and the men accomplished their mission, returning with plenty of gratefully received water, suffering only minimum casualties. One was Pvt. Mike Madden from "Dude Troop" K, whose right ankle and lower leg were shattered by a bullet. His comrades managed to get him back to the defences but his wound was untreatable so Dr. Porter made the decision to amputate the limb below the knee. A big, tough Irishman, over six feet tall, Madden accepted this gamely, and, with no anaesthetic, was glad to gulp down an offer of brandy before Porter started sawing. With the injured limb removed, he was given more brandy, which seemed to please him. He was said to have grinned and smacked his lips, his eyes twinkling as he chuckled "Ehhh, doctor, you can cut off me other leg!" Most of these water carriers would later be rewarded with the Medal of Honour, although, for some unknown reason, not the redoubtable Mike Madden!

Relieved by water and well entrenched, Reno's men were able to relax a little, especially as the Indian fire grew noticeably lighter as the afternoon drew on. The smell of dead animals in the day's heat was becoming offensive, but it was now obvious that the warriors were losing interest in the Long Knives on the hill, concentrating instead on breaking down their camp to move on.

By early evening, the warriors had set fire to the dry prairie grass in several places, the flames surging high and producing profuse clouds of smoke which obscured much of the valley. Through occasional breaks in the smoke, the troopers on Reno Hill could see thousands of Indians on foot and horseback, leading pack animals and dragging travois as they trekked south towards the Bighorn Mountains. This was a welcome sight, but the soldiers were understandably cautious, fearing a trick which might have been designed to draw them into the open. One of the last groups of warriors spotted in the valley, studying the hill and smoking a shared pipe, were a group who appeared to be led by a chief on a distinctive horse. Several of the 7th.'s veterans swore that this was Crazy Horse himself.

The firing died away completely and Reno gave orders for the dead to be buried. Most of the men shifted position to try and get away from the stench of the slain mules and horses, whilst others ventured down to the river again to collect more water. Reno had suffered further heavy casualties since setting up his hilltop defence, with about a dozen more killed and many wounded. Amongst these was Lt. Varnum, disabled by a shot through both legs, and Benteen who suffered a nominal wound in his right thumb. By the time the Indians packed up and left, Dr. Porter had about sixty patients in his care.

During the evening, a few more men, who had been thought lost in action, made it back to the hill. These included the interpreter Fred Girard and Lt. De Rudio who had spent a terrifying two days and a night evading the hostiles down in the undergrowth by the river. They were ravenous and exhausted, but otherwise unharmed. Although the pressing threat appeared to have evaporated, Reno's command spent a second nervous night on and around the bluffs, relieved yet totally bewildered by whatever events may be occurring nearby.

Tuesday June 27th. began peacefully with no further traces of hostile Indians in the valley. As the officers discussed what best to do, a large dust cloud was spotted to the north. Many present began speculating that it could be General Crook approaching although this was an odd conclusion as Crook would most logically have come from the south. Studying the advancing body through field glasses, it was soon apparent to Reno and Benteen that this new column was made up of white troops who before long proved to be those under the command of Terry and Gibbon. As this column drew close, the 7th.'s survivors began to cheer, but there was confusion as it became general knowledge that Custer's column was not with these new arrivals. If he had withdrawn, surely the "General" would have linked up with the advancing relief force.

Gibbon's chief of scouts, Lt. James Bradley, was one of the first to arrive at the hill with the advance guard. Although a cool customer and seasoned frontiersman, Bradley looked shaken as Lt. Godfrey rode out to greet him.

"Where is Custer?" asked K Co.'s commander, gingerly.

The answer he received would chill him to the bone.

"A SCENE OF SICKENING, GHASTLY HORROR"

Early on a sunlit morning, the day after the massacre, as the men on Reno Hill fought their defensive battle, Lt. Bradley became the first outsider to learn of the disaster.

Leading his own Crow scouts in advance of Terry's column, Bradley was making his way up the Bighorn valley, following the course of the river. Finding pony tracks, the party rode on until they spotted a small group of Indians on the far bank. Familiar figures, because these three men were Crows who had ridden under Bradley's command in the Montana column before Custer had poached them. White Man Runs Him, Hairy Moccasin and Goes Ahead seemed apprehensive and were reluctant to cross the river, but they spoke in sign language about terrible events which they had witnessed and were still taking place further up the valley.

Bradley was shocked, hoping against all reason that the scouts were either mistaken or exaggerating, but he wasted no time in riding back to General Terry and Col. Gibbon. This news of heavy, disastrous fighting ahead was received soberly by the commander, but at this stage no one knew the exact details. The Crows had left a defeated Reno on the hill but what had become of Custer was anyone's guess. Terry gave orders to push on with haste into the valley. By late afternoon they could see vast clouds of smoke to the south. Could this mean that Custer had succeeded in overcoming the Indians and was now burning their village?

Darkness fell and, vocalising their theories and brimming with excitement, Terry's men made camp for the night. The general feeling was that Custer had "jumped the gun", stealing the glory for himself. Even though hostiles had been seen earlier in the distance, taunting the advancing column as they rode around wearing looted cavalry uniforms, an atmosphere of optimism (plus some resentment at having missed out on the action) dominated the camp.

At first light the next morning they were pushing on again, anxious to solve this riddle. On the east bank of the Little Bighorn a particular hillside stood out from the others because it was dotted with groups of stark white objects, interspersed here and there with larger, dark objects. Could these be skinned buffalo? Bradley took his Crows and made off to cross the river.

Carrying on along the west bank, the main column soon came upon the first signs of the deserted Indian camp. It had obviously been occupied until very recently because many of the camp fires were still smouldering. Debris lay everywhere in a scene of utter chaos. A few scavenging dogs yelped, whined and loped away whilst here and there pitiful looking wounded ponies and horses stood around mournfully. Some of these animals were recognised as cavalry mounts. As Terry's men picked their way through this wasteland of horror, they began to find evidence of the disaster none dared to believe. Bloodstained underclothes were found with the name "Sturgis" etched in the waistband, and another trooper picked up the discarded gauntlets of Capt. Yates. Gibbon's medical officer, Dr. Holmes Paulding, came across a buckskin shirt which was saturated with dried blood. A bullet had torn through the right breast and exited via the right shoulder leaving a massive hole. The lining displayed the name "Porter-7th. Cavalry"; the "Wild I's" 1st. Lieutenant.

Numerous other items of regimental origin were discovered, including a small fortune in dollar bills scattered everywhere, but more disturbing were horrific finds like severed heads. Some were recognised but others had been burned. A few lodges were still standing, but these contained the corpses of Sioux warriors who had been killed in the battle. The Cheyenne dead had been taken away, as was their custom, for disposal along the trail. Lakota casualties were dressed in their finery, as usual, laid out carefully for their journey to the happy hunting ground, but, naturally, the newly arrived soldiers showed no respect. The bodies were soon looted and abused, the lodges set on fire, as vengeful troopers gave way to their frustration and anger.

As Terry, Gibbon and their staff sat contemplating the implications of all this, Bradley returned from his mission across the river. The objects seen on the hillside were not buffalo but the stripped bodies of approximately 200 cavalrymen, lying around the carcasses of many of their horses. Amongst them was the unmistakeable corpse of Lt. Col. George Armstrong Custer.

*   *   *

Well, at least more than half of the 7th. had managed to survive on Reno Hill over these last two days, but it was obvious that the regiment had taken a severe beating. Practically five entire companies wiped out. Such a blow, at the time, was beyond comprehension, so it is not difficult to imagine the extent of the shock suffered by the survivors.

Moving on through the village, finding more terrible evidence with every step, Terry's column finally managed to link up with Reno and Benteen, whose men had come down from the hill to the river. Stunned silence greeted the initial news of Custer's defeat, but soon the men had relaxed, relieved at their own salvation. Many had thought they would never leave that hill alive.

Benteen decided to take a detail out immediately to investigate the situation on Custer Hill. It is said that when he recognised the body of the "General" he had known for so many years, and yet despised, he muttered, "Well, there he lies, God damn him. He'll never fight anymore".

The rest of the day was spent clearing up the area around Reno Hill, tending to the wounded, burying any more army dead they could find and settling down for a night's sleep in relative safety. On the following morning, Wednesday June 28th., an organised plan was put into action to sweep the land towards the north, heading up to the site of Custer's Last Stand. The surviving companies rode out stretched across the bleak landscape in long lines, each one assigned a particular area to cover. First signs of disaster they discovered were just north of Medicine Tail Coulee, in and around Deep Coulee and particularly on Calhoun Hill. From there they went on up the slopes, passing over the site of the running battle where Keogh's battalion had died and finally to Custer Hill itself.

Lt. Godfrey, who commanded the men sweeping the left flank of the field, later wrote that it was a "scene of sickening, ghastly horror". Not only had most of the victims been stripped, scalped and savagely mutilated, they had also been lying exposed for three days in blistering heat. The bodies were bloated and blackened, the limbs of dead men and horses sticking out upright like stiffened dummies. Thousands of grotesque green flies swarmed over these corpses, massing upon the sticky, hideous wounds. The cloying, foul stench was overpowering and several of the newly arrived troopers began to retch.

The nature of the mutilations were fairly standard in most cases, according to the cult of Plains Indian warfare. Scalping was almost obligatory, as was the deep slashing of thighs, for this was a way of marking which tribe, or even warrior society, had been responsible for the kill. Heads were crushed usually as a way of administering a final death blow with a war club or tomahawk, although often the skulls were smashed as flat as a palm width, using rocks just out of spite. Hands and feet or whole arms and legs were removed sometimes as a way of disabling an enemy before he entered the spirit world, but it seems the squaws liked to cut off the genitals just for fun. It was also customary to pepper vanquished foes with many arrows so that they looked like pin cushions. Decapitation seemed fairly extensive on the Custer field, although, as a rule, this was a practice most popular among the Santee Sioux who were not present in large numbers at the Greasy Grass. The Ree scout Bloody Knife was beheaded and it was reported that a pair of young Sioux girls were seen in the village during the battle, swinging this gruesome trophy to and fro as they held a braid each!

The pattern of bodies stretched across Calhoun Hill and Battle Ridge, along with piles of discharged cartridge cases, seemed to confirm that this was the area where the most cohesive defence had taken place. Jimmy Calhoun was recognised lying with the men of Co. L, identified mainly by a distinctive dental filling. Nearby lay young Lt. Crittenden, the one eyed infantry officer who was only discovered because his killers had shot an arrow into his glass eye leaving splinters all over his torn and swollen face. The body of Lt. Harrington, who as commander of Co. C should have been in this area, was not found.

It was said that Keogh's body did not suffer mutilation and he was found, according to one soldier's account, lying beneath the body of his company's trumpeter. Around his neck he still wore the Pro Petri Sede medal which had been given to him by the Pope years ago, and perhaps it was the sight of such apparent powerful medicine that stopped the Indians from cutting him up. Co. I's Lt. Porter was not officially recognised, although quite a few of Keogh's "Wild" bunch were, (including 1st. Sgt. Frank Varden,) scattered in a fairly tight group around their tough captain.

Later to create something of a legend, Keogh's horse Comanche was found alive, close to his master's body. The story arose that Comanche was the only living thing left on the field but this was untrue as quite a few of the regiment's horses, the wounded ones anyway, were still around. Comanche did not look fit enough to survive much longer as he had been wounded severely in several places, his saddle having turned under his belly as he stood bleeding and woebegone. Some spoke of putting the suffering animal out of its misery but Pvt. Gustave Korn came to its rescue, Korn being one of the fortunate Co. I men whose lives had been saved by their own wayward mounts giving out or bolting. Korn led Comanche down to the river where he bathed his wounds and began the long process of nursing him back to health.

All over the slopes and in the gullies lay gruesome clues as to what had happened, although very often the evidence just led to confusion and controversy which has puzzled historians ever since. For instance, the body of James Butler, 1st. Sgt. Of Co. L, was located quite a way to the south of the main action, down in Deep Coulee alongside two to four other men from L. Some have speculated that he was killed here early in the fight, but this location was where Yates operated with companies E and F. Surely Butler would have been with his own company up on Calhoun Hill. A more likely scenario is that this experienced sergeant was entrusted with the task of trying to get through as a courier, perhaps in response to a sighting of Capt. Weir on the far off ridge. This theory is supported by the fact that Butler appeared to have an escort with him, customary practice when urgent messages were being relayed with high risk.

Between twenty to thirty men, mainly from Co. E, were found in the depths of Deep Ravine where they had been caught and slaughtered. It seems probable that some of them were the last to die. Near the summit of Custer Hill itself, on the slope facing the river, were found 42 men in a fairly tight group. There were also 39 dead horses here and it was apparent that several of these mounts had been led to a position where they were killed to form breastworks. Indeed, quite a few of these dead soldiers were still in their positions behind the fallen beasts where they had fought to the last. This had been the legendary Last Stand. Most of Custer's staff were identified here; Adjutant Cooke, Chief Trumpeter Voss, Colour Sgt. Hughes, Dr. Lord and probably Sgt. Maj. Sharrow. Also fallen together lay the bodies of Capt. Yates and lieutenants Smith and Reily, although the bullet riddled corpses of the two young civilians Boston Custer and Autie Reed were further down the slope. Mitch Bouyer was nearby too. Most of the identified enlisted men who died on this hill were from Co. F, although there would have been remnants from all companies.

Custer's thoroughbred horse Vic may have been killed heading up the slope from the direction of Keogh's position, so it seems that the "General" himself had perhaps been forced to cover the last hundred feet or so on foot. He and brother Tom had fought their last battle alongside each other and one cannot help wondering if it was a poignant moment for them at the end. Their courage had never been in question. Veterans of numerous dangers, I think it reasonable to assume that their stout spirit did not desert them, even when all hope was lost. Resigning themselves to their fate, maybe they had time for some last words or sentiments before the Lakota surged over them.

Tom had been dealt with very harshly. He lay face down and when he was turned over, it could be seen that his body had been split down the centre, his entrails spilling out. His arms and thighs were viciously slashed open and his throat had been cut. The entire head had been scalped, leaving just a little hair on the nape of the neck, the skull crushed so flat that the facial features were squashed into a mask of complete distortion. Many arrows had been shot into his head and body. For a while the witnesses were uncertain as to who this unfortunate soul might be, but in the end it was recognised as Tom by the unique tattoos on his arm; the initials "TWC" and an image of the goddess of liberty. Despite all this, there was no indication of the captain's heart having been cut out by Rain-in-the-Face, or anyone else for that matter.

As for Autie, he was found naked but for his socks, in a sitting position propped up between the stripped bodies of two of his troopers. His upper right arm was supported by one of these bodies, his forearm bent so that his head was resting in the palm of his hand as if he was asleep, in fact his expression appeared totally calm and untroubled. Even in death it seems he refused to let the hostiles faze him! There were two undoubted fatal bullet wounds, one near to the heart and the other in the left temple, neither of which bore signs of powder burns, so I think it fair to immediately scotch all malicious rumours of suicide. In any case, it would simply not have been in the man's nature to kill himself. It was long said that Custer's body was not mutilated at all but nowadays it appears fairly certain that such an impression was given to spare the feelings of Libbie. In fact there were other marks on the body although the "General" still escaped more lightly than most of his men. There was, apparently, a wound in his right forearm and a deep knife slash in one thigh, along with tales of a warrior who cut off one of Autie's fingertips. A Cheyenne woman told of how Long Hair was recognised in death as the soldier chief who years before had promised not to make war on her tribe, and so the squaws dug into his ears with sewing awls to enable him to hear what he was told more clearly! He was not scalped simply because his thinning, short hair would not have made a good trophy.

Terry had issued strict orders for the bodies to be buried as they were found, and this was done. The stench of the offensive, rotting corpses was such that everyone was keen to get them under the ground as soon as possible. However, the earth being hard and with proper tools in short supply, most of the dead were only interred a few inches below the surface, if they were lucky, for some only had sandy soil or sagebrush scooped over them where they lay. The only half decent burial was reserved for the two eldest Custer brothers, George and Tom, who were laid side by side in a wide eighteen inch deep grave on the spot where they were killed, covered by blankets and sections of canvas. When the pit was filled in, the whole thing was decorated with an upturned Indian travois brought up from the village which was pinned down by rocks and clearly marked. The recognised officer's graves were also numbered and named (so this did not include a known last resting place for Harrington, Porter or Sturgis), along with the graves of Boston Custer and Autie Reed, but all the others were simply marked anonymously with a plain stake to show that someone lay there.

*　　　　　　　　*　　　　　　　　*

It had been a day of despair and horror for Terry's relief force and the 7th.'s survivors as they dealt with the aftermath of the massacre and they were anxious to get away from the scene as quickly as they could. They were to spend one more stressful night there, gathering up the last remnants of what remained, destroying discarded equipment and abandoned Indian property, before heading back north. Terry and Gibbon (who had just recovered from a nasty stomach infection) had no intention of following the victorious Indians with the limited troops they had available. All enthusiasm for combat had evaporated once they had witnessed the terrible sights on the Greasy Grass and the emphasis was now placed on getting Reno's wounded back to civilization. Mule litters were constructed to transport these injured men and Terry had already sent word ahead to Captain Marsh, skipper of the steamer *Far West*, to bring his boat upriver to meet them. As the troops prepared to leave, Gibbon himself decided to take his first close look at Custer Hill. The route he took from his camp on the river led him in from the west across ground which had not been covered by the burial parties. There, all on its own, he stumbled upon the fully clothed, un-mutilated corpse of the reporter Mark Kellogg.

Actually, Marsh was by this time aware of something traumatic having happened to the column, for Curley had already arrived on the Yellowstone. Unable to speak English, the young Crow scout tried to relay in sign language what he had witnessed at the Little Bighorn but it seems he was only partly understood. In any case, sceptical of such bad news, those on the boat were not convinced to act until couriers arrived from Terry. Now Marsh jumped into action, applying steam immediately as he pointed the *Far West* down the Bighorn to the confluence of its small tributary. On the way, the boat was transformed into a floating hospital as prairie grass was spread thickly over the decks, then covered with tarpaulin like a giant mattress.

Terry marched his men carefully back up the valley, covering twelve miles before they reached the mouth of the Little Bighorn where the *Far West* was tied up waiting. The wounded were taken on board, which must have been a moment of great relief for them. By July 3rd. the steamer was ready to set off back down river for the long journey to Fort Lincoln. With them, cosseted in his own cosy stall which Capt. Marsh had set up between the steamer's rudders, was Keogh's long suffering horse, Comanche.

Terry was very distressed by the failure of his expedition and he took Marsh aside to tell him that he felt that all the wounded men were victims of a "sad and terrible blunder". Marsh steamed away at full speed, breaking records as he rushed his boat down the Yellowstone and Missouri rivers, covering over 700 miles in just 54 hours, finally mooring in Bismarck, Dakota. The terrible news spread like wildfire, reaching the far away east coast almost instantly by telegraph, just in time to mar the centennial celebrations which were just getting into their stride.

Newspaper headlines all across the nation gave sensationalist accounts of the demise of the heroic Boy General and his glorious regiment. It was called a massacre, an outrage, the perpetrators being nothing more than murderous savages who deserved swift and merciless retribution. Any sympathy which the Indian plight might have engendered seemed to vanish overnight. President Grant gruffly commented, "I regard Custer's massacre as a sacrifice of troops, brought on by Custer himself, that was wholly un-necessary".

As the American public clamoured for explanations and revenge, the army's top brass did their utmost to subtly shift the blame from one party to another. The surviving officers, especially Reno and Benteen, would soon become targets for accusations of dereliction of duty which led to Custer's death, but higher up the chain of command men like Terry, Gibbon and even Little Phil Sheridan were beginning to twist the truth to cover up their own possible contributions to the disaster. Scapegoats were badly needed.

On a deeply personal level, none felt the blow more strongly than Libbie Custer who received the news early on the morning of July 6th. when she was woken by her servant girl who told her that there were army gentlemen at the door. Gathering in the parlour of her Fort Lincoln home, accompanied by Autie's sister, Maggie Calhoun, and his niece, Emma Reed, Libbie absorbed the details of her husband's death with admirable dignity. The entire family had suffered a terrible blow with the multiple losses of the "General", Tom, Boston, Autie Reed and their brother-in-law, Jimmy Calhoun. Putting her outward grief on hold, Libbie pulled a shawl around her shoulders and absorbed herself in the unenviable task of helping to relay the dreadful tidings to the other women on the post who would be most affected by it. Apparently she showed great strength and did much to comfort them, although this in no way detracts from her own huge loss which showed itself in other deeper ways as the years progressed.

LAKOTA SWAN SONG

Custer dead and the army humiliated. It was simply too much to bear. Sheridan wasted no time in voicing his demands that the remaining forces in the field should strike back hard, but Generals Terry and Crook were reluctant to leave their supply bases until they had been hugely reinforced. It seemed that no one was willing to take chances anymore. Begrudging respect for Indian fighting ability had risen tenfold.

This meant that there was a delay of over a month before the U.S. Army was ready to fight again and by that time the former gigantic concentration of hostiles had disbanded. Immediately following the Custer massacre, Sitting Bull had led his followers into the area around the Bighorn mountains where they spent some time resting and celebrating. Feelings were mixed about the possible *wasichu* reaction to the battle and some Indians believed that the war was won in the way that Red Cloud had achieved temporary success back in the sixties. Others were more realistic and gave up early, accepting the fact that the Lakota and their allies had had their moment. As the weeks passed, various bands began to drift away from Sitting Bull, returning to the Rosebud country or, in the case of the Cheyenne, making their way back south along the Powder into Wyoming. Quite a few Indians even returned quietly to the reservations. Sitting Bull remained defiant, however, heading north east while Crazy Horse took his Oglala into the Black Hills where they amused themselves conducting sporadic raids against the gold miners.

Terry finally got moving at the end of July, leaving his Yellowstone base in command of an army of some 1,700 cavalry and infantry. Within a week, Crook was also back in action, pushing up from the south with an even bigger force numbering about 2,300. Amazingly, following the bloody nose he had received at the Rosebud, Crook seemed to lose his spirit and spent weeks idling his time away at Goose Creek, his men fishing and snoozing in the sunshine while they were so greatly needed further north. How different things would have turned out for Custer had Crook acted as he should have. The grizzled general's lame excuse was that he was awaiting instructions, reinforcements and re-supply.

By now the Indian trails were long cold and the ponderous columns of the two armies seemed uncertain of what to do. They knew they must be seen to be doing something so they blundered on and accidentally met each other on the banks of the Rosebud on August 10th.. Linking up, this vast force proved too cumbersome to be effective against the nimble hostiles who were far ahead of them anyway. Finding nothing and exhausting their supplies at an alarming rate, the two commanders were forced to halt for an extended period on the Yellowstone to await replenishment. Unco-operative and bickering, Terry and Crook split their forces again, the former carrying on up the Yellowstone while the latter headed east across the Little Missouri and then south towards the Black Hills. Pretty soon Crook's unwieldy force, beset by relentless rain, were desperate for supplies again so an advance party, under Capt. Anson Mills, was sent hurriedly down to Deadwood to find something. On the way there, by chance, this foraging party stumbled upon a Sioux camp at Slim Buttes which Mills decided to attack on September 9th.. The surprised Indians, Oglalas under Chief American Horse, were driven away and trapped in a ravine, while Mills and his troops ransacked their village for food. Mills and American Horse, facing a stalemate, both sent riders away to summon help, the first to arrive being the main body of the army with Crook. Indian reinforcements soon arrived, however, under Crazy Horse, who once again proved his fighting talents by keeping Crook pinned down with only about 300 warriors. American Horse was killed in the fighting but Crazy Horse succeeded in bloodying Crook's nose yet again before withdrawing. The general who had gained such a fine reputation for himself fighting the Apaches had proven, in this summer campaign, that he did not seem to possess the same ability to fight the Lakota. Demoralised and exhausted, Crook let Crazy Horse go, continued into Deadwood and withdrew his forces from the entire enterprise. (In the Slim Buttes village, soldiers found several 7th. Cavalry horses as well as items which included one of Keogh's gauntlets and the company guidon of the Wild I. Incidentally, not many of the big army mounts survived for long under Indian ownership.)

Terry, in the meantime, found nothing, and at Wolf Point on the Missouri River on September 16th. he also decided to give up. The pointless summer campaign was over, having achieved almost nothing except huge expense and more humiliation for the army. A very minor success had occurred in mid July when Buffalo Bill Cody, scouting for the 5th. Cavalry, had managed to shoot and scalp a Cheyenne chief named Yellow Hair (often mistakenly reported as Yellow *Hand*). Waving the oozing trophy at nearby cheering troops, Buffalo Bill, in true theatrical style had proclaimed this act the "first scalp for Custer". If nothing else, it was great propaganda and excellent for morale, and Cody could not resist incorporating a highly dramatized version of this incident in his touring Wild West Show.

As autumn advanced into winter, the fugitive hostiles, who were scattered far and wide across several areas, must have felt that they would be safe with the arrival of harsh weather. The army had made such a hash of their summer efforts they would surely not bog themselves down in a winter campaign when conditions would be so much more difficult. On the contrary. The dark, snowy months would prove to be the downfall of the Indians.

This was owing to a rapid rethink of strategy on behalf of the army. It had been proved pointless to try and harass the hostiles with large, unmanageable forces. More concerted efforts were made to fight the Indians on their own terms using native allies and the expertise of teams of experienced scouts. Crook was given another chance, launching a fresh expedition in mid November, assisted by Col. Mackenzie and over 400 friendly Indians, many of whom were Sioux and Cheyenne who had thrown in their lot with the whites. They succeeded in surprising the Cheyenne village of Chief Dull Knife, just south of the Bighorn Mountains, driving the battle's survivors out into freezing conditions where those who refused to surrender quickly succumbed to the elements or starvation.

Further north, Col. Nelson Miles had been placed in command of an independent operation to suppress the Sioux. The backbone of his force was actually the 5th. Infantry (who the Lakota called *walkaheaps*) and they were well equipped for the conditions in heavy buffalo coats. Miles proved to be a tenacious and wily Indian fighter, concentrating on the area which lay between the Yellowstone and Missouri rivers. Using informants and excellent reconnaissance, Miles kept on the backs of the fleeing Sioux, surprising and exhausting them with his persistence and the hardiness of his troops. There were several clashes with Sitting Bull's band until, in the end, desperate to shake off the untiring *walkaheaps*, the aging medicine man led those of his people who had not surrendered much further north across the Canadian border. Sitting Bull had heard that this land was ruled by a mighty white Queen from far over the distant waters who might offer him refuge.

Miles now turned his attention to Crazy Horse who was still running loose with a formidable band of aggressive warriors. Crook sent messages to this charismatic chief, appealing to him to surrender and making offers of a permanent homeland in the Powder River country, but the less conciliatory Miles determined to make a point of defeating him by force of arms. In early January 1877, the colonel came a big step nearer to achieving this by seizing Crazy Horse's village and supplies in a series of fiercely fought clashes, but still many of the hostiles got away. Fighting on with little food or shelter and no respite from the relentless Miles, even Crazy Horse eventually had to concede that further resistance was pointless. At Camp Robinson, Nebraska, in May, the great war chief finally surrendered, but it was a very dignified capitulation as he rode in proudly at the head of hundreds of his warriors, all armed and resplendent in their warpaint and feathered bonnets, singing as if they were the victors. Crazy Horse was not going to be a model prisoner and immediately the authorities viewed him with distrust.

Crook, who was admired and respected by the Indians, no doubt was sincere about his promise to Crazy Horse, but he was in the hands of more powerful forces within politics. Already Congress had acted against the Lakota, pandering to the public outcry over Custer's death, by forcing through an approbation act which effectively suppressed the entire Sioux nation. Ignoring the terms of previous treaties, the board was swept clean and the Sioux were forced or tricked into signing over virtually all rights to the Black Hills, the unceded territory and much of their reservation land. Military rule was imposed upon the reservations and the men of fighting age became virtual prisoners, unhorsed and disarmed, their every move under observation.

Crazy Horse was not the kind of man to submit to this kind of treatment and before long he and his followers had taken off again. Taking no chances, several companies of the 3rd. Cavalry, supported by a host of Indian scouts, were dispatched to bring this unruly chief in once and for all. Confronting him when he turned up unexpectedly at the Spotted Tail Agency, the soldiers persuaded him to come quietly, which he did, under escort back to Fort Robinson still carrying his weapons. Once within the confines of the fort, the army's gentle methods dissolved and scouts and soldiers began to manhandle Crazy Horse as they tried to disarm him. At this point he must have realised that he was to be treated harshly, a small cell within sight to be his destination, and so he pulled a knife to lash out at his captors. The response to this came from an army guard who instantly plunged his bayonet through the Oglala chief's body. Carried into a nearby office, Crazy Horse sang his death song and died during the night.

Sitting Bull remained at large in Canada until July 1881 when deprivation at last forced him to cross the border back into the United States. Life on the run had proved hard and he surrendered, following in the wake of Gall, Crow King and all the principal surviving chiefs. At Fort Buford, North Dakota, the great spiritual leader of the Lakota symbolically handed his Winchester rifle to his son, Crow Foot, so that it could not be stated that he personally surrendered his weapon to the *wasichus*.

"I wish it to be remembered," he said, "that I was the last of my tribe to surrender my rifle".

*   *   *

Sitting Bull did not adapt well to reservation life and his resentment at the Standing Rock Agency failed to impress the government administrator, James McClaughlin, who described the great Lakota in less than complimentary terms. Buffalo Bill, however, saw money making potential in this demoralized Indian and in 1885 offered Sitting Bull a role in his hugely successful Wild West Show which included a spectacular re-enactment of Autie's last battle. The wily old medicine man's hatred of the *wasichus* did not apparently extend to any reluctance to accept a salary of $50 per week so that he could be put on display as "the savage red chief who killed Custer". Touring the cities of the east, Sitting Bull was overwhelmed by the extent and grandeur of the white race's influence, but he was never able to understand how poverty could exist alongside such vast wealth. Consequently, he would give away much of his earnings to the numerous street urchins and beggars he encountered. He also learned to sign his name in English and would sell autographed pictures of himself for $1.50 a time.

Even so, much of his rebellious spirit remained intact. In 1887, he turned down Cody's offer to tour Europe, deciding instead to remain at home and play a part in some renegotiations over Sioux land. He stuck to a hard line during talks in Washington the following year, stubbornly refusing to sign anything. At one point he was heard to snarl, "Indians? There are no Indians left but me!"

Sitting Bull looked around at what his people had been reduced to and it must have been very disheartening for him. A great warrior race forced into farming and begging for handouts. It led to an almost total breakdown of the Lakota's ancient culture. Drunken-ness became rife and the ex-warriors could see no meaning to their lives. Life on the reservations was intolerable and Sitting Bull experienced another vision in which a meadowlark prophesied that he would die by the hand of his fellow Sioux countrymen.

Following years of this futile existence, 1890 brought a glimmer of hope which stirred the spirit of most tribes for the final time. Down south in Nevada, a Paiute medicine man named Wovoka had also been having visions of salvation which many were beginning to take seriously. Wovoka was a charismatic character who put his case across convincingly, for he said that his ethereal guidance had told him that the Great Spirit would come and make all dead Indians live again. All must then head into the high hills to await a huge flood which would roar across the country washing away all the white people and everything they stood for. The tribes could then re-inherit their homeland and live in peace forever. To make this happen, Wovoka said that all Indians must indulge in the Ghost Dance to create the necessary power.

Up at Standing Rock, Sitting Bull recognized the strength of Wovoka's message, and whether or not he totally believed it, he certainly saw it as a way of unifying his people once more. The Lakota, therefore, did begin to dance, day and night, a trend which spread throughout the entire Indian nation. Pretty soon most Sioux appeared to be overtaken by a trancelike state, wailing, dancing and wearing ghost shirts which were proclaimed to be immune to white men's bullets. Sitting Bull encouraged them enthusiastically, much to the horror of the authorities, especially McClaughlin who gave orders that the dancing must cease immediately.

Blatantly, Sitting Bull refused and as the influence of the Ghost Dance cult spread, the government realised that they were facing an explosive situation. McClaughlin decided to have Sitting Bull arrested and he sent a party of agency policemen to achieve this. This squad was made up almost entirely of Sioux braves who had sold out to the whites, about forty of them led by Lt. Bull Head and Sgt. Red Tomahawk, two Indians who had not fallen under Sitting Bull's spell and disliked him intensely. They arrived at the medicine man's log cabin at dawn on December 15th., bursting in and brusquely demanding that he surrender. Rudely awoken, Sitting Bull was, at first, co-operative, but, as he made ready to leave with his captors, many of his supporters began to gather outside the cabin demanding his release.

The Sioux policemen ushered their half dressed prisoner outside, hemming him in with a human shield. As the situation grew more tense and ugly, Sitting Bull's teenaged son, Crow Foot, called out to his father, inferring that he was a coward for allowing himself to be subdued so easily. Rising to this, the old chief's attitude changed, particularly since the policemen were now dragging him along roughly. Protesting and struggling, Sitting Bull appealed to his followers to rescue him.

A shot rang out from the crowd striking Lt. Bull Head, but as he fell, the officer fired a round into Sitting Bull's chest. Almost simultaneously, Sgt. Red Tomahawk blasted the old chief in the back of the head, killing him instantly. Within seconds, this needless violence resulted in a bloodbath with Sitting Bull's followers and the remaining policemen shooting, hacking and stabbing at each other. At the end of this melee, six policemen and seven of Sitting Bull's followers (including Crow Foot) lay dead. The meadowlark had spoken truly. Hunkpapa had killed Hunkpapa.

Although much of Sitting Bull's influence among the Lakota had diminished in recent years, news of his treacherous death was greeted with apprehension. Various Sioux leaders wondered who would be next on the hit list, especially the current Oglala and Minneconjou chiefs Hump and Big Foot. Tension increased and the ghost dancing carried on as army detachments were sent out to subdue any potential hostility.

Sixty years old and crippled by pneumonia, Big Foot took his band from their camp on the Cheyenne River from where he was reported to be heading for a rendezvous with Hump. Fearing this group to be hostile (Big Foot's case not being helped by the fact that he had taken in fugitives from the Sitting Bull debacle), the army tracked them down, intercepting them and leading them to a place called Wounded Knee Creek. The Lakota placidly submitted to this, or so it seemed, and by the freezing, snow dusted evening of December 28th. 1890, Big Foot's entire camp had been surrounded by eight companies of the 7th. Cavalry, many of whose troopers were no doubt brooding heavily about what had befallen their regiment at the hands of the Sioux just fourteen years before. The soldiers pitched their tents and wheeled up four heavy Hotchkiss guns onto the heights above the village where a white flag flew over Big Foot's tepee. Army strength stood at approximately 470 men (supplemented by Indian scouts) while the Lakota numbered about 340, only a little over 100 of them being warriors.

Dawn the following morning proved bitterly cold and everyone was keen to end this stand off. Col. James Forsyth, the cavalry commander, had explained to Big Foot that it would be necessary to disarm the warriors before escorting the whole band back to the agency. All Sioux men of fighting age were mustered together on a spot of high ground next to their camp where they were ordered to surrender their weapons. Some were sent back to their tepees in groups to collect any firearms which might be there, but after an hour of tense and resentful movement, barely a handful of useless guns had appeared. Forsyth had little time for this. His men were cold, hungry and impatient and the attitude of these Indians was beginning to goad him. Insisting that he knew the warriors were concealing a number of Winchester repeating rifles, the colonel sent a small party of officers and men into the village to carry out a search of the tepees. Once again, only a few fairly redundant weapons were found and, in the meantime, a Sioux medicine man had been drifting among the gathered warriors, stirring them up by reminding them that they were wearing ghost shirts so the soldier's bullets would not harm them.

Most of the warriors were seated together, wrapped in blankets to protect them from the biting cold, but Forsyth grew suspicious that they were concealing something. He ordered his troops to form up just a few feet in front of the assembled, grim faced braves as if hoping that such armed and determined presence would persuade them to submit. Tension was now at boiling point and afterwards many of those present spoke of a feeling that trouble was imminent. Finally it happened. Whether by pre-arranged signal or chance, someone (probably a warrior) opened fire and the Lakota men threw off their blankets to reveal the guns they had been hiding. In this way, the Sioux were able to loose a pre-emptive volley at point blank range into the soldier's ranks, causing heavy casualties, but the 7th. Cavalry were quick to respond. As the fighting gathered momentum, Forsyth ordered the Hotchkiss guns to commence firing and soon deadly explosive shells were crashing between the tepees, the hot metal tearing through anyone and everything indiscriminately.

When it was over, a blizzard blew over the corpses of 25 soldiers and at least 150 Sioux men, women and children, one of them being the infirm Big Foot. The ghost shirts had failed them, effectively ending Sioux resistance for good with one short, sharp blow. In addition, the 7th. Cavalry had been avenged.

To evoke the spirit within the words of that fine historical writer Dee Brown, indeed the heart of the Lakota would be buried at Wounded Knee.

FOR THE LOVE OF LIBBIE

"When I heard the news, I wanted to die," said Libbie, years after hearing of the loss of her beloved *darling boy*.

Indeed, Custer's widow was deeply affected. She was 34 years old, in the prime of life, with every reason to expect a golden future alongside her famous husband, but now all those assumptions had been blown away. Although the army and the general public expressed great sympathy for her plight, conditions were such that little time was wasted in ushering her, and the other widows, out of their Fort Lincoln homes. With the arrival of a new commanding officer, these grieving women were gently forced out within six weeks of the battle, barely having had time to gather their thoughts.

Deeply depressed, Libbie returned to the Monroe home she had inherited from her father where for months she wallowed in isolation, but practicality finally persuaded her to get a grip of herself. Regardless of Autie's fame and respect, he was no financier and his gambling and stock market dabbling had left his wife in debt to the tune of about $13,000. Insurance policies were not adequate to cover all this and it left Libbie struggling. For the first time in her life she was forced to seek gainful employment.

To her credit, she moved to New York City to begin a new life where she soon found a job as a secretary for the Decorative Arts Society. She had many friends in town who were anxious to help her and pretty soon she was writing articles for various newspapers. Largely, this was a response to the low mumbling of criticism which was beginning to grow against Autie's key role in the disaster. Libbie was particularly incensed by what she saw as a betrayal by General Terry who was trying to put himself in the clear by spreading the word that Custer had disobeyed orders. Determined to salvage her husband's reputation, Libbie, from then on, was to devote the rest of her long life to creating what became known as the "Custer Myth", portraying him as the perfect soldier, ideal husband and archetypal American; a "symbol of patriotism". Whether rightly or wrongly, there was a strong, general feeling in the military, even amongst the surviving participants from the battle, that the "General" had acted rashly, thereby bringing the disaster on his own head, but they mostly kept quiet out of respect for Libbie. In the meantime, she co-operated with a dime novelist named Whittaker who swiftly published Autie's first biography, *A Complete Life of General George A. Custer*, which was sycophantic in the extreme and laid all blame for the defeat on Reno and Benteen. Libbie supported this view with a passion, especially regarding Reno who she openly lambasted as a coward and a "man without honour". It was an image which the general public embraced and within a few years Custer had been immortalized as a hero in countless paintings, books, poems and songs. He would have loved it.

Just over a year after the battle, Libbie's influence succeeded in granting her request to have the 7th. Cavalry's officer's remains removed from their crude graves on the field for decent reburials back in civilization. With the exception of the three officer's bodies which were never found, and Lt. Crittenden whose father insisted that his son's body be left where it fell in action, this was done. The scant bones which were believed to be those of the "General" were brought back east and laid to rest, with great reverence and military ceremony, in the cemetery at West Point Academy. (In 1879, a statue of Autie was placed upon his tomb, but Libbie hated it so much that she had it removed a few years later.)

The great turning point in Libbie's career, however, occurred following the publication of a trilogy of very well received books which she wrote (between 1885-90) about her life with Autie, from which he emerged as an almost saint like figure. Fitting the image of the perfect widow, Libbie was soon in demand on the lecture circuit, a role which she took to with skill and grace as she toured the United States entertaining the crowds with her witty, enthralling and ultimately moving talks on frontier life. She seldom mentioned her husband's actual death but she did not have to. Everybody knew who she was and what she stood for. Eventually her popularity grew to the extent that she toured the world, visiting such countries as China, Japan, Egypt and much of Europe, making herself vast sums of money along the way. By the early 1900s she was living in style on Park Avenue in New York.

Aging gracefully, the widow Custer, revered by the nation and virtually beyond criticism, drew a parallel with Queen Victoria, such was the level of affection felt for her. In 1910, President William Taft himself was present at a grand ceremony in Monroe when Libbie unveiled a handsome $25,000 bronze statue of her husband on horseback. This time it was a glorious image which she approved of. Watched by surviving members of Autie's Wolverines and other regiments (especially the 7th. Cavalry), the president referred to Custer as a hero who, along with his kind, had made it possible to "settle the great west". It was a most moving occasion for Libbie and she spent much of the time gazing across at the First Presbyterian Church where, as a young, shy girl 46 years ago, she had married her dashing beau.

She lived to see him portrayed by actors on film, although she could never bring herself to visit the battlefield where he died. On the 50th. anniversary of the Last Stand she listened to a radio broadcast of the celebration live from the Little Bighorn. By this time, she was experiencing a very different world to the one she and Autie had known together. Not only had the raw West been embraced by civilization, the whole country had been taken over by a new technological age. Motor cars raced along highways, aeroplanes flew through the skies, people spoke across oceans by telephone, American soldiers had fought a Great War in Europe for the first time and prohibition had divided the nation. Outliving a succession of presidents, her long held bitterness against her husband's killers finally softened in 1924 when she calmly stated "I believe now that the Indians were deeply wronged".

A grand, dignified old lady, a national icon, Libbie suffered a heart attack and died in her apartment on April 4th. 1933, just days before her 91st. birthday. Franklin Roosevelt had just become the president and in far away Nazi Germany, Adolf Hitler was being swept into power as Reich Chancellor. What a changing world she had seen.

Buried alongside Autie at West Point, she would have been horrified that within a few years the critics and debunkers would emerge from the closet intent on demolishing the heroic image she had spent a lifetime constructing.

(Curiously, if not significantly, for *me* at least, my fascination with Custer has quite a few synchronistic tendencies. For instance, the girl I married shares the same birthday as Libbie, April 8th., and her middle name is *Elizabeth*. And my middle name? Yes … *George!*)

THE SURVIVORS

There were other victims of the Little Bighorn, quite apart from those who died violently on that hot, dusty June day. One was Maj. Reno whose role in the battle haunted him for the rest of his life.

During the chaos of shock and re-assignment immediately following the disaster, Reno was given field command of what remained of the 7th. Cavalry and he spent the rest of that summer leading them on a wild goose chase pursuing the Sioux. From then on his fortunes began a slippery slope to ruin. Always a heavy drinker, he hit the bottle with a passion and was often accused of being drunk on duty. There were those who said he was even inebriated during the defence of Reno Hill. As accusations of cowardice and poor leadership assailed him from numerous quarters, there is, perhaps, little wonder that such pressures led him to become involved in various scandals and scrapes. Over the next few months the unfortunate major's behaviour degenerated into alcoholism, improper conduct with a fellow officer's wife, insulting manners and several instances of physical brawls with other officers. This included a serious incident with Custer's chief of scouts, Lt. Varnum, which almost resulted in a duel. Court-martialled in early 1877, Reno escaped dismissal from the army but his loss of rank and pay for two years hit him hard financially. Only his previous twenty years of steady service saved him, but when he was finally restored to duty it did not take him long to get into trouble again.

First of all, however, having suffered the shame of seeing his name dragged through the mud by those who blamed him for Custer's death, Reno put in a request for a Court of Inquiry so that he could publicly put across his side of the story. The hearing convened for nearly a month in Chicago in early 1879 when many of the survivors from the battle expressed their opinions. Although Reno did not emerge from this testimony as any kind of hero, the conclusion was that under the circumstances he had not conducted himself shamefully. Several fellow officers held the view that had he pushed home his attack on the village, and not withdrawn from his defensive position in the timber, the disaster would have been much worse than it was. On this occasion, Reno was cleared of all potential charges, but the mud continued to stick and he still suffered from nagging criticism and a general contempt shown to him in social circles.

Serving at Fort Meade, close to the Black Hills, Reno supplied the final nail for his own coffin by offending no less than the commander of the regiment. Col. Sturgis was already bitter about the loss of his son at the Little Bighorn, openly blaming Custer yet clearly acknowledging Reno's role in the tragedy. The major had already drawn attention to himself again that year, obviously having failed to learn his lesson, because he was continually drunk, had damaged property and had got into a fight with a lieutenant following a billiard game. Pursuing some kind of "death wish", it seems, Reno could not resist peering into the window of the Sturgis household at the colonel's twenty year old daughter, Ella, as she relaxed in the parlour. Ella was terribly shocked and no amount of explanation or apology could save Reno this time. By the prim standards of the day, the major's act as a "peeping tom" was outrageous and he was charged with "conduct unbecoming an officer and a gentleman". Found guilty, recommendations by several of the judges (and General Terry) for clemency were ignored and Reno was dishonourably discharged from the army in April 1880.

Totally disgraced, Reno drifted to Washington where his second marriage ended within a few months. He could not even afford to attend his son's wedding although he did manage to secure a dreary desk job with the pension's bureau. By 1889 this sad, lonely, unlucky man had contracted cancer of the tongue, an unsuccessful operation for which led to his death at the age of 54. Few, if any, mourned his loss, and even as late as the 1920s, when a memorial was proposed for Reno Hill, the authorities, responding to objections from Libbie Custer, decided to omit the inclusion of his name. Many more years would pass before his case was re-examined, but a sympathetic descendant eventually succeeded in getting the disgraced major's name cleared when a new hearing agreed that he had been improperly dismissed. Ironically, in 1967, Reno's remains were transferred for reburial at the Custer National Cemetery where, rank posthumously restored, he joined Lt. Crittenden to become one of the only known officers who fought in the battle to end up resting permanently on the field.

Capt. Benteen emerged from the shame of the Little Bighorn with more distinction. Although he was criticized for failing to respond to Custer's direct orders to hurry and bring up the pack train, his initial lethargy and resentment had been replaced by a display of true leadership and courage during the siege of Reno Hill. He later stretched the truth and even lied to cover up his own failings during the early stages of the battle, but he did testify, albeit not over enthusiastically, for Reno at the Chicago inquiry. His considerable skills as an Indian fighter were put to further use during the campaign against the Nez Perce in 1877, where he distinguished himself at the Battle of Canyon Creek. Transferred to the 9th. Cavalry and promoted to major in 1882, he eventually echoed Reno's faults by getting himself suspended from duty on half pay for drunken-ness and disorderly conduct. Soon after this he was granted a medical discharge from the army owing to disabilities which he had apparently sustained during his long service. Retiring to Atlanta, Georgia, with his wife and son, he continued to harbour resentment for Custer by voicing his opinions privately, and in 1890 he was honoured by the brevet rank of Brigadier General as a reward for his gallantry during the Indian wars. In 1898, aged 63, he died following a stroke.

Capt. Tom Weir became an early victim of post Greasy Grass syndrome. Co. D's commander never came to terms with the loss of his revered commanding officer and despite his lone attempt to instigate a rescue mission, he somehow seemed to blame himself. His behaviour following the relief of Reno Hill grew increasingly bizarre and he suffered from severe depression. Recognising the stress he was under, his superiors withdrew him from active service and he was posted back east to help supervise recruitment. Nervous, unpredictable, secluding himself from company, this previously dashing officer who had once caught the eye of Libbie Custer, expired suddenly within six months of the battle, aged just 38. Just before he died, he wrote an emotive letter to Libbie in which he hinted that he had something of great importance to tell her. Unfortunately, this intriguing secret appears to have gone to the grave with him.

Also deeply affected by Custer's death was his faithful striker, Pvt. John Burkman. Following discharge from the 7th. Cavalry, Burkman worked as a teamster, angrily reacting to anyone who dared voice even the mildest criticism of his hero. Naturally, he had an emotional time during his attendance at the unveiling of Autie's statue at Monroe in 1910. For the last thirty years of his life, he lived as a cantankerous eccentric in Billings, Montana, so that he could be close to the site of the "General's" last battle, but in the end it all got too much for him and, in his 86th. year, he shot himself.

Custer's last two messengers made the most of their lucky escape by living into old age. Sgt. Kanipe served on until 1882, marrying the widow of Co. C's 1st. Sergeant, Edwin Bobo. He worked for twenty years for the U.S. Revenue Service in North Carolina before dying aged 73 in 1926, less than a month after the 50th. anniversary of the battle. The Italian trumpeter, Martini, stayed in the army until 1904, transferring to the artillery and reaching the rank of sergeant. He then became a subway ticket seller in New York City, a faceless employee whose customers were oblivious to his historic past. In 1922 he died of pneumonia in Brooklyn, 69 years old and fluent in English at last.

Lieutenants Varnum and Hare, Custer's scouting officers, both followed distinguished military careers for many years, becoming colonels and professors of military science at the universities of Wyoming and Texas, respectively. Hare fought in the Philippines in 1899 and won two silver stars for gallantry, while Varnum was awarded the Medal of Honour for his actions against the Sioux just before Wounded Knee. Varnum also served in the Spanish American War in Cuba (1899) and both were active in the 1877 Nez Perce campaign and at Wounded Knee in 1890. Hare died in Washington, 1929, aged 78, and Varnum struggled on, battling long standing ill health, until he finally succumbed at the grand old age of 86 in San Francisco.

Lt. Bradley, Gibbon's efficient chief of scouts, did not fare so well for he was killed at the Battle of Big Hole fighting Chief Joseph's Nez Perce barely a year after the Little Bighorn. Lt. Wallace, the lanky and prophetic engineer officer, ironically suffered a similar fate. He survived the Nez Perce campaign, having been promoted to regimental adjutant to replace Cooke, and served on, fairly uneventfully, until Wounded Knee. Now a captain, Wallace was one of the officers appointed to search the village for weapons and he fell in the first barrage of gunfire, shot several times through the body and head. He was 41.

Gustave Korn, by now a sergeant, was also killed at Wounded Knee, and he was sorely missed by Keogh's horse, Comanche. For fourteen years Korn tended the legendary mount, nursing him back to health and accompanying him in his role as "only living representative of the Custer tragedy" at numerous ceremonial occasions. Col. Sturgis announced in 1878 that the recovered Comanche was never to be ridden again and the horse spent the rest of its 29 years pampered and revered, his only role being to walk solemnly at the head of the restored Co. I during special parades. With Korn dead, Comanche began to pine and within a few months he had faded away. Not wishing to lose their symbolic mascot, the regiment had him stuffed and put on display at the University of Kansas.

The doctor who did such an admirable job caring for the wounded on Reno Hill, Henry Porter, carried on with his distinguished medical career, returning to private practice and occasional army contracts. As a civilian, he was eventually awarded $125 compensation for the loss of his horse in the retreat to the bluffs. He became vice president of the Society of Veterans of Indian Wars and spent the latter part of his life touring the world, during which he died in 1903, in Agra, India, where he was laid to rest.

Curley, the young Crow scout who escaped from Custer Hill at the last moment, was to suffer ridicule and contempt from whites as well as his fellow Indians. This was unjust, for his early accounts of what he had witnessed were misinterpreted and many people began to consider him a liar. Unable to speak English and thereby defend himself properly, Curley had to endure the ordeal of words being put into his mouth. Even the other Crow scouts resented him, largely out of jealousy because of the attention he was attracting. Eventually, he refused to discuss the battle and retired to his log cabin near the Crow Agency, within a short distance of the battlefield. He died there, aged about 67, in 1923. Nowadays, unbiased and pedantic historians have managed to unravel the truth behind Curley's verifiable accounts and his testimony is now a valued part of the Custer saga.

Sioux chiefs like Gall and Rain-in-the-Face, once they had been forced to surrender, had no choice but to submit to reservation life. Rain spent the rest of his life mischievously avoiding a definite admission to any connection with Tom Custer's heart, but he largely took to his role as the "tamed savage", gawped at by mesmerised city dwellers during his visits to the east. Gall, the powerful, handsome and charismatic warrior, became obese with the advancing years but he never lost his sparkle of charm and leadership. Most whites who met him felt instant respect and many of them could not help liking his affable, yet proud, nature. Even Libbie considered him a "fine specimen of a warrior". He died on what would have been Autie's 54th. birthday,

December 5th. 1893, and was around the same age himself.

To conclude this random sample of the fates of battle participants, let us look at the career of Lt. Edward Godfrey, the officer who represented the 7th. Cavalry at just about every phase of its existence from its creation through to his death in 1932. Godfrey was steady, courageous, moral and seemingly beyond criticism and he was eventually to wear the mantle of grand old mentor of the regiment. Following the Little Bighorn, Godfrey was promoted to captain and took Weir's place as Co. D's commander. He received the Medal of Honour for his service in the Nez Perce campaign, became an instructor in cavalry tactics at West Point and was involved at Wounded Knee. Working his way up through the senior ranks, he served in Cuba and the Philippines, where he commanded the 9th. Cavalry, ending up a brigadier-general and commander of the Department of the Missouri before retiring in 1907. He terminated his impressive career at Fort Riley, the 7th. Cavalry's original home, having served in the U.S. Army for 46 years.

General Godfrey became a close friend and supporter of Libbie's, always referring to her late husband in positive terms. In 1892, *Century* magazine published an article he had written entitled *Custer's Last Battle*, in which he largely blamed Reno for the disaster. He and Libbie continued to cast aspersions on the major's name for years after his death and were both responsible for applying the pressure which kept his name off of the monument which was to grace the hill Reno (along with Godfrey and the other survivors) had defended. Godfrey escorted Libbie at the unveiling of Custer's statue in Monroe and was a driving force in the organisation of several commemorative reunion events at the battlefield. The last one he was involved with was particularly significant.

1926 was to see the 50th. anniversary of the Battle of the Little Bighorn and a national feeling arose that something special should be done to mark the occasion. There had been ceremonies on the battlefield before, but this one was to be on a grand scale, especially as it was recognised that veterans from the battle were becoming fewer with each passing year. Here lay an ideal and symbolic opportunity to underline the West's greatest Cavalry/Indian fight for posterity.

It was a grand affair, heavily covered by the media. Although Libbie was emotionally unable to attend, June 25th. 1926 saw the battlefield and national cemetery festooned with an estimated 50,000 spectators, basking in the glorious sunshine of a cloudless blue sky. Many of them arrived in new fangled motor cars as a squadron of military bi-planes soared overhead to give an aerobatic display. The modern 7th. Cavalry was present too, still on horseback but this time dressed in khaki as they rode in columns of two across the field. Veterans who had once worn the frontier blue arrived stooped and grey haired, yet proud of their history. Thousands of Indians, no longer a threat, camped once more in the valley. Even Western silent movie star William S. Hart was present.

The celebrations lasted for three days and included speeches, concerts and a rodeo, but the highlight fell on the morning of June 25th. itself when old General Godfrey led a solemn procession on horseback along Battle Ridge. Godfrey was 82, yet he sat upright in the saddle like the proud military man he had always been. Beside him rode White Man Runs Him, the sole surviving Crow scout. In one hand Godfrey carried a stars and stripes banner while in the other he held his sabre.

From the other direction came a very different group of riders, colourfully clad in their traditional tribal best and feathered head-dresses. These were the representatives of the Sioux and Cheyenne, about eighty of whom had actually fought in the battle. When the two columns met, many in the crowd could not help feeling tense, but a wave of relief swept over them as the old enemies exchanged greetings. White Man Runs Him stared at the Sioux leader, White Bull, before presenting him with a peace pipe, then Godfrey, having sheathed his sword, offered the American flag to the elderly Lakota. White Bull, clutching his long, hooked coup stick, nodded, acknowledging the peaceful gestures by accepting these gifts and handing over one of his own, a beautifully woven Sioux blanket.

Dismounting, Godfrey marched to the summit of Custer Hill where a granite monument now stood, but he was not alone. With him came seven aged veterans of the 7th. Cavalry, all of whom had fought to defend Reno Hill, representing companies C, D, G, H and M. One of them, Peter Thompson, had been fortunate enough to have his horse give out as he rode towards this spot with Custer, thereby saving him from a different, and shorter lived, kind of immortality. Another, Charles Windolph, had been wounded in the buttock during the siege but lived on until 1950, making him the last white survivor of the battle. Together, these old soldiers laid wreaths around the monument, their eyes looking down in respectful silence as they stood immersed in their memories. Long gone comrades and lucky escapes for all who gathered here today.

The whole event was covered by numerous photographers and even a film unit from Universal Pictures, but none of the images have remained more poignant than the shot of Godfrey and White Man Runs Him standing together on Reno Hill. The General has his right hand on the top of a white wooden cross which marks the spot where a memorial (minus Reno's name) would soon be erected. He is incongruously dressed in a suit and tie, like some civil servant, but his bowed head and sombre expression beneath his huge, snow white moustache seems to say it all. Knees bent, shoulders stooped, he appears to be bearing a huge weight of guilt and sorrow. By contrast, an amazingly youthful looking White Man Runs Him, stunningly dressed in full tribal regalia and magnificent feathered bonnet, has his arms and eyes raised to the sky.

Honoured at last. Maj. Reno's grave in the Custer National Cemetery.

HONOURING THE DEAD

Casualty figures for the U.S. Army at the Little Bighorn are, based on various sources of evidence, pretty reliable. Including Autie himself, probably 210 men of his command died on or around Custer Hill with another 53 dying in action over the separate two day battle in the valley and on Reno Hill. Indian casualties are much more uncertain because the tribes kept no official records and were reluctant to talk about their dead. Over the years, various individual braves have been identified but a figure of 32, supplied by one historian, even under the circumstances of the disaster, seems improbably low. Although Custer's and Reno's men were largely routed, elements of them without doubt put up a spirited fight. Indian dead were carried away, remember, and not all were laid to rest in burial tepees in the abandoned village. Many other wounded warriors would have died along the trail as the tribes dispersed, so the total number will probably never be known. Whatever, we can be reasonably sure that the Sioux and Cheyenne did not lose anywhere near as many men as the 7th. Cavalry.

As previously described, the relief force and the survivors were anxious to get away from the terrible stench and aura of the battle as quickly as possible so the initial burials were hastily done. For more than a year the battlefield was abandoned to the elements, visited only by perhaps the odd adventurer and groups of curious Indians. During that time, the shallow graves of the cavalrymen and others were savaged by a cruel Montana winter with driving rain and snow, which eroded the soil and exposed many of the bodies. Then along came skulking scavengers like buzzards and coyotes which fell upon these decaying corpses, dispersing bones over an ever widening area. By the time the first official government expedition arrived in July 1877, the field looked like a slaughterhouse with the bleached white skeletons of horses and parts of dead soldiers scattered all over. Here and there hideous grinning skulls peered, half hidden, from their graves. The expedition was made up of troops sent from a newly built garrison at the mouth of the river (destined to be named Fort Custer), and their commander was Col. Michael Sheridan, brother of Little Phil. Their mission was to carry out Libbie's request to locate the bodies of as many officers as possible, but the task proved more difficult than anticipated, even when it came to identifying the "General" himself. In the end eight sets of remains were gathered together from around Custer Hill and three from the Reno site for shipment back east. To this day there is still uncertainty as to whether the incomplete bones which lay at West Point are actually the remains of Custer. It could be that Libbie rests alongside some faceless trooper. Perish the thought!

Another expedition in 1879, complete with a photographer, made an effort to clean up the battlefield, gathering together all the horse bones which had been left lying around and placing them inside a tower of logs which was erected on the summit of Custer Hill. They also put up wooden markers, complete with names, on the old grave sites of the identified officers and civilians. The graves of enlisted men remained anonymous. This work was improved upon in 1881 when a proper effort was made to create a permanent site of hallowed ground. With Fort Custer now close enough to enable fairly regular supervision of the battlefield, a detachment of the 2nd. Cavalry was sent to place an eighteen ton granite memorial on the hill to replace the tower of logs. This pyramid like shaft is carved with the names of all but two of the men who fell with Custer, a pure mistake. As many human bones as possible were disinterred from the soldier's individual graves and reburied en-masse in a deep trench around the base of the memorial, but an effort was made to mark the original resting places.

Five years later, ex-participants of the battle met on the site to recognise the 10th. anniversary. It was a gathering full of nostalgia, sadness and more than a little heavy drinking. Godfrey was there, also Benteen, Edgerly, McDougall and Dr. Porter, as well as a few enlisted men. Sitting Bull was invited but could not make it because he was on tour with Buffalo Bill, but Gall turned up, swapping stories and opinions with his erstwhile enemies. Apparently the atmosphere was cordial and philosophical.

In 1890 a government directive led to permanent markers being erected across the battlefield, but the commander of this expedition was faced with a problem. He had made the long journey to the site with wagon loads of heavy marble headstones, but only those of the identified dead officers were inscribed with names. Guided by a scout who had been with the 1881 party, the soldiers carefully placed the markers on and around Custer Hill, later to claim that they were as accurate as possible. No doubt they were sincere, but the fact remains that 249 markers were placed across a battle ground where only 210 bodies were found.

Over the years, a few more markers were placed to honour odd individuals and occasionally more bones would be unearthed. A house was built near to the site in 1893 for the first superintendent and he became known to the Crows as the "ghost herder" because they believed that when he lowered the flag in the evening, the spirits of the slain would rise from their graves. An official cemetery was also established there, just to the north west of Custer Hill, and as various military forts closed down across the frontier, the remains from their graveyards were transferred for re-burial in this newly established Custer Battlefield National Cemetery. Eventually this hallowed spot would contain the bones of nearly 5,000 individuals from numerous frontier conflicts, as well as army family members, military personnel, Indian scouts and victims from wars as recent as Vietnam.

Originally managed by the Bureau of Indian Affairs, the Little Bighorn area was overseen by the War Department until 1940 when it came under the jurisdiction of the National Park Service. It is now part of the Crow Agency.

In 2002 a stone memorial was finally erected, close to the 7th. Cavalry monument, to honour the Sioux and Cheyenne dead.

The 7th. Cavalry memorial on Custer Hill.

The markers on Custer Hill looking south west towards the river. Custer's body was found where the black faced marker stands.

OFFICERS, STAFF, SERGEANTS AND CIVILIANS, UNDER CUSTER'S DIRECT COMMAND, KILLED AT THE BATTLE OF THE LITTLE BIGHORN DURING THE LATE AFTERNOON OF JUNE 25th. 1876 ON AND AROUND THE SLOPES OF CUSTER HILL.

Lt. Col. George Armstrong Custer (Born New Rumley, Ohio, U.S.A.,1839)
Adjutant 1st. Lt. William Winer Cooke (B. Mount Pleasant, Ontario, Canada, 1846)
Aide-de-camp Capt. Thomas Ward Custer, Co. C (B. New Rumley, Ohio, U.S.A., 1845)
Asst. Surgeon George Edwin Lord (B. Boston, Massachusetts, U.S.A., 1846)
Sgt. Maj. William Sharrow (B. Yorkshire, England 1845)
Chief Trumpeter Henry Voss (B. Hanover, Germany, year unknown)
Battle flag bearer Colour Sgt. Robert Hughes, assigned from Co. K, (B. Dublin, Ireland, 1840)
Quartermaster/scout/interpreter Michel "Mitch" Bouyer (B. Missouri territory, U.S.A., 1837)
Quartermaster Boston Custer (B. New Rumley, Ohio, U.S.A., 1848)
Harry Armstrong Reed (B. Monroe, Michigan, U.S.A., 1858)
Newspaper reporter Marcus Henry Kellogg (B. Brighton, Ontario, Canada, 1833)

Company C
1st. Lt. James Calhoun, assigned to command Co. L during battle (B. Cincinnati, Ohio, U.S.A., 1845)
2nd. Lt. Henry Moore Harrington, commanding C during battle (B. Albion, New York, U.S.A., 1849)
1st. Sgt. Edwin Bobo (B. Franklin County, Ohio, U.S.A., 1845)
Sgt. George August Finckle (B. Berlin, Germany, 1844)
Sgt. Jeremiah Finley (B. Tipperary, Ireland, 1841)

Company E
1st. Lt. Algernon Emory Smith, assigned from Co. A (B. Newport, New York, U.S.A., 1842)
2nd. Lt. William Van Wyck Reily, assigned to Co. F during battle (B. Washington, U.S.A., 1853)
1st. Sgt. Frederick Hohmeyer (B. Darmstadt, Germany, 1848)
Sgt. William James (B. Pembrokeshire, Wales, 1848)
Sgt. John Ogden (B. Newberry, Massachusetts, U.S.A., 1845)

Company F
Left Wing battalion commander Capt. George Wilhelmus Mancius Yates (B. Albany, New York, U.S.A., 1843)
1st. Sgt. Michael Kenney (B. Galway, Ireland, 1849)
Sgt. John Groesbeck (B. Toronto, Canada, 1847)
Sgt. Frederick Nursey (B. Bungay, Suffolk, England, 1848)
Sgt. John Wilkinson (B. Salem, New York, U.S.A., 1847)

Company I
Right Wing battalion commander Capt. Myles Walter Keogh (B. County Carlow, Ireland, 1840)
1st. Lt. James Ezekiel Porter (B. Strong, Maine, U.S.A., 1847)
1st. Sgt. Frank Varden (B. Yarmouth, Maine, U.S.A., 1845)
Sgt. James Bustard (B. Donegal, Ireland, 1846)

Company L
2nd. Lt. John Jordan Crittenden, assigned from the 20th. Infantry (B. Frankfort, Kentucky, U.S.A., 1854)
2nd. Lt. James Garland Sturgis, assigned from Co. M (B. Albuquerque, New Mexico, U.S.A., 1854)
1st. Sgt. James Butler (B. Albany, New York, U.S.A., 1842)
Sgt. William Cashan (B. County Queens, Ireland, 1845)
Sgt. Amos Warren (B. Brooklyn, New York, U.S.A., 1849)
  Plus 175 other ranks (corporals, trumpeters, farriers, blacksmiths, saddlers and privates). Highest loss suffered by Co. L with 45 killed.

THE GREASY GRASS TODAY

As I walked up Custer Hill for the first time, my heart was pounding. I could scarcely believe I had actually made it here, at last. It was late afternoon on Wednesday, May 3rd. 2000, almost 124 years since Autie and his men had died on these slopes.

Like The Alamo which I would experience almost a year later, the site of Custer's last battle is now a haven for tourists and enthusiasts, but the main difference is that the famed mission lies in the centre of a teeming city while the Greasy Grass is still located in the middle of nowhere. A visitor to the Little Bighorn Battlefield National Monument has to be determined to make his or her way there. Located on the edge of the Interstate 90, which cuts its way north across the bleak landscape like a livid scar, the battle ground is pretty much as it would have been in 1876. Of course, there are many signs of civilization there now like the visitor centre and the neat green lawns of the cemetery, but one can still experience an intense feeling of exposure and harshness surrounded by those endless rolling hills and gullies.

Still standing on these slopes, dotted singly and in groups, are the white markers which were placed by the 1890 expedition to preserve the spots where the slaughtered 7th. Cavalrymen originally lay. As stated before, one cannot rely on the accuracy of all of these markers, but their placement does give a general impression of the deployment and rout of Custer's doomed troopers. As I made my way to the summit of the hill, two of the first markers I passed, standing alongside one another, were dedicated to Boston Custer and Autie Reed, who had met their deaths a fair way down the slope from their more famous relative. Custer's marker lies a few yards from the hilltop, on the western slope, surrounded by those naming most of his clique; brother Tom, Cooke, Yates, Smith, Reily ….. It is the only marker to be distinguished by solemn black facing, immortalized with the words

G. A. CUSTER
LIEUT. COLONEL
BVT. MAJOR GENERAL
7 U.S. CAV.
FELL HERE
JUNE 25, 1876

Most of the others just say *U.S. SOLDIER-UNKNOWN*, or something similar. The 7th. Cavalry monument is somewhat weather worn these days but you can still read the names of almost all the men who died under Custer's command, including those who were with Reno. For some reason Harry Reed is mistakenly remembered as "Arthur" and the black interpreter Isaiah Dorman is honoured only by his first name, but mostly this imposing obelisk can be relied upon. One is not permitted to walk on the lush green grass which surrounds it because the remains of most of these men still lie there.

This patch of green, and the much larger one at the nearby cemetery, stand out because the area is generally covered, as far as the eye can see, by acres of scrubby, dry grassland, straw coloured and interspersed with spiky sagebrush. The soil is hard and gravelly and I was quickly able to appreciate one of the major problems faced by Custer's men. There are many treacherous gullies and ravines, impossible country for the effective deployment of cavalry. Movement would have been terribly restricted whilst furnishing the attacking Indians with excellent cover. The 7th. Cavalry were sitting ducks and must have been mown down like a turkey shoot. Looking south east towards the Little Bighorn river you can see Deep Ravine where most of E Co. were wiped out.

Driving the battlefield road which winds for about four miles along undulating ground to Reno Hill, I passed various other significant spots including Calhoun Hill where L Co. had put up such a fight. Close by there is a cluster of markers where Keogh and the "Wild I" fell. Further on, having passed over Weir Point, from which you could clearly have seen the debacle on Custer Hill, I paused at the spot which claims to be where Custer and his men were last seen by Reno's attacking force, waving down into the valley. There is also a marker close by devoted to the unfortunate farrier Vincent Charley of D Co. who was left to a grisly fate when the troops retired from Weir Point.

I noted that the monument on Reno Hill is still devoid of the luckless major's name, but walking the path which takes you on a tour of the defences, I was pleased to see that some of the old rifle pits have been preserved. A black cross on a white stone marks the area in the central depression where Dr. Porter struggled to tend to the wounded. Looking down Water Carrier's Ravine towards the river, I shuddered to think of the bravery of those troopers who risked their lives exposing themselves to hostile fire as they ran the gauntlet to fill canteens for the wounded. Far away in the haze of the distant south east I tried to locate the Crow's Nest.

Back at Custer Hill it was about 5.00pm. on a hot cloudless day and I suddenly realised that these were virtually the same weather conditions, and exact time, of the final struggle. Of course, it was a lot more peaceful now, but only a few visitors strolled around under the watchful eyes of the ever present park rangers. One of my only real disappointments was that I was not permitted to walk down to many of the places I would like to have visited, for much of this land is privately owned.

The visitor centre is superb. Filled with battle related artefacts and personal items which had belonged to Custer, it is a dream for Western history buffs. Interpretive film and informative artwork gives an overall impression to even the most uninformed of what took place there. In recent years much new information has been gleaned from the archaeological work which took place in the early 1980s following a grassfire which cleared much of the battle ground. Using the latest computer technology, it has been possible to recreate the facial images of battle victims by working on skulls which have recently been unearthed. One of the most exciting discoveries in recent years was of some bone fragments along with a civilian style mother of pearl button on the lower reaches of Custer Hill. The most complete section of these remains consisted of facial bones which included the left side of the cheek and part of an eye socket, along with the nasal cavity attached to several upper front teeth. Close study revealed that the man had been of mixed race, aged between thirty to forty, with the wear on the teeth being indicative of a pipe smoker. Researchers slowly began to realise that they had probably identified one of the prime participants in the battle, a fact which was confirmed when they superimposed the partial skull with computer enhancement over the only known photograph of this particular individual. It was a perfect match. The remains of Mitch Bouyer had emerged like a ghost from the past. His, and all other recently discovered remains, have since been re-buried in the Custer National Cemetery.

The cemetery itself is a poignant place and a truly fascinating "who's who" of Western history. It has a tranquil beauty too, with its lines of well ordered white gravestones nestling amidst groves of imported cedar trees. Some of the graves are additionally marked with fluttering miniature Stars and Stripes flags and here you can find the last resting places of such figures as Capt. William Fetterman, who met his doom when he and his command were overwhelmed by the Sioux some ten years before Custer's fall. Also buried here are several of Custer's Crow scouts, including the much maligned Curley, and Lt. Crittenden whose father had insisted that his body be left where it had fallen. This wish was granted until 1932 when the re-routing of the battlefield road made it necessary to move the one eyed lieutenant's bones to the cemetery. Custer's striker John Burkman lies here too, as well as Maj. Reno, forgiven, officially at least, at last.

I eventually found myself standing before a bulky memorial which honours those troopers of the infantry and cavalry who died in the largely forgotten Nez Perce campaign of 1877. This affair is worthy of mention because it is an incredible story which underlines the courage and tenacity of the Indian spirit. Chief Joseph of the Nez Perce tribe, who originally settled in far distant Oregon to the west, fell victim to government pressure in the volatile months following Custer's death. Essentially craving peace with the whites, Joseph was forced into a situation where he had to lead his people on a long, eventful trek across the north western states in his quest for escape from hounding by the army. He and his warriors fought several pitched battles with vastly superior numbers of troops, succeeding in holding them off and evading capture for months before finally succumbing. This monument actually names the enlisted men who were killed in the Battle of Bear Paw Mountain, one of whom was of especial significance to me. This soldier had been Capt. Weir's 1st. Sgt. in Co. D and had survived the defence of Reno Hill. Born in Dublin, Ireland, in 1835, he had been killed by a shot in the head ironically on the very morning Chief Joseph surrendered. He was my namesake, Mike Martin.

My next trip to the Greasy Grass was about a week later and this time I was completely alone on the battlefield. I made sure I got there first thing in the morning for my plan was to be able to experience the place in solitude. By 8.00am. I was once again trudging up Custer Hill towards the monument.

The skies were clear again heralding the advent of a beautiful day, but there was a chill in the crisp, early air. Looking down once more at Custer's marker, the stillness of the moment was disturbed only by a light breeze which rustled through the coarse grass on that barren slope. Even the chirruping of a few birds and crickets seemed to take on an added intensity. I felt a wave of emotion sweep over me as I began to really connect with this place. It was spiritual, a truly peak experience. Eventually I would experience similar feelings at The Alamo and San Jacinto, but they did not compare to the depth of this. Let the cynics scoff, but I *know* that I experienced something very special during those quiet moments on Custer Hill.

By the time I got to Reno Hill there were a few more visitors around but I spent a long time exploring the defence site, frustrated that I was not permitted to walk down to the river. I was tempted to take a chance but the gun toting rangers take their duty very seriously. Down there I would have been able to locate where Lonesome Charley, Isaiah Dorman, Bloody Knife, Lt. Hodgson and Tosh McIntosh fell. Symbolically, I suddenly spotted a rattlesnake slithering through the grass as if warning me not to stray from the allotted areas. I had to content myself with a panoramic distant view of the wide plain down in the valley across which Reno's companies had charged towards the Hunkpapa circle.

Shortly before I was ready to leave, I got into conversation with a pleasant old gentleman who, it transpired, was a retired officer from the U.S.A.F.. As we stood together on the edge of the bluffs in the centre of B and M Co.'s firing lines, peering down at the tree lined river's edge where the Indian village once stood, he asked me, "So, what do you think of all this?"

I continued to stare into the valley before turning my gaze south towards the snow capped Bighorn mountains. "Ethereal," I said.

The old gent glanced at me quizzically. "Yep, that's the word," he replied, "*whatever* it means."

*   *   *

I love travelling across the old frontier areas of the American West and have devoted a lot of time to doing so. However, a whole life's span would not enable me to see everything I wish to see. That said, I am trying!

There is so much to experience, spread over a landscape so vast that it makes your head spin. Only by driving across the Great Divide, which seems to go on forever, can you absorb any sense of the exhausting journeys undertaken by the original pioneers who were heading into the unknown, not the next motel. How wonderful it was for me to cross the North Platte for the first time and roam the Powder River country.

Fort Laramie, still remote, is largely preserved and cared for by historical re-enactors who spend their time sitting around in authentic 2nd. Cavalry uniforms, living their dream. The nearby tiny hamlet which serves as a town apparently has a population of 250, but I only saw about a dozen of them. Finding a place which looked like it had some life in the deserted main street, I wandered into a downstairs bar which was hung with saddles, lanterns and gingham. A line of stetsoned cowboys sat along the bar, their conversation ending abruptly as I entered. It was like a scene from a Howard Hawks movie when John Wayne saunters into the saloon.

An Elly May Clampett look-alike behind the bar answered my enquiry about food by shouting down the room to a haunted looking figure who leaned over his beer, face hidden by a huge hat and a soup-strainer moustache.

"Hey, Roy," she drawled, "feller here wants to eat."

Roy looked up, his voice bemused. "You wanna eat *here*?!!"

The meal they rustled up actually turned into a great experience as I found myself surrounded by interesting characters who wanted to chat and be friendly. These included a couple of fierce looking bikers and an old widow who regaled me with stories of her life in the wilds.

In the Black Hills I felt the presence of long gone Lakota, the stark beauty of the forest and hills somehow emitting a forlorn sense of injustice. Deep in a tree lined gully I found the sleepy town of Deadwood where Wild Bill Hickok was shot in the back by a sneaky assassin named Jack McCall in the Number 10 saloon just six weeks after Custer's defeat. The town Hickok knew burned down but it has been rebuilt and still retains a lovely old-timey feel. Above the town, crowned by Lookout Point, is the Mount Moriah cemetery, Deadwood's very own "Boot Hill" where Wild Bill's remains lie in a sacred little fenced enclosure. Just behind him is the gravestone of Calamity Jane whose dying words were "Bury me next to Bill". She always liked to give the impression that she had a romantic connection with the legendary gunfighter, but the truth is he just humoured her.

Many miles to the west I spent more solitary time at the site of Fort Phil Kearny which was besieged by Red Cloud. Not much of the old fort remains (except for some charred timbers which are being excavated) because the Sioux burned it, but the memories linger alongside the memorial to Portugee Phillips, commemorating the incredible ride he made to bring relief to the fort. Nearby are the sites of the Wagon Box Fight and the Fetterman Massacre. The first of these sites is where a small wood cutting party from the fort came under attack by hundreds of warriors, defending themselves by taking up positions in a circle of fourteen wagons with the wheels removed. On this occasion the army were successful, inflicting huge casualties on the Sioux whilst losing only three men themselves, unlike the previous year when Fetterman had ridden into that trap alongside the nearby Peno Creek and subsequently lost all of his command. The Wagon Box site is virtually as barren as it would have been in 1867, save for the stone memorial and replica of one of the wagon boxes. A tall column of stones immortalizes Fetterman and his men, towering high on a hill which overlooks a well marked trail. Follow this trail and you can read a line of placards which trace the course of the slaughter. Turn a full 360 degrees and you see nothing but hills and plains.

Stunning scenery further north took me along the Chief Joseph Scenic Highway, the route taken by the Nez Perce when they were trying to reach Canada, fighting off the army all the way. I also stayed in the town of Cody about fifty miles to the east of Yellowstone National Park, a place of such eye popping natural grandeur that mere words cannot do it justice. Buffalo Bill founded this town as a gateway to the park and it was a joy to take a room in the old Irma hotel which he built and named after his daughter. He used to hold court on the veranda. The long, ornate redwood bar was a gift from Queen Victoria. Cody also has the Buffalo Bill Heritage Centre, a massive multi layered museum which was purpose built to preserve the spirit of the Old West, a task it achieves to perfection. Here there are whole areas dedicated to the Plains Indians, a massive firearms display, the Whitney Gallery of Western Art (which is filled with emotive original paintings by the likes of Russell and Remington), the stagecoach which ran from Deadwood to Cheyenne in the 1870s, many items which belonged to the famous scout and heaps of other fascinating material. I was even able to handle and read actual letters which were written by survivors of the Custer Battle. One was penned by General Terry, sent from the Little Bighorn the day he arrived to relieve Reno, describing his first harrowing impressions. Another is a detailed description by Lt. Godfrey of the condition of the dead as found on Custer Hill. Hair raising stuff.

The Old Trail Town nestles on the western limits of Cody, custom built for the tourists, yes, but quite a gem because it is constructed almost entirely from old cabins and other buildings which were dismantled at sites all over the West and brought here to recreate an authentic frontier settlement. The interior of each building is wonderfully laid out too, with furnishings from the period, weapons, stuffed animals and pelts. Here you will find the Rivers saloon, as used by Butch Cassidy's "Hole in the Wall" gang of outlaws, complete with genuine bullet holes in the door. Also preserved, with many of his belongings, is the cabin built by Custer's Crow scout Curley, in which he lived for many years. This Trail Town also has a small graveyard where various frontier characters lie. Men like legendary buffalo hunter Jim White and "Liver Eatin' Johnson", who got his name following a long vendetta he carried out against the Crow tribe after they had killed his wife and unborn child. It was said that whenever Johnson claimed a Crow scalp he would take a bite out of his victim's liver! When Robert Redford made a movie about this character, he conveniently omitted that little detail.

So many highlights on the road. Wyoming's Devil's Tower (as seen in Spielberg's *Close Encounters*), Yellowstone's majestic spouting geysers (especially Old Faithful), foaming, gigantic waterfalls, sweeping valleys, wildlife and the Great Plains. Memories which will live with me forever, like swimming in desert lakes by moonlight, riding a bicycle for thirty miles across the rugged Grand Staircase Escalante, camping beneath the stars in the Arizona wilderness, trekking down the Angel Trail into the Grand Canyon, jamming along with singing cowboys on the Williams Flyer train en route to Flagstaff, driving through a snowstorm in the Bighorn mountains and meeting many truly wonderful and fascinating people. I stayed with the Navajo on their reservation in Nevada and may I say they were much more outgoing and friendly than the Crow up at the Little Bighorn. My experience of Custer's old allies was that they appeared aloof and did not wish to allow me into their confidence, regardless of my interest. Maybe they resent their role in history. Whatever, it seemed to me that they like to keep to themselves.

There is so much more I could say and the temptation to do so is great. However, space and common sense conspire to convince me to hold back, and so I come to the end of this potted history. The facts are here but this has been a very personal view of events surrounding a small, yet meaningful, slice of the past. Ultimately we must all reach our own conclusions.

We are born, live our lives, achieve (hopefully) and die, before moving on to whatever great mysteries may lie beyond. Those who knew and loved us will mourn our passing and remember us fondly but, eventually, the vast majority of we humble humans will merge into the jumble of the past, insignificant to future generations as the individuals we have been. Very few reach the pinnacle of immortality. Whatever we may think of them as people, or what they may, or may not, have done for the species, Davy Crockett and General Custer have earned their place in history and will be remembered. For that alone they deserve respect.

Finally, from me, Davy and Autie, a personal thank you, for what it is worth, for furnishing me with this lifelong obsession. At last, I can let it lie.

Across this ground, fleeing troopers from companies C, I and L fought a desperate running battle. The bodies of Keogh and his "Wild I" were found close by.

Water Carrier's Ravine, looking down to the river from Reno Hill. The distant plain is the one across which Reno made his charge, left to right, towards the village.

BIBLIOGRAPHY

Sources of research for this book were multifarious but here are some which were particularly noteworthy.

A LINE IN THE SAND: Randy Roberts and James S. Olsen (Touchstone)
A TIME TO STAND: Walter Lord (Longmans)
THE ALAMO: Albert Nolfi
THE ALAMO AND THE TEXAN WAR OF INDEPENDENCE 1835 -1836 : Philip Haythornthwaite and Paul Hannon (Osprey)
ATLAS OF THE SIOUX WARS: Combat Studies Institute; U.S. Army Command
THE AMERICAN PLAINS INDIANS: Jason and Richard Hook ((Osprey)
THE AMERICAN INDIAN WARS, 1860 -1890: Philip Katcher and G.A. Embleton (Osprey)
BLOOD OF NOBLE MEN (The Alamo Siege and Battle): Alan C. Huffines (Lakin Press)
BOWIE: Randy Lee Eickhoff and Leonard C. Lewis (Forge)
BURY MY HEART AT WOUNDED KNEE: Dee Brown (Vintage)
CRAZY HORSE AND CUSTER: Stephen E. Ambrose (Pocket Books)
THE CRIMSONED PRAIRIE: S.L.A. Marshall ((MacDonald)
CUSTER: Will Henry ((Leisure)
CUSTER; CAVALIER IN BUCKSKIN: Robert M. Utley (Salamander)
CUSTER'S FALL: David Humphreys Miller (Meridian)
CUSTER'S LAST CAMPAIGN - MITCH BOUYER AND THE LITTLE BIG HORN RECONSTRUCTED: John S. Gray (Bison)
DIGGING INTO CUSTER'S LAST STAND: Sandy Barnard (AST Press)
1876 FACTS ABOUT CUSTER AND THE BATTLE OF THE LITTLE BIG HORN: Jerry Russell (Savas)
1836 FACTS ABOUT THE ALAMO: Mary Deborah Petite (Savas)
FLASHMAN AND THE REDSKINS: George MacDonald Fraser (Pan)
I GO WITH CUSTER (The Life and Death of Reporter Mark Kellogg): Sandy Barnard (Bismarck Tribune)
LAST STAND! FAMOUS BATTLES AGAINST THE ODDS: Bryan Perrett (Cassell)
LITTLE BIG HORN 1876: Peter Panzeri (Osprey)
LITTLE BIG MAN: Thomas Berger (Bantam)
MEN WITH CUSTER - BIOGRAPHIES OF THE 7th. CAVALRY: Ron Nichols (CBHMA Inc.)
SCALP DANCE: Thomas Goodrich (Stackpole)
SON OF THE MORNING STAR: Evan S. Connell (Pimlico)
THREE ROADS TO THE ALAMO: William C. Davis (Harper Perennial)
U.S. CAVALRYMAN 1865 - 1890: Martin Pegler (Osprey)
WILD BILL HICKOK: Richard O'Connor (Mayflower Dell)
WONDROUS TIMES ON THE FRONTIER: Dee Brown (Arrow)

Plus the writings of Elizabeth Bacon Custer and numerous specialist periodicals, especially issues of *BATTLEFIELD DISPATCH* (CBHMA), *GREASY GRASS* (CBHMA) and *THE CROW'S NEST* (CAGB).

ISBN 141201878-1